Longman Geography
for GCSE

Authors
John Pallister
Ann Bowen
Roger Clay
Carmela Di Landro
Olly Phillipson

Edinburgh Gate
Harlow, Essex

Contents

UNIT 1 — Tectonic activity

	Focus photo: Kobe quake aftermath (1995)	5
1.1	Plate tectonics	6–7
1.2	Volcanic activity	8–9
1.3	Faults and earthquakes	10–11
1.4	Tectonic hazards: the Kobe earthquake, 1995	12–13
1.5	Tectonic hazards: the eruption of Mount Pinatubo	14–15
1.6	Fold mountain building: the Himalayas	16–17
1.7	Using volcanoes: Iceland and southern Italy	18–19
1.8	The East African Rift Valley: cradle of life	20–21
1.9	Activities	22–23
1.10	Sample examination questions	24

UNIT 2 — Rivers and the hydrological cycle

	Focus photo: Victoria Falls, Zambezi River	25
2.1	River systems and processes	26–27
2.2	The river and its valley in the uplands	28–29
2.3	The river and its valley in the lowlands	30–31
2.4	River floods	32–33
2.5	People, rivers and floods	34–35
2.6	A river and its valley: the River Tay	36–37
2.7	Floodplain and delta: the River Ganges	38–39
2.8	River management in a LEDC: the River Ganges	40
2.9	River management in a MEDC: the River Mississippi	41
2.10	Flooding in the United Kingdom: the River Ouse	42
2.11	Water supply: Kielder reservoir	43
2.12	Activities	44–45
2.13	Sample examination questions	46

UNIT 3 — Coasts

	Focus photo: storms along the south coast of Britain	47
3.1	The power of the sea	48–49
3.2	Cliff erosion	50–51
3.3	Building beaches	52–53
3.4	Changing sea levels	54–55
3.5	Coastal change and management: the Suffolk coast	56–57
3.6	Using a coastal area: Milford Haven	58–59
3.7	Pollution: Italy's Adriatic coast	60–61
3.8	Coastal tourism in a LEDC: sustainable development along the Tanzanian coast	62–63
3.9	Activities	64–65
3.10	Sample examination questions	66

UNIT 4 — Ice landscapes

	Focus photo: Matterhorn peak in the Alps	67
4.1	Landscapes eroded by ice	68–69
4.2	Glaciation in the lowlands	70–71
4.3	A glaciated area: the Lake District	72–74
4.4	Human activity in a glaciated area: the Lake District	75
4.5	Solving problems in the Lake District	76–77
4.6	Activities	78–79
4.7	Sample examination questions	80

UNIT 5 — Weather, climate and ecosystems

	Focus photo: satellite image of the World	81
5.1	Measuring weather	82–83
5.2	Factors affecting climate	84–85
5.3	World climates	86–87
5.4	Weather and climate: the United Kingdom	88–89
5.5	Climatic hazards: tropical storm Gordon	90
5.6	Urban microclimates: London	91
5.7	World soils	92–93
5.8	Ecosystems	94–85
5.9	Grassland ecosystem: tropical savanna in the Sahel	96
5.10	Ecosystem change: desertification in the Sahel	97
5.11	A grassland ecosystem: North America's prairies	98
5.12	How vegetation adapts: tropical rainforest in Brazil	99
5.13	Deforestation: tropical rainforest in Brazil and Malaysia	100–101
5.14	Activities	102–103
5.15	Sample examination questions	104

UNIT 6 — Population

	Focus photo: crowded street in India	105
6.1	Distribution and density	106–107
6.2	Population change	108–109
6.3	Migration	110–111
6.4	Population structure	112–113
6.5	Population distribution: the United Kingdom	114–115
6.6	Internal migration: the United Kingdom	116
6.7	Internal migration: Brazil	117
6.8	An ageing population: France	118
6.9	Population policy and population control: China	119
6.10	Population contrasts: the USA and Mexico	120–121
6.11	Activities	122–123
6.12	Sample examination questions	124

Settlement

	Focus photo: Chicago	125
7.1	The nature and growth of settlements	126–127
7.2	Patterns of land use	128–129
7.3	Changing cities	130–131
7.4	Changes around the city	132–133
7.5	World urbanisation	134–135
7.6	Urban growth in a MEDC: London and the South East of England	136–137
7.7	Out-of-town shopping centres: the United Kingdom	138
7.8	An out-of-town shopping centre: the MetroCentre, Gateshead	139
7.9	Urban growth in a LEDC: São Paulo	140–141
7.10	Urban transect: Manchester	142–143
7.10	Urban problems: LEDCs	144
7.11	Shanty town improvement: Lima, Peru	145
7.13	Activities	146–147
7.14	Sample examination questions	148

UNIT 8 Industry

	Focus photo: using robots in factories	149
8.1	Types of work	150–151
8.2	Industrial location	152–153
8.3	Industrial change	154–155
8.4	Global industry: multi-nationals	156–157
8.5	Industrial change: South Wales	158–159
8.6	A multi-national corporation: Nike	160
8.7	A newly industrialising country (NIC): Malaysia	161
8.8	Industry in a LEDC: India	162–163
8.9	Industry in the EU: the M4 corridor in the UK	164–165
8.10	Activities	166–167
8.11	Sample examination questions	168

UNIT 9 Farming as an industry

	Focus photo: market gardening in southern Spain	169
9.1	Types of farming	170
9.2	Farming in rich and poor countries	171
9.3	Soil erosion – a world wide problem	172
9.4	Farming in Britain	173
9.5	Lowland and upland farming in Britain	174–175
9.6	The changing face of farming	176–177
9.7	Farming and famine	178–179
9.8	Rice for subsistence: the Indian subcontinent	180–181
9.9	Commercial coffee growing in Tanzania	182–183
9.10	Shifting cultivation in Papua New Guinea	184
9.11	Intensive market gardening: the Netherlands	185
9.12	Appropriate technology: farming in Peru	186
9.13	Large-scale technology: irrigated farming in California	187
9.14	Activities	188–189
9.15	Sample examination questions	190

UNIT 10 World development

	Focus photo: contrasting cities	191
10.1	Measuring development	192–193
10.2	World trade	194–195
10.3	Global citizenship	196–197
10.4	Development project in a LEDC: improving the supply in Moyamba, Sierra Leone	198
10.5	The benefits and problems of aid	199
10.6	Countries with different levels of development: Brazil and Italy	200–201
10.7	Contrasts in development within countries: Italy and Brazil	202–203
10.8	A trading nation: Japan	204
10.9	Primary product dependency: Dominica	205
10.10	Assisting development: British overseas aid in Bangladesh	206–107
10.11	Activities	208–209
10.12	Sample examination questions	210

UNIT 11 Energy

	Focus photo: a North Sea oil rig	211
11.1	World energy resources	212–213
11.2	Non–renewable energy	214–215
11.3	Renewable energy	216–217
11.4	The changing demand for energy in the UK	218–219
11.5	Wind power: Haverigg Wind Farm, Cumbria	220
11.6	Energy in Africa: fuelwood	221
11.7	Hydro-electric power: the Three Gorges Dam in China	222–223
11.8	Nuclear energy	224–225
11.9	Activities	226–227
11.10	Sample examination questions	228

UNIT 12 Managing environments

	Focus photo: Antarctica	229
12.1	The global environment	230–231
12.2	Global problems and pressures	232–233
12.3	Transport development: roadbuilding in the UK	234
12.4	New road schemes: the Newbury bypass	235
12.5	Marine pollution: Europe	236
12.6	Oil spills: the *Sea Empress* disaster	237
12.7	Farming leading to desertification: Namibia	238
12.8	Sustainable and non-sustainable development	239
12.9	A National Park in the UK: the Lake District	240–241
12.10	A National park in a LEDC: Etosha National Park, Namibia	242–243
12.11	Protecting a fragile environmet: Antarctica	244–245
12.12	Activities	246–247
12.13	Sample examination questions	248
	Glossary	249–250
	Index	251

PEARSON EDUCATION LIMITED

Edinburgh Gate, Harlow, Essex, CM20 2JE, and associated companies throughout the world.

© Pearson Education Limited 1997, 2001

The right of Ann Bowen, Roger Clay, Carmela Di Landro, John Pallister and Olly Phillipson to be identified as authors of this work has been asserted by them in accordance with the Copyright, Designs and Patents Act of 1988.

All rights reserved. No part of this publication may be reproduced, stored in a retrieval system, or transmitted in any form or by any means, electronic, mechanical, photocopying, recording, or otherwise, without either the prior written permission of the Publishers or a licence permitting restricted copying issued by the Copyright Agency Ltd, 90 Tottenham Court Road, London W1P 9HE

First published 1997
This edition 2001

ISBN 0582 447445

Produced in Great Britain by Scotprint, Haddington

The Publishers' policy is to use paper manufactured from sustainable forests.

Design and production by Moondisks Ltd, Cambridge

Illustrations by Judy Brown, Tom Cross, Hardlines, Nick Hawken, Moondisks Ltd, Pat Murray/Graham Cameron Illustration, Oxford Illustrators

We are grateful to the following for permission to reproduce photographs and other copyright material.

Ace Photo Agency/Benelux Press, page 185; Aerofilms, page 74; Art Directors & TRIP, pages 18 *below* (Tibor Bognar), 51 (Hazel Rose), 198 (J Highet), 223 *above* (B Ashe); Barnabys Picture Library, page 37; Big Pit, Blaenafon, Gwent, pages 158, 214 *above*; John Birdsall, page 130; Ann Bowen, pages 71 *above*, 95; Len Brown, page 225; Vincent Bunce, pages 144 *above*; 205, 124, 227, 248; CAFOD, page 156; Cephas, page 139 (Mike Herringshaw); Chorley Handford, pages 33 *below*, 34 *above*, 56; Roger Clay, pages 8, 20, 21, 50 *above & left*, 57, 63 *left*, 171 *left*, 182, 183; John Cleare Mountain Camera, page 29; Stephanie Colasanti, page 163; Colorific!, pages 19 *right* (Enrico Ferorelli), 121 (Alon Raininger), 128 *above* (Steve Benbow), 189 *left* (Heiner Mulier-Elsner/Focus); Sylvia Cordaiy, pages 39, 48 (John Farmer); Sue Cunningham/SCP, pages 172 *above left*, 196 *below*, 199 *above*; James DavisWorldwide, page 169; Department For International Development, © Crown Copyright, pages 197 *above left & above right*, 206, 207; Ecoscene, pages 17 *left* (Andy Binns), 53 (John Farmer), 86 (Richard Glover), 98 (Andrew Brown), 172 *below* (E.J. Bent), 184 *centre*, 218; Experian Goad, pages 50 *below right*, 54 *right*, 55 *above right*, 64, 66; Eye Ubiquitous, pages 83 *above* (Paul Seheult), 171 *right* (Gerald Fritz); Fundu Lagoon, Pemba Island, page 63 *right* (Ken Niven); Geographer's A-Z Map Company Ltd, © Crown Copyright, page 148; GeoScience Features, pages 52, 82 *below*, page 93 *above, centre & below*; Green & Black's, page 179 *below*; Sally & Richard Greenhill, page 155 *below*; Robert Harding Picture Library, pages 16, 105 (Jeremy Bright), 107 *above* (J.H.C. Wilson), 184 *above*, 190 *left*, 190 *right* (Martyn Chillmaid), 215 *below*, 242, 244; Nick Hawken, pages 210, 241; The Hutchison Library, pages 68, 135 (Edward Parker), 144 *below*; The Image Bank, page 151 (G. Covian); Images Colour Library, page 32; Intermediate Technology, page 186; International Rice Research Institute, Philippines, page 181 *below*; Katz Pictures, pages 12 (Shigeo Kogure/Time Magazine), 14 (Garcia); Landform Slides, page 54 *left*; Magnum Photos, page 191 *left* (E Reed); Met Office, London, page 89; Mikes-Eye, page 175 *left*; National Meteorological Library, page 83 *below* (G.A. Robinson); Oxford Scientific Films/Survival Anglia, page 172 *above right* (Alan Root); PA News, page 42 (John Giles); PA Photos/European Photo Agency, page 18 *above*; John Pallister, pages 26, 31, 46, 107 *below*, 110, 113, 126, 128 *centre & below*, 131,133, 142, 145, 155 *above*, 157 *above*, 160 *above*, 161, 164, 165, 217 *above right*, 219, 229; Panos Pictures, pages 60 (Dylan Garcia), 160 *below* (Jeremy Hartley), 191 *right* (Sean Sprague); O.M. Phillipson, pages 238 *below*, 242; Planet Earth Pictures, pages 33 *above* (Mark Mattock), 67 (John Lythgoe), 170 *right* (P.N. Raven), 187 (William Smithey), 247 (Jonathan Scott); Popperfoto/Reuter, pages 5, 15, 170 *left* (Patrick Price/Reuters), 237; Rex Features, pages 47 (Richard Austin), 61 (Sipa Press/D E Pasquale), 149, 152 (Sipa Press), 184 *below*; Ryston Estate, page 174; Science Photo Library, pages 7 (CNES, 1989 Distribution Spot Image), 10 (David Parker), 23 (NRSC Ltd), 81 (European Space Agency), 82 *left* (Jerry Mason), 90 (Noaa), 215 *above* (Maximilian Stock Ltd), 230-1 (Tom Van Sant/Geosphere Project, Santa Monica); Sealand Aerial Photography, pages 43, 91; Skyscan Photolibrary, pages 49 (R & R Photography), 55 *above left* (Patrick Roach), 59 *below right* (Bob Evans), 76, 136, 153, 176 *below left* and 176 *below right* (Skyviews Aerial Archives), 216 *below* (Patrick Roach); South American Pictures, pages 140, 196 *above* (Bill Leimbach); Still Pictures, pages 17 *right* (Jorgen Schytte), 77 (Dylan Garcia), 96 (Olivier Langrand), 97 *left* and 97 *right* (Mark Edwards), 99 *left* (Alan Watson), 101 (Nigel Dickinson), 112 (Mark Edwards), 177 (Thomas Raupach), 197 (Teit Hornbak), 199 *below* (Jorgen Schytte), 215 *centre* (Mark Edwards), 216 *above* (Edward Parker), 217 *above left* (David Brain), 217 *below left*, 220, 221; Stone, pages 6 (Alan Kearney), 21 *left* (Nicholas Parfitt), 25 (Ian Murphy), 38 (Herb Schmitz), 59 *above* (Jeremy Walker), 87 *above* (Paul Harris), 87 *below* (Hugh Sitton), 99 *right* (Gary Braasch), 125 (Mark Segal), 175 *right* (Penny Tweedie), 211 (Arnulf Husmo), 213 (Joseph Pobereskin), 214 *below* (Wayne Eastep), 217 *below right* (Chris Kapolka), 233, 236 (Jeremy Walker); Telegraph Colour Library, pages 155 *centre* (Charles Briscoe-Knight), 238 *below*; Topham Picturepoint, pages 11 (Associated Press), 19 *above*, 19 *below left*, 179 *above* (Associated Press), 235 (Press Association), 240; Tropix, page 157 *below* (Ian Spark); University of Dundee, page 89 *inset*; Tony Waltham, pages 70, 71 *below*; Xinhua News Agency, London, page 223 *below*; Zefa, pages 34 *below* (K. Kerth), 181 *above* (M. Prabhu).

Maps reproduced from Ordnance Survey mapping with permission of the controller of Her Majesty's Office, © Crown Copyright, Licence No. 100027767

Front cover and title page: NASA image of largest ever ozone hole over Antarctica. Corbis

UNIT 1

Tectonic activity

Unit Contents

- Plate tectonics
- Volcanic activity
- Faults and earthquakes
- Tectonic hazards: the Kobe earthquake, 1995
- Tectonic hazards: the eruption of Mount Pinatubo
- Fold mountain building: the Himalayas
- Using volcanoes: Iceland and Southern Italy
- The East African Rift Valley – cradle of life

A survivor of the 1995 Kobe earthquake. What will be the short- and long-term effects on such survivors?

1.1 Plate tectonics

The earth's crust

The crust of the earth is made up of a number of **tectonic plates** (Source 1). These plates move over the surface of the globe. When two plates are moving apart, for example in the oceans, the margin between them is called a **constructive plate margin**. It is called this because new crust is being created, for example, along the mid-ocean ridge in the Atlantic Ocean. When two plates move towards each other, like the Nazca plate and the South American plate, the margin between them is called a **destructive plate margin**.

Source 1 — The world's tectonic plates

Key:
- constructive (divergent) plate margin
- destructive (convergent) plate margin
- direction of plate movement

Plates labelled: North American plate, Pacific plate, Nazca plate, South American plate, Antarctic plate, African plate, Eurasian plate, Indo-Australian plate, Philippine plate.

Along the plate margins powerful forces are at work. These forces change the landscape and cause serious hazards:

- They push up whole landscapes into high mountains by bending or folding the rocks, for example the Cascade Mountains in North America (Source 2) and the Himalayas (see Unit 1.6), which have been crumpled up as the Indian plate crashes into the Eurasian plate.
- They create hazards like the **earthquake** which hit the Japanese city of Kobe in 1995 (see Unit 1.4).
- They cause **volcanoes** to erupt, such as Pinatubo (see Unit 1.5).
- They rip open the earth's crust into deep **rift valleys** such as in East Africa (Source 3 and Unit 1.8) and **faults** like that of San Andreas (see Unit 1.3).

Source 2 — Tectonic forces push up mountains

The volcanic peak of Mount Rainier rises above the folded Cascade Mountains in North-West USA where the North American and Pacific plates meet.

Forces beneath the crust

It is hot beneath the surface of the earth. The heat is so great that the rocks below the crust are molten. This molten rock is called **magma**.

At particular places, called 'hot spots', magma rises to the surface in a series of **convection currents**. When the currents reach just below the crust they can rise no more. Instead, the hot currents spread out and carry the crust in a series of plates across the globe, as shown in Source 4.

As the convection currents spread out they pull the crust apart (A in Source 4). At this point a crack in the crust is formed, called a **rift valley**. Molten magma reaches the surface through this crack, producing volcanoes and, under the ocean, **ocean ridges**. Here, new crust is being constructed, hence the name 'constructive plate margin'.

Convection currents also move the crust towards other plates. One of the plates will be forced down beneath the other at the **subduction zone** (B in Source 4). The rocks left on the other plate are crumpled into high **fold mountains**. The crust which has been dragged beneath the surface is destroyed – hence these margins are called 'destructive plate margins'. In fact some of the lost crust is heated up to form new magma which eventually finds its way back to the earth's surface.

Wherever the tectonic plates are being pulled apart or crushed together, earthquakes can occur. Shock waves travel through the rocks causing violent movements of the land which destroy settlements and may also lead to loss of life.

Sometimes the plates pass alongside each other, neither colliding nor pulling apart. These plate margins are known as **conservative plate margins**, since crustal material is neither being created nor lost. However, the crust may crack and faults like San Andreas will be created, along which other earthquakes occur like that in San Francisco in 1906.

Source 3 | Satellite view of part of the East African Rift Valley – tectonic forces are tearing apart the earth's crust

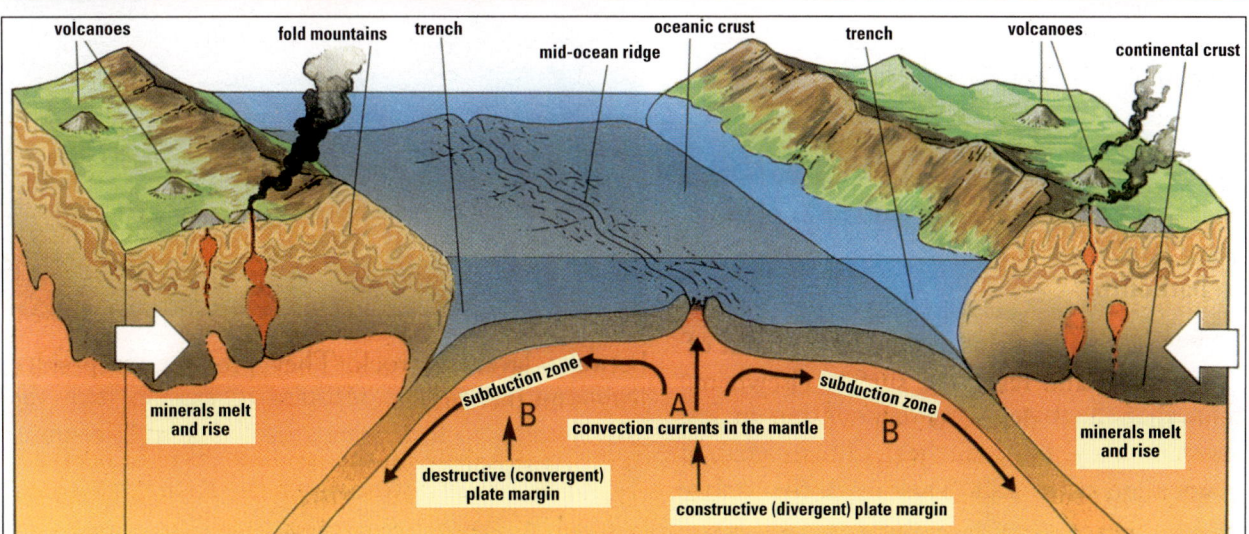

Source 4 | Forces beneath the earth's crust produce mountains, volcanoes and ocean ridges

1.2 Volcanic activity

Volcanic activity is important right across the earth's surface. There are over 500 active volcanoes which still erupt from time to time. Each year there are around 30 or 40 eruptions. Some eruptions are slight, but others have serious effects, causing loss of life and damage to land and property.

Volcanic activity can be divided into two types (Source 1):

- **intrusive volcanic activity** – where **lava** (molten rock) cools and solidifies beneath the surface
- **extrusive volcanic activity** – where lava reaches the earth's surface before it cools and solidifies.

Source 1 Intrusive and extrusive volcanic landforms

Intrusive volcanic activity

A whole range of landforms result from intrusive volcanic activity (Source 1). On the left of the diagram there are examples of landforms which have been produced by molten rock cooling and solidifying beneath the surface. When it is under the earth's surface the molten rock is called **magma**.

When a large amount of liquid rock pushes up towards the earth's surface it will cause all the surface rock to bulge up into a dome or plateau. Such a large mass of solidified magma is known as a **batholith**.

Sometimes smaller veins of magma push out of the batholith and reach the surface elsewhere. Some are called **dykes**, which will stand up above the surrounding land if they resist erosion more than the surrounding rocks; if they are less resistant they form ditches. Other veins of magma are called **sills**. They reach the surface

Source 2 Upstanding dyke in northern Scotland

by forcing their way between layers of rock. They produce steep-sided ledges on the surface.

Source 2 is a dyke on the island of Skye in northern Scotland. It is more resistant to erosion than the surrounding rock. It stands up like a 'wall' running across the land.

Tectonic activity

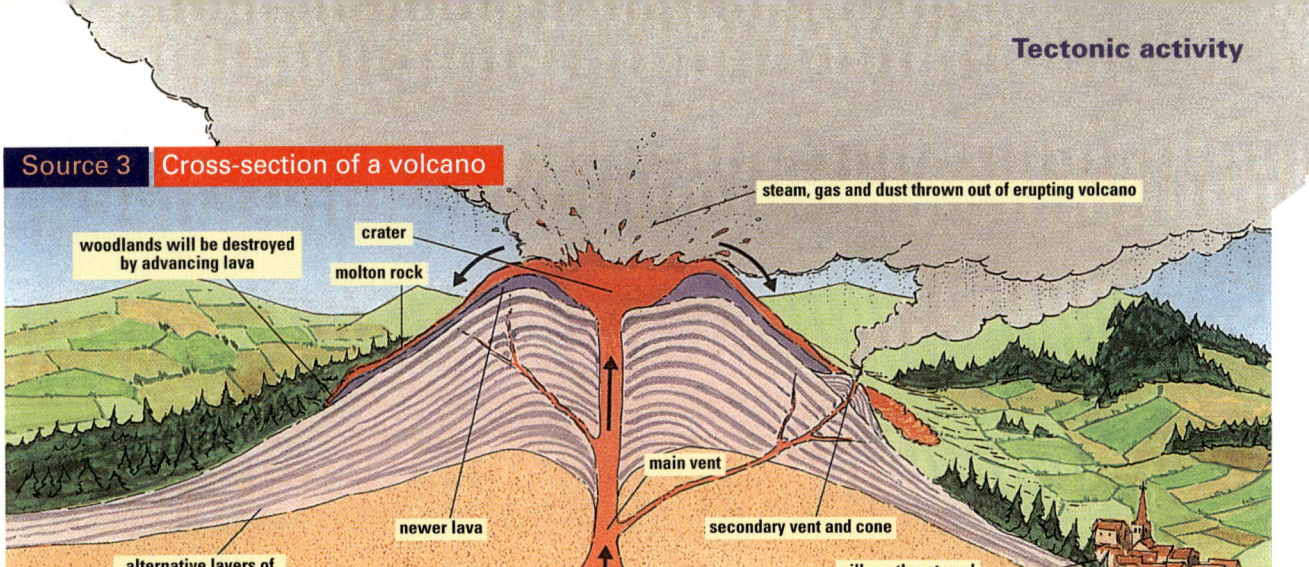

Source 3 — Cross-section of a volcano

Extrusive volcanic activity

On the right-hand side of Source 1 are extrusive volcanic landforms. A volcano is a crack in the earth's surface which provides an outlet for lava, steam and ash. The lava passes through a pipe called a vent from inside the crust to the earth's surface where it erupts (Source 3). After the eruption a crater is left on the surface. Lava which has erupted hardens on the surface.

The escape of lava from a volcano can take place under pressure, resulting in explosions of steam, gas and dust. These are hurled high in the air and molten rock pours down the volcano's sides.

Eruptions may damage property – houses, roads and farmland. The dust which reaches the upper layers of the atmosphere can cause climatic change on a global scale, blocking out the sun's heat and increasing rainfall. An example of a very destructive volcano is Mount Pinatubo in the Philippines (see Unit 1.5).

Volcanoes can also have positive effects. Ash and lava turn into fertile soils. Hot magma beneath the surface heats up underground water, providing steam for heating and power. Examples of these positive effects are described in Unit 1.7.

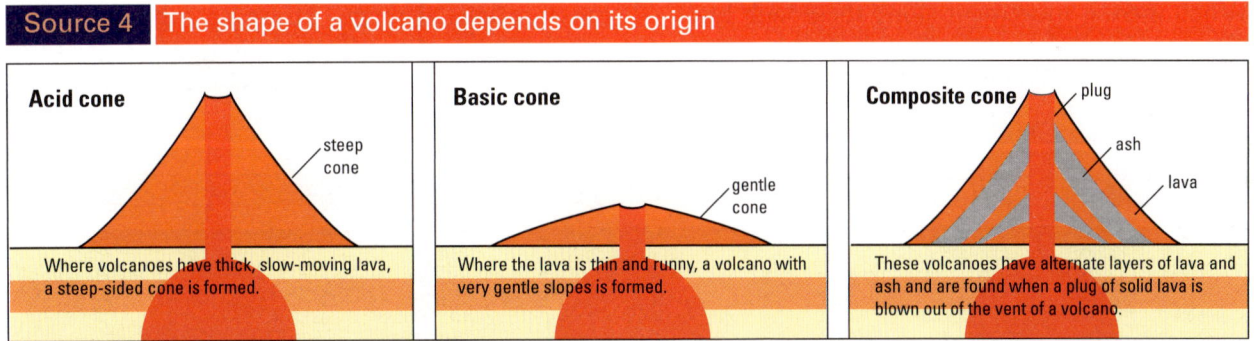

Source 4 — The shape of a volcano depends on its origin

There are many different kinds of lava. Some are very thick and 'sticky' (viscous). Others are thin and 'runny'. Lava which is made up of mainly acid minerals is viscous. When it flows out it solidifies quickly forming steep-sided **acid cones**.

Basic cones are formed by less acid lavas which flow across the landscape forming gentle slopes or, sometimes, flat plateaus.

9

1.3 Faults and earthquakes

Faults

Tectonic plates may move towards each other, away from each other or slide against each other. When they do move they make the earth's crust crack. These cracks are called **faults**.

Source 1 shows three types of faults. One is known as a **lateral fault**. This is when the crust at A is sliding along the crust at B. This is what is happening along the San Andreas fault in California, USA (Source 2). Another type of fault shown in Source 1 is the **vertical fault**. Here, the crust at B has slipped down and away from the crust at C.

Sometimes, when the crust is being pulled apart (tension), two **parallel faults** are formed. The land between these faults slips down. A steep-sided, flat-bottomed valley is created. This is a rift valley. The East African Rift Valley, part of a great tear in the earth's crust, is examined in Unit 1.8 (see also Source 3, Unit 1.1).

When there is movement along these fault lines, the jagged rocks catch against each other. Each movement may only be a millimetre at any one time. However, over the years the pressure on the 'caught' rock will build up and become extreme. Eventually the rocks will spring apart. When they do so, earthquakes happen.

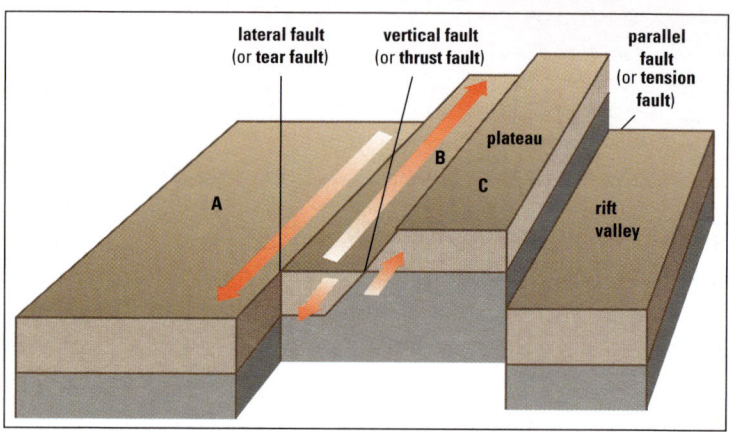

Source 1: Tear, thrust and tension faults create new landscapes. How has the plan helped us to understand the processes?

Earthquakes

Every year, several thousand earth movements are detected around the world. Usually only 40 or 50 of these movements are violent enough to cause serious damage. However, when they do occur, earthquakes like the one in 1993 near the village of Killari in India (Source 3) can result in loss of life.

Source 2: The San Andreas fault runs down the western side of California

Tectonic activity

Source 3 — The destruction of Killari by the 1993 earthquake

Disaster at Killari

At 4 o'clock in the morning on 30 September 1993, the village of Killari in central India was destroyed by a severe earthquake. Killari is 450 km east of Bombay. Several of the villages around Killari were destroyed, 30 000 people lost their lives and many more were left homeless. The quake measured 6.4 on the Richter Scale.

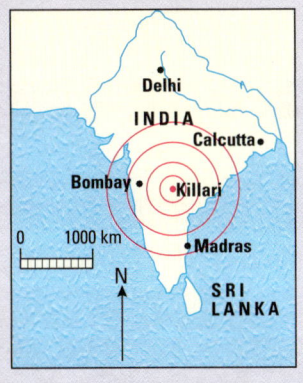

When earthquakes occur, the point underground where rocks spring apart is known as the **focus**. From the focus (Source 4), shock waves travel through the rocks in all directions. As the shock waves reach the surface they will damage houses, factories and roads.

Most damage will be caused on the earth's surface closest to the focus. This point, directly above the focus, is called the **epicentre**. By the time the shock waves have reached the surface further away, they have lost most of their energy and less damage is caused.

How far the damage extends depends, also, on the nature of the rocks. Hard, resistant rocks will quickly reduce the energy of the shock waves. Softer rocks will buckle and bend, and the shock waves will be able to carry their destructive power to places further away.

Earthquakes in less economically developed countries (LEDCs) are much more damaging than those in more economically developed countries (MEDCs). Often the buildings cannot resist the shock waves as they have been poorly built. They are often made of heavy, local rock. When the buildings collapse the people inside have little chance. Few LEDCs are able to mount a quick rescue operation – their emergency services are usually few in number and not well trained. Many people died in Killari (Source 3) because the Indian government did not have the resources to respond quickly enough.

Source 4 — Earthquake shock waves are measured by the Richter Scale which is used to determine the likely damage caused by an earthquake

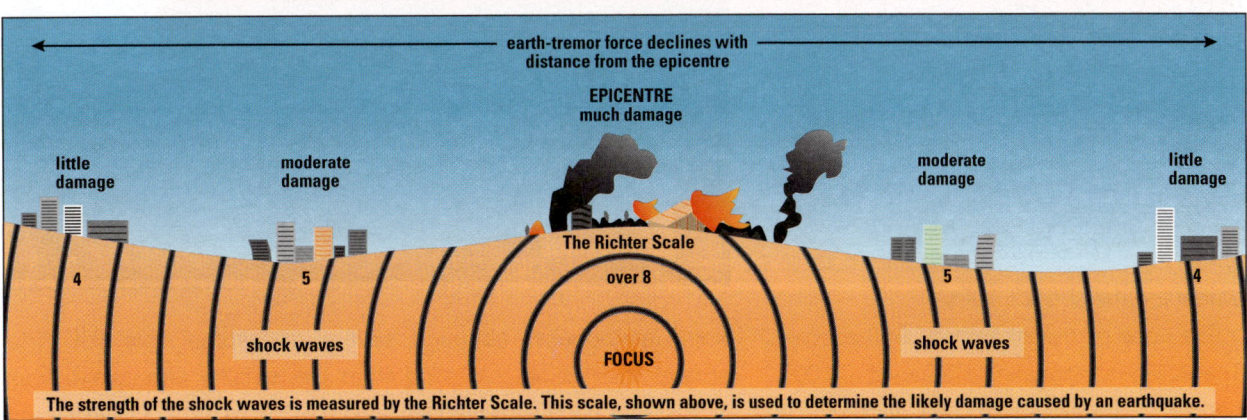

1.4 Tectonic hazards
the Kobe earthquake, 1995

Early in the morning on Tuesday 17 January 1995 the shock waves of a huge earthquake roared through the city of Kobe. Measuring 7.2 on the Richter Scale, it was the worst earthquake to hit Japan for 50 years.

- More than 3500 people were killed.
- Some 20 000 houses were destroyed.
- About 250 000 people were left homeless.
- Operations at Japan's largest port (Kobe) ceased.
- An area of over 100 hectares was completely destroyed by fire.
- The cost of the damage was over US$50 billion.

This earthquake was caused by the Philippine plate moving beneath the Eurasian plate (Source 1). The rocks had locked together many years ago and the pressure had built up each year since then. Suddenly they jerked free, and the shock waves were released. The destruction is shown in the photograph on page 5, in Sources 1 and 2, and is also described in the newspaper article in Source 3.

The epicentre of the earthquake was near Awaji Island. Here only buildings were destroyed. The greatest destruction was where most people live – in the cities of Kobe, Akashi and Ashiya. The famous bullet train tracks, motorways and bridges were all badly damaged. Broken gas pipes and electricity lines caused fires to rage throughout the built-up areas – especially among the many wooden houses built to withstand the shock waves.

The Kobe earthquake killed 3500 people. The Killari earthquake killed over 30 000 people. Whereas the Kobe earthquake measured 7.2 on the Richter Scale, the Killari earthquake, although severe, measured only 6.4. The greater loss of life resulting from the smaller earthquake was almost entirely due to the inability of LEDCs to protect themselves from such natural disasters.

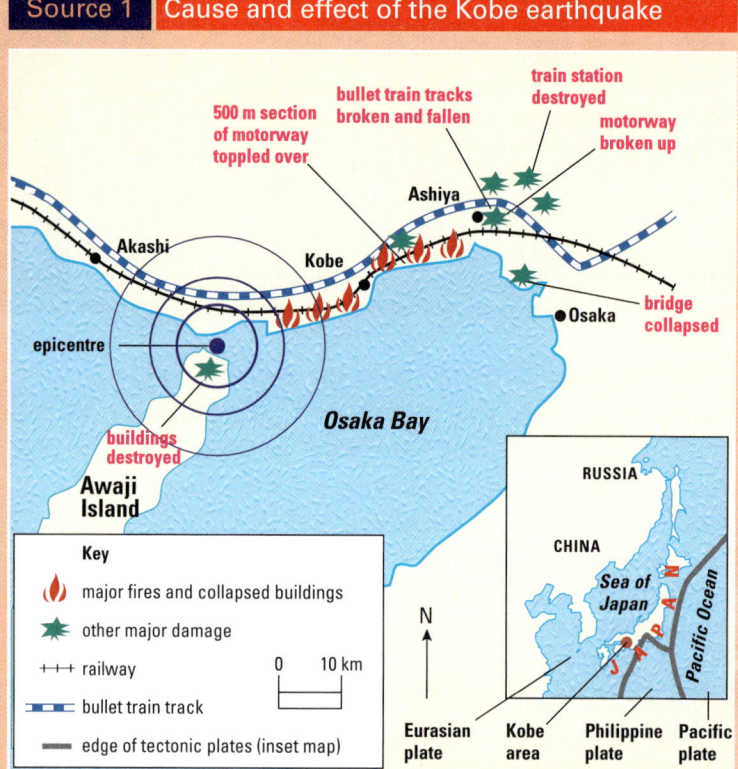

Source 1 — Cause and effect of the Kobe earthquake

Source 2 — The Kobe earthquake caused severe damage

Tectonic activity

| Source 3 | Newspaper report of earthquake damage |

Kobe – the quake's aftermath

An empty noodle shop, in Kobe's central shopping and entertainment district, suddenly caught fire yesterday. The blaze, one of many hampering earthquake relief efforts, quickly consumed 10 surrounding buildings.

Police and Japan's military forces later tried to clear some of the damage in the district, where the walls of Daimaru, a department store, fell on the main road.

Most of the initial fires ignited by Tuesday's quake have been damped. Yesterday, firefighters were trying to kill the last of the flames. Shop signs, melted and mangled from the heat, were strewn about and dust and smoke filled the air.

Construction workers tried to overhaul parts of the elevated Hanshin Expressway collapsed on to the main road between Osaka and Kobe. The damage has blocked part of the road, forcing traffic to follow other routes and causing severe jams.

Although trucks, cranes, power shovels and workmen gathered, nobody seemed to know what to do with the giant concrete structure on its side, and the massive uprooted pillars, their steel foundations exposed.

And while emergency supplies arrived by trucks from throughout the country, many people blamed the government for its slow reaction. "What are we paying taxes for?" asked a woman. "Isn't it for times like this?"

Predicting earthquakes

Scientists know where earthquakes will strike – along the active plate margins. They find it much more difficult to say when they will happen. Before an earthquake the land may be seen to rise or tilt. Sometimes the water level in wells is seen to fall. If local people notice these changes they can alert everyone to reach places of safety, well away from buildings.

If these changes do not occur, or are not seen, there is very little chance of predicting earthquakes. There have been recent improvements in detecting changes in electrical signals and in registering radioactivity emissions. In order to register such changes many more scientific stations or satellites capable of recording these indicators are needed.

| Source 4 | Building to survive earthquakes |

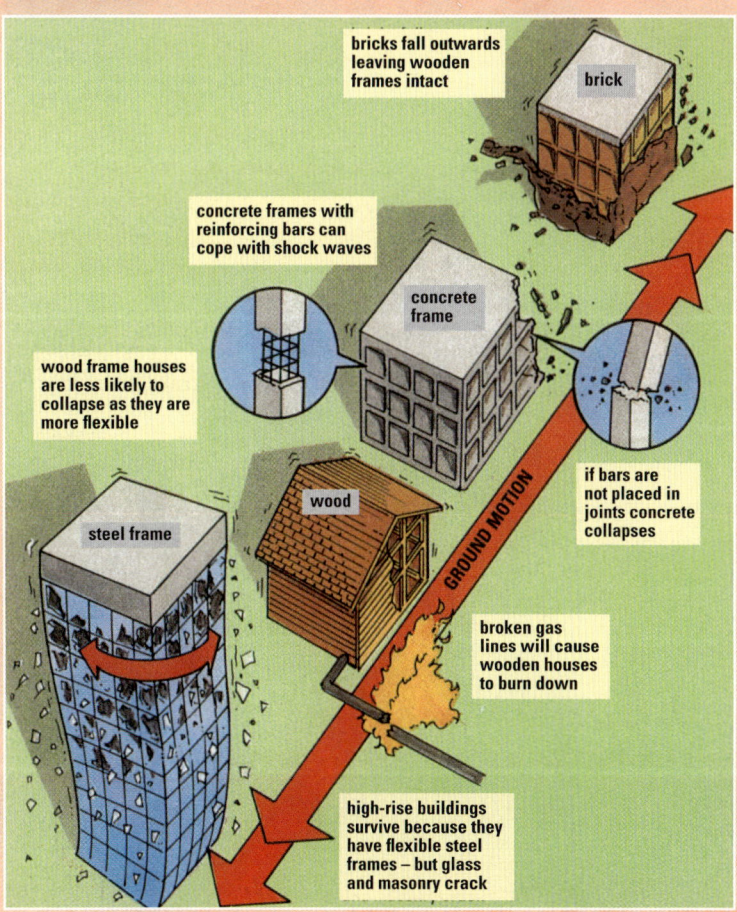

Resisting earthquakes

If scientists were able to predict when earthquakes are likely to happen, many lives would be saved. Even if earthquakes could be predicted accurately, they would still damage buildings. Recent earthquakes in different parts of the world have allowed town planners to form a picture of what types of buildings can resist earthquakes.

Source 4 shows how different building materials respond to shock waves.

- Wooden houses may burn in the aftermath of an earthquake, as they did in Kobe.
- Bricks fall out of buildings, so they are not good materials in earthquake zones.
- Concrete is much better, as long as it is reinforced by strong, flexible steel bars.
- High-rise buildings with flexible steel frames do survive, but falling glass and bricks can cause injury and death.

These are the lessons which the people of Kobe must pay attention to as they rebuild their city.

1.5 Tectonic hazards
the eruption of Mount Pinatubo

Mount Pinatubo is a volcanic mountain located about 100 km north-west of Manila, the capital of the Philippines (Source 1). By June 1991, the volcano had been peaceful for more than six centuries. During this time the ash and lava from previous eruptions had weathered to become fertile soil which was used to cultivate rice. Then, suddenly, the volcano came to life (Source 2).

Advance warning that the volcano was about to erupt gave the authorities time to evacuate thousands of people from the nearby town of Angeles. Some 15 000 American airmen and women also left the nearby Clark air base. The level of activity increased and finally on 12 June the volcano sent a cloud of steam and ash some 30 km up into the atmosphere.

More deadly than the steam and ash were the **pyroclastic flows**. These are the burning gases that descend from the volcano at speeds of over 200 kilometres an hour. They engulf and burn everything in their path. It is the main killer of people and destroyer of wildlife in volcanic eruptions (see Unit 1.7 on Vesuvius).

Source 1 — Mount Pinatubo in the Philippines

Source 2 — Pinatubo erupts in June 1991 – a lorry tries to outrun the rapidly advancing pyroclastic flow

Fact File

- Ash fell to a depth of 50 cm near the volcano, and over a 600 km radius of the volcano it was still over 10 cm deep.
- The volume of ash in the atmosphere turned day to night and hampered the rescue operations.
- Torrential rain accompanied the eruption, and much of the ash was rained back to earth as mud, causing thousands of buildings to collapse under its weight.
- Power supplies were cut and roads and bridges were left unusable, as was the water supply which was quickly contaminated.
- Some 350 people were killed, mostly by pyroclastic flows.

Tectonic activity

When a volcano erupts much cinder, ash and lava falls on the slopes. The lava solidifies, and the cinder and ash remain in a loose and unstable condition on the upper slopes.

This is what happened after the 1991 eruption of Mount Pinatubo.

At a later date heavy rain washed this loose material down the volcano sides. This occurred after typhoons hit the Philippines in 1993 and 1995. The local people were inundated with mud avalanches – the **lahars** (Source 3).

Source 3 Filipinos flee the lahar, 5 September 1995

Boiling mud swamps towns

Philippines. Hundreds of Filipinos were plucked from the roofs of their houses yesterday after walls of boiling mud swamped towns.

Torrential rain from Tropical Storm Nina loosened a torrent of volcanic debris, called lahar, from Pinatubo volcano which swept into towns. More than 65 000 people were forced to flee the area.

A spokesperson for the regional disaster office said: 'We had already been hit by a 10 ft lahar last week. And then Bacolor got hit with another 10 feet of lahar today.'

Bacolor, a town of 20 000 people, was turned into a wasteland of mud and ash. Houses were buried, forcing residents to haul their beds, cooking pots and clothes to the roof.

Helicopters evacuated scores, but many refused to go, not wanting to leave their belongings behind.

The long-term effects

The effects of the eruption were felt long after the volcano became dormant again. With thousands of people living in refugee camps, malaria and diarrhoea quickly spread. Huge quantities of dust, some 20 million tonnes, were left in the atmosphere. Scientists believe that the dust has resulted in a lowering of average temperatures, and that it will delay global warming.

The cost to the Philippines was immense. Crops, roads and railways, business and personal property were destroyed, amounting to over $450 million.

Looking towards recovery

The Philippines is a LEDC and has little money to spend on rebuilding the part of Luzon devastated by the eruption.

The response of the authorities of Central Luzon needs to focus on:

- protecting against further lahars and flash flood damage by building dykes and dams
- establishing new work for the farmers and other workers, for example those working at Clark air base, well away from the danger area
- creating new towns and villages away from the danger area.

The great cost of these needs cannot be borne by the people of Luzon alone. Here is a good example of how the international aid agencies, such as OXFAM, can be used to provide development funds in LEDCs.

1.6 Fold mountain building
the Himalayas

Source 1 shows how the Indian plate collided with the Eurasian plate. The softer sedimentary rocks lying on top of the plates along this constructive (convergent) plate margin were scraped up and folded to produce the highest mountain range in the world. Mount Everest (8848 metres) and K2 (8611 metres) are the two highest peaks.

The Himalayas stand in the way of the warm, wet summer monsoon winds. These winds sweep up from the Indian Ocean and the Bay of Bengal. As they rise up the mountain sides they produce torrential rain and, at higher levels, blizzards of snow.

The great rivers of the Indus, Ganges and Brahmaputra feed off this rain and snow. They bring valuable water to the dry lands of Pakistan and India – which is used to grow the rice and other crops to feed the huge populations of these countries.

Source 1 The Himalayas were created when the northward moving Indian plate slid below the rigid Eurasian plate and the soft sedimentary rocks lying on the plates were scraped off and folded into mountains

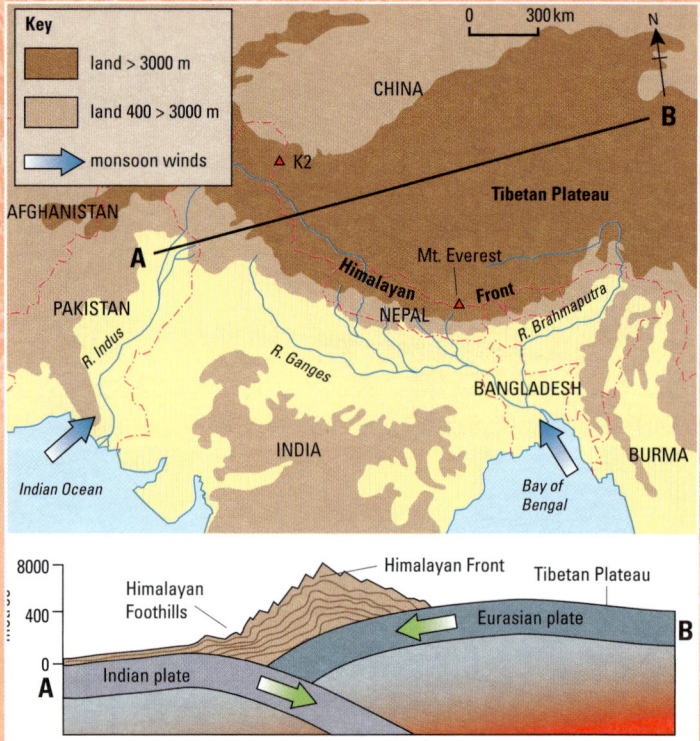

Source 2 The unstable slopes of the high Himalayas

- The snow-capped Himalayan peaks release tonnes of water in the spring
- Loose scree collapsing down the slope
- Road building undermines the mountain slopes

The natural threat to the mountains

Such a large amount of water creates problems. Rivers regularly burst their banks as they are fed by the summer rains and melting snows. Half of Bangladesh lies in the great delta formed by the rivers Ganges and Brahmaputra. Each year people lose their homes, farmland and often their lives as they battle the floods.

The heavy rains and snows on the steep slopes of the mountains create another problem. The water is washing away the rocks. Source 2 shows the loose rock (**scree**) collapsing down the sides of the mountains.

Nowhere in the world is there greater removal of rock by natural forces than in the Himalayas. Every year ice and rain carry millions of tonnes of weathered rock down the steep slopes.

Tectonic activity

The impact of people on the mountains

People, too, have helped increase the erosion of the land. The Himalayas have long been a barrier to travel and trade between countries to the south, such as India, and countries to the north, such as China. Roads now link these countries across the mountains. The Karakoram Highway (Source 4) is the highest road in the world. During its construction mountainsides were blasted away leaving the road sitting on loose scree. This scree is a constant landslide threat.

These roads have helped tourists reach the higher mountains. Climbers, trekkers and sightseers are welcomed by the local people because they bring much-needed foreign currency to the region. Unfortunately they often leave unwanted marks on the landscape like litter and eroded footpaths. The eroded footpaths channel streams down the mountainside and so increase the removal of the land.

Source 3 Hazards of the Himalayas

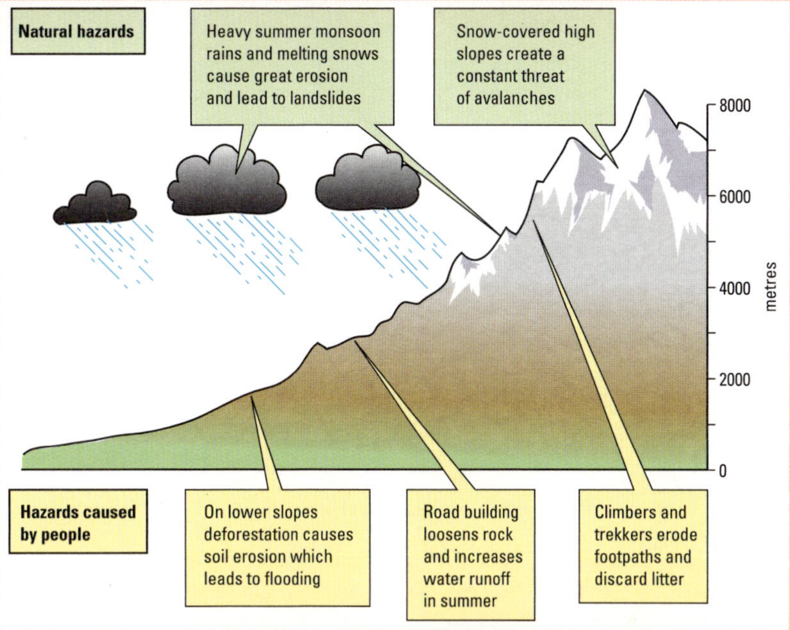

- **Natural hazards**
  - Heavy summer monsoon rains and melting snows cause great erosion and lead to landslides
  - Snow-covered high slopes create a constant threat of avalanches
- **Hazards caused by people**
  - On lower slopes deforestation causes soil erosion which leads to flooding
  - Road building loosens rock and increases water runoff in summer
  - Climbers and trekkers erode footpaths and discard litter

On the lower slopes there are more roads. These have been built as the local people have expanded their farming and fuelwood collection into the hills.

Source 4 The Karakoram Highway heads towards the Tibetan Plateau from the mountains – note the lack of tarmac on the surface of this remote highway

Source 5 This Himalayan hill slope has lost all its vegetation and is now collapsing

As the number of villages has grown so has the removal of the protecting trees (**deforestation**). These trees help hold the soil on the slopes. Without them the soil is lost, leaving bare hill slopes (Source 5).

Using volcanoes
Iceland and Southern Italy

Volcanoes are usually destructive. Eruptions often lead to loss of life and may also damage property and crops. However, volcanic activity can also have positive results.

Iceland

Iceland is situated in the North Atlantic Ocean. It is also located on a major plate boundary – the mid-Atlantic ridge (Source 1). As a result of this, there is a lot of volcanic activity on the island.

- It has over 200 volcanoes (Source 2).
- There are over 800 hot springs and geysers.
- Ten per cent of the land surface is lava fields.
- New land is being created as the two plates (the Eurasian and North American plate) separate along the ridge.

Source 2 | Mount Hekla erupts in February 2000

Source 3 | Bláa Lónið – the 'Blue Lagoon' near Reykjavik – Icelanders take advantage of these naturally heated waters which vary in temperature between 33°C and 45°C

Source 1 | Iceland on the mid-Atlantic ridge

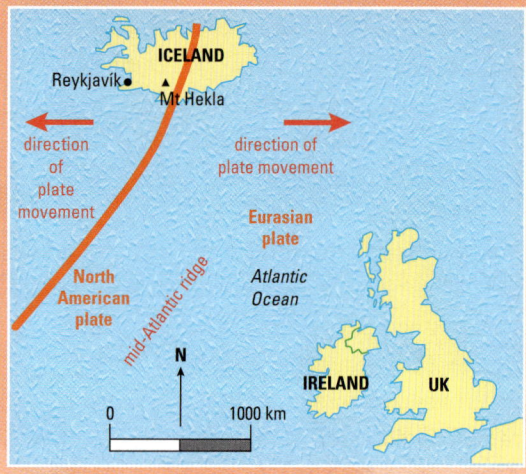

Volcanic activity in Iceland has some positive effects:

1. **Hot spring water** is carried by pipeline to Reykjavik, the capital of Iceland, giving most people a cheap and reliable form of energy which does not damage the environment. Much of the water used in the city today comes from a borehole 45 km away, which yields water at over 300°C. Hot water at a lower temperature provides recreational opportunities for Icelanders and tourists alike (Source 3).

2. **Electricity is generated** from the geothermal resources of hot water which lie under the ground in many parts of Iceland. Steam from the hot water deposits found underground is used to power turbines, which in turn generate electricity for factories and homes.

3. **Greenhouses** not far from Reykjavik are geothermally heated, allowing some Icelanders to produce vegetables, fruit and even flowers.

Tectonic activity

| Source 4 | Petrified body excavated from the ash at Pompeii |

| Source 5 | Land use on the fertile soil surrounding Vesuvius |

Southern Italy

In southern Italy, volcanic activity has brought different benefits. Over 1900 years ago, in AD 79, the volcano Vesuvius erupted. The town of Pompeii was completely destroyed. The eruption sent burning gases (pyroclastic flows) down the sides of the volcano killing the people of the town. Ash from this eruption, together with many smaller ones that have taken place since, has covered the landscape in this part of southern Italy. Source 4 shows the petrified remains of a child killed by pyroclastic flows from Pompeii in AD 79.

Over many years, the ash has weathered to produce fertile soils. This has led to many people settling around the volcano, where the soils are used to grow olives, fruit, vines and nuts as well as a variety of market garden produce (Sources 5 and 6). Villages and towns circle the higher, sterile slopes, where the lava has not yet weathered, so nothing can be grown. In other places where the ash and lava are loose, forests have been planted to stop slope erosion.

The slopes of Vesuvius, in spite of the ever-present danger of new volcanic eruptions, will always provide rich soils to encourage farmers to work the land.

| Source 6 | Mechanisation on the rich farmland surrounding Vesuvius |

Predicting volcanic eruptions

Like Vesuvius, volcanoes may erupt only after hundreds or thousands of years of being quiet (**dormant**). So it is very difficult to predict eruptions. There are warning signs, however. Near the time of an eruption the magma beneath the volcano comes close to the surface. This will cause:

- the escape of gases, particularly sulphur dioxide, which can be monitored with special equipment
- a number of small earthquakes which can be measured with special equipment
- swelling of the sides of the volcano.

The problem is that monitoring equipment is very expensive and could be in place for generations without detecting any signs. Perhaps the best way is for people living near volcanoes to keep a regular watch on any changes which may indicate a coming eruption.

1.8 The East African Rift Valley
cradle of life

Source 1 The location of Lake Natron in the Great Rift Valley in northern Tanzania

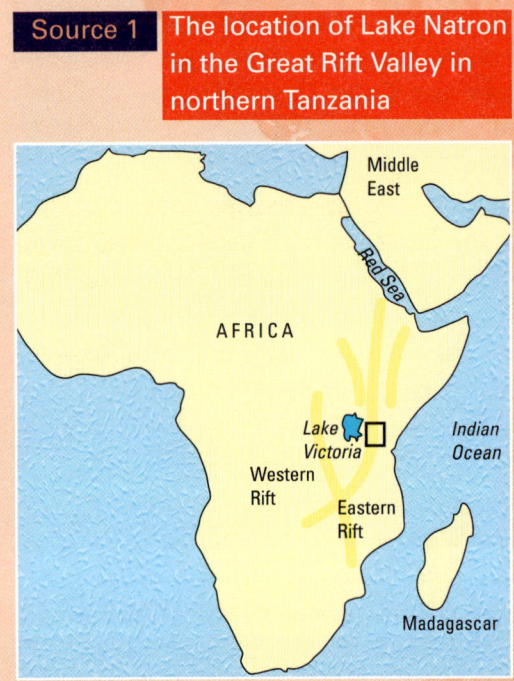

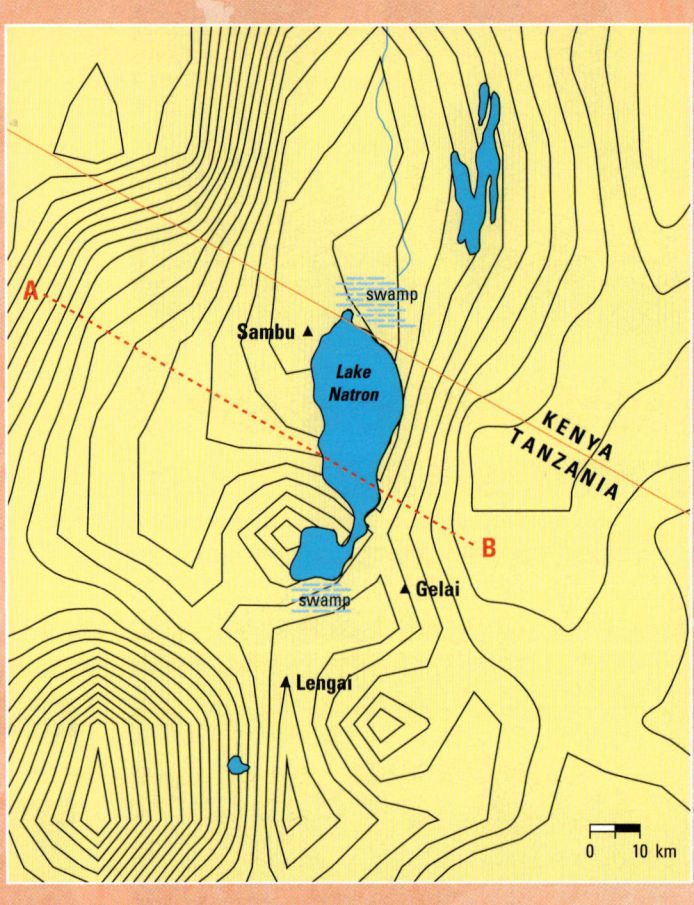

Around 1.5 million years ago small groups of people wandered across the dry grassland near Lake Natron.

These were our earliest ancestors. Why was this part of the Rift Valley the origin of modern humans?

From the Red Sea, all the way down through East Africa the earth is being torn apart. A great number of cracks have weakened the crust. The hot magma beneath has forced its way up to the surface and volcanoes and faults are strewn along the line of cracks.

As the surface domed up it pushed the edges of the crack apart creating steep-sided slopes known as fault escarpments. Source 2 shows part of the fault escarpment overlooking Lake Natron. The lavas from the volcanoes flowed across the valley lying between the escarpments. Rivers flowed down the sides of the escarpments and created lakes, like Natron.

The lavas weathered to form soil. Tall grasses and scattered trees began to cover the land. Large herds of wildebeest, zebra and other grass-eating animals (herbivores) roamed the valley floor. They were preyed on by lions, hyenas and many other flesh-eating animals (carnivores). People left the forests of the slopes and began to scavenge what was left by the carnivores. Before long, they began to hunt for themselves. In this part of Africa 'the hunter' was born.

Source 2 The fault escarpment overlooking Lake Natron

Tectonic activity

Shaping the Rift Valley

Source 1 shows the three volcanoes which lie around the edge of the Lake Natron rift – Gelai, Lengai and Sambu. The volcanic lavas forming the land over which early people walked came from Sambu 1.5 million years ago. It has not erupted since. The only active volcano is Mount Lengai which last erupted in 1966 (Source 3).

Source 3 Mount Lengai

Today, away from Lake Natron, the floor of the Rift Valley is a dry, desolate place (Source 4). At best it is a dry grassland with a scattering of thorny shrubs. The high sides of the escarpments block the rain-bearing winds, which deposit their moisture high above the valley. Here, rainforest is to be seen.

Source 5 The 'badland' floor of the Rift Valley above Lake Natron

Small movements of the land cause local faulting. In Source 5 plateaus (A) are separated by fault-line valleys (B). The dry land is rapidly eroded by the few heavy showers of rain – this is a 'badland' landscape.

Source 6 Masai in the Rift Valley

Today, only the semi-permanent Masai cattle and goat herders live in this desolate landscape (Source 6). Each day they move their herds around to take advantage of what little vegetation is to be found.

Source 4 Vegetation zones in the Natron Rift Valley

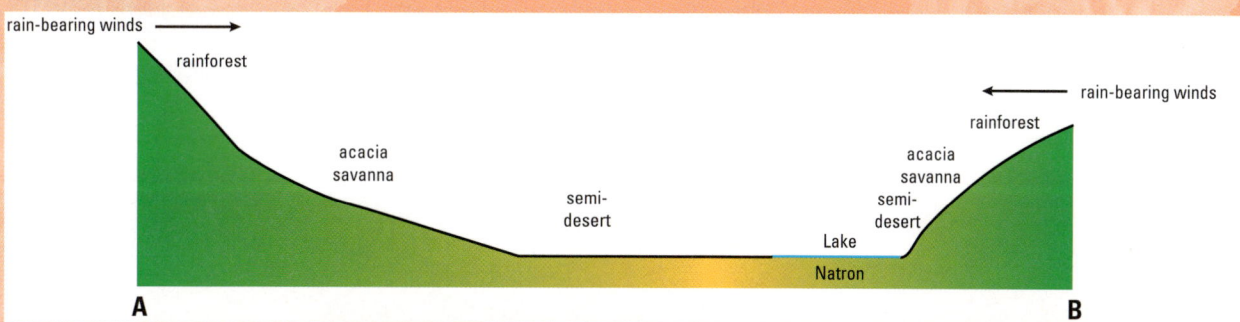

1.9 Activities

1 Copy the following passage into your book filling in the blank spaces.
The earth's crust is made up of a number of _____ _____. Where these _____ move apart a _____ _____ _____ is formed. Where these _____ push together a _____ _____ _____ is formed.

Beneath the earth's crust is molten rock called _____. This molten rock is brought to the surface by _____ _____. As the molten rock spreads outwards, it pulls the crust apart creating _____ _____. Beneath the sea the molten rock rises to the sea floor producing _____ _____.

Where the moving crust meets another part of the crust, one of them will sink below the other. This junction is called a _____ zone. As it sinks the crust heats up, turns back to molten rock and is forced up as an erupting _____. Other rock is crumpled by these crustal collisions and _____ mountains are built.

2 Make a copy of the volcano (Source 1).
   a Label the following features: magma chamber; main vent; crater; steam; gas and dust; layers of cooled lava.
   b Describe the landforms of intrusive volcanic activity.
   c Explain how and why a volcano erupts.
   d Describe the different shapes of volcanoes and explain how each is formed.

Volcano

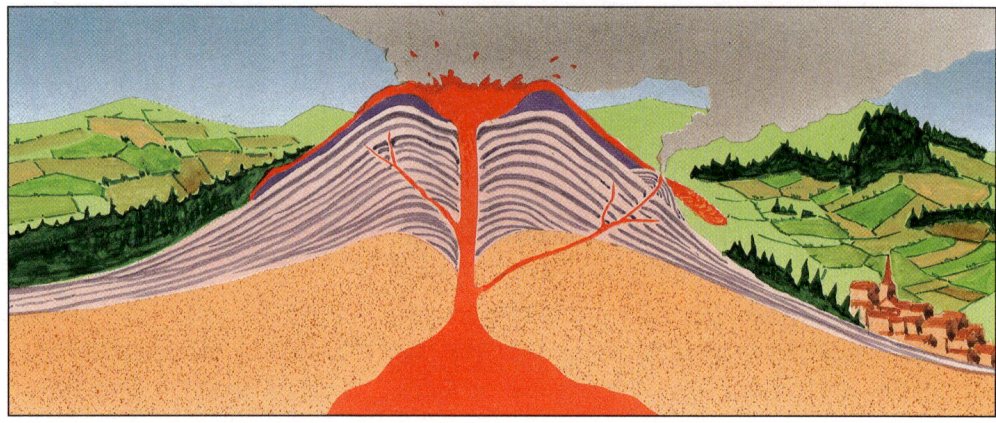

3 a Draw a simple diagram showing the difference between a lateral and vertical fault. Name a specific example of one fault you have studied.
   b Describe what happens at the focus of an earthquake.
   c How does the Richter Scale help us to estimate the amount of damage which earthquakes cause?
   d Explain the ways in which MEDCs are less likely to suffer severely from earthquakes than LEDCs.

4 a Read the newspaper article on the Kobe earthquake on page 13 and, with the help of other evidence in 1.4, make a list of the damage caused.
  b Using the information from 1.3 and 1.4, explain why the smaller Killari earthquake in India caused many more deaths than the larger Kobe earthquake in Japan.
  c The main cause of loss of life in an earthquake is the collapse of buildings. Describe the ways in which town planners can reduce earthquake damage to buildings.

5 a Mount Pinatubo is a tectonic hazard. When it erupted in 1991 it released pyroclastic flows. In 1995 heavy rainstorms released lahars. Explain the origin and destructive effect of these two hazards.
  b Iceland is built by volcanoes. Describe how the people who live on the island use the volcanic resources to their benefit.
  c Vesuvius destroyed the city of Pompeii in AD 79. Since then people have settled around the volcano. What are the advantages of living so close to such a dangerous volcano?

6 a Look at Source 1 on page 20 and refer back to Source 1 on page 6. Describe the earth movements that have created the East African Rift Valley.
  b Explain why volcanoes are to be found along the line of the Rift Valley.
  c Explain why the volcanic activity has been important for both wildlife and people in the Rift Valley.
  d Describe how and explain why the vegetation changes across the Rift Valley.

7 a Study Source 2 below. In which direction from the peak of Vesuvius is the modern city of Naples located? How is this different from the location of the ancient settlement of Pompeii? Why do you think this is?
  b Examine the rural land uses surrounding the volcano. Make a list of these and describe how each is distributed, for example distance from peak, compass directions from peak.
  c How have road routes been influenced by the presence of the volcanic cone?

Source 2 | Satellite view of Vesuvius and surrounding area

1.10 Sample examination questions

1 a Draw a diagram of a volcano and label on it Crater, Vent and Layers of lava.
(*3 marks*)

b State two differences between volcanoes along constructive and destructive plate margins. (*2 marks*)

c Describe what happens when an earthquake occurs. (*2 marks*)

d Explain how ranges of fold mountains are formed. (*3 marks*)

(Total: *10 marks*)

2 a Source 2 shows the effects of the eruption of Mount St. Helens in 1980.

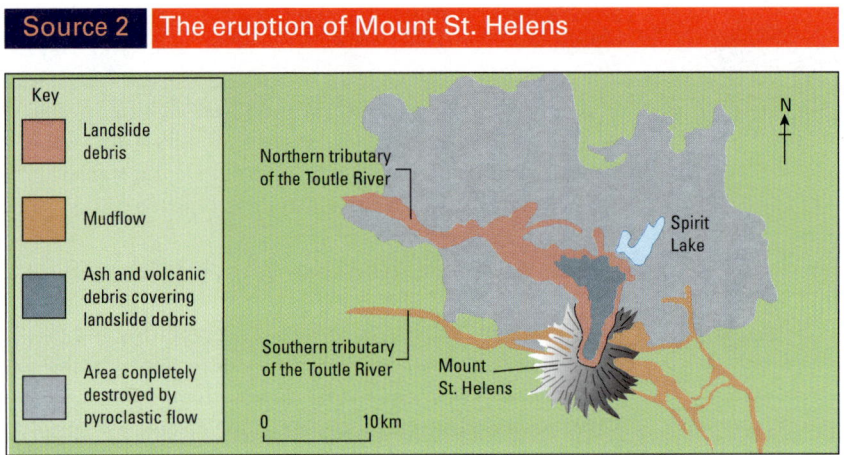

Source 2 — The eruption of Mount St. Helens

i Describe how the tributaries of the Toutle River were affected by the eruption. (*2 marks*)

ii Explain how landslides are caused by volcanic eruptions. (*2 marks*)

iii What is a 'pyroclastic flow'? Why is it so destructive? (*2 marks*)

b In the long term volcanic areas can benefit people. Describe, using examples, any three ways in which people have taken advantage of living in volcanic areas. (*4 marks*)

(Total: *10 marks*)

3 a Describe the ways in which people try to predict earthquakes and volcanic eruptions. (*5 marks*)

b Explain why earthquakes and volcanic eruptions are often much more damaging in LEDCs than in MEDCs. Give examples. (*5 marks*)

(Total: *10 marks*)

UNIT 2

Rivers and the hydrological cycle

Unit Contents

- River systems and processes
- The river and its valley in the uplands
- The river and its valley in the lowlands
- River floods
- People, rivers and floods
- A river and its valley: the River Tay
- Floodplain and delta: the River Ganges
- River management in a LEDC: the River Ganges
- River management in a MEDC: the River Mississippi
- Flooding in the United Kingdom: the River Ouse
- Water supply: Kielder reservoir

The Victoria Falls on the Zambezi River, Africa. Where and why do rivers form spectacular waterfalls?

2.1 River systems and processes

Fresh water is essential for life on earth. Water that reaches the land surface forms part of the **water cycle**, also called the **hydrological cycle** (Source 1). The main input into the system is **precipitation**. This is usually rain, but in high mountain areas snow is frequent as well. Water may flow quickly through the system as **runoff** on the surface, in the form of rivers transferring water from land to sea. Energy from the sun **evaporates** sea water: it changes liquid water into water vapour in the atmosphere. As the water vapour is drawn higher up into the atmosphere, it is cooled. The water vapour may **condense** into water droplets which can be seen as clouds. Precipitation falls from clouds that are sufficiently tall and thick, and the water cycle begins all over again.

The water cycle is more complicated than this, however. Some of the rain water may never reach the sea; instead it is lost directly back into the atmosphere from the leaves of plants. This process is known as **evapo-transpiration**. Some of the rain water is **intercepted** by trees so that its flow is delayed. Precipitation that falls as snow can be stored in glaciers on the surface (Source 2). Rainwater may be stored in lakes. Some rain water seeps down through the soil. This is the process of **infiltration**. Some of the infiltrated water seeps further down to fill empty spaces in the rock, which is known as **percolation**. The water can only do this until it reaches the level called the **water table**. Below this level the spaces in the rock have already been filled with water. At this point the water flows sideways as **groundwater flow**, as Source 1 shows.

Source 2 | Perito Moreno glacier

Source 1 | Processes, flows and stores in the hydrological cycle

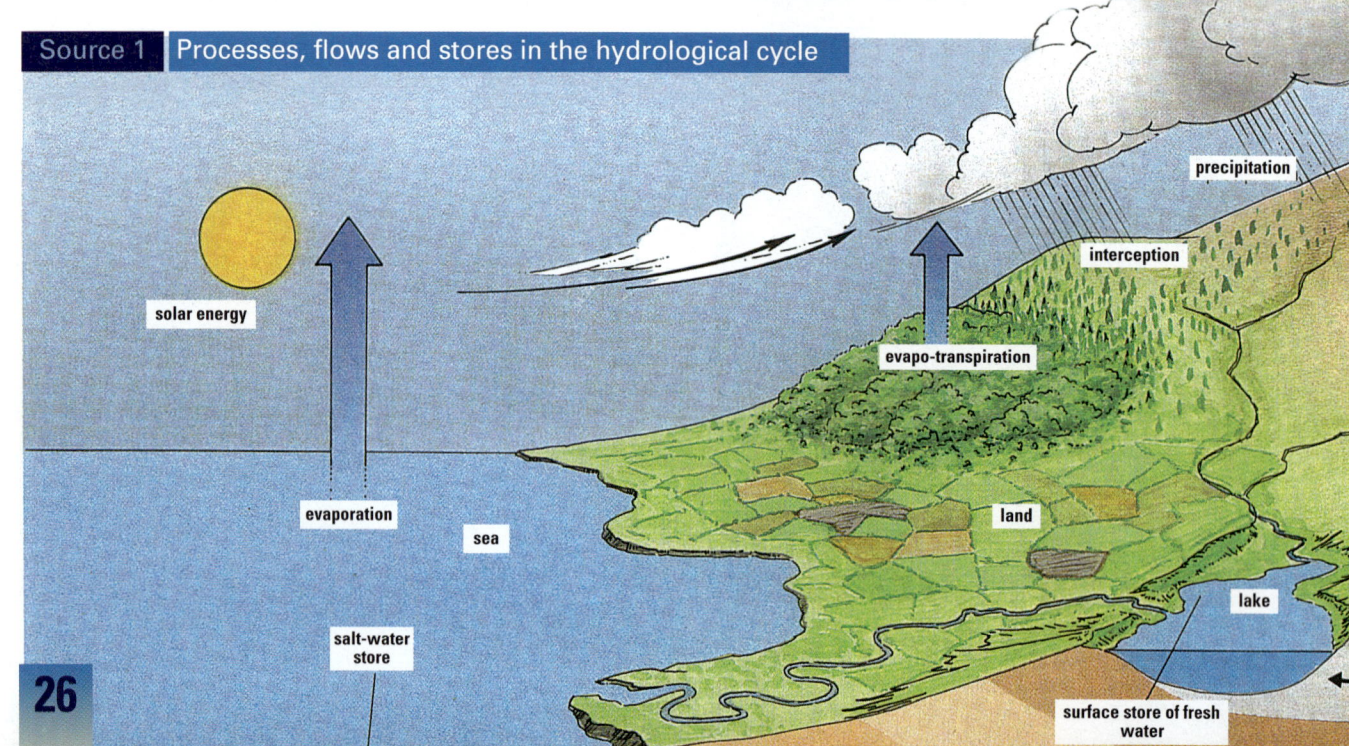

Rivers and the hydrological cycle

Source 3 The drainage basin

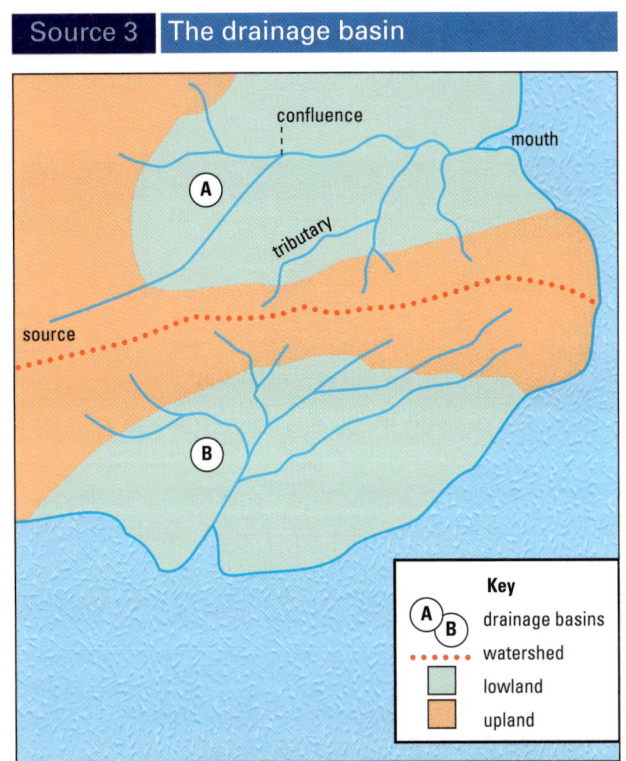

Source 4 Factors affecting the rate of runoff

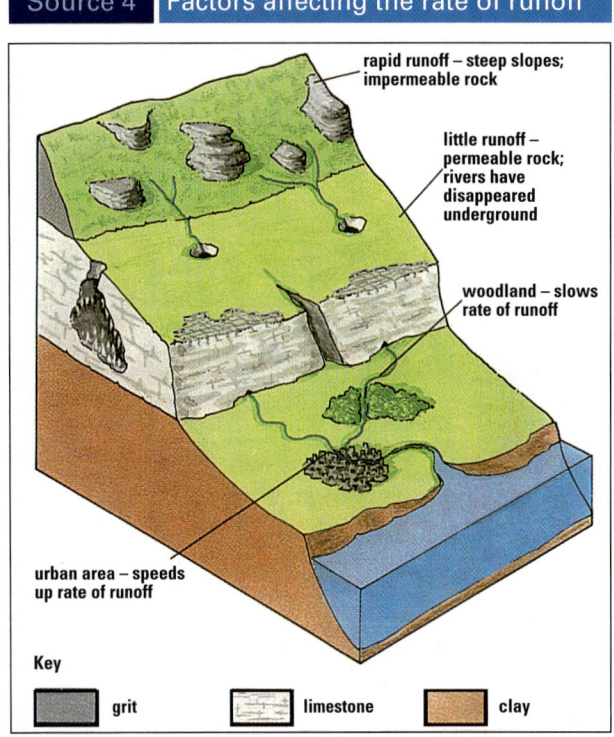

Each river has its own **drainage basin**. Each drainage basin has its own inputs, flows, stores and outputs. As Source 3 shows, it is possible to draw a definite dividing line between each drainage basin. It follows the tops of the hills and is called the **watershed**. The main river has its source in the higher parts of the basin where most precipitation falls. Smaller streams or **tributaries** join up with the main river; they meet at a **confluence**. The **mouth** of the river is where it meets the sea.

Each drainage basin has its own features of rock type, relief (shape of the land) and land use and these affect how quickly or how slowly the water moves through the basin. Source 4 shows how the features of a drainage basin can affect runoff. The rock type and relief are physical factors over which humans have little influence. However, land use is different. Land uses can be changed by people. Urban areas increase the rate of runoff. The rain water hits solid surfaces such as roofs, pavements and roads; the water is led into drains which speed up its overland flow into rivers.

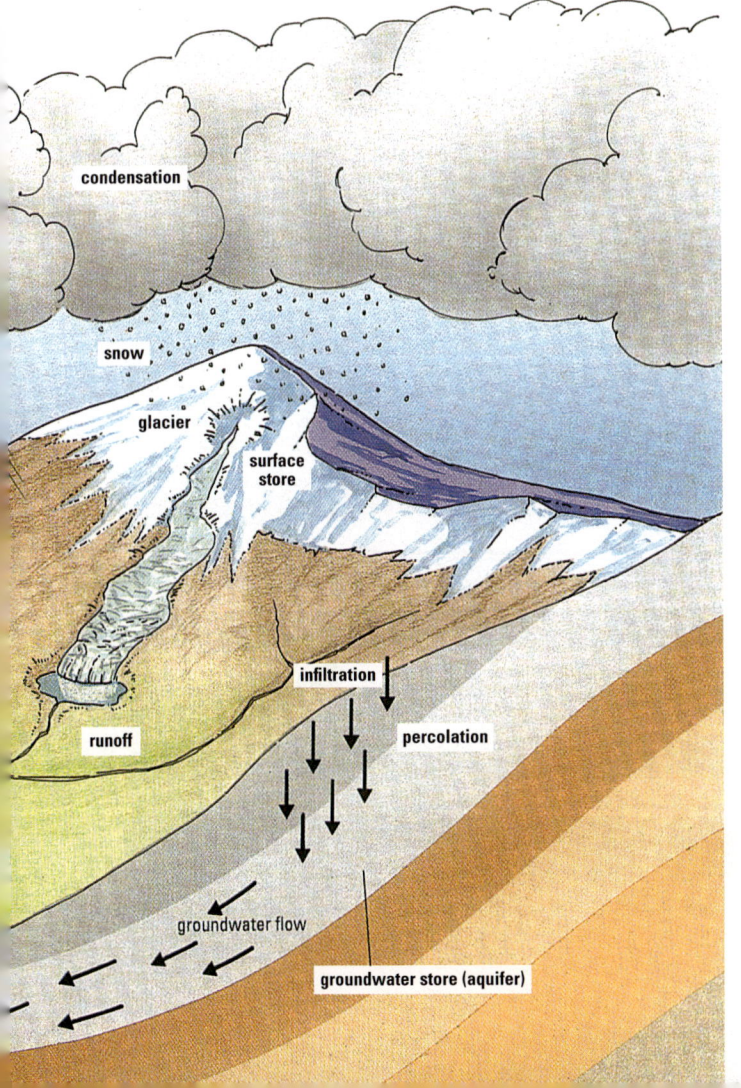

27

2.2 The river and its valley in the uplands

The river's course from source to mouth is summarised by its **long profile** (Source 1). The profile is steep and irregular when the river is flowing well above sea level in the uplands, but much gentler and smoother as the river nears the sea.

The main work of any river is to transfer rain water from land to sea. Most of its energy is used simply to keep the water flowing, because it needs to overcome the friction of the river's bed and banks. It may have some spare energy to transport its load of fine material and pebbles. There are four ways in which a river transports its load: solution, suspension, saltation and traction. Source 2 shows how each of these works.

The river is, therefore, an **agent of transport,** carrying material from upland to lowland regions. It is also an **agent of erosion.** There are four ways in which a river undertakes the work of erosion (Source 3).

Source 1 | River long profile

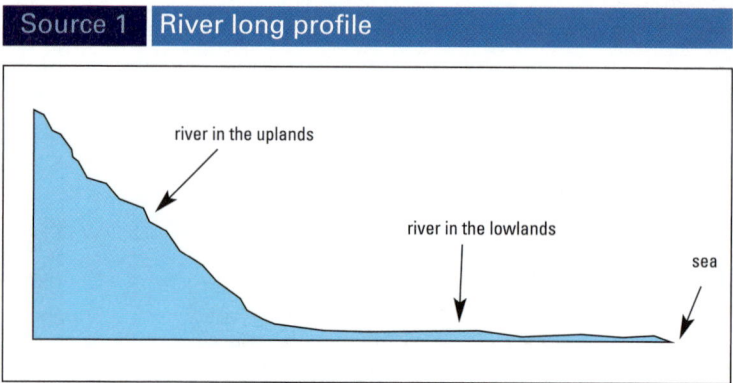

Source 2 | Ways of transporting the river's load

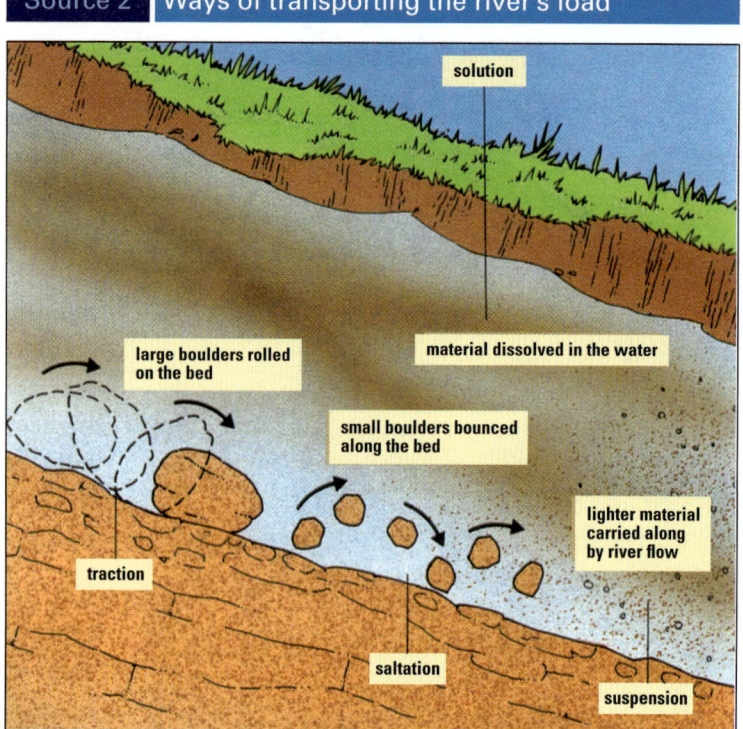

Source 3 | Process of river erosion

Abrasion or corrosion	Hydraulic action
The pebbles being transported remove material from the bed and banks of the river channel, by wearing them away.	The sheer force of the water by itself may be sufficient to dislodge material and erode the bed and sides of the channel.
Solution or corrosion	**Attrition**
Some rocks are subject to chemical attack: chalk and limestone, for example, slowly dissolve in water.	The particles are knocked about as they are being transported. They are reduced in size to sand and eventually to even smaller silt-sized particles. These are more easily moved by the water.

Source 4 shows a river in the uplands. Labels have been added which describe the channel and valley features.

Source 4 — Moffat Water in the Southern Uplands

Source 5 — Formation of valley landforms in upland areas

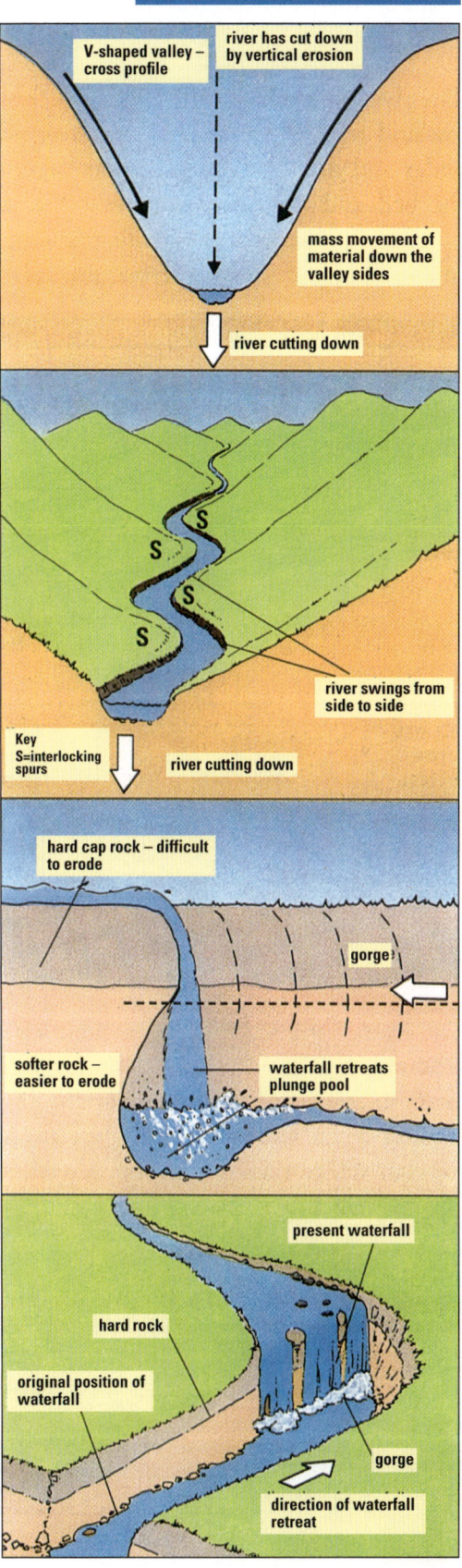

River landforms in the uplands

The main landforms found in the uplands – steep **V-shaped valley, interlocking spurs, waterfall** and **gorge** (Source 5) – have all been formed by the processes of river erosion already referred to.

The steep-sided V-shaped valley is formed by **vertical erosion**. The river is flowing so high above sea level that its main work is cutting downwards, which is what vertical erosion means. By the processes of abrasion and hydraulic action, the river erodes the rocks on its bed making the valley deeper. There is mass movement of material down the sides of the valley because the valley is so steep and deep.

Interlocking spurs are formed where the river swings from side to side. Again the main work of the river is vertical erosion into the rock on its bed by abrasion and hydraulic action. This means that the river cuts down to flow between spurs of higher land on alternate sides of the valley.

Waterfalls occur where a hard band of rock outcrops which is much more resistant to erosion than the softer rock below it. The river can only slowly erode the hard band of rock; it can erode more quickly the soft rock below. The soft rock is eroded also by the force of the water as it falls, which creates a **plunge pool** at the bottom of the falls. The waterfall gradually retreats upstream leaving a gorge below it. The gorge is protected from erosion by its capping of hard rock.

2.3 The river and its valley in the lowlands

The river and valley features (Source 1) change as lowland regions are reached: the river channel is wider and deeper; there are fewer large stones in the bed and river flow can be as fast as in the uplands despite the more gentle gradient; the plan of the river is less straight because of the many **meanders**; the river can often split up into **distributaries** near the sea to form a **delta**; the valley cross-section is wider and flatter, and includes the **floodplain** where the distinctive landforms include **levees** and **ox-bow lakes**.

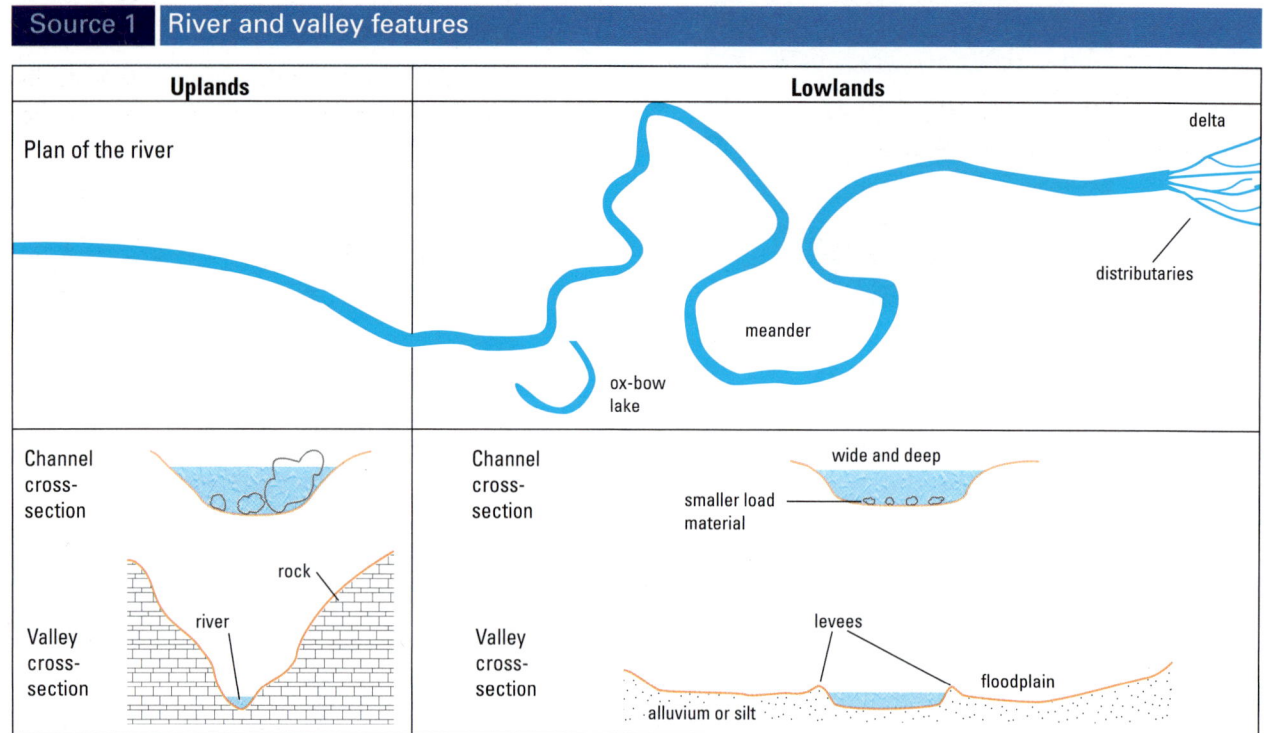

Source 1 River and valley features

The river is still an agent of erosion, but vertical erosion is less important because the river is too close to sea level. More important is **lateral erosion** where the river wears away the sides of the channel, especially on the outside of bends.

The river becomes an agent of **deposition** as well. Such a large load of material has been picked up that, once the river loses energy, it drops some of the material it is transporting. Energy is lost when the river flow gets slower, such as on the inside of a bend or where the river meets the sea.

The greatest thickness of river-deposited material, called **alluvium**, is on the floodplain. As its names suggests, the floodplain is an area of flat

Source 2 Formation of the floodplain and levees

Rivers and the hydrological cycle

land formed by flooding. Every time the river leaves its channel, it is slowed down and begins to deposit **silt** across the valley floor. A great thickness of alluvial material builds up. The largest amount of deposition is always on the banks of the channel, which builds up to a greater height than the rest of the floodplain to form levees (Source 2).

Meanders and ox-bow lakes

A study of the formation of meanders and ox-bow lakes shows how the river both deposits and erodes laterally (Source 3).

The force of the water undercuts the bank on the outside of a bend to form a steep bank to the channel, called a **river cliff**. An underwater current with a spiral flow carries the eroded material to the inside of the bend where the flow of water is slow. Here the material is deposited to form a gentle bank, called a **slip-off slope**.

The bend of the meander becomes even more pronounced as lateral erosion continues (Source 4). Especially in times of flood, when the river's energy is much greater, the narrow neck of the meander may be broken so that the river flows straight again. This forms an ox-bow lake by cutting off the old meander loop. Deposition during the flooding may seal off the edges of the lake. The lateral erosion on the outside bank of the meander helps to widen the floodplain.

Source 3 Formation of meanders and ox-bow lakes

Source 4 A meandering river

Most British rivers are relatively small and go out to sea through estuaries. There are often one or two deep water channels between extensive deposits of sand and mud. An example is the River Tay on pages 36–7. Bigger rivers in other parts of the world may split up just before reaching the sea and form a delta. The River Ganges, which is described on pages 38–9, does this.

2.4 River floods

Causes of river floods

After a rainstorm, there is an increase in the river's **discharge** (the amount of water flowing in the river). This can be shown on a storm hydrograph (Source 1).

Most rainstorms will do no more than fill up the river channel, as shown for point B in Source 1. Flooding only occurs when the river channel has reached bankfull level and more water is still reaching the channel. The river reaches bursting point at C and floods the surrounding land at D (Source 2). Weather conditions which favour the greatest amount of runoff in the river's drainage basin are the main cause of flooding. Imagine that the rainstorm shown in Source 1 gave more rain and lasted longer. A point will be reached when the river discharge will be too great for the channel (Source 2). This is happening to the river in Source 3.

Three weather conditions are likely to cause extensive flooding.

1. **Large amounts of rain day after day** – rain saturates the ground so no more rain can infiltrate or percolate into the ground.

2. **A cloudburst in a thunderstorm** – the rain droplets are so large and hit the ground so fast that there is little chance of any seepage into the ground.

3. **Melting snow and ice** – a sudden increase in temperature can begin a rapid thaw to the point where the river cannot cope with the increased amount of water.

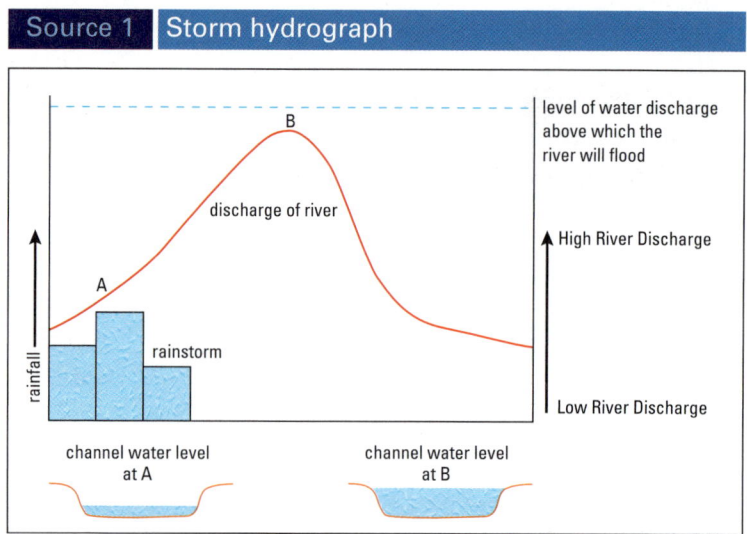

Source 1　Storm hydrograph

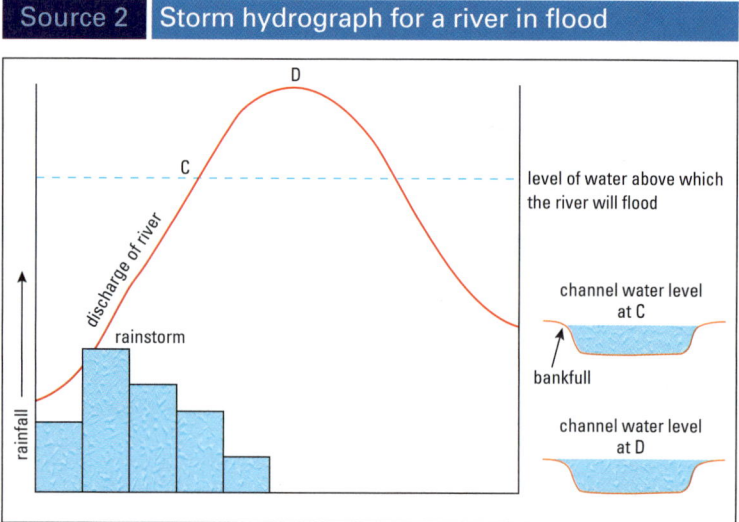

Source 2　Storm hydrograph for a river in flood

Source 3　A river in flood

Rivers and the hydrological cycle

Source 4 | Immediate effects of river floods

Effects of river flooding

Flooding greatly increases a river's energy so that it can do more work. In times of flood, the deeper and faster river increases its load dramatically. Most rivers turn brown when in flood because of the large amount of material they are carrying in suspension. The amount of erosion by hydraulic action and abrasion is greatly increased. Many of the valley landforms in lowland areas have been formed by flooding. Levees and floodplains are formed by deposition after the river overflows its banks. Ox-bow lakes are cut off when the force of the river enables it to break through the meander neck.

River floods can cause a lot of damage. As with all the natural hazards, there are both immediate and long-term effects. The immediate effects of a river flood include loss of life, destruction of property and crops, and the disruption of communications (Source 4). The consequences can be serious. Many lives have been lost in floods along the big rivers in China – the Huang Ho is called 'China's sorrow' because its devastating floods have killed thousands of people. During the Rhine floods in early 1995, people in some Dutch villages had to be evacuated and the river current was too strong for barges to use the river safely.

In the longer term there is the cost of replacing what has been lost and damaged. In rich countries the risks may be covered by insurance. The poor in the less economically developed countries, however, may lose everything. With crop land ruined and animals lost, widespread famine can result. The need for emergency food aid in these circumstances becomes urgent.

2.5 People, rivers and floods

Responses to floods

Flood protection measures are in operation along most big rivers. Where the costs of damage from flooding could be enormous, the scheme may be big and expensive such as the Thames Barrier which protects the city of London (Source 1).

Along most rivers the aim is to alter the channel or banks so that the river can carry more water without flooding. The most common measure of flood protection is to increase the height of the natural levees along the banks. This makes the channel deeper so that it can hold more water. Another measure that is often taken is to clean out the channel by dredging to make the river flow more efficiently.

On a much larger scale is the building of dams. In times of great runoff dams hold back water, and the river discharge in the area below the dam can be controlled. Dams can be a very effective measure of flood control but they are an expensive solution. They are often built as part of a scheme of **river basin management**. Not only is there flood control, but the water stored behind the dam can be used to supply houses and factories, irrigate crops and for recreation and shipping, as well as for HEP

Source 1: The Thames Barrier

(hydro-electric power). This is called a **multi-purpose scheme**. The River Rhône in France is an example of a managed river (Source 2).

Often, however, prevention is better than cure. By cutting down trees and by ploughing up and down slopes people have increased the rate of runoff in some areas, such as on the sides of the Himalayas in Nepal. The frequency and scale of flooding have been increased as a result. More care and attention given to the way in which the land in a drainage basin is used would reduce the risks of floods occurring in the first place.

Source 2: River Rhône: river basin management

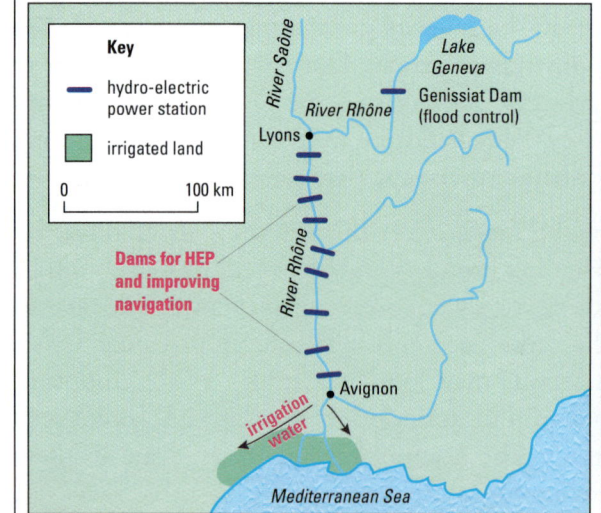

Rivers and the hydrological cycle

Human activities in river valleys

One of the reasons why the hazard of river floods affects so many people in so many different countries is because rivers attract people to their sides. Some of the many uses of rivers are illustrated in Source 3.

River valleys offer attractive locations for settlements. It is easier to build on the more gently sloping land. The valley floor is sheltered and warmer than the slopes above. The variety of land uses and the amount of settlement tend to increase as you move from the uplands to the lowlands.

In the uplands, opportunities for farming are restricted by the narrow valley floor, steep slopes and poor climate. It is colder, more cloudy, wetter and windier than on the lowlands. Often only sheep will survive, with cattle grazing the better grasses on the valley floors. There may be good sites for building dams and storing water or even generating hydro-electric power. The flat land on the floodplain, underlain by a great thickness of silt, offers a much better environment for farming. Towns and industries often grow up on the sides of the estuary where the water is deep enough to be navigated by ships. Unfortunately, so many farms, industries and towns next to rivers can create problems of pollution.

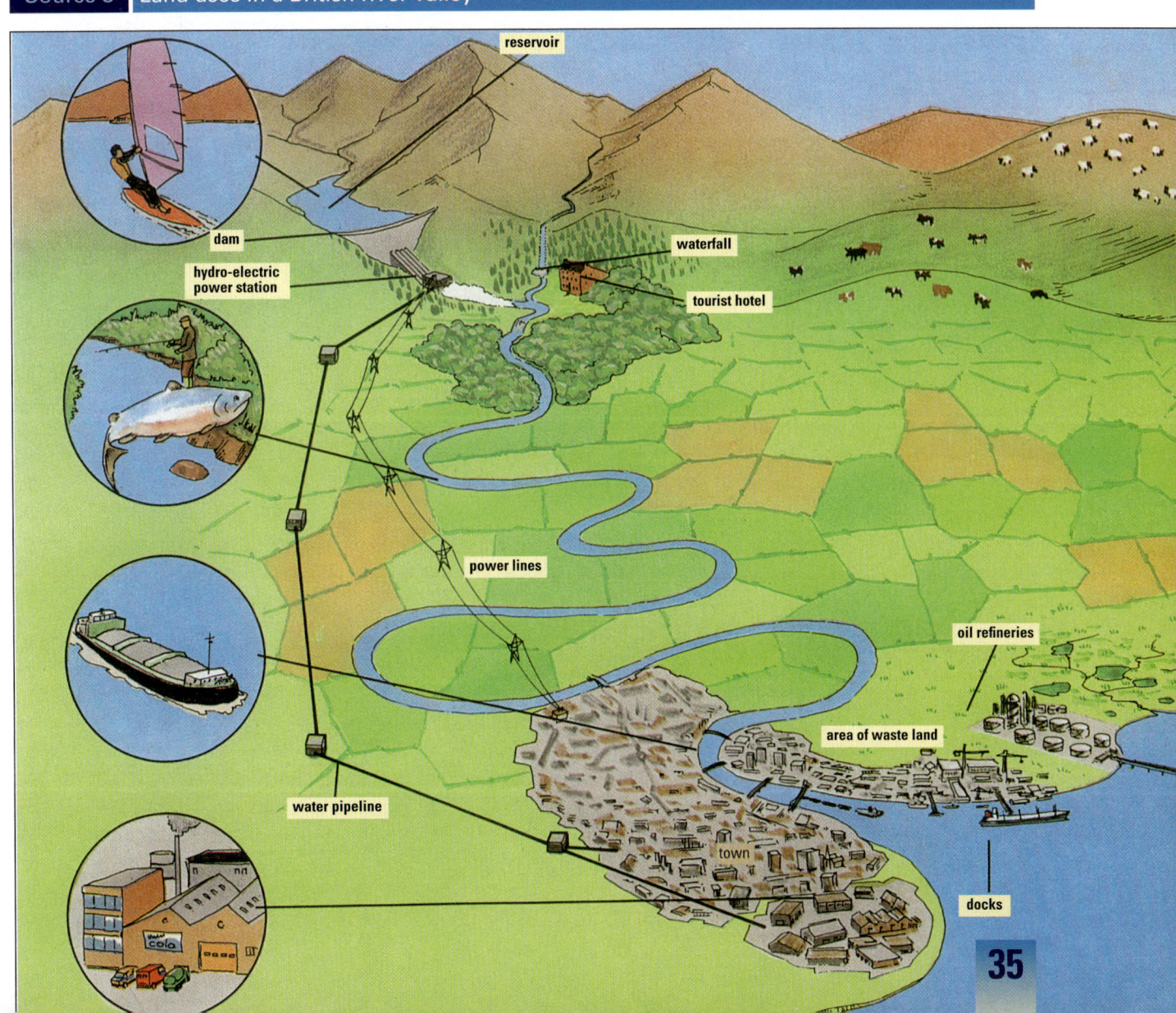

Source 3 Land uses in a British river valley

2.6 A river and its valley
the River Tay

In the uplands
The River Tay is fed by streams which drain the slopes of the Grampian mountains in the Highlands of Scotland. Precipitation in the upland parts of the drainage basin is high (well over 1000 mm per year) and slopes are steep, which gives high amounts of runoff. It is already a big river, about 100 metres across in that part of its course shown on the Ordnance Survey map extract (Source 1).

The valley cross-section is shown in Source 2a. It is V-shaped and steep-sided. The river fills the valley floor. The cross-section shows that the river is still flowing at some height above sea level; it is cutting down into the valley floor by vertical erosion.

As for the land uses shown on the map (Source 1), the small settlements and roads are concentrated on the less steep and more sheltered land in the Tay valley.

To the north of the river much of the land is likely to be used for nothing better than rough grazing for sheep and deer. South of the river coniferous (evergreen) woodland is the land use which covers the largest area.

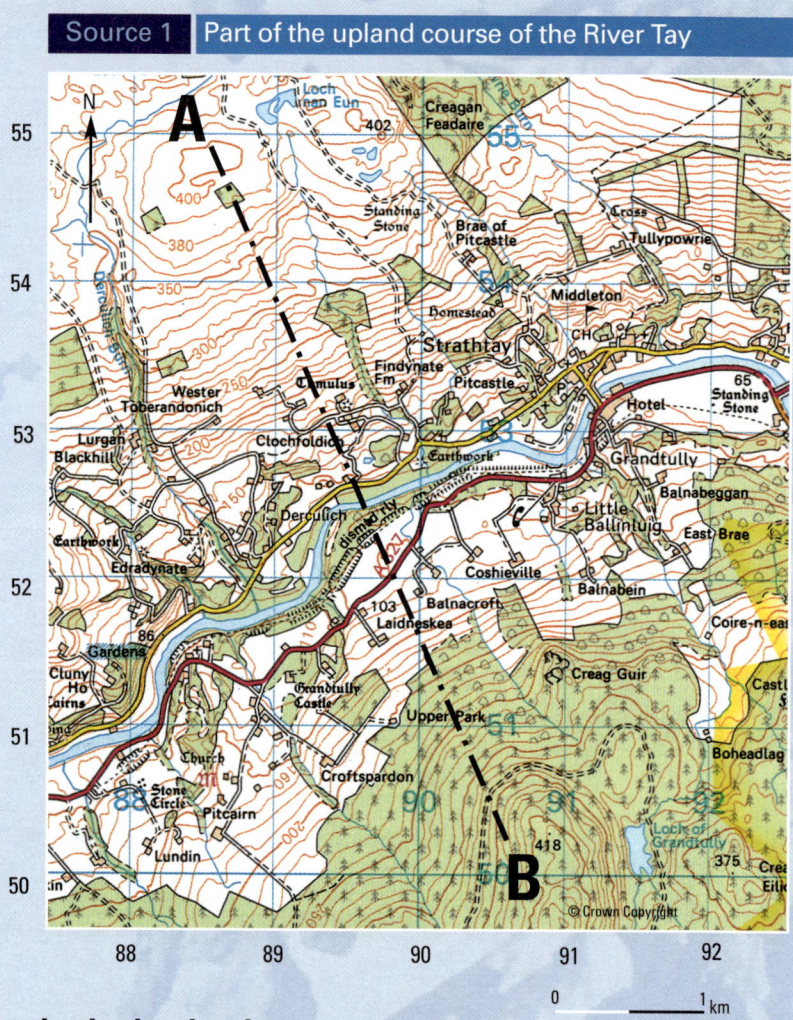

Source 1 Part of the upland course of the River Tay

In the lowlands
Source 2b is the valley cross-section near the sea. The flat and low-lying land is the floodplain. It is 0.6 km wide where the tributary River Earn meets the main River Tay.

Source 2 Cross-sections across the Tay valley

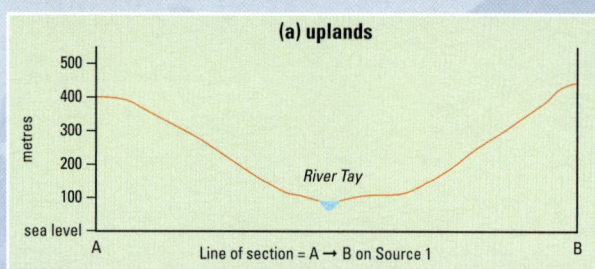
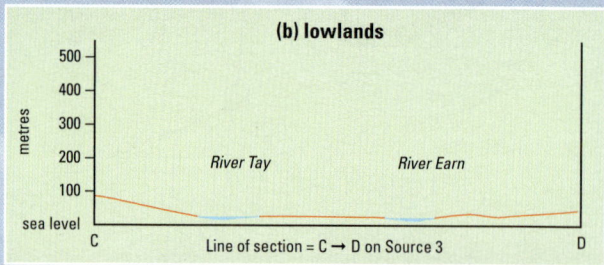

Rivers and the hydrological cycle

Source 3 Part of the floodplain and estuary of the River Tay

The River Tay has many of the typical estuary features that can be found at the mouths of rivers in other parts of Britain, including:

- a wide channel – up to 2 km
- sand and mud banks – Abernethy Bank
- some areas of marsh – in square 2119
- channels of deeper water – North Deep.

On reaching this tidal part of the river, a river's flow is reduced. The river loses much of its energy to transport its load and deposits it as sand and mud. These estuaries are difficult to navigate and to bridge, but they are good wildlife habitats. The River Earn has many features of a river in the lowlands (Source 4). Notice the big meander loop through squares 1718 and 1717 (Source 3). The black dashes marked around its edges show the levees. Settlements are larger than those in the uplands, but the danger of flooding means that they were carefully sited towards the edge of the floodplain where the risk of flooding was lower. The location of Abernethy is an example of this.

Source 4 Floodplain of the River Earn

37

2.7 Floodplain and delta
the River Ganges

The source of the River Ganges is in the Himalayas. The Ganges flows across its floodplain for over 1500 km through northern India. The Ganges delta is found at the mouth of the river as it flows into the Bay of Bengal. The Indian city of Calcutta lies on the western side of the delta, but most of the delta is in Bangladesh (Source 1).

Within the zone covered by the floodplain and delta of the Ganges live some 10 per cent of the total world population. This area is one of the most densely populated parts of the world (see unit 9.1). Most people living here are farmers for whom rice is the main food crop.

The **monsoon** climate brings summer rain, which fills up the River Ganges (Source 2). For centuries the Ganges flooded the land around it between July and October. Each flood left another layer of fertile silt so that there is a great thickness of very rich and easy to work alluvial soils. Today a number of dams control the flooding of the river and supply water for winter crops. There is a neat landscape of tiny fields from which the farmers try to gain the highest possible output by hard work and by using high yielding varieties of rice, wheat and maize seeds (Source 3).

Source 1 The River Ganges

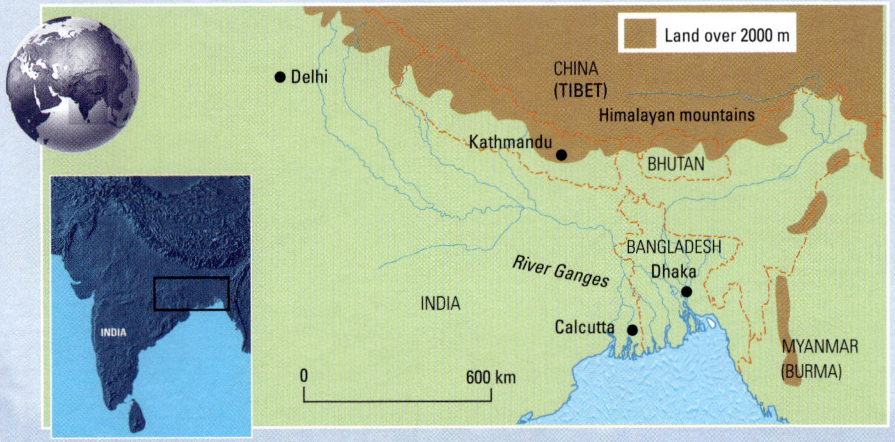

Source 2 Average discharge of the River Ganges

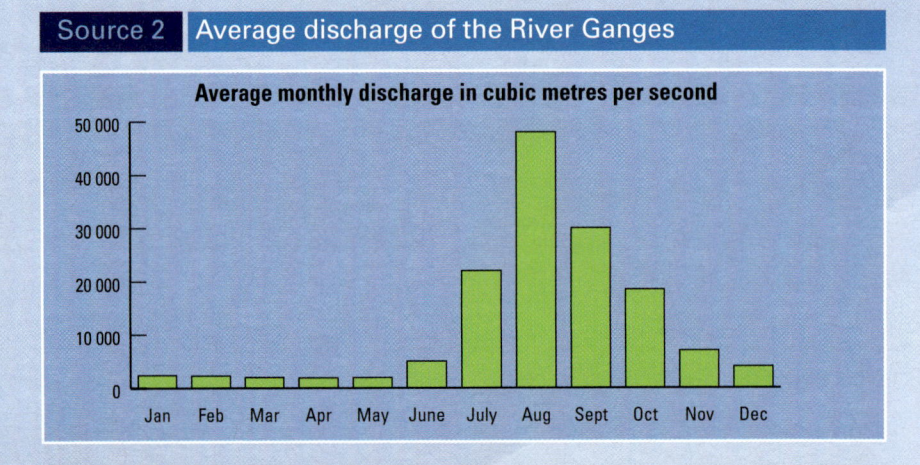

Source 3 The Ganges floodplain is intensively farmed

38

Rivers and the hydrological cycle

Fact File	The Ganges delta

The delta is an example of a landform of river deposition. The physical features of the delta are labelled on the map and the reasons for the formation of the delta are written below.

Formation of a delta
1. The Ganges carries a large load of sediment.
2. The flow is slowed down by meeting the denser sea water.
3. Sediment is deposited faster than the tides can remove it.
4. River flow is blocked by so much deposition that the river splits up into distributaries.
5. Distributaries deposit sediment over a wide area, extending new land into the sea.

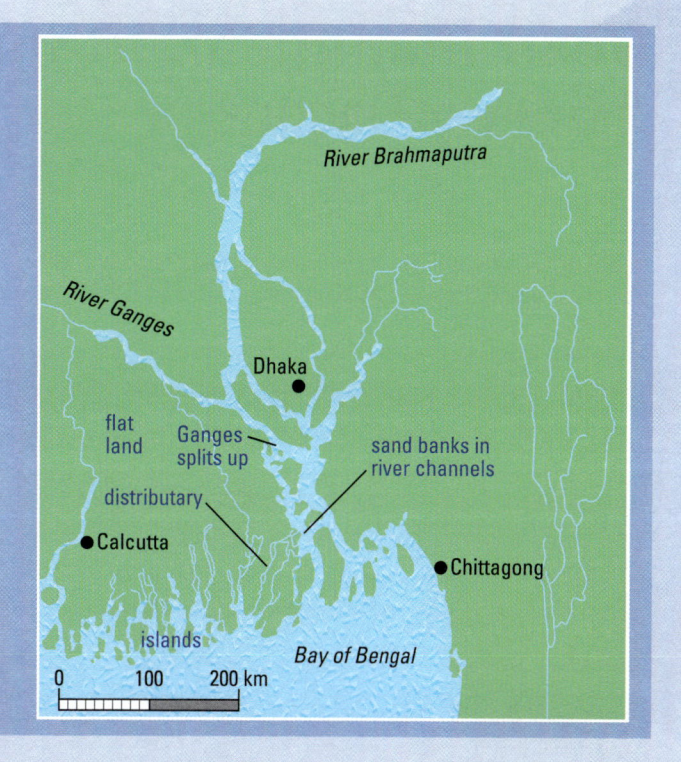

The *advantage* of the Ganges delta to the people of Bangladesh is that the land is very fertile. The silty soils are also easy to work. All the land is low lying (Source 4). There is water in the channels for irrigation during the dry season so that two or three crops can be grown. Many people can be fed each year.

The *disadvantage* is that the Bangladeshis live in a hazardous physical environment. The risk of being flooded is always present and many people have died. There are so many wide rivers to cross that land transport is slow and difficult. Access for ships is not easy because many channels are blocked by sand and mud. A wet environment in the tropics is a breeding ground for many diseases. Perhaps worst of all, Bangladesh is at the mercy of people living further up river. Nepal has cleared a lot of its forests; the higher rates of runoff in the mountains near the source have increased the severity of floods in Bangladesh at the river's mouth. India also uses the river for disposal of its waste products.

Source 4	View of the Ganges delta

2.8 River management in a LEDC
the River Ganges

Three problems make effective management of the River Ganges difficult to achieve.

- **Climatic:** About 80 per cent of the yearly rainfall which supplies the Ganges falls in just four months of the year. As Source 2 on page 38 shows, the Ganges suffers either from low flow (too little water for everyone's needs) or high flow (too much water causing flooding).
- **Political:** The River Ganges flows through three countries, which do not share the same interests. The source of the River Ganges is in Nepal; what happens there has knock-on effects for both India and Bangladesh. For example, removing forests from valley sides in Nepal increases surface runoff, which also increases flood risks in India and Bangladesh downstream.
- **Economic and social:** All three countries are relatively poor. They do not have unlimited amounts of money to spend on river management. There have been decades of high population growth and increased demands for food from the land.

Source 1 | Management issues and methods along the Ganges

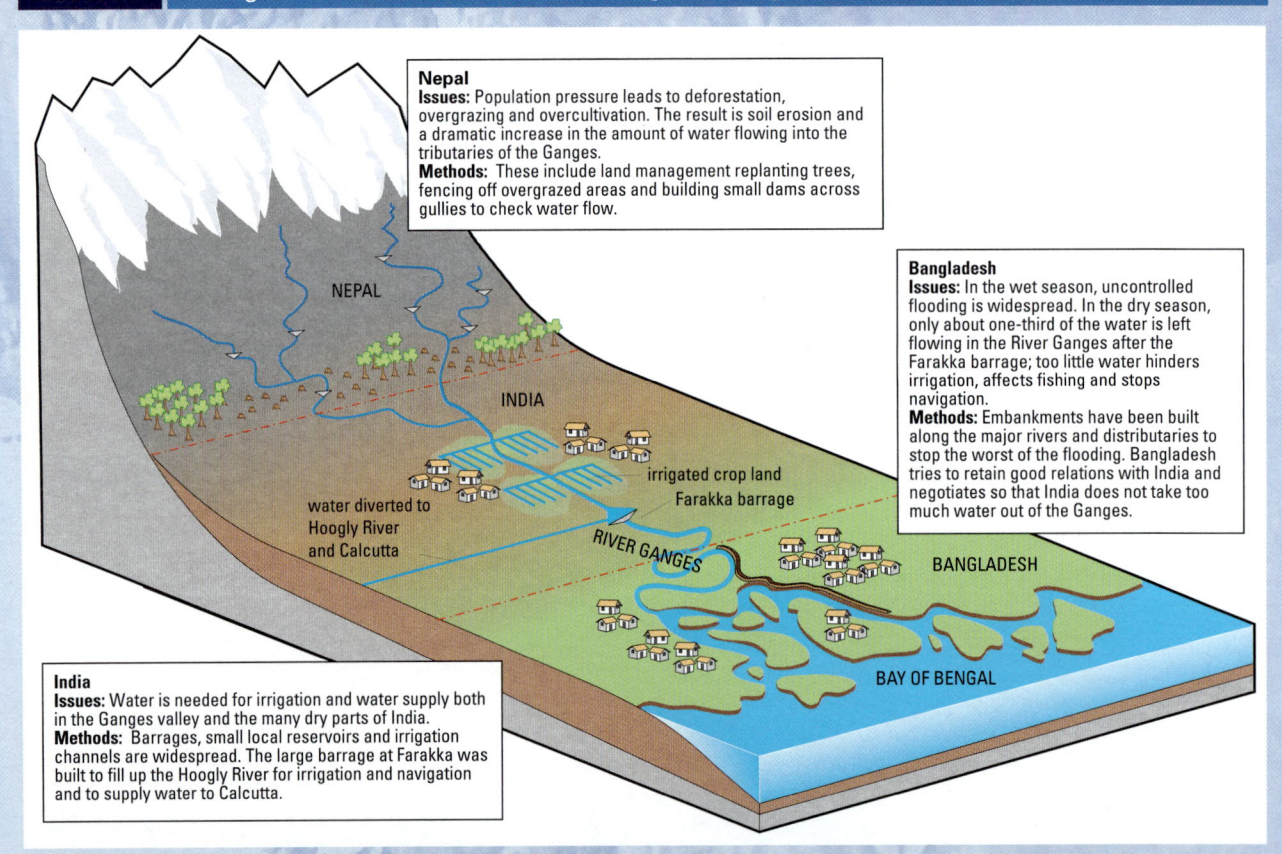

Nepal
Issues: Population pressure leads to deforestation, overgrazing and overcultivation. The result is soil erosion and a dramatic increase in the amount of water flowing into the tributaries of the Ganges.
Methods: These include land management replanting trees, fencing off overgrazed areas and building small dams across gullies to check water flow.

Bangladesh
Issues: In the wet season, uncontrolled flooding is widespread. In the dry season, only about one-third of the water is left flowing in the River Ganges after the Farakka barrage; too little water hinders irrigation, affects fishing and stops navigation.
Methods: Embankments have been built along the major rivers and distributaries to stop the worst of the flooding. Bangladesh tries to retain good relations with India and negotiates so that India does not take too much water out of the Ganges.

India
Issues: Water is needed for irrigation and water supply both in the Ganges valley and the many dry parts of India.
Methods: Barrages, small local reservoirs and irrigation channels are widespread. The large barrage at Farakka was built to fill up the Hoogly River for irrigation and navigation and to supply water to Calcutta.

The floods are vital to the prosperity of most farmers in Bangladesh – they add another layer of fertile silt and water the land. However, how can floods be stopped from increasing beyond normal levels and ruining crops? This is almost impossible. Many of the flood protection schemes in Bangladesh are in urgent need of repair. Many embankments are of little use. Some have been washed away and others have merely diverted the water to other parts of the country.

River management in a MEDC 2.9
the River Mississippi

The Mississippi is a major river system, draining most of the USA (Source 1). The Central Plains are an attractive area for agriculture and settlement, but the flood risk from the Mississippi has always been high as its flood record shows (Source 2). After every big flood, protection measures have been increased in size and numbers (Source 4).

- Everywhere levees, the high embankments on the river sides, have been increased in height, so that in places they are 15 metres high.
- Artificial channels have been cut across the necks of meanders so that the water flows straighter and quicker.
- Spillways have been built to take away excess water during floods.
- Over 100 dams have been built to control water flow on tributary rivers such as the Missouri, Ohio and Tennessee.
- Slopes have been afforested to reduce surface runoff.

Source 2 — The flood record of the Mississippi

1900	Flooding from Cairo to the Gulf of Mexico
1927	Flooding up to 150 km wide around the river
1937	Flooding of an area the size of Scotland
1993	Flooding of almost everywhere north of Cairo

Source 3 — Causes and consequences of the 1993 flood

THE MISSISSIPPI FLOODS OF 1993

It rained all spring and summer in the upper Mississippi and Missouri river valleys. 'Boy did it rain'. In some places it rained every day for two months. Most places had two to three times the usual amount of rain. There was nowhere for the water to go except into the rivers. The ground was waterlogged. By July an area the size of England was under water. Over 50,000 people were forced out of their homes. Many people were put up in schools and public buildings, which were used as temporary shelters. Nearly 50 people died. Crop losses were estimated at over $6 million and damage to property was put at $10 million.

Source 1 — The drainage basin of the Mississippi

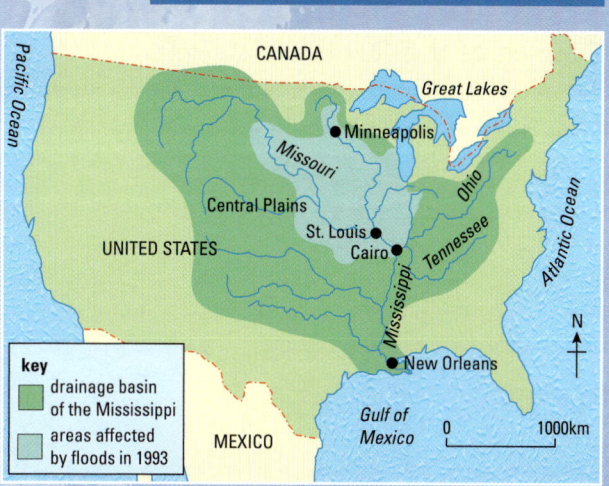

Only a big and rich country could afford this amount of flood protection. The scale is enormous; for example, the levees stretch more than 3000 kilometres.

Considering the amount spent on flood protection measures, the size and scale of the floods in 1993 came as a big shock. People living in cities on the river banks and farmers in the Corn Belt states believed that they were no longer at risk from river floods. In 1993 it was the upper rather than the lower basin that was attacked, where flood protection was less. However, what these floods showed is that it is impossible to give a guarantee that a big river can be stopped from flooding, even in a wealthy MEDC.

Source 4 — Methods of flood protection along the Mississippi

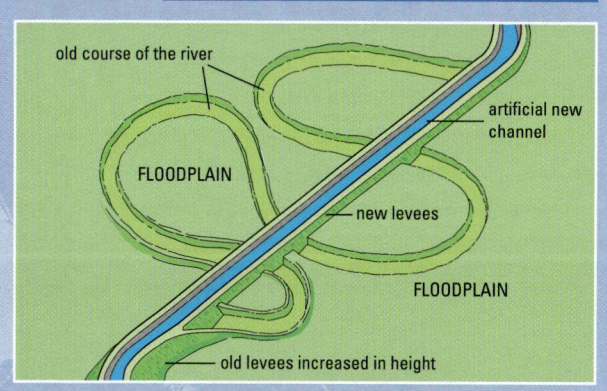

41

2.10 Flooding in the United Kingdom
the River Ouse

The River Ouse in Yorkshire floods during most winters. The floods in 1991 were worse than usual.

Causes of the flooding

The River Ouse has many tributaries originating in the higher parts of the Pennines where precipitation is high. In 1991, there was a month of heavier than average rainfall in the Pennines, followed by heavy snowfall. When the snow melted, the ground was already saturated. This meant a great runoff into the Pennine rivers, which transported more water into the River Ouse than its channel could hold (Sources 1, 2 and 3). In early June 2000 the River Ouse again swamped the centre of York. Within the first four days of June, over 75 mm of rain had fallen over much of North Yorkshire – already well above the average for the month of June. Insurance companies put the cost of clearing up at tens of millions of pounds. The same area in York was flooded again in November 2000 after the wettest autumn for over 200 years. Businesses and home owners are being refused insurance against future floods.

Source 1 Causes of the Ouse floods

Flood prevention measures

Embankments and flood walls line the sides of the River Ouse. The flood prevention scheme designed to protect the main commercial properties cost £8 million. Unfortunately, the flat, low-lying nature of the Vale of York near to the tidal part of the River Ouse means that freedom from flooding can never be guaranteed, even after spending millions of pounds.

Source 2 Newspaper report

ARMY CALLED IN TO RESCUE STRANDED RESIDENTS

York, 26 February 1991

Soldiers, equipped with aluminium boats, were called in to help residents stranded in flood-stricken York. The River Ouse was 4.5 metres higher than normal. Houses, shops and offices next to the river are still under water. More than 70 residents had to be evacuated. 'The streets were like canals,' said one of the army officers. At high tide yesterday the Ouse broke its banks south of York covering farmland, blocking roads and disrupting train services.

Source 3 Floods in York

Water supply 2.11
Kielder reservoir

Source 1 — Kielder reservoir: for water supply and recreation

Kielder reservoir in Northumberland, which opened in 1982, is the largest artificial lake in western Europe (Source 1). It is over 10 km long and contains 190 million litres of water.

It was built as a water store to supply industry, particularly companies such as ICI and British Steel, located on Teesside, which were expected to expand.

The site selected in the Cheviot Hills was chosen for several reasons.

- It has a large flat-bottomed valley with steep sides.
- The area has a high annual rainfall (1370 mm per year).
- It is a sparsely populated area – only a few families needed to be moved out when the dam was finished and the North Tyne valley was ready to be flooded.
- The land was marginal in quality, and could only be used for forestry and rough grazing.

Fact File — Kielder reservoir

Construction period	7 years
Number of trees felled	1 500 000
Height of dam wall	50 metres
Length of dam wall	1.2 km
Surface area of Kielder Water	1084 hectares
Supply capability	up to 1.2 million m³ of water a day
Length of shoreline created	43 km

Source 2 — The distribution of Kielder Water

Who uses the water?

While the reservoir was being constructed, the steel and chemical industries went into decline and did not need Kielder Water. However, Source 2 shows how the water can be distributed to all the main centres of population in North-East England by both rivers and pipelines. The presence of Kielder Water has meant that there have been no hosepipe bans or restrictions on water use in North-East England, even in the summer drought of 1995. Indeed water is exported – both to the Middle East and to Yorkshire. After the water shortages in Yorkshire in 1995, Yorkshire Water paid for a pipeline to take water from south of the River Tees into the Yorkshire heartland.

43

2.12 Activities

1 a Draw a labelled diagram to show the main features of the hydrological cycle.
  b Explain the differences between each of the following pairs:
    i evaporation and precipitation
    ii runoff and groundwater flow
    iii interception and percolation.
  c What is meant by evapo–transpiration?
  d Give the reasons why trees and impermeable rocks decrease the amount of runoff in the drainage basin.
  e Name two features of a drainage basin which favour a large amount of runoff. Explain why.

2 a State two ways in which the long profile of the river in the uplands is different from that in the lowlands.
  b Name and describe the ways in which the river is likely to transport the following:
    i pebbles and boulders
    ii sand and silt.
  c Make notes on the four different processes of river erosion.
  d i Describe the features of the Victoria Falls shown on page 25.
    ii State the different kinds of rock which are needed for a waterfall to form.
    iii What is a plunge pool? How is it formed?

3 a Describe how a river changes when it reaches the lowlands.
  b i Name two features formed by river deposition.
    ii Explain why rivers deposit their load in the lowlands.
  c With the aid of labelled diagrams, explain the formation of meanders and ox-bow lakes.

4 a Explain when and why rivers flood.
  b Describe as many disadvantages of flooding as you can.

5 a Draw a labelled diagram to show one way in which people try to prevent river floods.
  b With reference to the River Rhône in France:
    i describe the type of work people have undertaken along the river to prevent flooding
    ii state and explain three advantages of the scheme.
  c How can people be one of the causes of river floods?
  d Explain why people live close to rivers despite the risk of being flooded out.

6 a Use the OS map on page 36 to answer the following.
    i Imagine you are walking between points A and B. Describe the changes in relief (shape of the land) you would notice on your walk.
    ii How many square kilometres of the land are used for coniferous woodland?
    iii Suggest reasons why trees are a common type of land use in an area such as this.
    iv Name five different land uses shown in square 9153.
  b Use the OS map on page 37 to answer the following.
    i Draw a sketch map of the River Tay estuary to the east of easting 20. Show and label on your map four physical features commonly found in a river estuary.
    ii Suggest the advantages and disadvantages of this river estuary for shipping. Use map evidence to support your answer.

7 a i From Source 1 on page 40, describe the course of the River Ganges, naming the countries through which it flows.
   ii Explain why passing through different countries makes management of the River Ganges more difficult.
 b Most of Bangladesh consists of the delta formed by the Ganges and Brahmaputra rivers.
   i Describe how the delta is different from other sections of a river's course.
   ii Explain the formation of the delta in Bangladesh.
 c At certain times of the year Bangladesh suffers because there is low water in the Ganges.
   i When during the year is this most likely to happen?
   ii Why does it happen?
 d At other times of the year there is too much water in the Ganges in Bangladesh.
   i When during the year is this most likely to happen?
   ii Why is it difficult to stop the Ganges from flooding?
 e Give reasons why some of the world's highest densities of population are found on the floodplain and delta of the River Ganges.

8 a Make notes on the Mississippi case study using the following headings:
   i Location of the Mississippi river basin and its major tributaries
   ii Methods of flood protection used along the river and its tributaries
   iii Causes of the major flood in 1993.
 b Where would you feel safer living – on the floodplain of the Mississippi in the USA, or on an island in the Ganges delta in Bangladesh? Give reasons for your answer.

9 a Using the flooding of the Ouse in 1991 on page 42 as a case study for river flooding, make brief notes using the headings:
   i causes of the flooding
   ii effects of the flooding
   iii flood protection measures used.
 b Why is it unlikely that it will ever be possible to stop river flooding in the Vale of York?

10 a Look at Source 2 on page 43.
   i Describe the location of Kielder Water in relation to the rest of North-East England.
   ii State the route by which water is taken from Kielder reservoir to Middlesbrough.
 b Explain why it was a good site for building a reservoir.

2.13 Sample examination questions

1. The values below give the average amount of water in a European river at different times of the year.

Months	J	F	M	A	M	J	J	A	S	O	N	D
Amount of water (cubic m)	500	450	620	700	750	820	900	840	650	580	550	530

   a Draw a bar graph to show the monthly amounts of water in the river. (4 marks)
   b State the difference in amount of water between the months with the largest and smallest amounts. Show your working. (2 marks)
   c Name the season of the year in which this river is most likely to flood. (1 mark)
   d The source for this river is high in the mountains. How does this help to explain the season in which the river is likely to flood? (3 marks)
   (Total: 10 marks)

2. Source 1 is a map of the Iguaçu Falls on the border between Brazil and Argentina. Source 2 is a photograph of the Iguaçu Falls.

   Source 1 Map of the Iguaçu Falls

   Source 2 The Iguaçu Falls

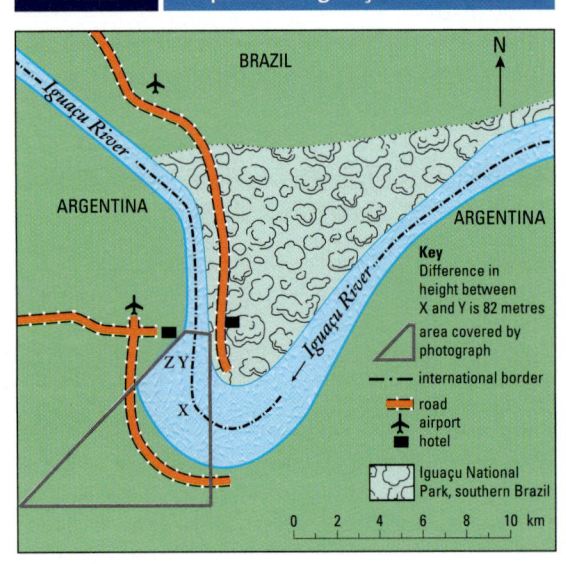

   Key
   Difference in height between X and Y is 82 metres
   area covered by photograph
   — · — · international border
   road
   airport
   hotel
   Iguaçu National Park, southern Brazil
   0 2 4 6 8 10 km

   a Look at Source 1.
     i Name two facilities provided for tourist visitors to the area. (2 marks)
     ii State the height of the Iguaçu Falls. (1 mark)
   b In which direction was the camera pointing when the photograph in Source 2 was taken? (1 mark)
   c Describe the attractions of the area for tourist visitors. (3 marks)
   d Suggest reasons why the site marked Z in Source 1 could make a good site for a hydro-electric power station. (3 marks)
   (Total: 10 marks)

3. Look at Source 2.
   a Make a frame and draw a labelled sketch to show the physical features of the area shown in the photograph. (5 marks)
   b Explain how the features shown in Source 2 are formed by river erosion. (5 marks)
   (Total: 10 marks)

UNIT 3

Coasts

Unit Contents

- The power of the sea
- Cliff erosion
- Building beaches
- Changing sea levels
- Coastal change and management: the Suffolk coast
- Using a coastal area: Milford Haven
- Pollution: Italy's Adriatic coast
- Coastal tourism in a LEDC: sustainable development along the Tanzanian coast

Coastal storms batter homes along the south coast of Britain

3.1 The power of the sea

The coastline is like a battle zone. It is here that the sea comes into direct contact with the land. Powerful waves crash against the rocks and cliffs and help to shape beaches. A complex set of processes allows the sea to erode the land, transport the eroded material and deposit it elsewhere. A series of coastal landforms are created – some of them by **erosion**, others by **deposition** (Source 1).

Some waves erode the shore; others build up the shore (Source 2).

Coastal erosion

Destructive waves are responsible for many spectacular landforms, including **cliffs**, **arches** and **stacks** like those in Source 3. Many different processes help to form and shape these landforms.

Source 1 Coastal landforms of erosion and deposition

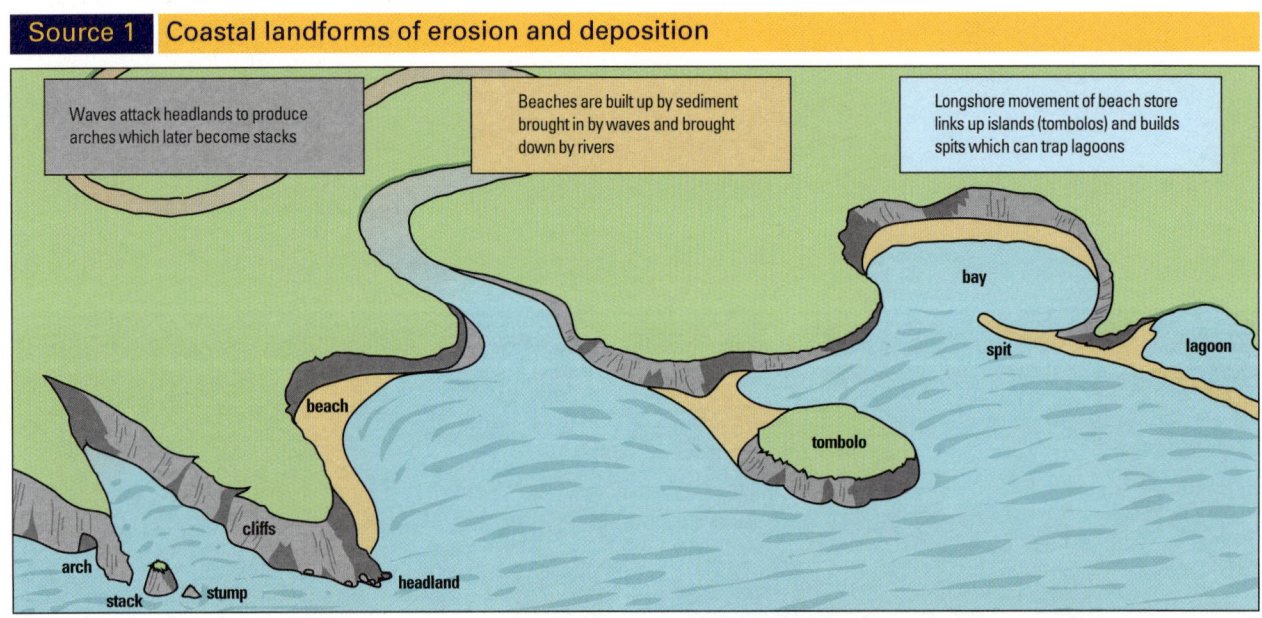

Waves attack headlands to produce arches which later become stacks

Beaches are built up by sediment brought in by waves and brought down by rivers

Longshore movement of beach store links up islands (tombolos) and builds spits which can trap lagoons

Labels: arch, stack, stump, cliffs, beach, headland, tombolo, bay, spit, lagoon

Source 2 Different waves shape the shore in different ways

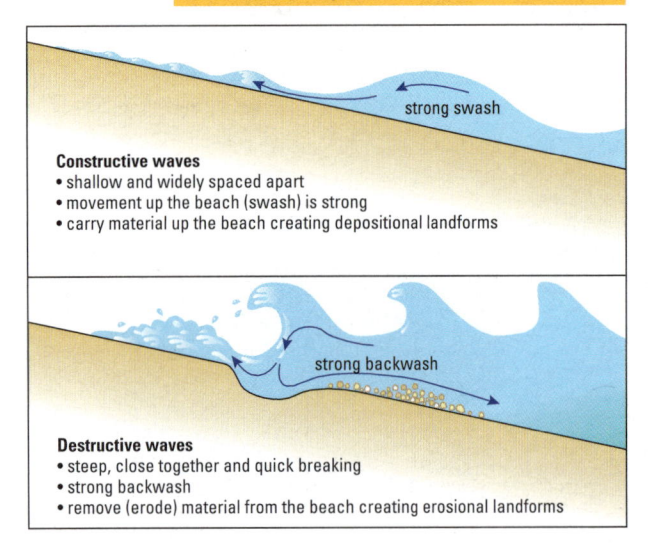

strong swash

Constructive waves
- shallow and widely spaced apart
- movement up the beach (swash) is strong
- carry material up the beach creating depositional landforms

strong backwash

Destructive waves
- steep, close together and quick breaking
- strong backwash
- remove (erode) material from the beach creating erosional landforms

Source 3 Wave erosion creates steep cliffs, arches and stacks

Labels: cliffs, arch, stack

Coasts

Erosion occurs when powerful waves crash against the cliffs. The waves hurl sand, shingle and pebbles against the cliff. This breaks up the rock – a process called **corrasion**. The waves trap air in crevices in the rock, causing large pieces to break off – a process called **hydraulic pressure**. The rocks and pebbles from the eroded cliffs crash into each other in the waves and are reduced in size into sands and gravels – a process known as **attrition**. Vegetation on cliffs also plays a part. Rain and sea water dissolves acids from the vegetation and these help erode some rocks like chalk. Vegetation can also protect the cliffs from mass movement.

Harder rocks usually form cliffs. Softer rocks are more easily eroded, and wear back more quickly. Cliffs tend to stand out as **headlands**. When waves approach headlands they are bent or **refracted**. As a result they attack the headlands on three sides (Source 4B). Weaknesses in the rock will be eroded first, with small sea caves being formed. If the waves break through on both sides of the headland they form an **arch**. When the roof of the arch collapses an isolated tower of rock called a **stack** is left. This stack will eventually be worn away leaving a **stump**.

Source 4 Coastal processes

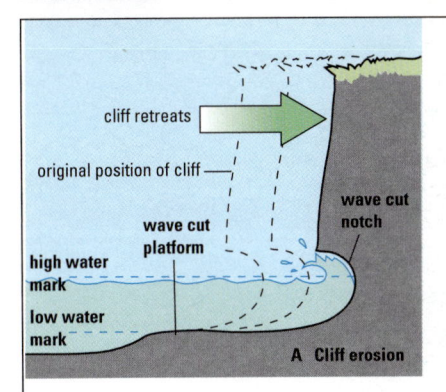

A Cliff erosion – Destructive waves cut a deep notch at the base of the cliff causing the cliff to collapse

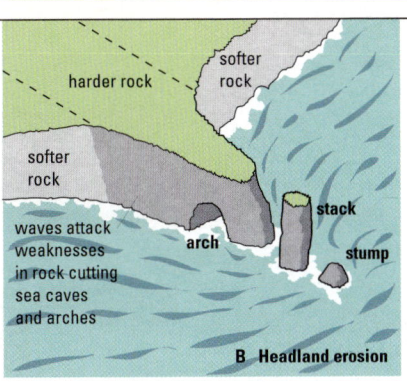

B Headland erosion – Waves erode headland from both sides forming an arch – the roof of the arch will collapse leaving a stack

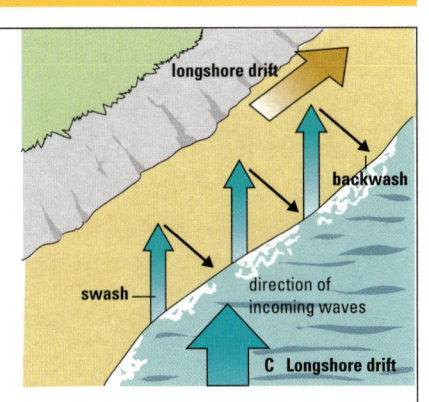

C Longshore drift – Constructive waves reach the beach at an oblique angle, the water then drains off at right angles – this motion pushes beach particles along the beach

Source 5 Spurn Head – the growth of a spit

Coastal deposition

Other waves, known as **constructive waves**, carry the pebbles and sands from which most beaches are formed. The pebbles and sands are the remains of eroded cliff faces. Waves carry this material along the coast by a process called **longshore drift** (Source 4C).

The waves approach the shore at an angle. The **swash** pushes the sand and pebbles up the beach at the same angle. The **backwash** flows back at right angles to the sea, moving some of the sand and pebbles with it in a series of 'zig zags'.

Sometimes the shoreline changes direction. Longshore drift continues to push the sand and pebbles and they now form a new beach roughly parallel to the shore called a **spit**. Spits continue to grow in a series of curves and may divert rivers or lock up **lagoons** of water between them and the main shoreline. As the spit grows it may find an offshore island which it will join, forming a **tombolo** (Source 1).

3.2 Cliff erosion

Burton Cliff in Dorset (Source 1) is made of sandstone which has been laid down in a number of layers or **strata**. The sandstone is hard and resists wave erosion. The effect of wave action is seen in the **wave attack zone**, which causes the cliff to be undercut. This is why there is a marked cliff overhang, resulting in such a steep cliff being formed.

When waves attack, they do most damage at the weakest points. These are between each layer of sandstone. This is where the most marked **wave cut notch** is seen. Undercutting means that large blocks of the cliff will collapse. This debris can be seen as the **rock platform**.

Here, the backwash of the waves is stronger than the swash, so smaller pieces of debris are removed from the foot of the cliffs. This is why there is such a narrow beach beneath the cliff.

Within the space of just 500 metres, Burton Cliff turns into Burton Beach. The map (Source 2) shows how close these two coastal features are to each other.

Source 1 Burton Cliff, Dorset – horizontal sandstone strata eroded by waves into an irregular vertical cliff

Source 2 The contours illustrate the difference between Burton Cliff and Burton Beach

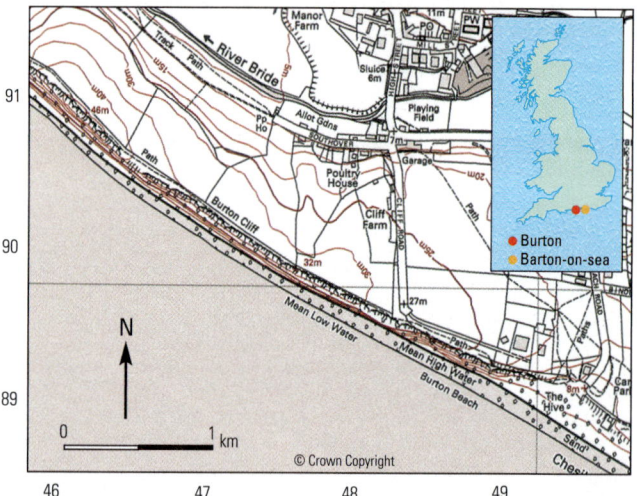

Source 3 Burton Beach – the cliff is less steep and the beach is wider

At Burton Beach (Source 3) there is a wide beach of fine sand and shingle. This has been moved from the foot of Burton Cliff by longshore drift. Here the swash of the waves is becoming stronger and the backwash weaker. The low cliff made of clay has slumped into a gentle slope.

Coasts

Source 4 — The effect of rock structure on the shape of cliffs

A horizontal rock layers: flat cliff top, steep cliff face with small overhangs, resistant rock, soft rock, wave erosion

B rock layers dip towards sea: rugged cliff top, gently sloping cliff face with few overhangs

C rock layers dip away from sea: cliff top slopes steeply down inland, steep cliff face with many overhangs, wave erosion

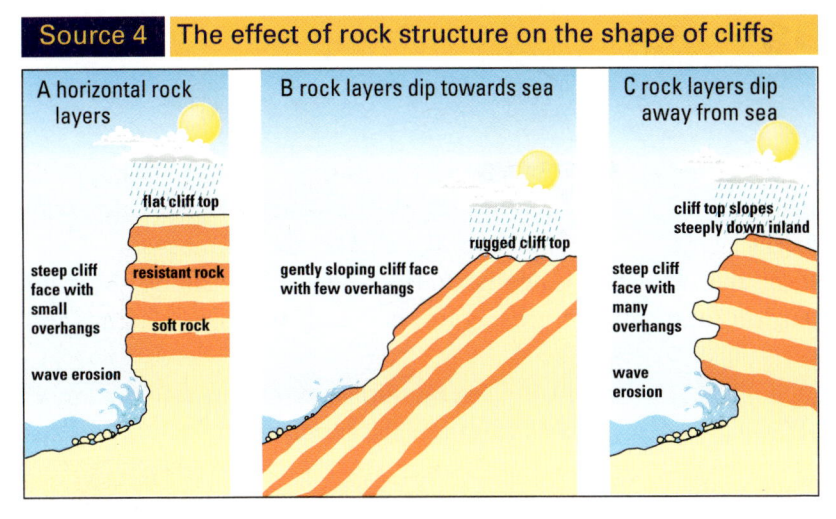

Behind the beach is a cliff, but it is quite low and not as steep as Burton Cliff. In fact, the material making the cliff has slumped down on to the beach. The land here is made of clay. The cliff has not been eroded by the sea at all. Instead, rain falling on the clay has made it **saturated**. When this happens the cliffs become unstable and begin to slump. This slumping is known as **mass movement**. The sea then carries away the clay that has been washed down on to the beach.

Wave action is not the only process shaping cliffs. The cliffs are also shaped by the actions of rain, ice, heat and wind. These actions are called **sub-aerial** weathering and erosion. In Source 4, the top of the cliffs is being weathered and eroded by sub-aerial actions. Only lower down the cliff does wave action take over.

Most rock is laid down as **sedimentary rock**. In the past, the seas covered much of the present land. Beneath these seas layer upon layer of sediments have been deposited. These sediments were hardened into rock by the pressure of overlying sediments. Some rock, such as sandstone, became very hard. Other rock, such as clay, remained soft.

When the rock was pushed up out of the sea it was usually tilted one way or another. The effect of this is seen in Source 4. A series of hard and soft rock layers are tilted towards or away from the sea, or may be left horizontal.

Sub-aerial weathering and erosion break up and remove the soft rock faster than the hard, resistant rock. If the rock layers are horizontal the weathering and erosion act equally across the layers of rock. If not, then the alternating weathering of hard and soft rock creates an uneven top surface of the cliff (Source 4B).

Lower down the cliff face, the waves are also affected by the lie of the rock layers. If the layers are horizontal (Source 4A) the cliff face will be steep with overhanging ledges – like Burton Cliff. If the layers dip towards the sea (Source 4B) the cliff face will have a gentle slope. If the layers dip away from the sea (Source 4C) there will be an uneven and steep cliff face.

Cliff erosion at Barton-on-Sea

A few kilometres east of Burton (Source 2) is an example of cliff slumping at Barton-on-Sea. There have been many attempts at protecting the cliffs, but much land has already been lost.

The rocks forming the cliffs are gravels and sands overlying clays. Rainwater seeps through the gravels and sands into the clay. The clay becomes waterlogged and moves in a mass down the slope (Source 5).

Human activity has not helped. A few kilometres west of the beach groynes have been built to stop sand and shingle moving along the coast. Therefore sand and shingle is removed by humans and is no longer available to protect the shore. The sea attacks the base of the cliffs, removing the slumped beach material.

Source 5 — Mass movement results in cliff slumping at Barton-on-Sea

The saturated loose cliff deposits have slumped onto the beach

3.3 Building beaches

The beach store

Beaches are made up of all the material lying between high water and low water marks. This material is known as the **beach store**. Source 1 shows how the beach store is built. There are four main sources of beach store:

- at A, erosion of the cliff is providing broken rock for the beach
- at B, longshore drift is carrying sand and small pebbles from the cliff to the main beach
- at C, **constructive waves** are pushing the sand and pebbles up the beach to make it higher and wider
- at D, the river mouth is providing fine muds and gravels to add to the beach store.

Source 1 The effect of longshore drift on the beach store

Source 2 shows a typical beach store at Slapton Sands in South Devon. The shape of the beach can be clearly seen. It rises in a series of ridges, called **berms**. These ridges are built by constructive waves pushing the pebbles up the beach. If there is a very high tide the berm will be created high up the beach. Lower berms will be created nearer the water from constructive waves during lower tide levels.

The waves push up the larger pebbles at high tide, leaving them stranded high up the beach. When the water from the waves flows back to the sea only the smaller particles are removed. This is why the higher berms are composed of larger particles than the lower berms.

Source 2 Longshore drift and constructive waves in Start Bay, Devon, have produced a beach store and clearly marked lines of berms

Coasts

Source 3 | Beach form and composition changes from south to north along Start Bay, Devon

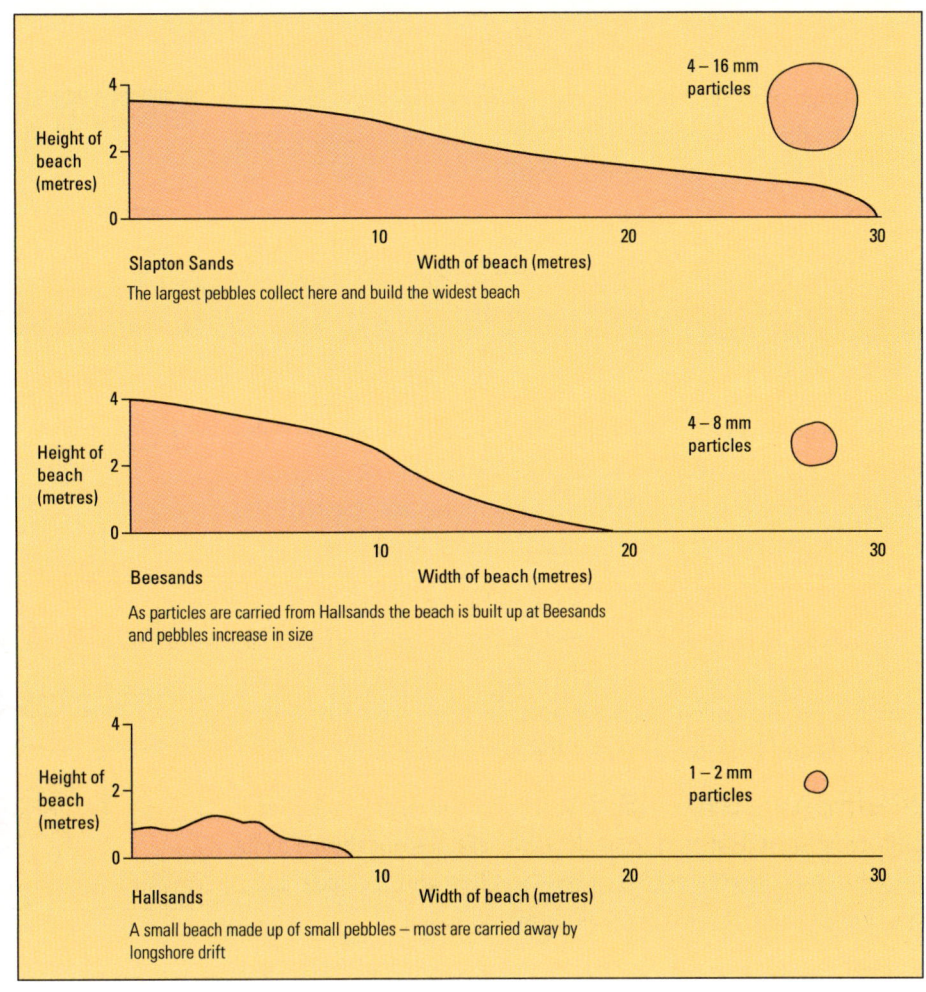

Slapton Sands — 4–16 mm particles
The largest pebbles collect here and build the widest beach

Beesands — 4–8 mm particles
As particles are carried from Hallsands the beach is built up at Beesands and pebbles increase in size

Hallsands — 1–2 mm particles
A small beach made up of small pebbles – most are carried away by longshore drift

The changing beach

Source 3 shows the long beach of Start Bay on the South Devon coast. The diagrams alongside the photograph show the size and shape of different beaches along the bay. Not only do the beaches become higher and wider from south to north, but the pebbles lying on them become larger. Why do these beaches change from south to north?

At Hallsands, to the south, the weathering and erosion of the cliff face is providing the beach store (A in Source 1). The waves are breaking down the rocks into pebbles. Then, as fast as they collect, the pebbles are being carried along the beach by longshore drift. So there is only a small beach, made up of a few pieces of unbroken rock and a thin covering of fine sand.

At Beesands, halfway along Start Bay, the picture is different. Here, a small stream is bringing fine muds and gravels down to the beach. The pebbles being moved along the beach have blocked the mouth of the stream, which empties into a small lagoon (D in Source 1). The beach here is wider and higher than Hallsands, with larger pebbles.

The widest and highest beach, with the largest pebbles, is found at Slapton Sands. This beach catches all the pebbles which are being brought from the south. Here are found all the very largest pebbles which are thrown up on to the beach by constructive waves.

3.4 Changing sea levels

Over long periods of time the level of the sea changes relative to the land surface. Every time there is a change, new cliffs and beaches are created. Sea level changes for two reasons.

1. If there is more or less water in the sea, the level will rise or fall.
2. If the land moves up or down, the level of the sea will fall or rise.

For two million years the polar ice caps advanced over the seas and land. The ice held water which would normally feed the sea. The sea level fell. Later, when the ice melted, the volume of water in the sea increased and its level rose.

The effect on the coastline is shown in Source 1. In A, the sea erodes cliffs and creates beaches. When the sea level falls, as shown in B, the cliffs and beaches are left stranded above sea level. These are called abandoned cliffs and **raised beaches**. New cliffs and beaches are cut at the new sea level.

When the sea level rises again it will cover the new beaches and cliffs, creating a drowned coast. If the level does not return to its original place, there will be raised beaches and old cliff lines remaining above the sea level, as shown in C.

Source 1 The fall and rise of the sea changes the face of the shore

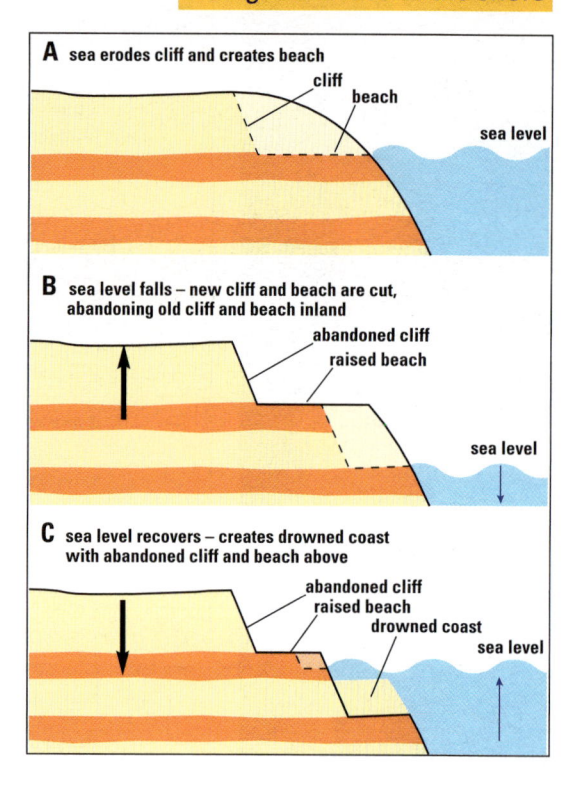

A sea erodes cliff and creates beach

B sea level falls – new cliff and beach are cut, abandoning old cliff and beach inland

C sea level recovers – creates drowned coast with abandoned cliff and beach above

Rias and fiords

When the sea level rises, as we have seen, it creates a drowned coast. Sea water floods into estuaries and inlets. This happened in southern England when the glaciers melted at the end of the last Ice Age. Many drowned river valleys, known as rias, were created in Devon and Cornwall. This is what has happened in the case of the valley near Port Quin in Cornwall (Source 2).

Source 2 Small ria near Port Quin, Cornwall

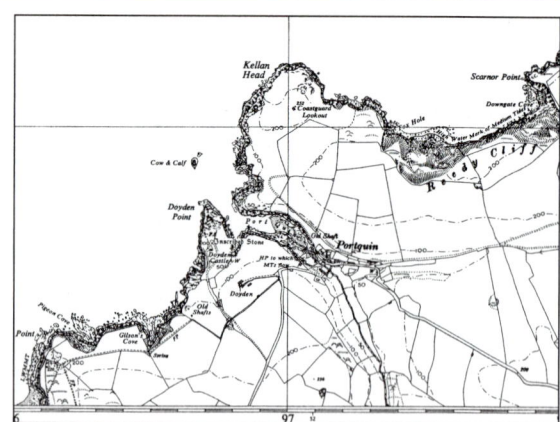

Coasts

Source 3 Fiord in Scotland

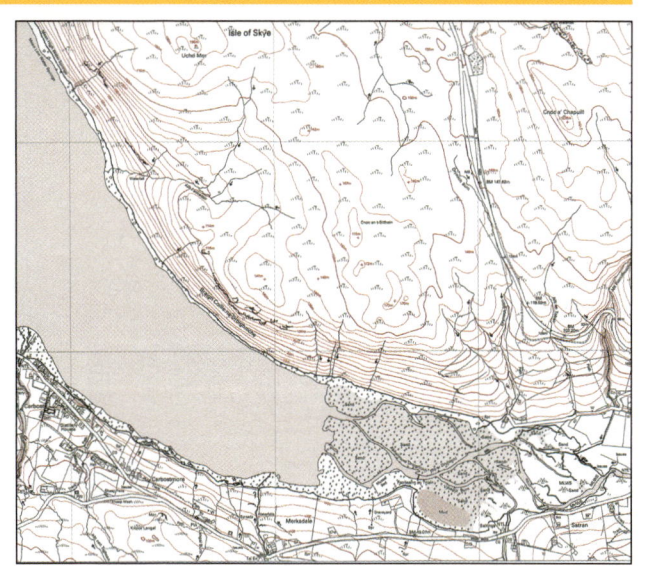

Source 4 Cross-section of a fiord

- steep valley sides
- glaciated or U-shaped valley
- section across width
- steep back wall
- shallow entrance
- deepest part close to backwall
- section along length

Source 5 Cross-section of Port Quin ria

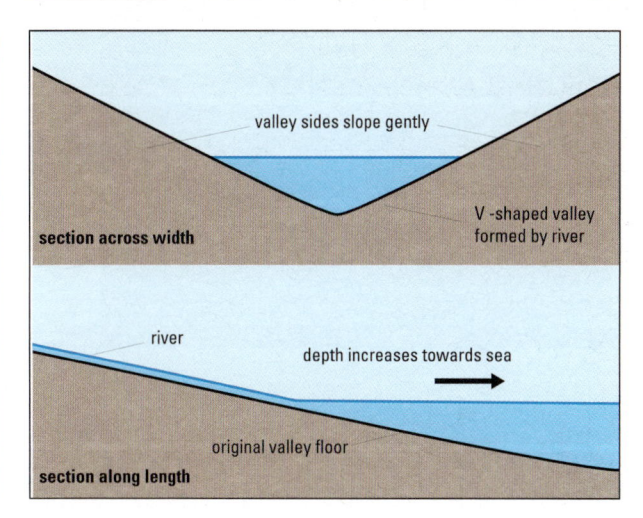

- valley sides slope gently
- V-shaped valley formed by river
- section across width
- river
- depth increases towards sea
- original valley floor
- section along length

In other parts of Britain, where ice cut into valleys which were later flooded, **fiords** were formed (Source 4). These are drowned glaciated valleys and differ from rias (Source 5).

In Scotland, events since the Ice Age have been more complicated. During the Ice Age glaciers cut deep valleys. The ice sheets were so thick that the land on which they rested was depressed. The sea level had already fallen. When the ice melted, the sea level rose and began cutting beaches and cliffs. Relieved of the weight of the ice, the land began to rise back to its old level. It carried up with it the new beaches and cliffs cut by the sea.

The increase in temperatures which is resulting from global warming may cause the polar ice caps to melt more rapidly. This will lead to another rise in sea level, drowning many coastal landforms seen today.

3.5 Coastal change and management
the Suffolk coast

Source 1 The Suffolk coastline around Aldeburgh is being reshaped by longshore drift and longshore currents

Source 2 The Suffolk coastline around Aldeburgh

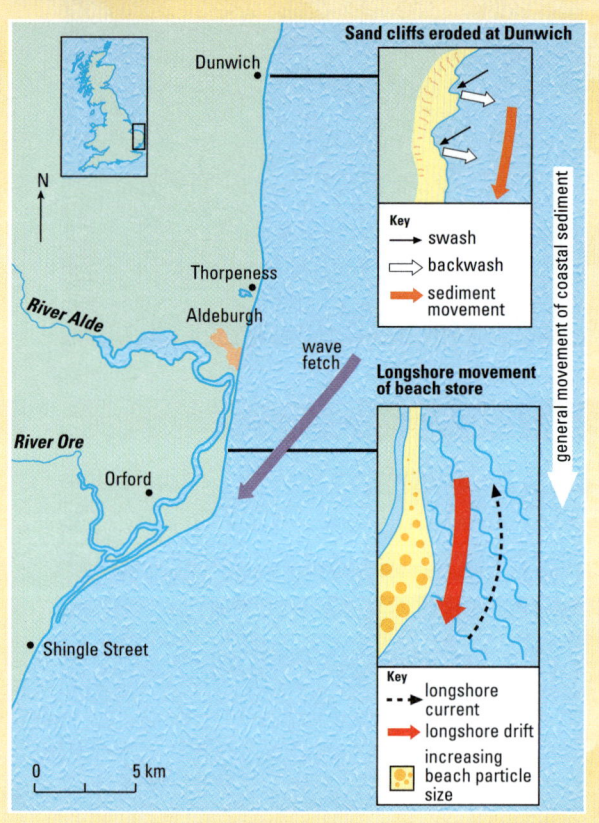

The Suffolk coastline is changing as a result of the powerful effects of the sea. The effects are both constructive and destructive. Cliffs are being eroded along one part of the coast, and the material is carried by longshore drift and deposited as a pebble spit further south.

Change: the building of Orford Ness

Orford Ness is a coastal spit in East Anglia (Source 1). The spit has been built up from beach store eroded to the north, around Dunwich, and further north up the coast. The Rivers Alde and Ore have been deflected southwards by the growth of the spit, the end of which lies off Shingle Street.

The spit is still growing in a southerly direction (Source 2). Destructive waves approach the land from the north-east, where the greatest **fetch** (the distance over the sea that the wind has blown) is to be found.

At Dunwich there are low cliffs made of soft sands. These sands are eroded by storm waves and are carried south by longshore drift. Shingle and pebbles also move southwards. Only the very fine sands are brought back north by the actions of the weaker longshore current. These are the reasons why the beach store particles become larger further south along the spit.

At Thorpeness the coastline changes direction from south to south-west. The sand and shingle have continued to be moved south. Aldeburgh was on the mouth of the River Alde until the spit began to deflect the river south over 1000 years ago.

Now, the spit near Aldeburgh is being used by the waves to provide beach store for the further extension of the spit. There are real fears that the present beach may be removed. **Groynes** and **rip-rap walls** have been built to try to stop this further erosion.

Coasts

Source 3 The eroding sand cliffs at Dunwich provide the beach store for the building of Orford Ness spit

Source 4 Groynes at Aldeburgh try to hold back the removal of the beach store

In spite of the groynes beach material is still being lost

Source 5 This rip-rap wall south of Aldeburgh helps absorb the energy of the waves and reduces the loss of beach

Problems and solutions

The cliffs at Dunwich are being eroded (Source 3). There has been no attempt to stop this. Many people believe that the only effective way to stop erosion is to allow the waves to create a new beach. This would mean losing some of the shore and, perhaps, the village of Dunwich itself.

Aldeburgh is the main town along this stretch of coast. As the beach dwindled away, groynes were built to stop the southward movement of sand and shingle. This is not always successful, as Source 4 shows. The lower levels of the groynes appear to be losing the battle.

Another approach to dealing with erosion along this coastline has been the building of rip-rap walls (Source 5). These aim to lessen the force of the destructive waves. As the waves break on the shore they fall against large boulders or concrete blocks. The many gaps in between the blocks absorb the energy of the waves.

Rising sea levels along the East Anglian coast

The British Isles is still recovering from the last Ice Age. The mountainous coast in the north and west is rising as it recovers from the weight of ice that covered the land in the recent past. In contrast, the south and east coast is sinking. This sinking is made worse by the rising sea levels resulting from the melting of the ice caps as the world's climate heats up.

Some scientists predict that sea levels will rise as the burning of fossil fuels (coal, oil) warms up the atmosphere. This could lead to the melting of the polar ice caps and a gradual rise in sea level. Some say that sea levels will rise by up to 1 metre in the next 100 years. Such a rise would drown many coastal beaches and estuaries around the world.

The East Anglian coast would suffer. Much of the coast behind the Orford Ness spit would be flooded and the Dunwich cliffs would completely disappear. Building and maintaining barriers like groynes and rip-rap walls would prove too costly – the coast would have to be abandoned to the sea, and the town of Aldeburgh and the surrounding villages would be lost.

3.6 Using a coastal area
Milford Haven

The landscape of the haven

Milford Haven in South Wales (Source 1) is a ria. As sea levels rose after the last Ice Age, water drowned this wide river valley. From the shore, the land rises steeply as cliffs. Out in the water lie many stacks, like Stack Rock and Thorn Island.

This whole coast is a deep water coast. The waves from the Atlantic Ocean that pound the cliffs are very destructive. The high, rugged coastal cliffs provide a habitat for much wildlife. People visit the area to enjoy the scenery and to take advantage of the recreational opportunities offered by walking, rock climbing and watersports.

This valuable natural resource is under pressure. Milford Haven is protected by the Pembrokeshire National Park Authority. The Authority is responsible for managing sites of special interest, such as woodlands and sand dunes. In addition there are a number of **nature reserves**, which were set up to protect the rare birds and mammals that use the coast.

Source 1 Milford Haven has attracted oil terminals and refineries, a power station and many other smaller businesses

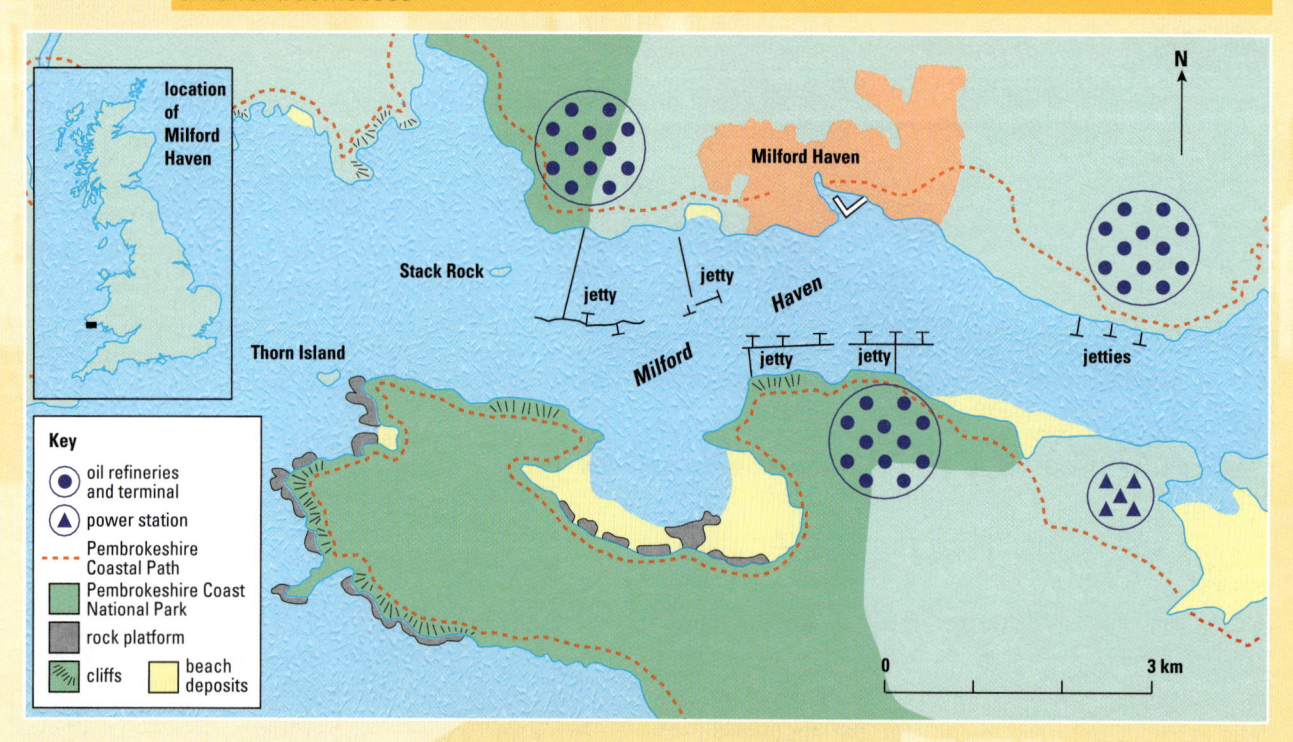

Industry in the haven

The inlet of Milford Haven (Source 1) allows giant oil tankers to offload their cargoes in safe deep-water harbours. To the west is the Atlantic Ocean which links Britain with the world's main oil-producing countries.

The jetties stand out in the deep water so that the oil tankers can offload without fear of striking the many rocks beneath the surface. Some oil is processed in the large **oil refineries** that have grown up around the inlet. One such refinery is shown in Source 2. The rest of the oil is sent by pipeline or by smaller tankers to other refineries in Britain.

The oil refineries have encouraged the development of other industries including a power station. In the town of Milford Haven itself, businesses such as shops, insurance offices and transport services have grown up as employment in the oil industry has grown.

Disaster in the haven

In February 1996, the *Sea Empress*, a huge oil tanker, hit rocks and ran aground on its approach to Milford Haven (Source 3). The disaster could not have come at a worse time for the area, which at this time of year is visited by many species of birds such as gannets and red-throated divers before they fly north. Large stretches of the Pembroke coastline were affected by the spill, including areas of National Park and Sites of Special Scientific Interest (SSSI).

It was feared that this contamination of the coast would be great. Not only was the wildlife at risk, but the coastline is also a favourite resort for many holidaymakers. The earnings of those who make a living from tourism were at risk.

The haven is also an important fishing area – particularly shellfish along the coast. It was feared that these fishing grounds would be so badly affected they could not be used again for a long time.

The people of this Pembrokeshire coast worked hard to contain the oil spill. In the event the extent of the damage was contained. Today the coast is clean again.

Source 3 An oil spill off Milford Haven

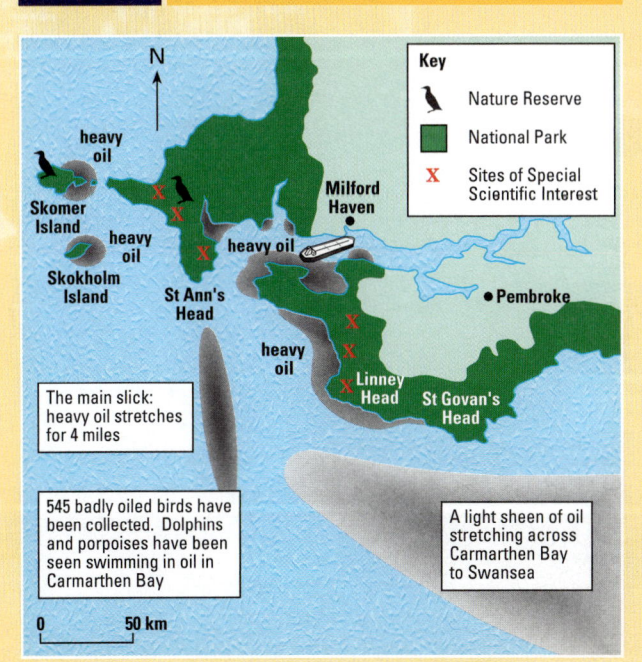

Source 2 An oil refinery looms over small villages in the haven

Conserving the haven

The Pembrokeshire Coastal Path (Source 4) surrounds the inlet of Milford Haven. The path takes walkers past some of the most attractive coastal scenery in Britain and attracts visitors to the area all year round.

This is a wild coast and the path can be made unsafe either by sea erosion or by too many people trampling it. The Pembrokeshire Coast National Park Authority is responsible for repairs and maintenance of the path.

Source 4 Pembrokeshire Coastal Path

3.7 Pollution
Italy's Adriatic coast

Mediterranean Europe is a popular destination for summer holidays. Each year millions of tourists from all over Europe travel down to the Mediterranean coast to enjoy the seaside in the sun. There are hotels and popular resorts from Venice south to Rimini.

The Adriatic Sea is an arm of the Mediterranean. As Source 1 shows, it is a narrow, enclosed sea. The River Po empties its waters into the sea south of Venice. As it flows through the lowlands between the Alps and Apennines, it passes through a rich farming area with many large towns.

Source 2 shows some of the sources of pollutants into the Adriatic Sea.

The Po basin

The waters of the River Po are used as a dumping ground. About 37 per cent of Italian industry is located in the Po Basin, which has a population of 16 million people. Large quantities of industrial waste and domestic sewage are found in the coastal waters of the Adriatic. The heavy industry near Venice is one source of industrial pollution (Source 2). However, the biggest polluter is agriculture. The Po valley is Italy's largest stretch of flat land, so agriculture is a popular activity here. The farmers use fertilisers and pesticides heavily and some of these inputs eventually find their way into the rivers and ultimately into the shallow coastal waters.

Source 1 Coastal pollution in the Adriatic

Source 2 Industry as well as farming sends pollutants to the Adriatic

Coasts

Source 3 Eutrophication – the result of pollution

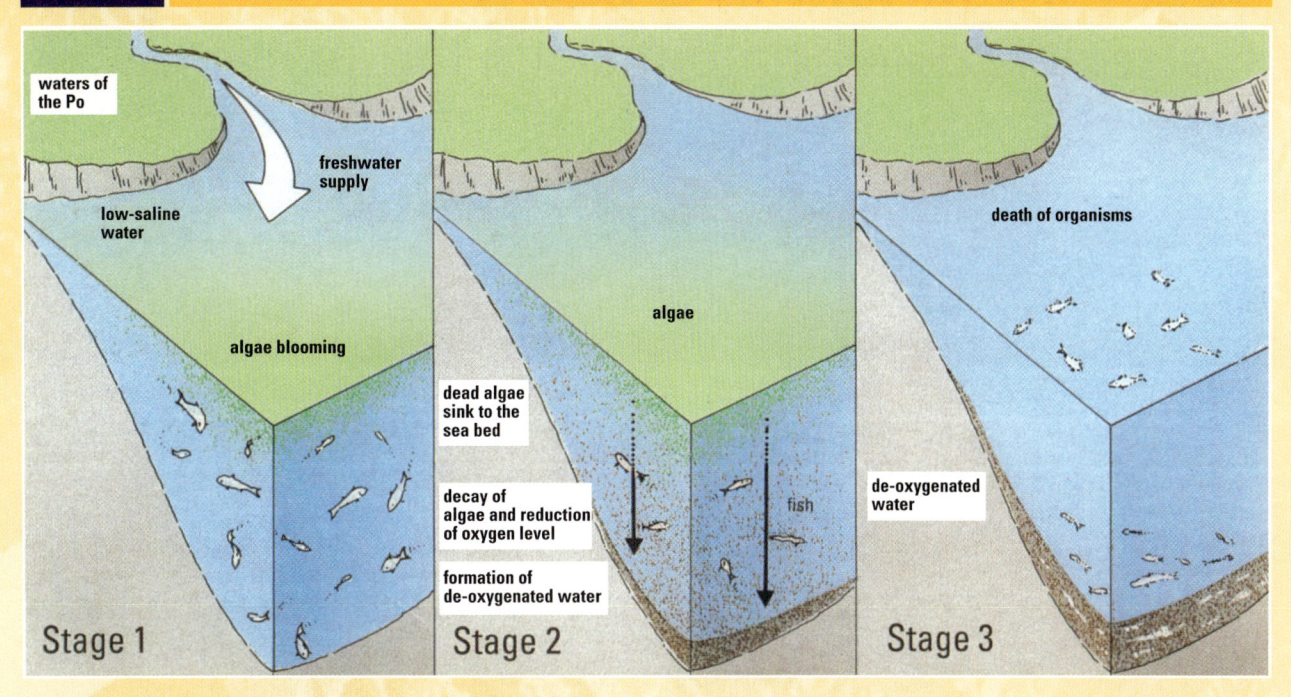

Stage 1: waters of the Po; freshwater supply; low-saline water; algae blooming

Stage 2: algae; dead algae sink to the sea bed; decay of algae and reduction of oxygen level; formation of de-oxygenated water; fish

Stage 3: death of organisms; de-oxygenated water

In recent years the waters in summer along this coast have turned into a green slime. Phosphorus and nitrogen seep into the River Po from urban sewage works and the fertilisers used in the fields. Source 3 shows the effects which these chemicals have when they reach the shallow, warm waters of the Adriatic (Stage 1). Being nutrients, the phosphorus and nitrogen feed the minute, green water plants called algae which grow on the surface – this is what gives the coastal waters their green, slimy appearance.

Source 4 Holidaymakers face thick slime on the beaches

When the algae die they fall to the sea bed, where they decay. The decaying algae remove the oxygen from the water (Stage 2). Without oxygen the other sea creatures cannot survive. Fish and plant life die, sinking to the bed, using up even more oxygen as they also decay. The result, as seen in Stage 3, is that the shallow coastal water loses all its oxygen. This is known as **eutrophication**. The waters are dead.

Cleaning up the River Po

Due to increased coastal pollution, holidaymakers are already declining in numbers (Source 4). Earnings from tourism are also falling. Fewer tourists will visit Italy's Adriatic coast and its resorts if the rivers, beaches and coastal waters are polluted and unpleasant. If the people living near the Adriatic wish to benefit from tourism in the future, they must spend money to stop the pollution. They need to:

- reduce the use of fertilisers and pesticides
- build effective sewage works
- stop industrial and urban wastes being poured into the river systems.

One source of hope for the region's future is that the Po basin does now have a river authority which is responsible for improving water quality

3.8 Coastal tourism in a LEDC
sustainable development along the Tanzanian coast

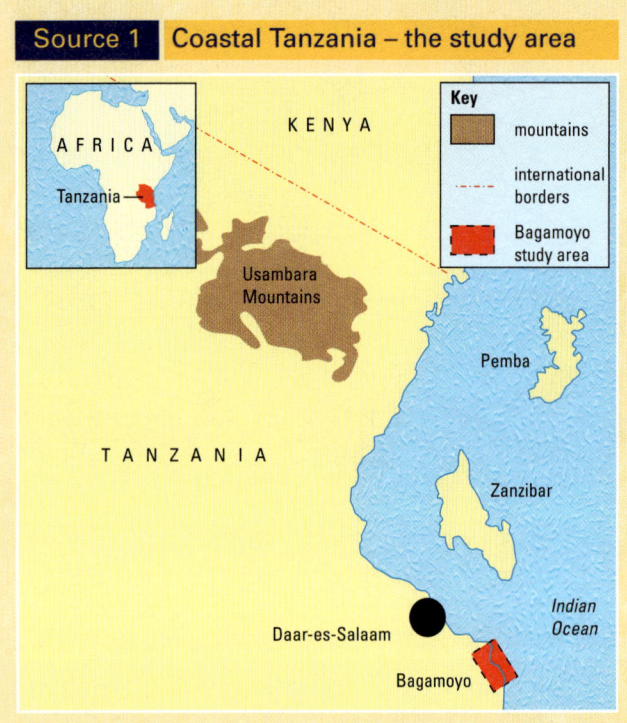

Source 1: Coastal Tanzania – the study area

Tanzania is one of the poorest countries in Africa. It has a Gross Domestic Product per person of only $700. Tourism is one way to develop the country. If more foreign tourists come to Tanzania they bring much needed dollars and other foreign currency to spend.

Tanzania has a coastline and islands with sandy beaches and coral reefs which give tourists the chance to relax and explore. If coastal tourism is to make a large contribution to development it must be managed. Sustainable development will depend on preserving the coastal resources.

Bagamoyo – can tourism take the pressure off coastal resources?

South of Dar-es-Salaam the coastal area of Bagamoyo is under siege. Mangroves, salt and coral reefs provide the large and growing population with their main resources outside peasant farming.

Mangroves provide wood for building as well as fuel wood, charcoal and fishing stakes. Medicinal plants are also collected. Too much mangrove forest is being removed. Areas of mangrove swamp are left to evaporate to produce salt. Now these salt ponds are in decline as cheaper imported salt has become available.

The coral reefs around Mwamba Kuni and Mwamba Mshingwi, and elsewhere, are also under severe threat. The local people depend upon fishing. The waters around the reefs are the main fishing grounds. Illegal dynamiting, trampling on the coral and removal of shells for sale are destroying this resource. At the same time the use of fine mesh nets means that juvenile fish are caught before they have time to reach maturity and breed.

Source 2: The location and resources of the Bagamoyo area

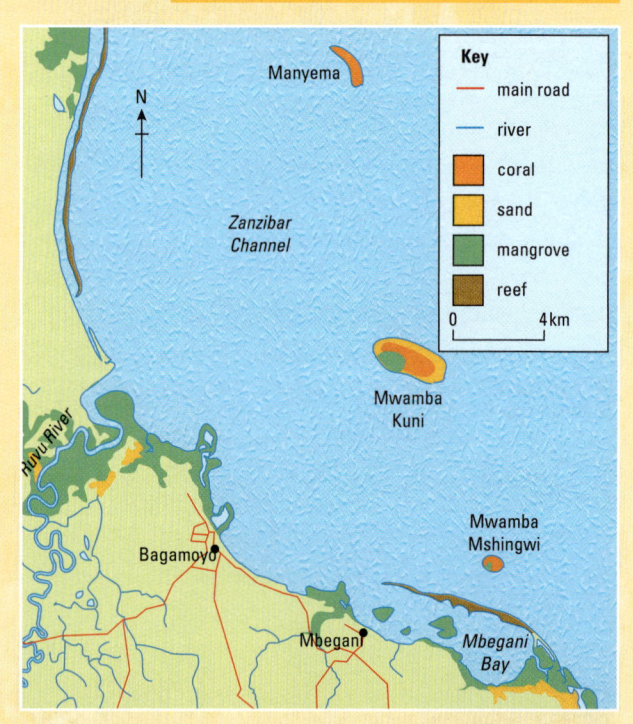

At present only five hotels have been built. The local fishermen are prevented from using the waters in front of the hotels. Little employment is to be found in the tourist industry as yet. However, as the resources dwindle it may be that a more developed tourist industry will not only provide more jobs, but also help protect these endangered resources.

Coasts

Zanzibar – the tourist paradise?

The recent growth in foreign tourists has been dramatic – an increase of over 300 per cent. Foreign currency earnings have swelled from US $13 million in 1970 to US $730 million in 1999. The island of Zanzibar is a fast-growing tourist 'honeypot'. It needs to be. The population is growing at 3 per cent per annum and by the year 2015 is expected to reach 1 500 000. This will mean a population density of over 600 per square kilometre.

Pemba – the future paradise?

North of Zanzibar is the relatively undeveloped island of Pemba. Like Zanzibar, it is blessed with excellent coral reefs. Unlike Zanzibar, it is not yet a tourist 'honeypot'. There are few hotels on Pemba, but the first high-quality hotel has just been opened.

Pemba has the opportunity to limit the pressures on the environment and encourage more environmentally friendly tourism. Masali Island off the west coast is a coral-fringed, protected nature reserve. The newest hotel, Fundu Lagoon, is built to blend in with the forest and mangrove trees – a good example of **ecotourism** (Source 7).

Pressure on the beaches and coral reefs is growing. Most resorts offer diving and snorkelling. The reefs must be protected if tourism is to continue. Some 23 000 local fishermen rely on the coral reefs as their fishing grounds and provide the main source of protein for local people. Both the tourists and the fishermen are threatening the reefs. Coral is damaged by tourists who trample on it and collect it illegally. The reefs are damaged by boat anchors and polluted by hotel effluents. Now the government is creating protected areas to safeguard these fragile resources.

Source 3 Growth of tourism in Tanzania 1970–1999

Source 4 Water-based tourist resources on Zanzibar

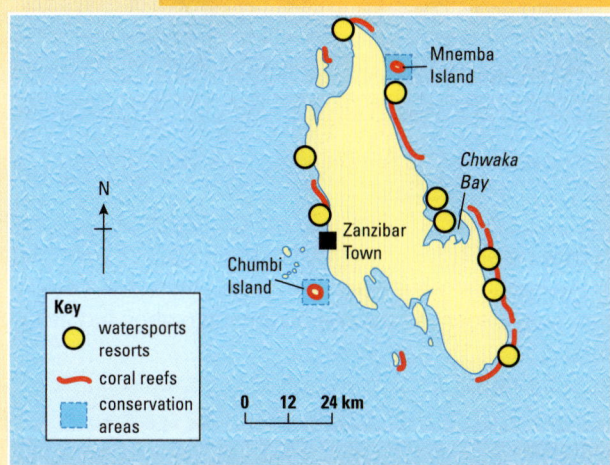

Source 5 Zanzibar offers tropical beaches and coral reefs

Source 6 Water-based tourist resources on Pemba

Source 7 Blending tourism and environment – ecotourism on Pemba

3.9 Activities

1. Explain the following terms:
   - constructive waves
   - destructive waves
   - cliffs
   - headlands
   - arches and stacks
   - abrasion
   - hydraulic pressure
   - longshore drift
   - swash and backwash
   - coastal spit
   - coastal lagoon

2. Study Source 1.

   Source 1 OS map of Burton Cliff and Burton Beach

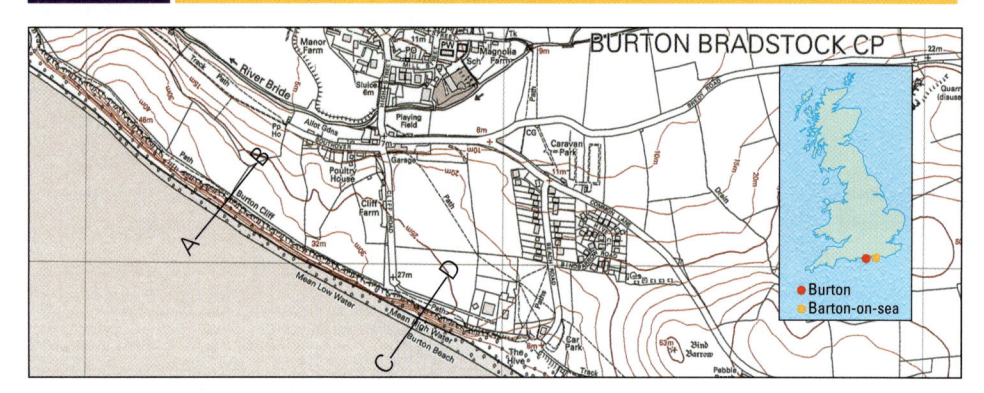

   a Draw on a suitable scale the two coastal profiles A—B and C—D shown above.
   b Describe the differences between the two profiles.

3. a i What does the term **beach store** mean?
      ii Describe four ways in which the beach store is built up.
   b i Using a simple diagram explain why beaches become wider and higher and have larger pebbles along some coasts.
      ii Describe how beach berms are formed.

4. a Describe the following coastal landforms:
      - raised beach
      - abandoned cliff
      - ria
      - fiord
   b Describe the sequence of changes in levels of land and sea over the last 2 million years.
   c How are people's activities affecting sea levels and what steps can we take to reduce these effects?

5. a Make a labelled sketch drawing showing the coastal processes affecting the Suffolk coast.
   b Describe the ways in which attempts are being made to reduce the removal of beach material by the sea from the Suffolk coast around Aldeburgh.

6. a Suggest reasons why industry has been attracted to Milford Haven.
   b What dangers to the environment are posed by industry in and around Milford Haven?
   c What steps are being taken to conserve the natural landscape around Milford Haven?

7. a Draw a simple labelled diagram to show the causes of pollution in the Adriatic Sea.
   b Describe the process known as eutrophication.
   c What steps are being taken to overcome pollution problems in the Adriatic Sea?

8 a Describe why tourism is so important to the economy of Tanzania.
  b In what ways are the coastal resources under threat in Tanzania?
  c Define what you understand by the term 'sustainable development' and what Tanzania must do to sustain its tourist industry.

9 Study the map of 'Rivermouth' in Source 2. 'Rivermouth' was once a thriving fishing harbour. Recent decline in fish stocks due to pollution and overfishing has resulted in little work for most of the fishing boats.
The town council wants to revive the fortunes of the area. Talks have been started between council members and the directors of a leisure company who want to build a holiday camp and recreation centre.
Some council members are greatly opposed to the scheme, fearing that it would change the nature of the coastal area for the worse.
  a Present a case for building the holiday camp and recreation centre. In your proposals you should:
  - suggest a site for the centre
  - locate routes for the access roads leading to the centre
  - describe how this coastline can be used for leisure and recreation
  - identify any parts of the coast which you would expect to be protected by the developers.

  b Look critically at your proposals and put the case for the opponents of the scheme. Make detailed reference to the expected damaging impact on specific sites which you think, from map evidence, are worthy of conservation.

Source 2 'Rivermouth'

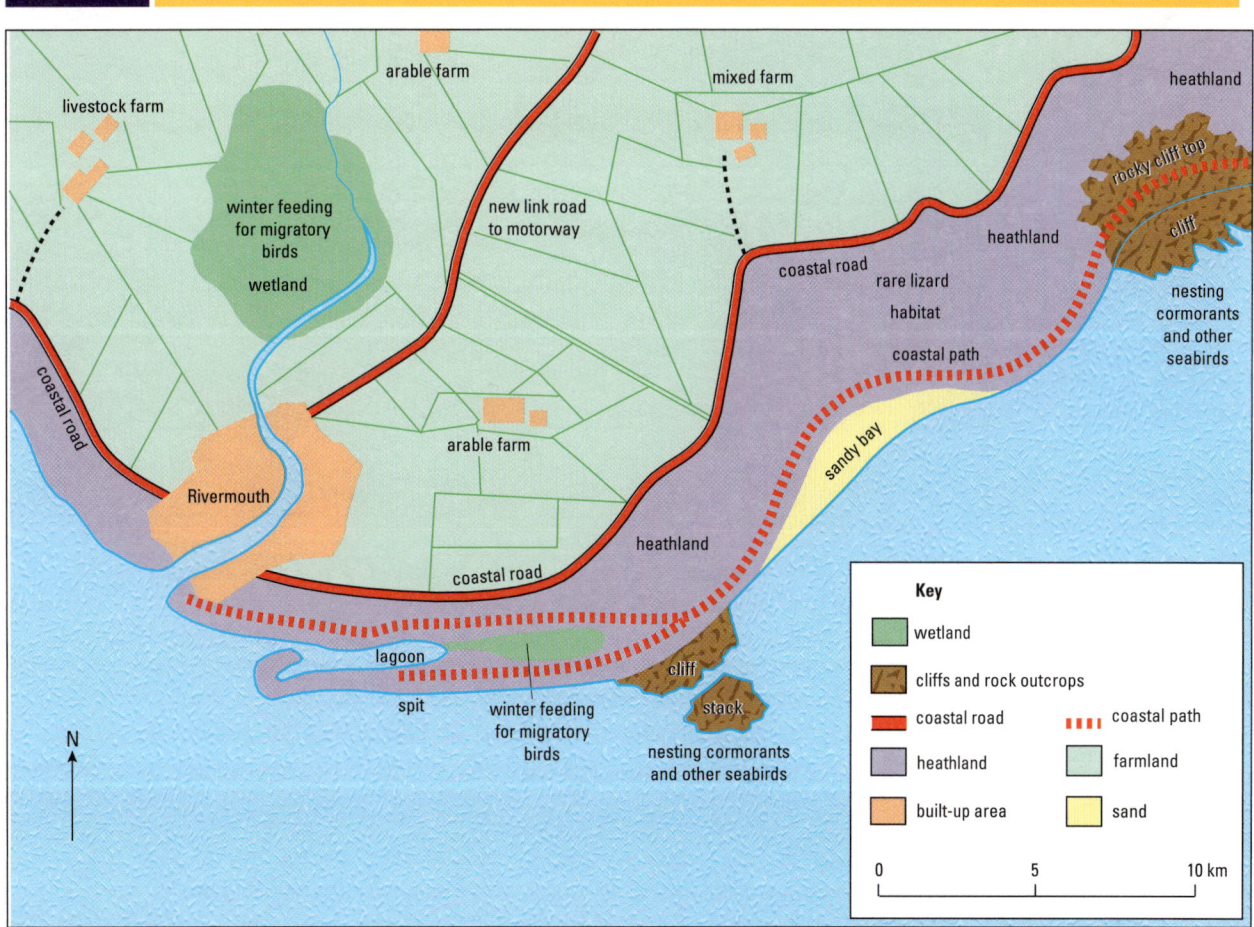

3.10 Sample examination questions

1 a Source 1 shows coastal landforms.

Source 1 | **Coastal landforms**

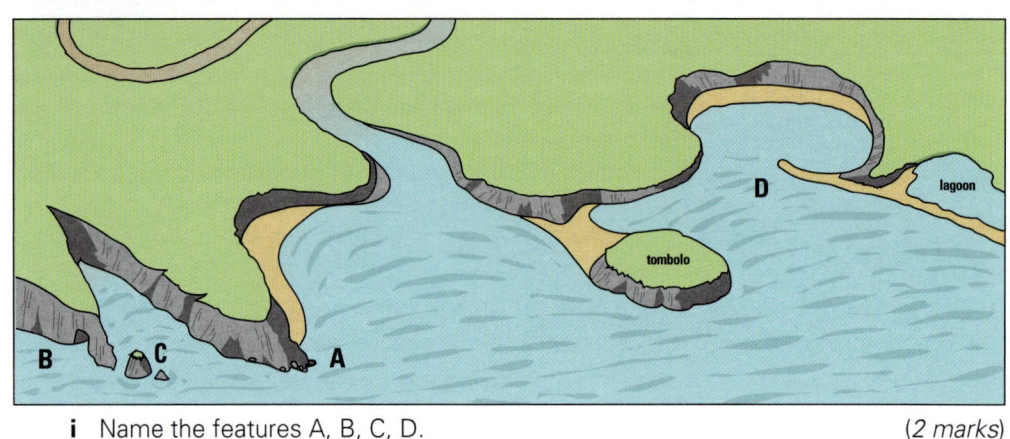

[Diagram showing coastal landforms labelled A, B, C, D, tombolo and lagoon]

    i Name the features A, B, C, D. *(2 marks)*
    ii Describe how feature B has been formed. *(2 marks)*
    iii Explain how the tombolo and lagoon have been formed. *(2 marks)*
b Draw a labelled diagram showing how longshore drift produces coastal landforms. *(4 marks)*

(Total: *10 marks*)

2 a Study Source 2 which is an OS map extract showing part of the Milford Haven estuary in South Wales.

Source 2 | **OS map of part of the Milford Haven estuary**

[OS map extract of Milford Haven estuary showing Pembroke Dock]

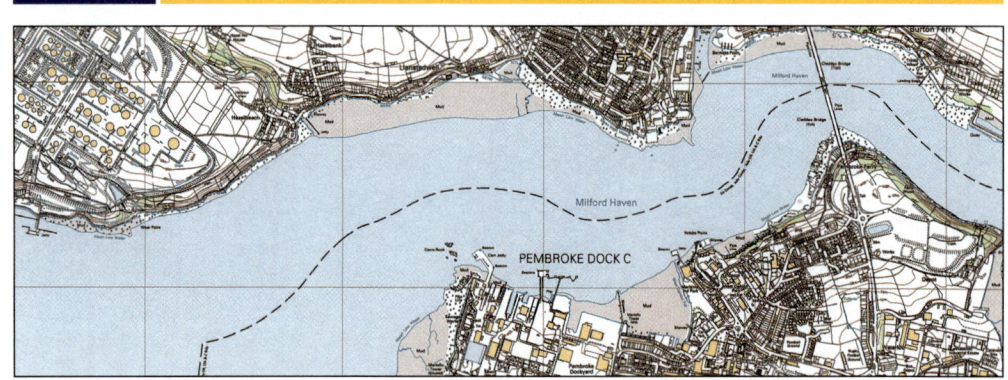

    i This estuary is a ria. Describe how rias are formed. *(2 marks)*
    ii Using evidence from the map, describe three ways in which industry uses the land on either side of the estuary. *(3 marks)*
    iii Describe two ways in which people's use of the land around the estuary may be a threat to the landscape and wildlife in the area. *(2 marks)*
b Name a coastal area (other than Milford Haven) that you have studied which is suffering from industrial pollution, and describe attempts being made to overcome this problem. *(3 marks)*

(Total: *10 marks*)

3 a Draw a sketch map to locate a stretch of coast under threat from erosion which you have studied and describe how measures are being taken to protect the shoreline (use labelled diagrams where appropriate). (Total: *10 marks*)

UNIT 4

Ice landscapes

Unit Contents

- Landscapes eroded by ice
- Glaciation in the lowlands
- A glaciated area: the Lake District
- Human activity in a glaciated area: the Lake District
- Solving problems in the Lake District

A photograph of the Matterhorn (4505 m) in the Alps. In the Alps there are many examples of landforms created by glacial erosion and deposition. Can you recognise the arêtes and pyramidal peak in the photograph?

4.1 Landscapes eroded by ice

In the last Ice Age, 2 million to 10 000 years ago, the climate was much colder than it is today. In the upland areas of the UK, the winter snow was retained all year. Each year more snow was added and it slowly compressed into ice. In some places, like north-west Scotland, the whole landscape was covered by huge ice sheets, as shown in Source 1. In some places the ice only filled the valleys, forming **glaciers**.

Today permanent ice is only found above the **snowline** in areas such as the Arctic and Antarctic and the higher parts of mountain ranges such as the Alps and Himalayas.

Ice sheets

These are huge masses of ice which move very slowly. At their edges there may be glaciers and in the sea they often form icebergs. As an ice sheet moves it scrapes and scratches the rock below. Areas of harder rock are rounded and smoothed. Areas with softer rocks are eroded to a greater depth forming basins which sometimes fill with water. These are called 'lochans' (Source 2). As the ice sheets melted and retreated they deposited all the material they had eroded. Huge quantities of **boulder clay** were laid down in the lowland areas.

Valley glaciers

Glaciers form in hollows on the sheltered sides of mountains. These are usually the north and north-east facing slopes in the northern hemisphere. As ice collects in a hollow, the pressure builds up. The ice bulges and begins to flow downhill. As it flows, it moves over obstacles, and splits occur called **crevasses**.

As the ice moves it erodes the landscape by the processes of **abrasion** and **plucking**.

Abrasion is when the rocks and boulders in the base of the glacier act like a giant file scratching and scraping the rocks below.

Source 1 Glaciated landscapes in the UK

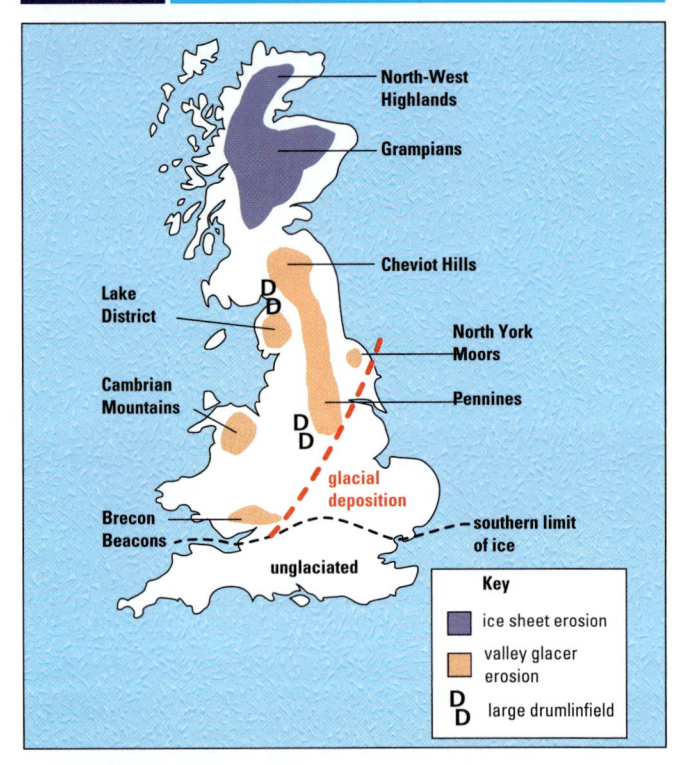

Source 2 Ice-rounded hills, and lochans

Plucking occurs when the ice freezes to the rock below. As the ice moves it pulls the rock away with it. This is very effective if the rocks have been

Ice landscapes

loosened by freeze-thaw weathering, which occurs when water freezes in cracks in rocks. As the water freezes, it expands causing the cracks to widen and the rock to break up. It helps to create arêtes and screes (Source 3).

The erosion produces many different features which are shown in Source 4.

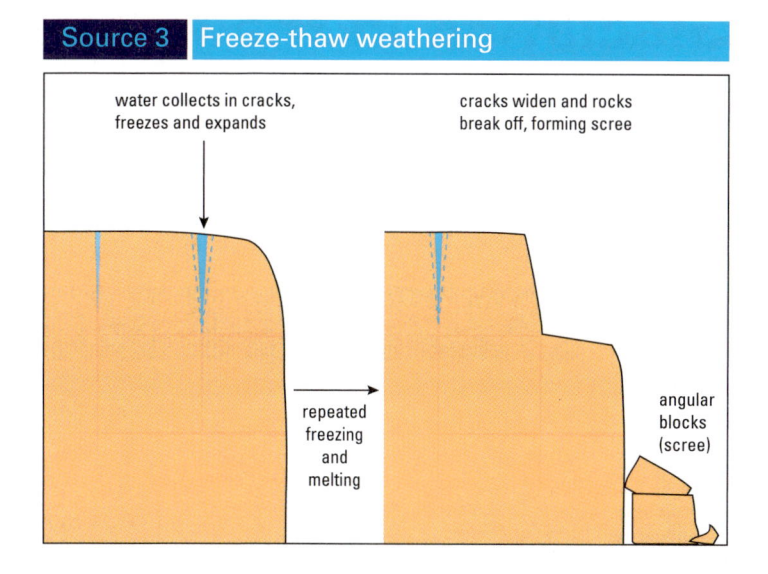

Source 3 Freeze-thaw weathering

water collects in cracks, freezes and expands → cracks widen and rocks break off, forming scree

repeated freezing and melting

angular blocks (scree)

Source 4 Features of glacial erosion

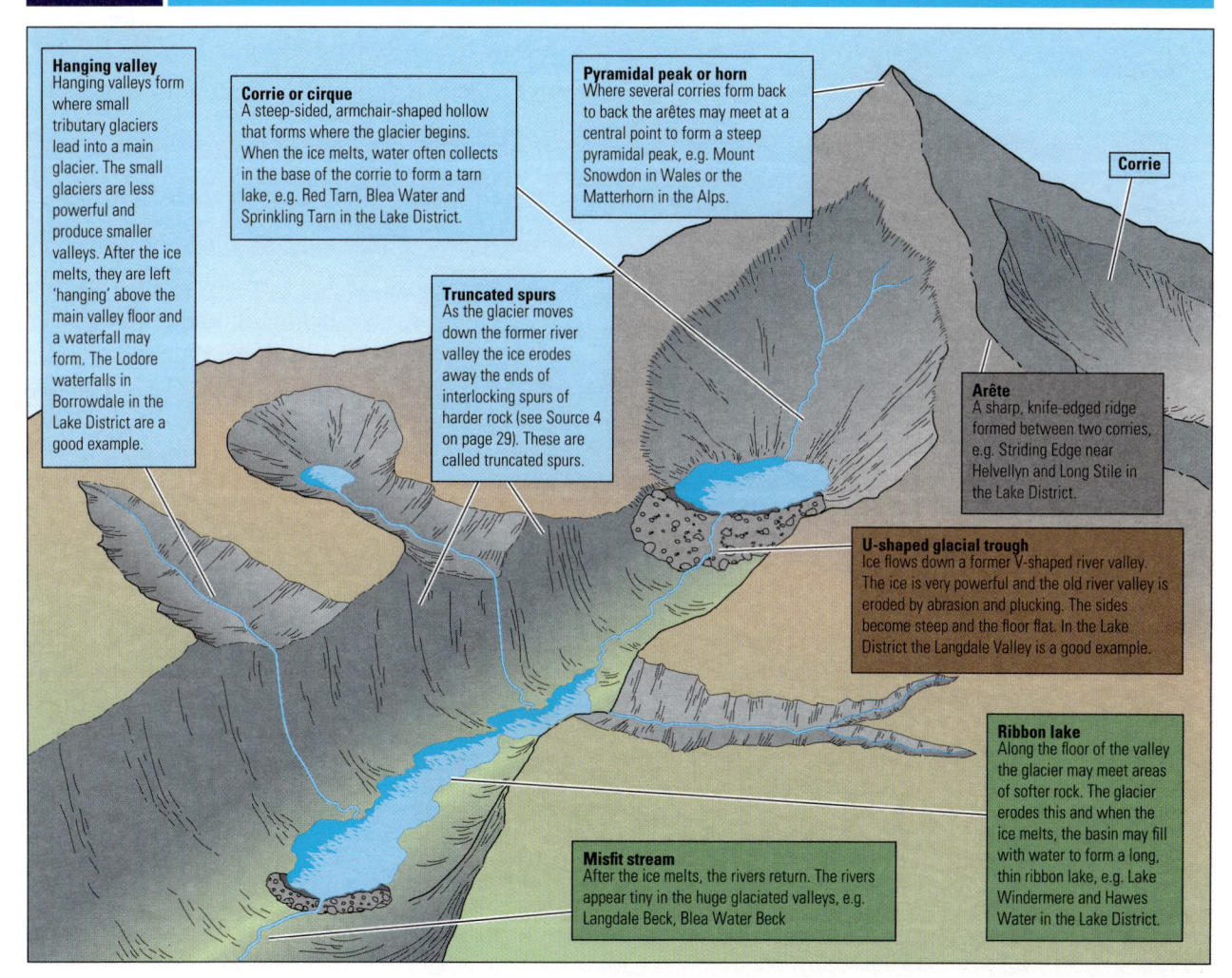

Hanging valley
Hanging valleys form where small tributary glaciers lead into a main glacier. The small glaciers are less powerful and produce smaller valleys. After the ice melts, they are left 'hanging' above the main valley floor and a waterfall may form. The Lodore waterfalls in Borrowdale in the Lake District are a good example.

Corrie or cirque
A steep-sided, armchair-shaped hollow that forms where the glacier begins. When the ice melts, water often collects in the base of the corrie to form a tarn lake, e.g. Red Tarn, Blea Water and Sprinkling Tarn in the Lake District.

Pyramidal peak or horn
Where several corries form back to back the arêtes may meet at a central point to form a steep pyramidal peak, e.g. Mount Snowdon in Wales or the Matterhorn in the Alps.

Corrie

Truncated spurs
As the glacier moves down the former river valley the ice erodes away the ends of interlocking spurs of harder rock (see Source 4 on page 29). These are called truncated spurs.

Arête
A sharp, knife-edged ridge formed between two corries, e.g. Striding Edge near Helvellyn and Long Stile in the Lake District.

U-shaped glacial trough
Ice flows down a former V-shaped river valley. The ice is very powerful and the old river valley is eroded by abrasion and plucking. The sides become steep and the floor flat. In the Lake District the Langdale Valley is a good example.

Ribbon lake
Along the floor of the valley the glacier may meet areas of softer rock. The glacier erodes this and when the ice melts, the basin may fill with water to form a long, thin ribbon lake, e.g. Lake Windermere and Hawes Water in the Lake District.

Misfit stream
After the ice melts, the rivers return. The rivers appear tiny in the huge glaciated valleys, e.g. Langdale Beck, Blea Water Beck

4.2 Glaciation in the lowlands

Glaciers pick up large amounts of eroded material or moraine. The moraine is transported by ice along glacial valleys to the lowland areas. The moraine is given different names depending on where it is found (Source 1).

Source 1 Types of moraine – notice how the moraines are named according to their location on the ice

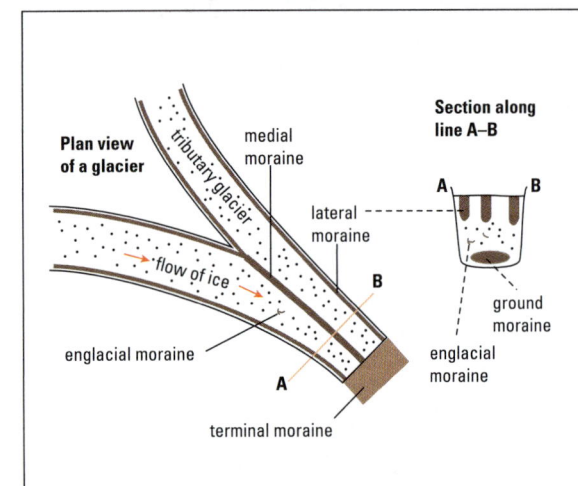

Ground moraine – at the base, a result of abrasion and plucking of the valley floor

Lateral moraine – at the sides, a result of ice erosion of the valley sides and freeze-thaw weathering on the bare rock above

Englacial moraine – in the ice. Rocks carried by meltwater over the surface and from rock falls are frozen into the ice

Medial moraine – forms at the junction of two lateral moraines where tributary glaciers meet

Terminal moraine – marks the furthest point the ice reached

Source 2 Boulder clay in a moraine on the Isle of Arran, Scotland

As the climate warms up, the ice begins to melt. The glacier can no longer carry all the boulders, clay and sand it has picked up, so it begins to deposit material (Source 2). This usually happens in the lowland areas where the climate is warmer.

The deposited material is a mixture of **boulder clay** and very fine material called **rock flour**. Boulder clay is a mixture of sand, stones, clay and boulders. All the material is angular, not smooth, and rounded like river sediments. Boulder clay covers large areas in England especially in East Anglia where it forms fertile soils which are good for crop growing.

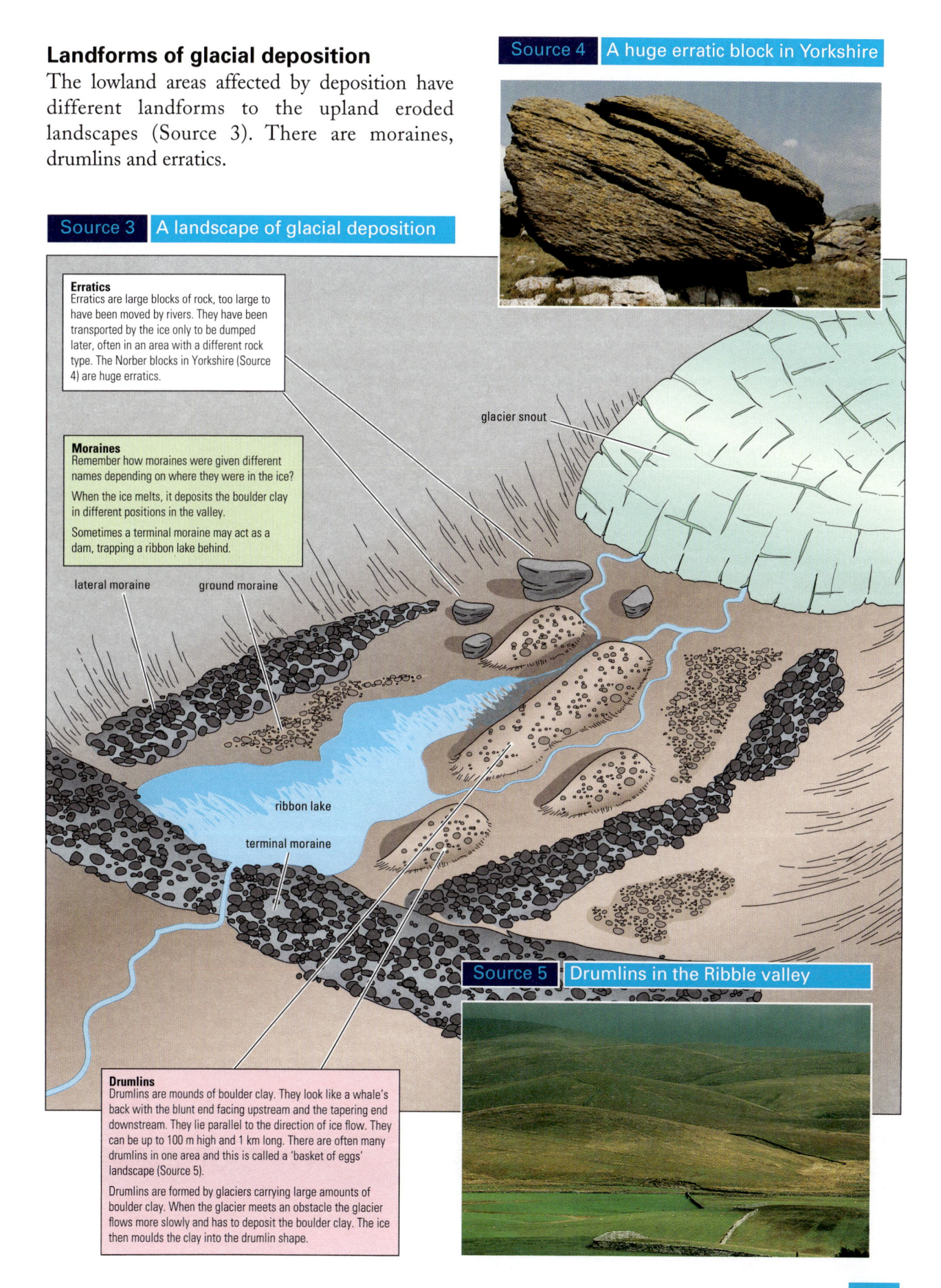

Ice landscapes

Landforms of glacial deposition

The lowland areas affected by deposition have different landforms to the upland eroded landscapes (Source 3). There are moraines, drumlins and erratics.

Source 3 A landscape of glacial deposition

Source 4 A huge erratic block in Yorkshire

Erratics
Erratics are large blocks of rock, too large to have been moved by rivers. They have been transported by the ice only to be dumped later, often in an area with a different rock type. The Norber blocks in Yorkshire (Source 4) are huge erratics.

Moraines
Remember how moraines were given different names depending on where they were in the ice?

When the ice melts, it deposits the boulder clay in different positions in the valley.

Sometimes a terminal moraine may act as a dam, trapping a ribbon lake behind.

lateral moraine
ground moraine
glacier snout
ribbon lake
terminal moraine

Source 5 Drumlins in the Ribble valley

Drumlins
Drumlins are mounds of boulder clay. They look like a whale's back with the blunt end facing upstream and the tapering end downstream. They lie parallel to the direction of ice flow. They can be up to 100 m high and 1 km long. There are often many drumlins in one area and this is called a 'basket of eggs' landscape (Source 5).

Drumlins are formed by glaciers carrying large amounts of boulder clay. When the glacier meets an obstacle the glacier flows more slowly and has to deposit the boulder clay. The ice then moulds the clay into the drumlin shape.

4.3 A glaciated area – the Lake District

The Lake District lies in north-west England (Source 1). It has some of the most spectacular glacial scenery in Britain. During the Ice Age, glaciers developed on the higher slopes of the mountains especially on the colder north and north-east facing slopes. The glaciers eroded the rock by abrasion and plucking, forming deep hollows and huge U-shaped valleys (Source 2).

Hawes Water in the Lake District

Source 3 and Sources 4 and 5 on page 74 show the area around Hawes Water in the Lake District. Hawes Water is a long, thin **ribbon lake** which fills the valley floor of the **glacial trough**. The lake formed after the ice had carved out an area of softer rock creating a depression. Source 2 shows the long profile of the glacial trough after the ice has melted. Notice how the upland areas have features formed by glacial erosion, while the lowlands have more depositional features. The large depression has also been filled with water to form the ribbon lake called Hawes Water.

Two small **corrie** tarns can be seen in Source 5 on page 74, Small Water in the far left and the larger Blea Water Tarn to its right. Both these tarns lie in corries – large, armchair-shaped hollows carved out by the ice. From Blea Water Tarn a small beck (stream) flows down into Hawes Water. Notice how small the beck is in relation to the valley. It is a **misfit stream**. Can you see any more? Find these features in Sources 4 and 5 on page 74.

Source 1 The Lake District

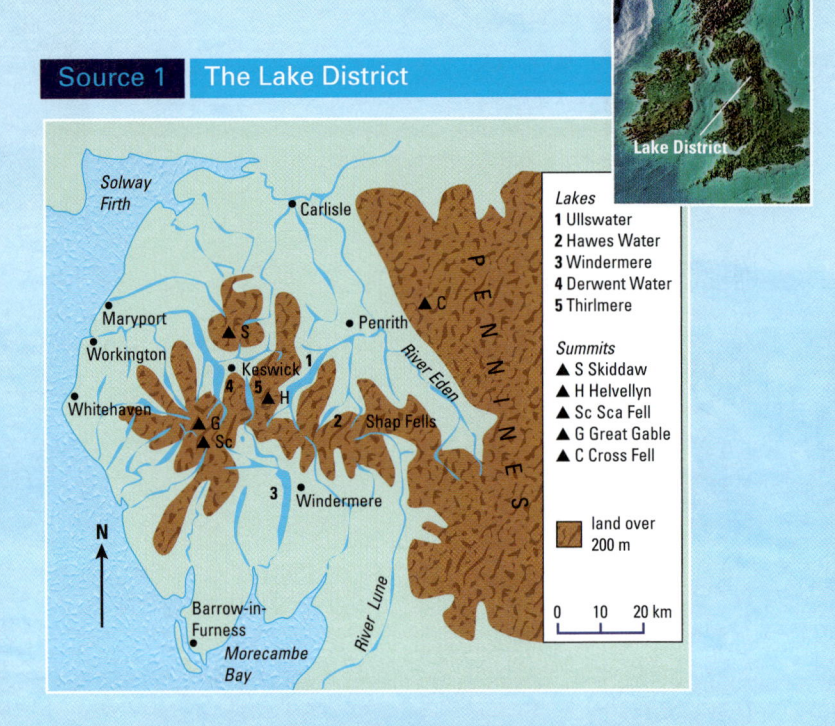

Source 2 Long profile of a glaciated valley

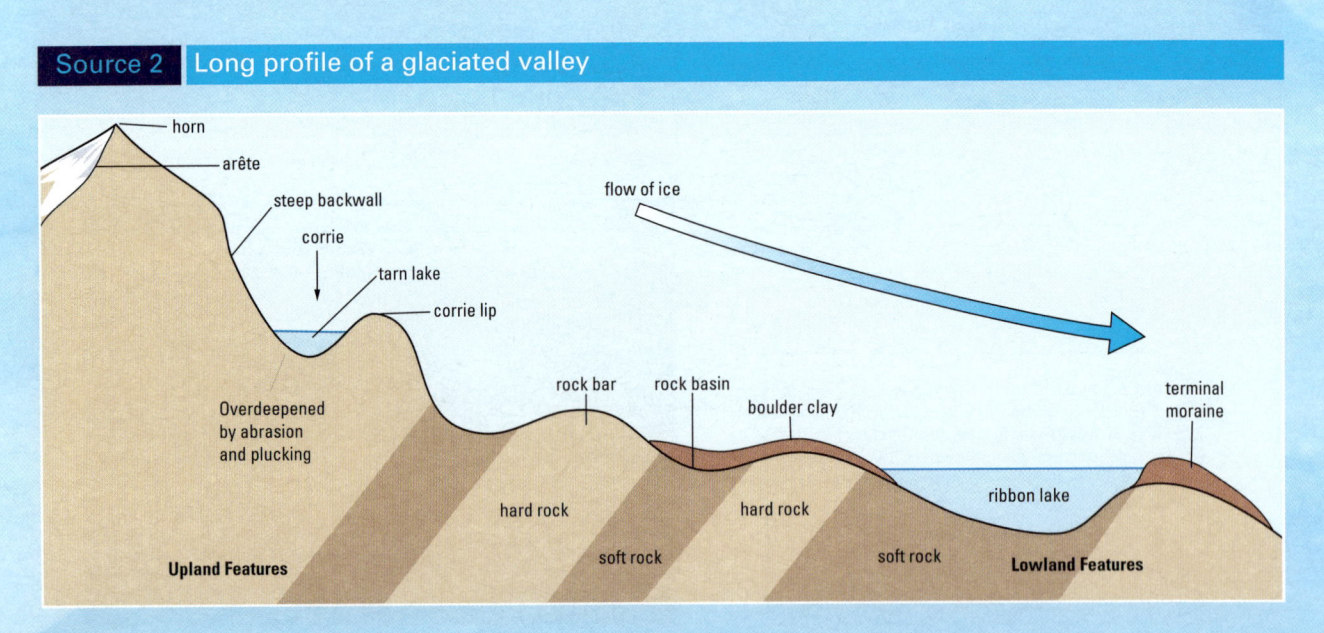

Ice landscapes

Source 3 — OS extract of the area around Hawes Water in the Lake District

Ice landscapes

Between Blea Water Tarn and the large glacial trough to the right, called Riggindale, there is a knife-edged ridge called an **arête**. The arête is called Long Stile. Behind Long Stile is another arête called High Street. Its highest point is 830 metres above sea level.

Today Hawes Water is at a higher level than it used to be. In 1929 the Manchester Corporation which owned the area built a small dam to raise the level and lengthen the lake to provide a water supply for Manchester. The village of Mardale with its dairy farms and pub was drowned as the reservoir filled up. Large coniferous woods were planted and the valley has completely changed.

In the Lake District valleys, and around the fringes, features produced by glacial deposition can also be found. Lake Windermere, for example, is dammed by a **terminal moraine** and many of the valleys contain deposits of boulder clay. There are **erratics** like the huge Bowder Stone in Borrowdale. In the Eden valley there are over 600 small oval hills all about the same size and shape and all in an area of 300 square km. This is a 'basket of eggs' landscape – a swarm of **drumlins** made up of boulder clay.

Source 4 The area around Hawes Water

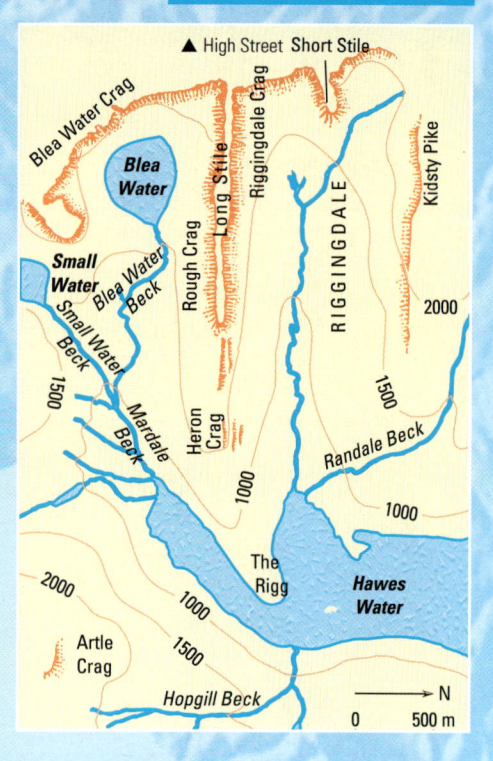

Source 5 Aerial photograph of Blea Water Tarn

Human activity in a glaciated area
the Lake District

4.4

The Lake District is the workplace and home for many people as well as a temporary home for over 12 million visitors each year. In the Lake District there are opportunities to work in farming, forestry, quarrying, water supply and service industries including tourism. Look at Source 1 to find out more about human activity in the Lake District.

Source 1 What are the opportunities for work and for leisure in this sketch of a Lake District valley? How might some of the activities shown cause conflicts between visitors and locals?

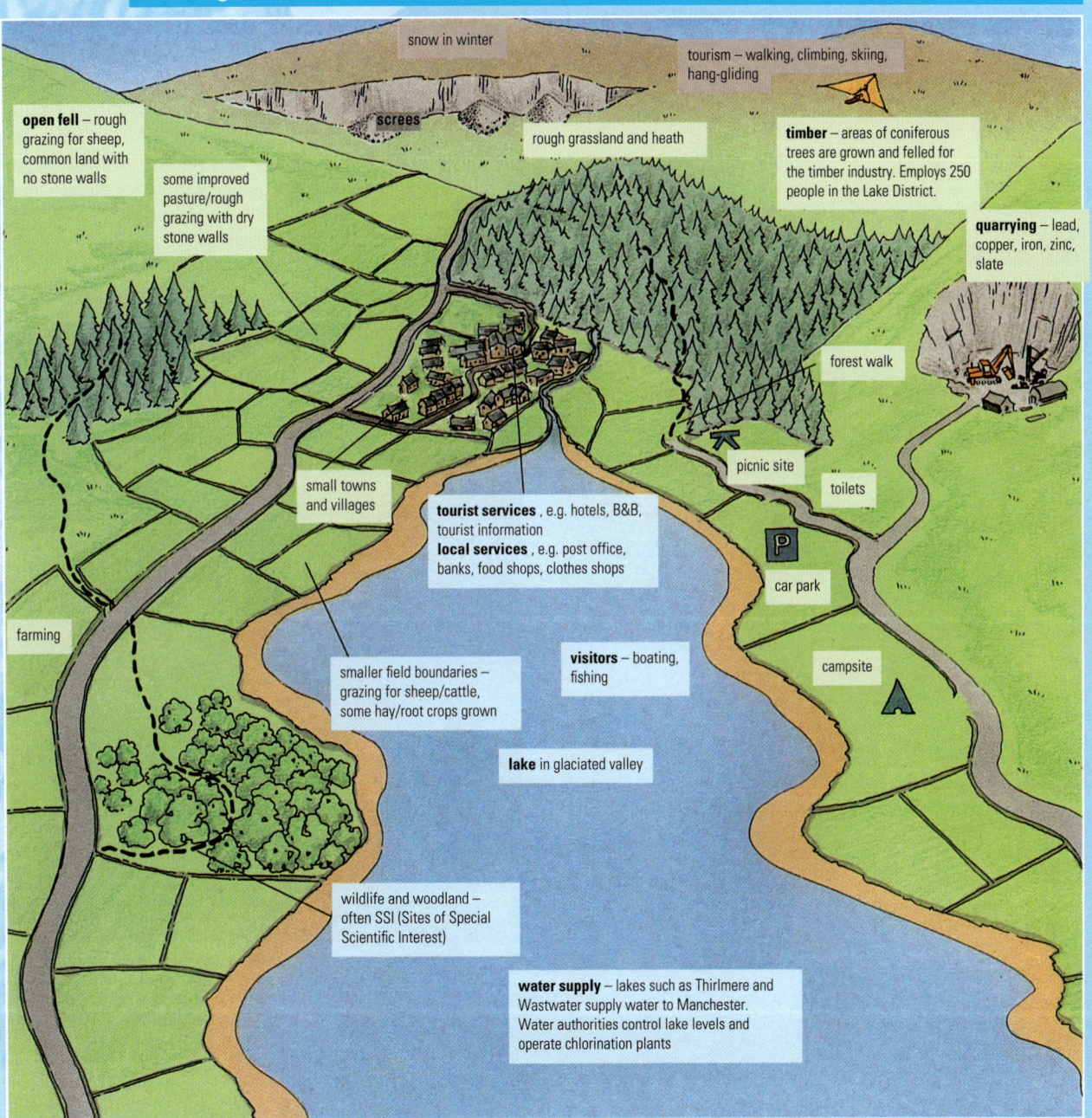

- snow in winter
- screes
- rough grassland and heath
- tourism – walking, climbing, skiing, hang-gliding
- **open fell** – rough grazing for sheep, common land with no stone walls
- some improved pasture/rough grazing with dry stone walls
- **timber** – areas of coniferous trees are grown and felled for the timber industry. Employs 250 people in the Lake District.
- **quarrying** – lead, copper, iron, zinc, slate
- forest walk
- picnic site
- toilets
- small towns and villages
- **tourist services**, e.g. hotels, B&B, tourist information
- **local services**, e.g. post office, banks, food shops, clothes shops
- car park
- farming
- smaller field boundaries – grazing for sheep/cattle, some hay/root crops grown
- **visitors** – boating, fishing
- campsite
- **lake** in glaciated valley
- wildlife and woodland – often SSI (Sites of Special Scientific Interest)
- **water supply** – lakes such as Thirlmere and Wastwater supply water to Manchester. Water authorities control lake levels and operate chlorination plants

75

4.5 Solving problems in the Lake District

In recent years there have been problems and conflicts (see Source 1) in the Lake District National Park:

Environmental problems
- Large numbers of visitors cause traffic congestion and park on private land
- Footpaths are becoming badly eroded
- Visitors may leave gates open, trample vegetation and drop litter
- New tourist developments spoil the countryside, for example camping and caravan sites (Source 2), signposts cluttering the verges.

Socio-economic problems
- Farmers and other locals object to the strict planning controls of the National Park Authority
- Many houses are bought as second homes forcing prices upwards and making housing too expensive for local people
- Developments of new industries that would provide much-needed jobs are restricted because they may damage the tourist industry
- The collapse of farm prices and BSE is causing bankruptcy and forcing farmers to sell up.

Source 1 What would you do to solve these problems?

Source 2 Camping site near Windermere

TAKE-AWAY THREAT TO AREA'S IMAGE
Fish and chips shops and hot-dog stands are spoiling the Lakeland. One of Britain's best landscapes is being cheapened. Planners need to be stricter.

'MAJOR IMPACT' FEAR OVER CHALET VILLAGE AT ENNERDALE
Building 40 timber chalets would destroy the character of the area. Plans by the Forestry Commission include a car park, service buildings and a swimming pool.

Source 3 shows the results of a questionnaire of 6000 groups of people visiting the Lake District. The table shows that the Windermere/Bowness area is least enjoyed because it is too crowded, too commercialised and too like a seaside resort. Some visitors also complain that the area lacks car parks and other facilities. How do you think the local people will react to plans for more facilities for tourists such as bypasses, holiday chalets and cable cars?

Ice landscapes

Source 3 Lake District visitors survey results

Place no longer enjoyed	% no longer enjoying visit	Reasons					
		too commercialised	too crowded	like a seaside resort	too much traffic	not enough car parks	lack of facilities
Windermere/Bowness	26.2	616	914	103	49	15	3
Keswick	7.4	136	278	9	32	8	1
Ambleside	5.8	109	237	20	27	5	2
Coniston	1.0	12	20	3	3	1	3
Tarn Hows	0.7	10	25	1	5	1	3

Solving the problems

The Lake District is a National Park and an area of great beauty. Visitors to the National Park create much-needed jobs and incomes for many local people. Local trades people and farmers may also rely on the visitors to buy the local produce. However, the visitors can also cause problems. There are conflicts between the visitors and the local residents, including farmers, but also between different groups of visitors, for example those who want to enjoy peace and quiet close to the lakes and others who wish to drive speedboats. It is the job of the National Park Authority to try to conserve the environment and manage the area to allow visitors access without causing damage. The aim is to manage the National Park in a sustainable way – to make sure that all developments and uses do not destroy or harm the environment so that the same amount of resources are available in the future as today. Source 4 shows how some of these conflicts and problems are being solved.

Source 4 Problems and conflicts in the Lake District

Conflict or problem	Solution
Overcrowding and traffic congestion	The Park Authority has developed certain parts of the Lake District into honeypot sites, e.g. Tarn Hawes, Pooley Bridge. Large numbers of tourists are expected in these areas and they are fully catered for with car parks, cafés, toilet facilities, etc. It is hoped that this will leave other parts less crowded. However, traffic congestion can still be a major problem. Other schemes are suggested for the future such as a bypass round Ambleside, limits on the numbers of cars allowed in, and banning all traffic that does not belong to locals or supply services in the Park.
Footpath erosion	New paths are being built using local materials to blend in with the environment. The paths reduce erosion by concentrating the walkers onto the footpaths. Some of this work is done by visitors and is an example of ecotourism.
Lack of affordable homes for locals	Special housing is being built at affordable prices and can only be sold to locals who live and work in the area.
Visitor use of Lake Windermere	New by-laws have been passed introducing a speed limit on the lake that limits power boating and water skiing. This led to a demonstration by powerboat owners on the lake.

Source 5 Affordable housing in the Lake District National Park

77

4.6 Activities

1. Copy and complete the paragraph below about glacial erosion. The three missing words are plucking, abrasion and freeze-thaw.

   Rocks in the base of a glacier act like a giant file scraping away at the rocks below. This is called _____. Ice can freeze on to rocks and when the ice moves the rocks are pulled away. This is called _____. Above a glacier the bare rock slopes are sharpened by _____ weathering. This is when the water in cracks expands as it freezes causing the rocks to break up.

2. Study the block diagram (Source 1) and write a list of the features shown marked A to L.

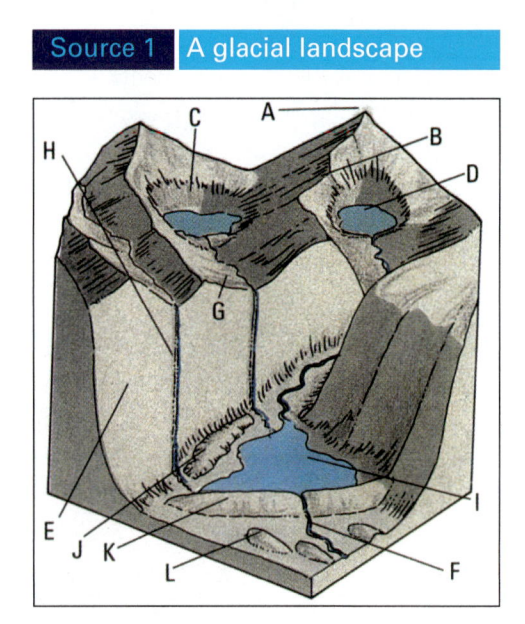

   Source 1   A glacial landscape

3. Copy the diagrams of a corrie in Source 2.
   a. Describe the main features of a corrie.
   b. Add the following statements to your diagram to show how a corrie is formed.

   Water moves down the crack and freezes in the base of the corrie.

   Plucking and abrasion erode the corrie floor.

   The glacier rotates deepening the corrie.

   The glacier flows out of the corrie leaving a lip.

   Above the ice the rocks are shattered by freeze-thaw weathering.

Ice landscapes

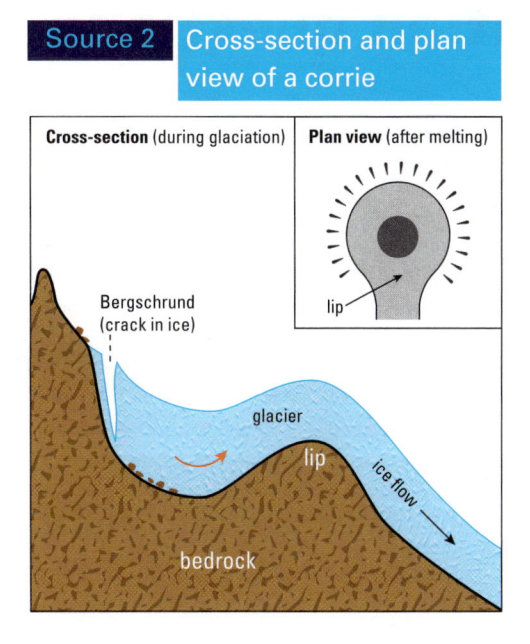

Source 2 Cross-section and plan view of a corrie

Cross-section (during glaciation)
- Bergschrund (crack in ice)
- glacier
- lip
- bedrock

Plan view (after melting)
- lip
- ice flow

4 Study the OS map of the area around Hawes Water (Source 3 on page 73).
  a Give the 4-figure grid reference for the parking area south of Hawes Water reservoir.
  b Give the 6-figure grid reference and the height of the highest point along High Street.
  c Name an example of a corrie tarn and give its grid reference.
  d There is often a small stream running from the corrie tarns. Name an example of one of these streams. Why are they often called 'misfit' streams?
  e Measure the width of Hawes Water reservoir along grid line 14.
  f What shape of valley is the reservoir in?
  g Write a few sentences to describe the human activities (past and present) shown by the map. Think about settlement, farming, forestry, tourism and water supply.

5 a Describe the location of the Lake District National Park.
  b Using an atlas describe how you would travel to the Lake District by car.
  c Describe the physical and human attractions of the National Park.

6 Study the page about human activity in a glaciated area.
  a List five jobs that the tourist industry will create.
  b Using Source 1 and the text on page 76 describe some of the problems and conflicts between the tourists and the local people.
  c Using Source 3 on page 77 draw a bar graph to show the figures for the percentage of people no longer enjoying the visit.
  d Explain why some people no longer enjoy going to Windermere and Bowness.

7 a List three advantages of tourism to the Lake District.
  b State three conflicts between different groups of people and suggest a solution to each one.
  c What are the aims of the National Park Authority?
  d To what extent are the solutions in Source 4 on page 77 sustainable?

4.7 Sample examination questions

1 The figures below show the numbers of boats launched from Ferry Nab, one launching site on the shores of Lake Windermere:

Months	J	F	M	A	M	J	J	A	S	O	N	D
Number of boat launches	18	11	275	326	843	1084	1119	1255	842	429	132	22

   a Draw a bar chart to show the number of boat launches each month. (4 marks)
   b Name the season of the year that is the busiest. (1 mark)
   c Suggest one reason why this is the busiest season. (1 mark)
   d Describe the problems large numbers of boats using Lake Windermere may cause. (4 marks)
       (Total: 10 marks)

2 Study Source 1 showing Blea Water and High Street in the Lake District.

Source 1 | Blea Water and High Street in the Lake District

   a Draw a labelled sketch to show the physical features shown in Source 1. (5 marks)
   b Explain how two of the physical features shown on the photograph have been formed. (5 marks)
       (Total: 10 marks)

3 Blea Water is shown in grid square 4410 in Source 3 on page 73. Use the map and Source 1 above to answer these questions.
   a Give the four-figure grid reference for one facility provided for visitors to the area shown on the map. (3 marks)
   b In which direction was the camera pointing when the photograph in Source 1 was taken? (1 mark)
   c What is the highest point shown on the OS map extract? (2 marks)
   d Using examples and grid references, explain why so few people live in the area shown on the photograph. (4 marks)
       (Total: 10 marks)

UNIT 5

Weather, climate and ecosystems

Unit Contents

- Measuring weather
- Factors affecting climate
- World climates
- Weather and climate: the United Kingdom
- Climatic hazards: tropical storm Gordon
- Urban microclimates: London
- World soils
- Ecosystems
- A grassland ecosystem: tropical savanna in the Sahel
- Ecosystem change: desertification in the Sahel
- A grassland ecosystem: North America's prairies
- How vegetation adapts: tropical rainforest in Brazil
- Deforestation: tropical rainforest in Brazil and Malaysia

In West Africa and across the Atlantic Ocean the cloud associated with equatorial areas stands out clearly on this satellite image. The Mediterranean Sea and the Sahara Desert are clearly visible. What does the satellite image show about the cloud cover in Britain?

5.1 Measuring weather

It is important to study the weather because it affects so many human activities. Airlines and ships need accurate information, so do farmers, skiers, walkers and the general public.

The weather is the state of the **atmosphere** at a certain time and it may change from hour to hour. A weather forecast often mentions the temperature, wind, rainfall, pressure and humidity. These are the elements of the weather. Around Britain there are many meteorological stations where weather is measured by special equipment. Source 1 shows the layout of a weather station with the instruments which are used. Weather stations are sited away from tall trees and buildings so that they are not sheltered from wind, rain or sun.

Today, the use of modern electronic equipment such as computers and radar means that the weather can be recorded continuously and forecasts are more accurate.

Source 1 | A weather station

Sunshine recorder
This records the hours of sunshine received in a day. This is the number of hours the sun actually shines, not just when it is light.

Maximum and minimum thermometer (Six's thermometer)
The thermometer contains alcohol and mercury and two metal indexes, one in each limb. When the temperature rises, the alcohol in the left-hand side expands and pushes the mercury up the right-hand side, which also pushes the index along. The maximum temperature is read from the bottom of the index in the right-hand limb. When the temperature falls, the alcohol contracts and the mercury flows in the opposite direction, pushing the index along. The minimum temperature is read from the bottom of the index in the left-hand thermometer – notice the scale is reversed.

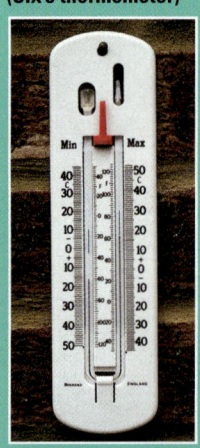

Wind speed and direction
Wind direction is measured by a wind vane. The rotating arm points to the direction from which the wind blows and the wind is named after this. So a westerly wind blows from the west.
Wind speed is measured by an anemometer. It has three or four cups on arms which rotate when the wind blows. The movement operates a meter which records the speed of the wind in kilometres per hour.

Weather, climate and ecosystems

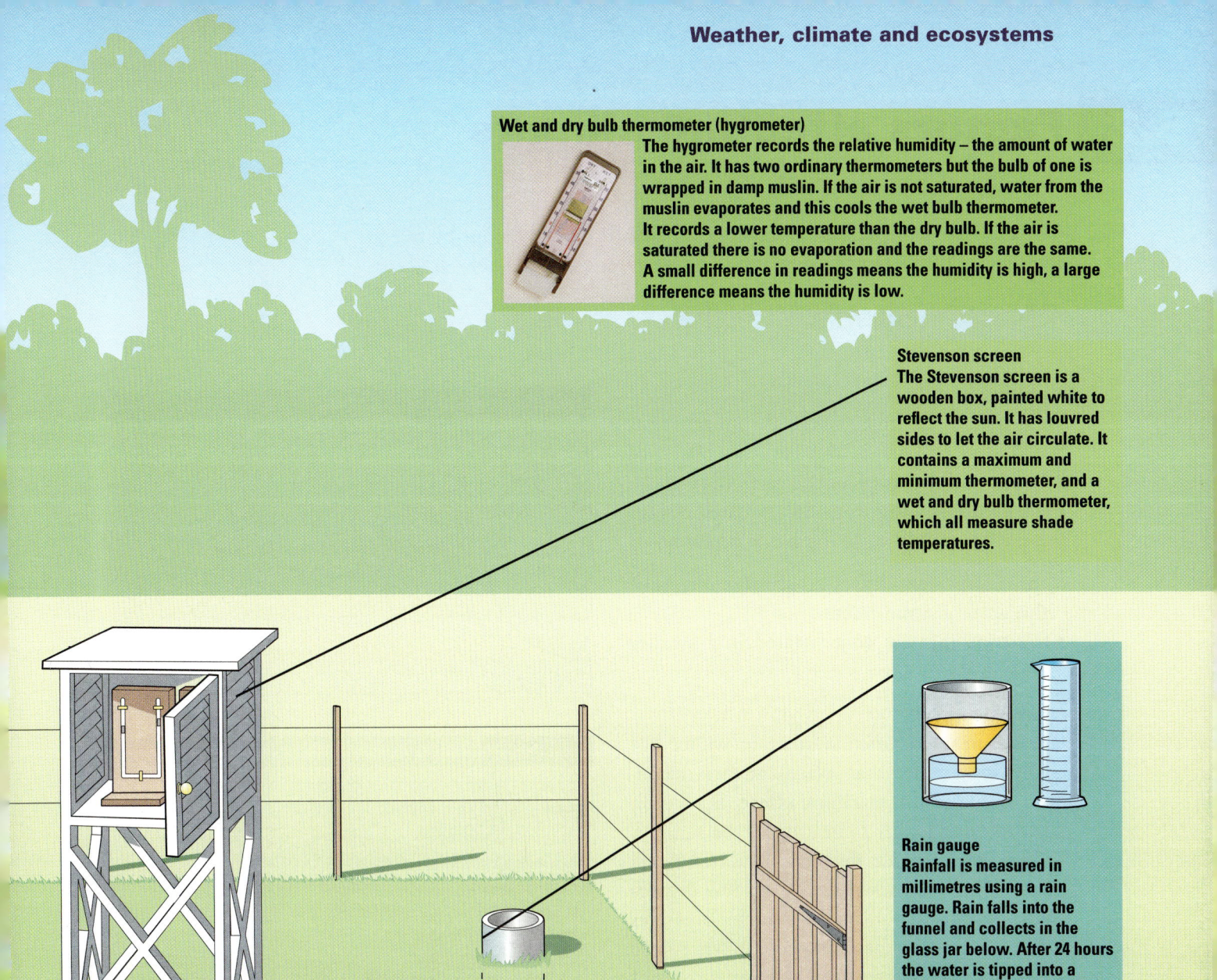

Wet and dry bulb thermometer (hygrometer)
The hygrometer records the relative humidity – the amount of water in the air. It has two ordinary thermometers but the bulb of one is wrapped in damp muslin. If the air is not saturated, water from the muslin evaporates and this cools the wet bulb thermometer. It records a lower temperature than the dry bulb. If the air is saturated there is no evaporation and the readings are the same. A small difference in readings means the humidity is high, a large difference means the humidity is low.

Stevenson screen
The Stevenson screen is a wooden box, painted white to reflect the sun. It has louvred sides to let the air circulate. It contains a maximum and minimum thermometer, and a wet and dry bulb thermometer, which all measure shade temperatures.

Rain gauge
Rainfall is measured in millimetres using a rain gauge. Rain falls into the funnel and collects in the glass jar below. After 24 hours the water is tipped into a measuring cylinder and the amount recorded. The rain gauge is in an open area with about 30 cm above the ground to stop splashing and to stop the sun evaporating moisture.

Air pressure
A barometer is used to measure air pressure in millibars. It can be located indoors since pressure is not affected by buildings. Inside the barometer, a small metal box contains very little air and its top moves very slightly as the air pressure changes. The movement is conveyed by a series of levers to a pointer which moves across graph paper recording the pressure changes.

5.2 Factors affecting climate

The **climate** is the average weather of an area. It is worked out by taking the average of the temperature and rainfall figures over a number of years.

The following factors affect the climate of an area.

Latitude
Polar regions are much colder than places near the Equator. This is due to the effect of **latitude** and the shape of the earth (Source 1). Places further away from the Equator receive less energy from the sun. Near the Equator:

- the sun's rays travel a shorter distance through the atmosphere
- the sun's rays are concentrated in a smaller area.

Maritime effect
Coastal areas are often warmer in winter but colder in summer than places further inland. This is due to the **maritime effect** (Source 2). The sea takes longer to heat up in the summer so the sea is colder than the land. Cool sea breezes form, so coastal areas are a few degrees colder than further inland in summer. In winter it takes longer for the sea to cool down, so the sea is warmer than the land. The west coast of the UK is particularly warm in winter because of the North Atlantic Drift, a warm ocean current.

Altitude
Uplands tend to be colder than lowlands due to the effect of **altitude** (Source 3). Temperature falls as altitude increases – usually by about 1°C every 160 metres. So a mountain 1600 metres high would be 10°C colder at the top than at sea level.

Prevailing winds
In the UK the **prevailing winds** are from the west. The west coast of the UK is in the path of the prevailing winds and so it tends to be much wetter than the east coast, which is more sheltered and in the **rain shadow** (Source 3).

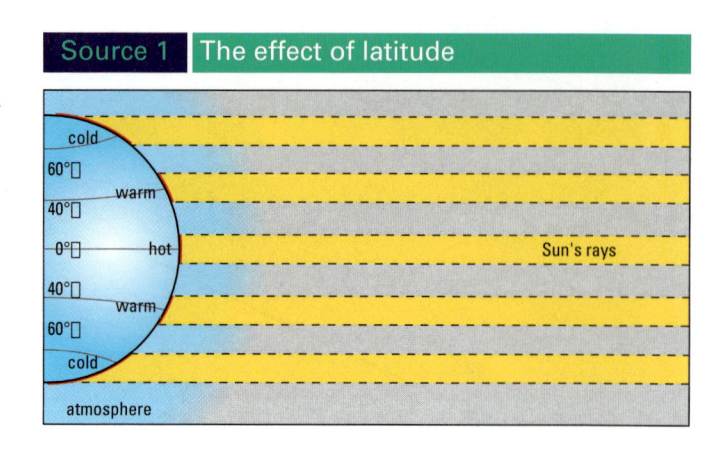

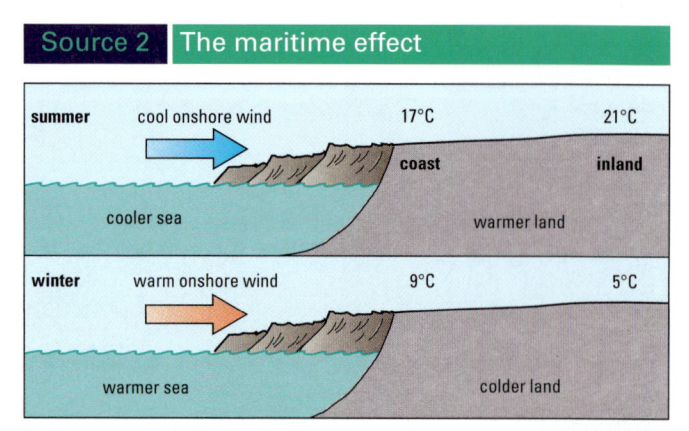

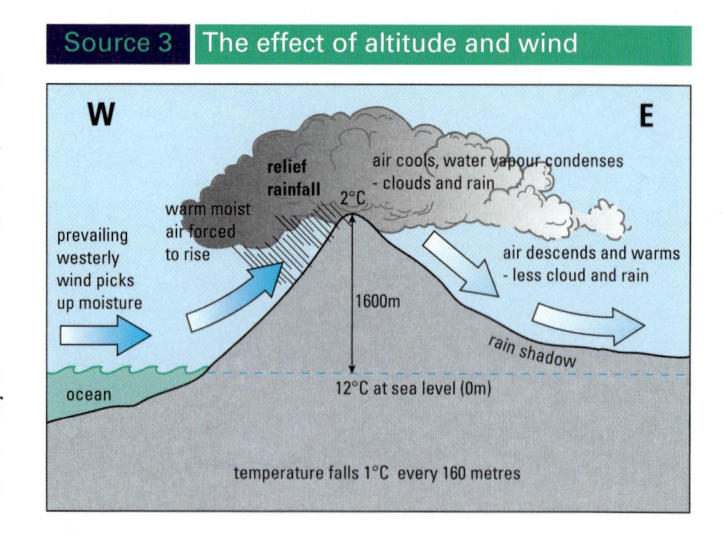

Source 1 The effect of latitude

Source 2 The maritime effect

Source 3 The effect of altitude and wind

Weather, climate and ecosystems

Air masses

Air masses are large bodies of air in the atmosphere. The area where they form is called the **source region**. In the source region the air mass remains stationary for a long time and picks up the temperature and moisture characteristics of the area. Warm air masses can hold more moisture than cold air masses.

Source 4 shows the main air masses which affect the UK. The tropical maritime air mass, for example, has its source over the sea in the tropics, so the air mass is warm and moist. Air masses move away from their source region and affect the weather in the area they invade.

Source 4 — Air masses affecting the UK

Polar maritime air mass
Source: Arctic Ocean
Mild and wet in summer; cold and wet (sleet/snow) in winter

Polar continental air mass
Source: Siberia (land)
Warm and dry in summer; very cold and possibly snow in winter

Polar air masses come from the north and are cold.

Maritime air masses form over oceans so they pick up moisture and often bring rain.

Continental air masses form over land so they are drier.

Tropical maritime air mass
Source: Azores (sea)
Warm and wet in summer; mild and wet in winter

Tropical air masses come from the south and are much warmer.

Tropical continental air mass
Source: North Africa (land)
Hot and dry in summer; mild and dry in winter

Anticyclones and depressions

The atmosphere pushes down on the earth's surface causing pressure. Warm air tends to rise and form **low pressure**. Cold, heavy air tends to sink and form **high pressure**. Areas of low pressure are called **depressions**. Areas of high pressure are called **anticyclones**.

On a **synoptic chart** (weather map) pressure is shown by **isobars.** These are lines joining places with the same pressure. Anticyclones and depressions greatly influence the UK's weather and climate (Source 5).

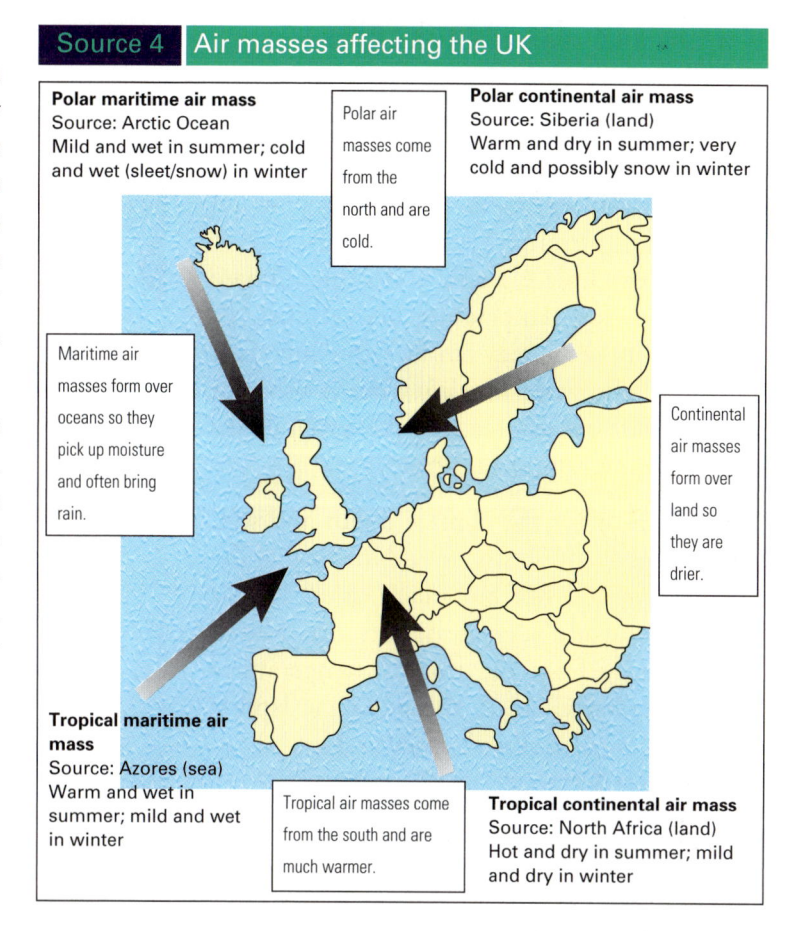

Source 5 — Anticyclones and depressions and the UK's weather

Anticyclones
There is only one air mass and so there are no fronts. Winds are light so the isobars are wide apart. Anticyclones bring stable, calm weather. In the UK they cause heatwaves in summer and cold, frosty days in winter.

high pressure
1012
1008
1004

cold sector
polar air mass
low pressure
981
988
992
996
1000
warm sector
tropical air mass
cold front
warm front

Depressions
In a depression the pressure is lowest at the centre. Warm and cold fronts separate two air masses. In the warm sector the air mass is tropical maritime, and in the cold sector it is polar maritime. Winds blow anticlockwise towards the centre of the low pressure. Depressions bring unsettled weather with cloud and rain.

5.3 World climates

The world can be divided into climatic regions or zones. Each region has its own temperature and rainfall pattern. The map in Source 1 shows three climate zones and some climate graphs showing temperature and rainfall. In the cold climates it may not be rain which falls but snow. The word **precipitation** is used for any moisture which reaches the ground, for example snow, rain, sleet, frost.

Near the Equator the climate is hot and wet. Further north and south around the tropics the climates are still hot but much drier. This is where the world's great deserts are found. Further away from the tropics, temperatures become cooler. Close to the poles the land is permanently covered with snow and ice.

The **wettest regions** in the world are:
- equatorial, which means close to the Equator, for example the Amazon Basin in South America
- monsoon regions, for example India, Bangladesh
- coasts facing onshore westerly winds, such as the west coast of Britain.

The **driest regions** in the world are:
- the interiors of Asia and North America
- the hot deserts, for example Sahara, Kalahari, Atacama
- the cold deserts, for example the Arctic and Antarctica.

Source 1 Three climate zones of the world

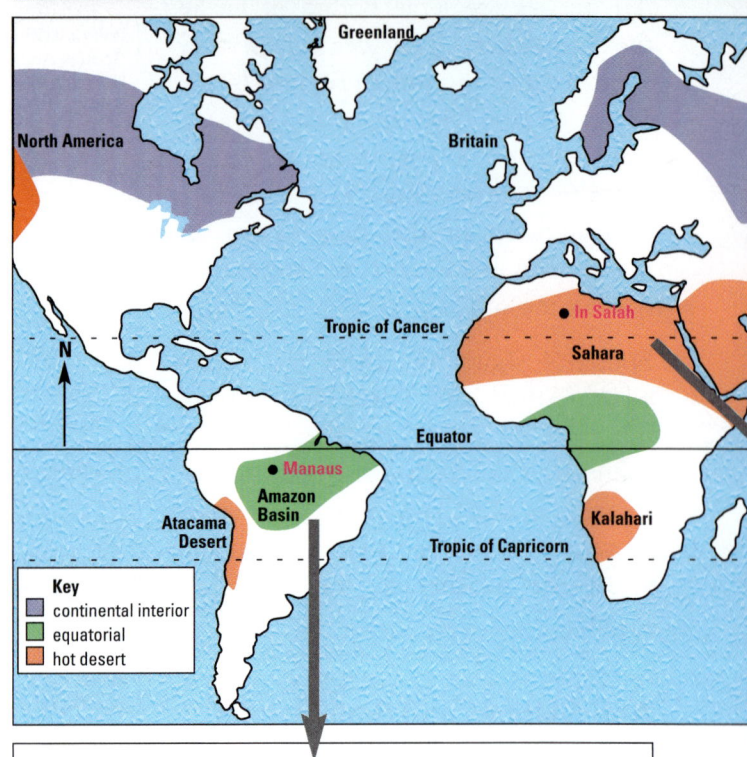

Key:
- continental interior
- equatorial
- hot desert

Equatorial climate
e.g. Manaus in the Amazon Basin

Features
- hot temperatures all year: 26°C
  low temperature range: 3°C
- high annual rainfall, evenly distributed: 2000 mm per year
- no seasons
- heavy rain with thunder and lightning in the afternoons
- high humidity: over 80%

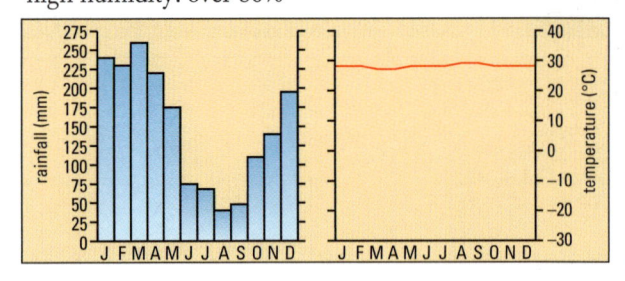

Reasons
This zone is very close to the Equator so the sun is nearly always directly overhead. It is an area of low pressure. The sun heats the ground surface. The hot air above rises and cools. The moisture in the air condenses forming tall thunderclouds called **cumulo-nimbus**. There is heavy **convectional rainfall** often with thunder and lightning.

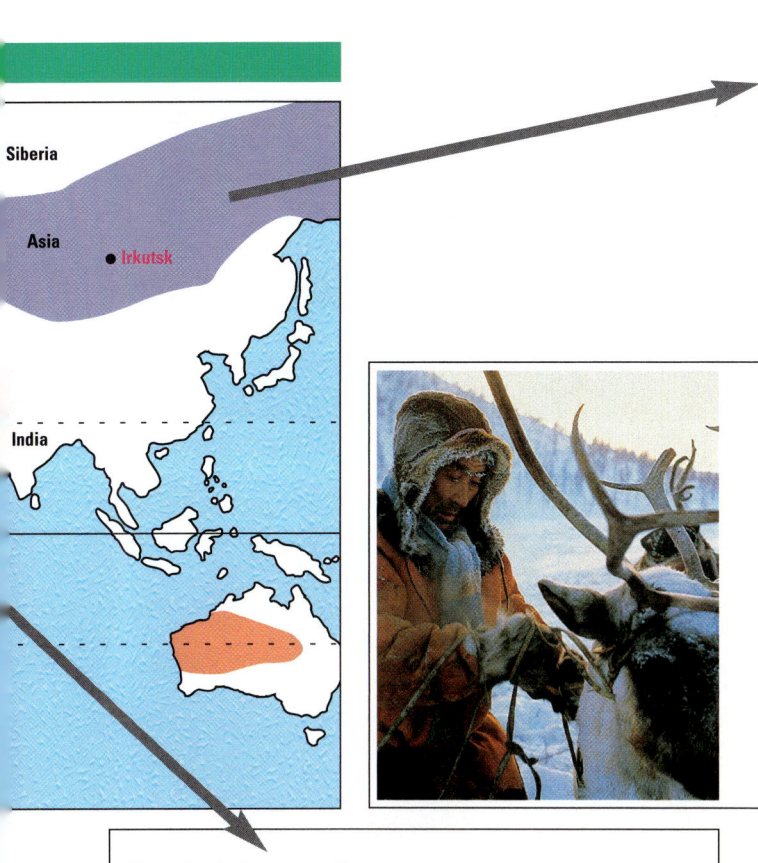

Weather, climate and ecosystems

Cold continental interior climate

e.g. Irkutsk in eastern Siberia

Features

- winter temperatures: reaching −40°C
- summer temperatures: +20°C
- large annual range of temperature: often over 55°C
- total rainfall quite low: about 400 mm per year
- winter precipitation falls as snow

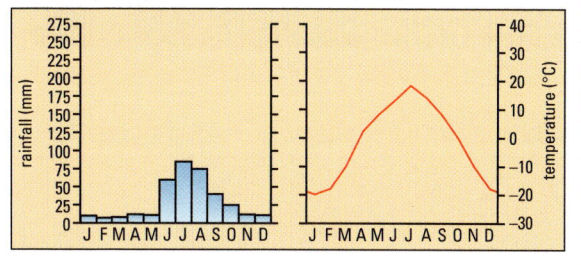

Reasons

Summer rainfall is convectional with thunderstorms caused by the land heating up and warming the air above. The hot air rises and cools. Moisture in the air condenses forming clouds and rainfall. The total rainfall is low because the area is dominated by high pressure. The high pressure brings clear skies so summer temperatures are high. Temperatures are cooler than in the hot deserts because of the effect of latitude – this zone is further away from the Equator. In the winter, temperatures are very low. The clear skies and long nights mean a lot of heat is lost by radiation. During the day the sun is so low in the sky that temperatures remain very cold.

Tropical desert climate

e.g. In Salah in the Sahara desert

Features

- rain is rare: less than 120 mm per year
- temperatures vary from 29°C in hot season to 10°C in cool season
- daytime temperatures may go over 38°C but fall to 5°C at night

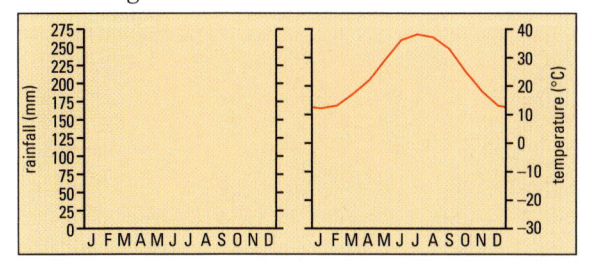

Reasons

The hot deserts are in an area of high pressure. Here the air sinks and warms. Warm, sinking air rarely produces rainfall. The **trade winds** which blow in most desert areas have blown over land so they are dry. The lack of cloud cover means that temperatures are very high during the day, but there is maximum heat loss by **radiation** at night.

5.4 Weather and climate
the United Kingdom

The UK weather is very variable. Colder, wetter weather is expected in the winter, and warmer, drier weather in the summer. Different parts of the country also have slightly different climates. Sources 1 and 2 show rainfall and temperature patterns across the UK. The rainfall map (Source 1) shows that:

- places in the west receive more rainfall than those in the east
- upland areas are wetter than lowland areas.

The west coast of the UK lies in the path of the **prevailing** westerly winds and approaching depressions. Reaching the west coast first, far more rain falls in these areas. The upland areas are also mostly in the north and west of the UK so **relief rainfall** adds to the total. Some areas receive over 2000 mm of rain per year. To the east, rainfall totals are generally below 650 mm. These areas are in the rain shadow of the uplands to the west. Newcastle, for example, lies in the **rain shadow** of the Pennines.

Source 1 Rainfall

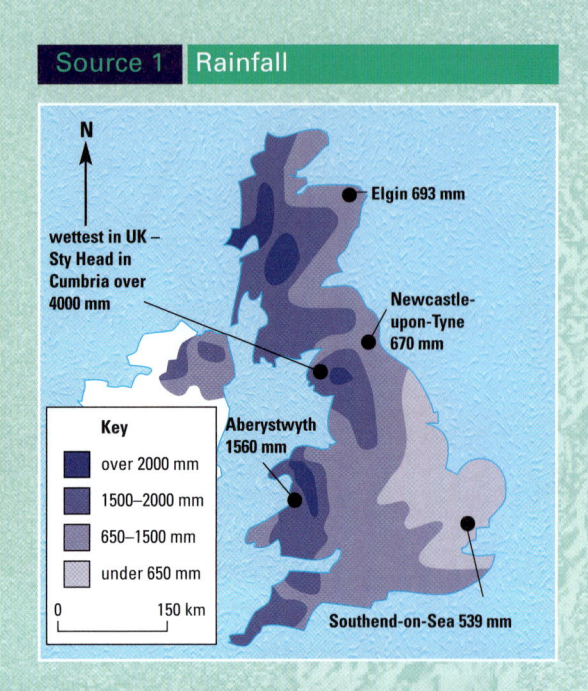

- wettest in UK – Sty Head in Cumbria over 4000 mm
- Elgin 693 mm
- Newcastle-upon-Tyne 670 mm
- Aberystwyth 1560 mm
- Southend-on-Sea 539 mm

Key:
- over 2000 mm
- 1500–2000 mm
- 650–1500 mm
- under 650 mm

Source 2 Winter and summer temperatures in °C

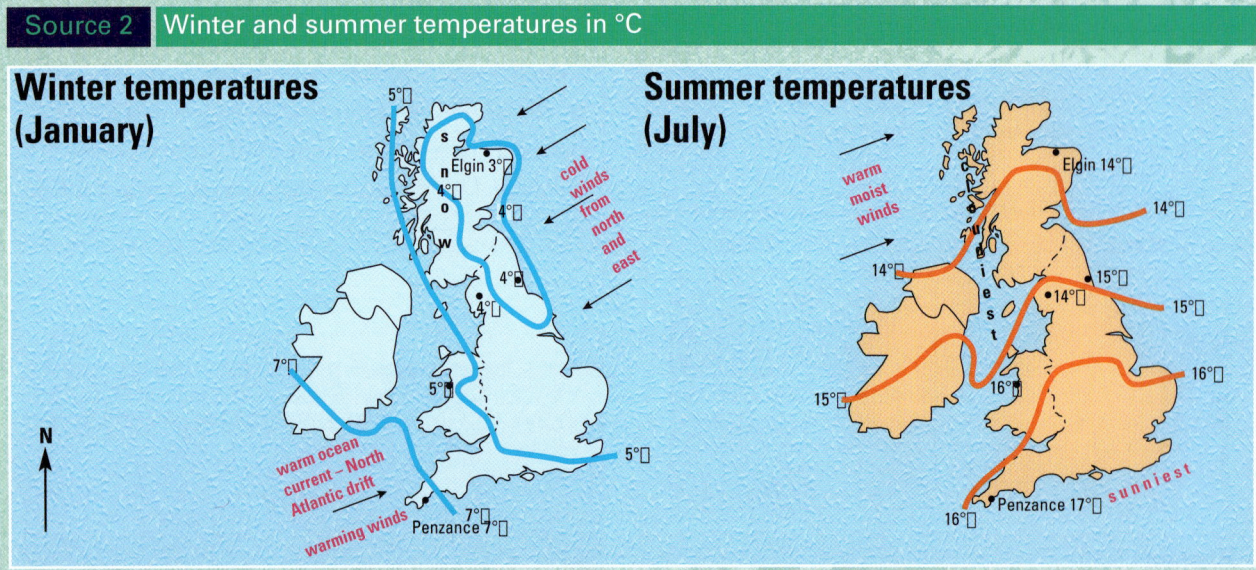

Winter temperatures (January)
Summer temperatures (July)

The maps in Source 2 show that:

- in summer, the north is colder than the south
- in winter, the west coast is warmer than the east coast.

In summer, the south of the UK is warmer than the north because it is closer to the Equator and receives more **solar radiation**. In winter, the sun is very low in the sky over the UK. Solar radiation is weak and **ocean currents** have a greater effect on the temperatures. The warm North Atlantic drift raises temperatures along the west coast. Cold winds from the north and east lower east-coast temperatures in winter. The Scottish Highlands receive heavy winter snowfall. Temperatures are often below freezing point because of the altitude and snow falls rather than rain.

Weather, climate and ecosystems

Depressions

Depressions affect the weather in the UK for much of the year. They are areas of **low pressure** which bring cloud, rain and wind. They form over the Atlantic Ocean where warm tropical air meets cold polar air. The two types of air do not mix and where they meet is called a **front**.

By the time a depression reaches the UK it has usually developed a warm and cold front. At the fronts the warm air is forced to rise. The rising air cools, and the moisture condenses forming cloud and rainfall. Source 3 shows a synoptic chart and satellite image of a depression near the UK.

A typical sequence of weather takes place when a depression passes over the UK (Source 4). As the warm front approaches, wispy cirrus clouds appear high in the sky. Gradually the clouds become lower and thicker leading to steady rainfall. As the warm front passes, the temperature rises. Winds change direction to south-westerly. At the cold front the air is rising quickly and steeply. Tall cumulus and cumulo-nimbus clouds form and they bring a shorter period of heavy rainfall. There may even be hail and thunder. As the cold front passes, the temperature falls and the pressure starts to rise. Winds change direction to the north-west and conditions become brighter and drier. Depressions move from west to east and take between one and three days to pass over the UK.

Source 3 | Synoptic chart and satellite photograph

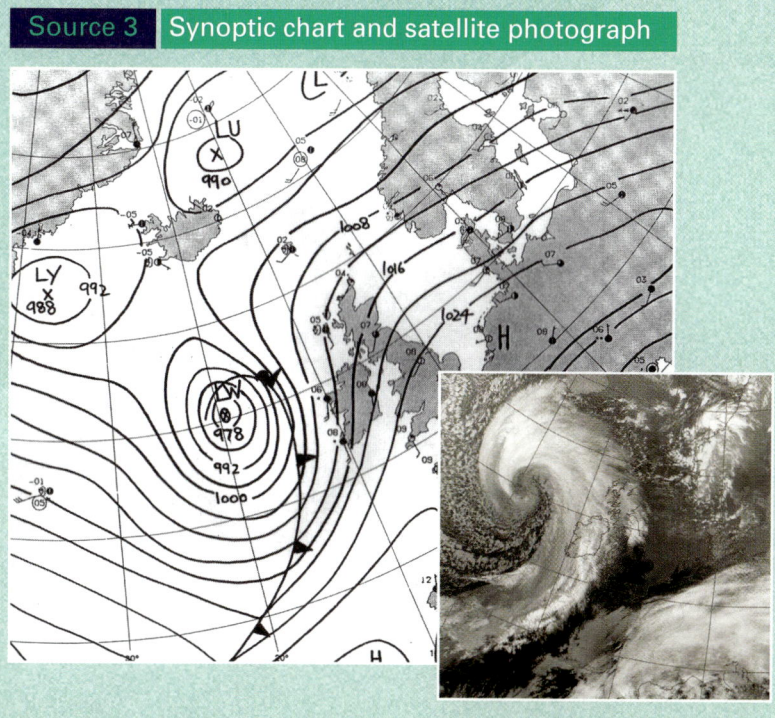

Anticyclones

Anticyclones bring much more settled weather to the UK. They are areas of **high pressure** in which air is sinking. As the air descends it warms and it can hold more moisture. An anticyclone is usually accompanied by clear skies which give very warm temperatures in summer and very cold temperatures in winter. During the night the clear skies allow heat from the ground to radiate back into the atmosphere. The ground becomes much cooler and air which is in contact with the ground cools and moisture condenses. If the temperatures are below 0°C frost forms and if they are above 0°C dew forms. Water particles suspended in the air form mist and fog.

Source 4 | Passage of a depression

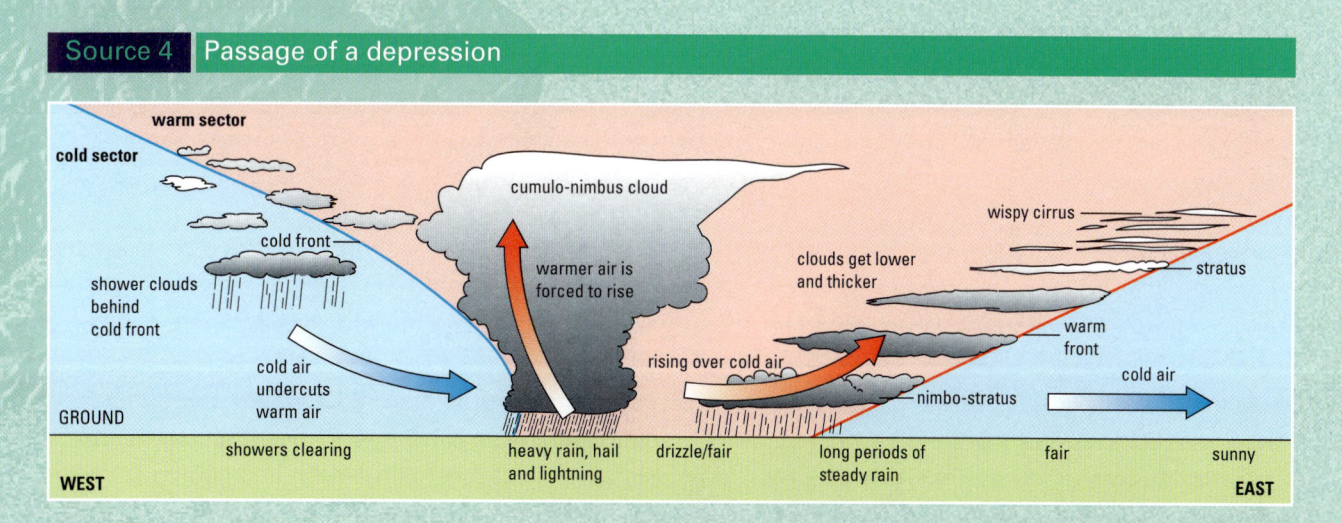

5.5 Climatic hazards
tropical storm Gordon

Tropical **cyclones** are very violent storms. The storms are accompanied by very strong winds and heavy rainfall and can be very destructive. Source 1 is a satellite photograph showing the swirling mass of cloud.

How do cyclones form?
Tropical cyclones form over the oceans where water temperatures are above 27°C. The air becomes moist and warm. Warm parcels of air rise very rapidly; the air around spirals inwards and upwards (Source 2). The air cools as it rises and the moisture condenses to form clouds and very heavy rainfall. The centre of the storm, called the 'eye', is calm. When a **hurricane** passes at first it is very stormy, followed by a short period of calm weather when the eye is overhead and then the storm begins again. Once on the land it is starved of its energy supply and it 'fizzles out'.

Tropical storm Gordon
Tropical storm Gordon left a trail of destruction in Cuba, Jamaica, Haiti and Florida in November 1994. The storm was not quite a hurricane as wind speeds were just below 120 km/hour. However, the effects were just as devastating. During the storm, 500 people were killed and the damage to homes, industry and crops ran into millions of pounds.

Modern remote sensing and satellite images can help to predict the track of a tropical storm. Local communities are warned of the storm's arrival by broadcasts on the TV and radio. But there is still enormous damage. People are drowned, or killed by falling trees and buildings. Crops are destroyed and animals killed. Power lines collapse and communications are disrupted. There are often landslides and the fast-flowing water erodes the soil, carving huge gulleys on hillsides.

The storm can whip up huge **tidal waves** sometimes over 25 metres high. These crash against the coastline destroying coastal villages. In 1970 in Bangladesh 250 000 people were drowned by hurricane storm waves.

Source 1 Satellite view of a tropical cyclone

Source 2 Section through a tropical storm

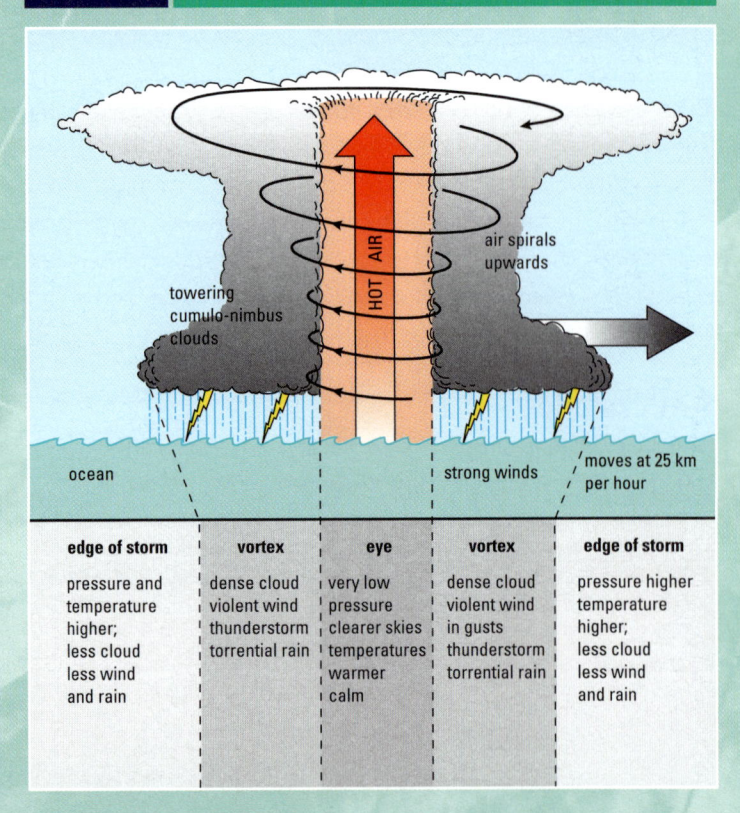

edge of storm	vortex	eye	vortex	edge of storm
pressure and temperature higher; less cloud less wind and rain	dense cloud violent wind thunderstorm torrential rain	very low pressure clearer skies temperatures warmer calm	dense cloud violent wind in gusts thunderstorm torrential rain	pressure higher temperature higher; less cloud less wind and rain

Urban microclimates
London

5.6

Source 1: London heat island

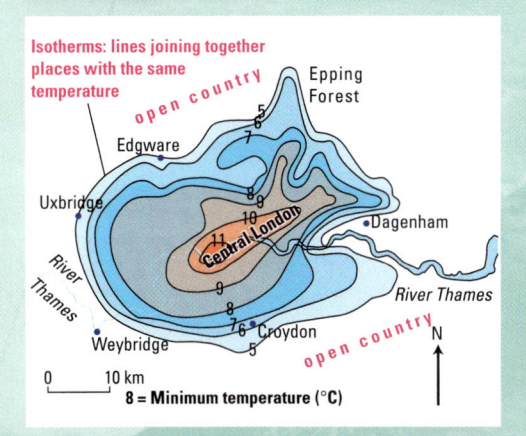

Isotherms: lines joining together places with the same temperature

open country

Epping Forest
Edgware
Uxbridge
Dagenham
Central London
River Thames
Weybridge
Croydon
River Thames

open country

0 — 10 km

8 = Minimum temperature (°C)

N

A large urban area like London, with its housing, industry, vehicles and people, creates its own **urban climate** which is different to the rural areas which surround it.

The urban heat island

The urban area tends to be a few degrees warmer than the surrounding area. This is called the **urban heat island** effect. The materials from which the roads and buildings have been made absorb heat during the day and, like a giant storage heater, release it at night. Factories, homes, offices and cars also release large amounts of heat. Source 1 shows that the inner area of London was over 6°C warmer than the surroundings on one day in May.

Source 2: London's microclimate

Wind speeds are lower in urban areas because of friction with the buildings, but in the centre of London and other large cities the very tall skyscrapers create 'canyons' along which the wind funnels.

London is cloudier than the rural areas nearby. The warm air rises and cools causing cloud formation helped by water vapour from chimneys.

Raindrops form around small dust particles so urban areas may have higher rainfall.

Urban areas like London receive less snowfall. Any snow melts quickly on the warmer streets.

Water vapour is released by burning fossil fuels, from cooling towers and from water surfaces like lakes.

There is more runoff in cities because of the impermeable surfaces, e.g. the tarmac and concrete. There is also less evapo-transpiration because there are fewer green areas.

The warmer atmosphere in the urban area causes convection. The rising warm air cools and condenses, leading to heavy rainfall.

5.7 World soils

Covering most of the world's land surface is a thin layer of soil. Soils contain five main ingredients (Source 1). These are:

- mineral particles from the breakdown or weathering of rocks
- humus – decayed plant and animal remains
- water – in the spaces between soil particles
- air – in the pore spaces
- living organisms – earthworms, bacteria.

Within a soil the amount of each of these ingredients varies. Soils are also formed on different rock types, in different climates and below different vegetation. Source 1 shows that there are many different soil types.

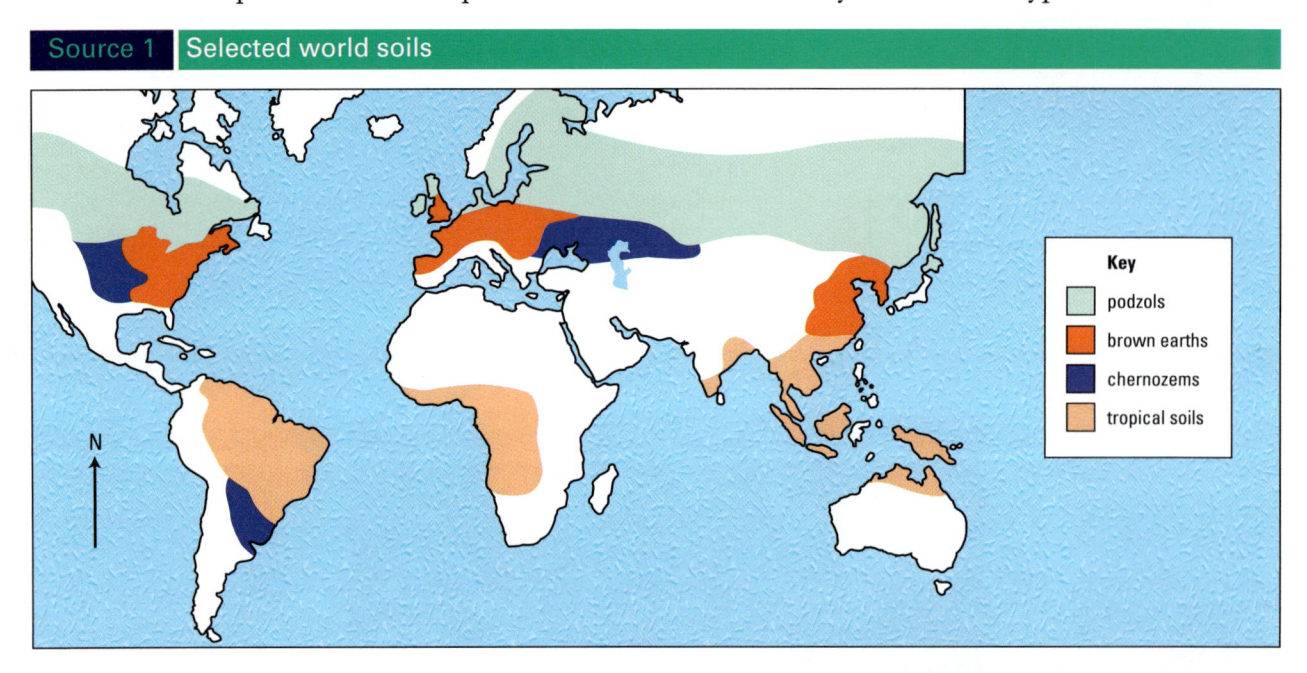

Source 1 Selected world soils

Key:
- podzols
- brown earths
- chernozems
- tropical soils

The soil profile

In order to study different types of soil a **soil profile** can be drawn. A soil profile is a section which looks at the soil from the earth's surface to the bedrock below. Most profiles have three layers which are called **horizons**. The horizons are lettered A, B and C in Source 2.

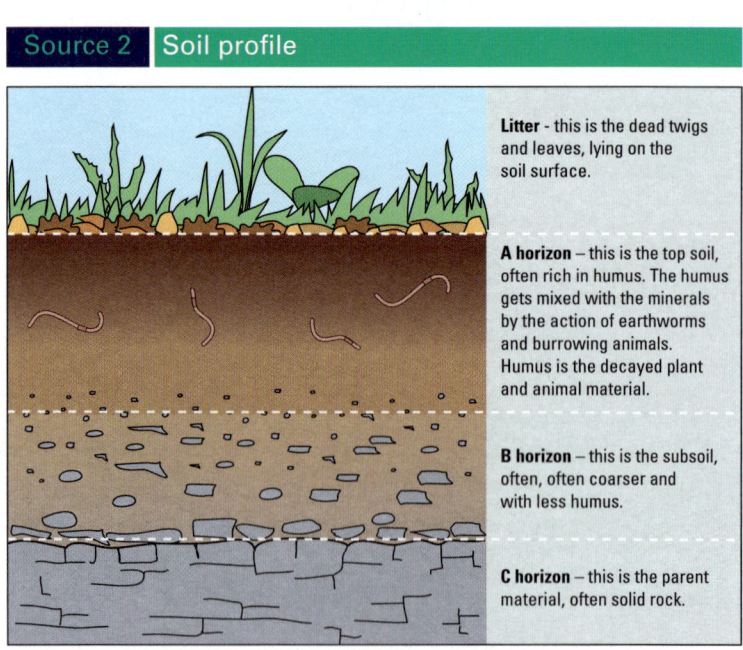

Source 2 Soil profile

Litter - this is the dead twigs and leaves, lying on the soil surface.

A horizon – this is the top soil, often rich in humus. The humus gets mixed with the minerals by the action of earthworms and burrowing animals. Humus is the decayed plant and animal material.

B horizon – this is the subsoil, often, often coarser and with less humus.

C horizon – this is the parent material, often solid rock.

Weather, climate and ecosystems

World soil types

Climate is the most important factor in soil formation and each major soil type matches up with a climate type. These major soil types are called 'zonal soils'. Study the information in Source 3 to find out more about three of the world's zonal soils.

Source 3 — Three zonal soils

Brown earths, e.g. lowland UK

Horizons
- A – Rich mixture of humus and minerals. Dark brown, crumb structure
- B – Mineral horizon with some humus
- C – Bedrock

deciduous forest
neutral pH (5–6.5)
moderate rainfall

How is it formed?
Grasses and deciduous trees add a lot of humus. This is well mixed by earthworms.
The A and B horizons merge into one another. There is no clear boundary because of the mixing by animals and the small amount of leaching. Little clay, iron or humus is washed down.

Podzols, e.g. central USA, Russia, uplands in the UK

Horizons
- A – Thin black layer of humus on top of light-coloured topsoil
- B – Red subsoil with black staining
- C – Bedrock usually acid

grasslands
acid pH = 4.0
heavy rainfall

How is it formed?
The surface layer is peaty. Plant remains do not rot away well because it is cold and wet and acid. The light layer has had the iron and aluminium removed by strong leaching (iron gives soil its brown colour) called podzolisation. There is a sharp change into the B horizon where the iron has been redeposited giving it its red colour. Sometimes the iron is deposited in a thin layer at the top of the B horizon. This is an iron pan.

Chernozems, e.g. continental interiors

Horizons
- A – Thick layer up to 1 metre. Black, crumb structure. Grades slowly into light-coloured zone. Notice the animal burrows (dark patches)
- C – Rich loess parent material. Fine, wind-blown and silty, high in calcium (white patches)

grasslands
neutral pH
light rainfall

How is it formed?
A large amount of humus from grass stems and roots.
Very dark humus in A horizon, well mixed by earthworm activity.
No B horizon. A horizon lies on top of C horizon, which is very rich in nodules of calcium. The dry summers and cold winters restrict the rotting of the humus. Rainfall is light but evaporation high so in summer water moves upwards through the profile causing calcification – the calcium is concentrated in the C horizon.

5.8 Ecosystems

Studying ecosystems is a good way to investigate the environment because they involve climate, soils, vegetation, animals and human activities. Source 1 shows a natural ecosystem. There are living organisms, such as the trees and animals, and non-living elements, such as the soil and climate. The elements in an ecosystem are linked together by a cycling of water, energy and nutrients.

People have always made use of ecosystems to provide themselves with resources such as fruit and nuts for food or timber for fuel and building materials. Even today primitive peoples still make use of ecosystems without disturbing or destroying

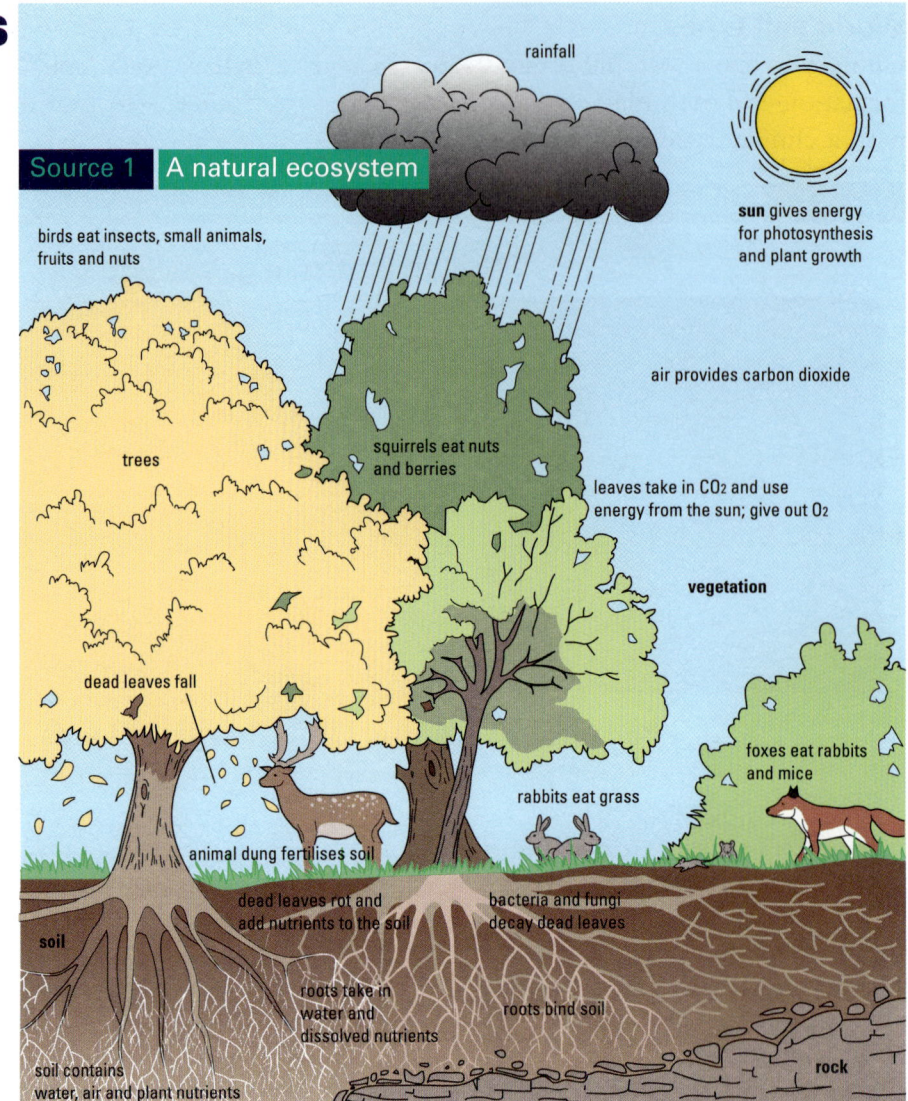

Source 1 A natural ecosystem

- rainfall
- **sun** gives energy for photosynthesis and plant growth
- birds eat insects, small animals, fruits and nuts
- air provides carbon dioxide
- squirrels eat nuts and berries
- leaves take in CO_2 and use energy from the sun; give out O_2
- trees
- vegetation
- dead leaves fall
- foxes eat rabbits and mice
- rabbits eat grass
- animal dung fertilises soil
- dead leaves rot and add nutrients to the soil
- bacteria and fungi decay dead leaves
- soil
- roots take in water and dissolved nutrients
- roots bind soil
- soil contains water, air and plant nutrients
- rock

Source 2 World vegetation zones

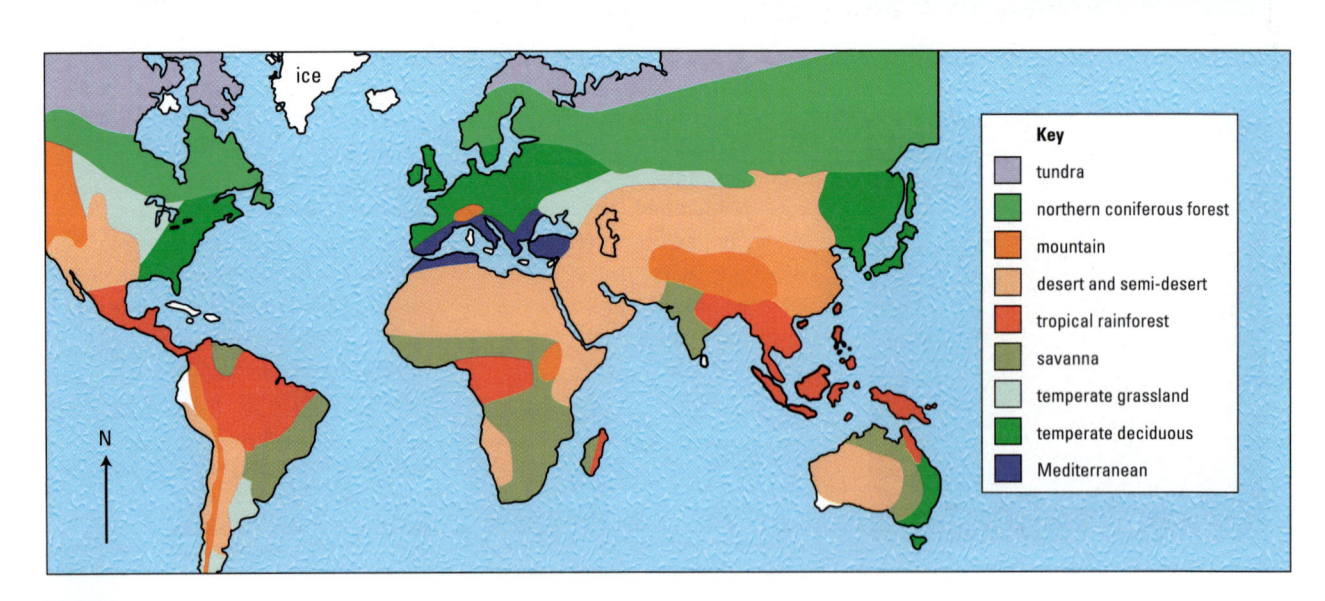

Key:
- tundra
- northern coniferous forest
- mountain
- desert and semi-desert
- tropical rainforest
- savanna
- temperate grassland
- temperate deciduous
- Mediterranean

Weather, climate and ecosystems

them. People like the Baka in Africa live in harmony within the tropical rainforest and their way of life is sustainable. However, in many places the natural ecosystems have been and are being seriously damaged. People have perceived them as a resource for human use and have destroyed them by over-exploitation. Today very little of the world's natural vegetation is left as people have cleared large areas of land for farming, settlement and industry.

Biomes

There are several types of ecosystem which are named after the main vegetation, for example: deciduous forest, tropical rainforest and grassland. Source 2 shows the distribution of world vegetation types. They are similar to the world climate and soil zones. These vegetation, soil and climate zones are called biomes.

Ecosystems can also be studied on a smaller scale, for example a pond, an oak wood or a hedgerow. This is useful because there are many small-scale variations in vegetation caused by slight changes in the climate or soil.

The coniferous forest ecosystem

Coniferous forests are sometimes called Boreal forests or taiga. They are mostly found in high latitudes across northern Europe and Asia and across northern North America (Source 2). These zones have cold climates with winter temperatures of below −20°C and only short summers up to +15°C. Precipitation totals are low, about 300 millimetres per year with most falling in the summer.

Most of the trees are **evergreen** conifers like those in Source 3. Some examples are spruce, pine and fir. The forests tend to be in single stands. This means they are all of one tree type.

The forests mostly grow in areas with **podzol** soils. The pine needles from the trees provide little humus. They rot very slowly because it is so cold. Although the rainfall is low there is very little evaporation, so most of the moisture can travel down through the soil causing leaching. Source 3 shows how the coniferous forests are well adapted to the long, cold, snowy winters.

Source 3 Coniferous forest ecosystem

- conical shape and flexible branches to allow snow to slide off
- evergreen (keeps leaves all year) – can begin to photosynthesise as soon as it is warm enough (short growing season)
- little undergrowth – frozen ground and little light
- podzol soils
- only one layer of vegetation
- needles not leaves to reduce water loss by transpiration
- thick bark and tough thick needles to protect from cold
- shallow roots to collect water
- subsoil frozen
- carpet of pine needles

5.9 A grassland ecosystem
tropical savanna in the Sahel

The Sahel is a narrow belt of land in North Africa. It borders the southern edge of the Sahara Desert (Source 1). The Sahel has a semi-desert climate shown in Source 2. Temperatures are always hot and there is a long dry season from June through to January. There is just enough rainfall for grasses to grow as well as some shrubs and trees.

The vegetation of grasses with some trees is called savanna. It is adapted to the hot temperatures and the drought during the dry season. A common tree in the Sahel is the Baobab or upside-down tree (Source 3). It has a swollen trunk where it stores water to help it survive the drought. Leaves and branches are small to reduce water loss through evapo-transpiration. Some of the vegetation has very long tap roots to reach down to underground stores of water. The grasses can grow up to 3.5 metres tall in wetter areas. These are called elephant grasses.

The savannas are the home of herds of large animals that graze on the grasses. People who live in the savannas are usually nomads who wander the land with their herds of cattle looking for the best grazing land.

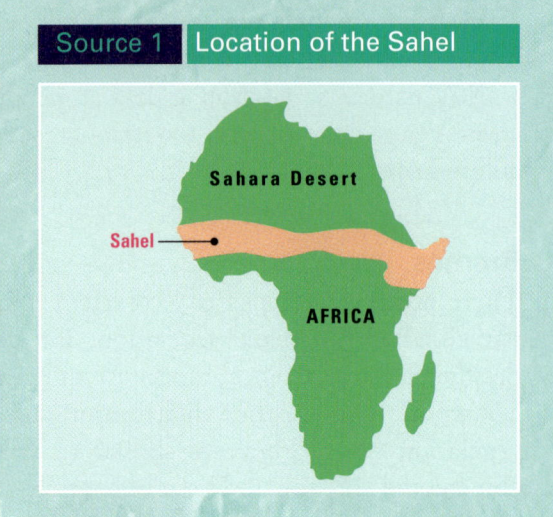

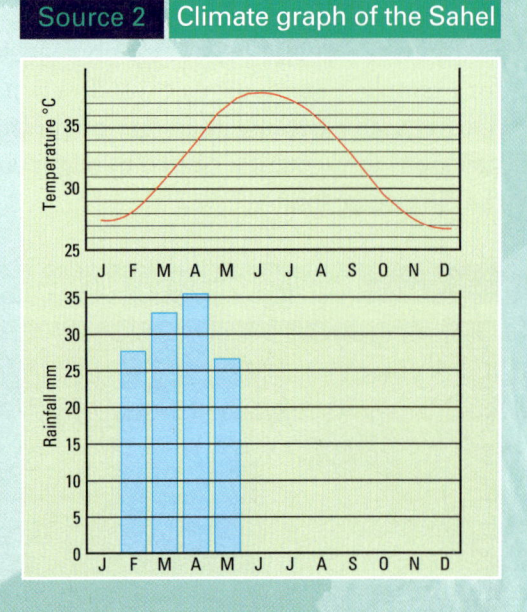

Source 1 Location of the Sahel

Source 2 Climate graph of the Sahel

Source 3 The Baobab tree

Ecosystem change 5.10
desertification in the Sahel

Desertification is used to describe the process by which land that once was covered in vegetation turns into desert. Both natural events and human activities may cause desertification.

In the Sahel there have been some years when less rain has fallen. Fewer grasses have grown and trees have died. The landscape becomes much more like desert. Study Sources 1 and 2 that show how desertification can affect land in the savanna.

This climate change is one cause of **desertification**. Desertification is also speeded up by human activity. Up until the 1960s there was more rainfall in the Sahel and the population grew. Water was plentiful so more crops were grown and numbers of animals increased. Wood was available to use as fuel and building materials.

In the drier years after the 1960s large areas of forest were removed for farmland and fuel supplies. People still tried to grow the same crops and rear the same numbers of animals. **Overgrazing** and **overcultivation** left the ground bare. Without vegetation less humus is added to the soil. The soil holds less water and dries out. The bare soil is quickly eroded by wind and flash floods. The land can no longer support any trees and plants and it turns to desert. Since 1970:

- there has been widespread crop failure
- over 100 000 people and millions of animals have died.

A variety of techniques can be used to prevent desertification and also to rehabilitate the land that has already been damaged.

New research using satellite images suggests that the deserts may not be spreading permanently. Some areas where rainfall has increased have now recovered. It is also difficult to decide whether it is the climate or the human activity which causes the changes. One thing is certain – the semi-arid lands are fragile environments and people must use them with care so that desertification is avoided.

Source 1 The Sahel before desertification

Source 2 The Sahel after desertification

5.11 A grassland ecosystem
North America's prairies

The temperate grasslands of North America are known as the **prairies**. They cover a huge area stretching from the Great Lakes in the east to the Rocky mountains in the west (Source 1). Large parts of the prairies are level and low lying. Most of the land in the east is less than 300 metres above sea level. The soils are deep, fertile chernozems (see page 93).

Source 1 The Prairie Provinces, Canada

Source 2 The natural landscape of the prairies

The area has a continental interior climate. Rainfall decreases from east to west but on average it is about 400 millimetres. Most of the rain falls in summer as convectional rainfall. Winter precipitation falls as snow. In the winter temperatures are as low as –20°C. High winds can cause blizzards. The soil is frozen for several months of the year.

In the spring, the warm 'chinook' wind comes from the west and can raise the temperature from –20°C to above 0°C in a few minutes. The snow melts and spring comes quickly! Summer temperatures rise to 20°C. The heating causes convectional rainfall and hailstorms.

The climate is too dry for trees to grow. Instead:

- the landscape is covered by tall prairie grasses with occasional trees along water courses (Source 2)
- the grasses are well adapted to the short growing season and the dry conditions (Source 3)
- the grasses are dormant in the winter but grow rapidly in spring and summer
- towards the Rocky Mountains, where it is drier, the grasses become shorter and more tussocky.

The prairies have excellent fertile soil, flat land and some summer rainfall. This makes them attractive to farmers for wheat growing. However, the farmers also have to cope with winter blizzards, summer drought, hailstorms, soil erosion and tornadoes.

Source 3 How the grasses adapt to the climate

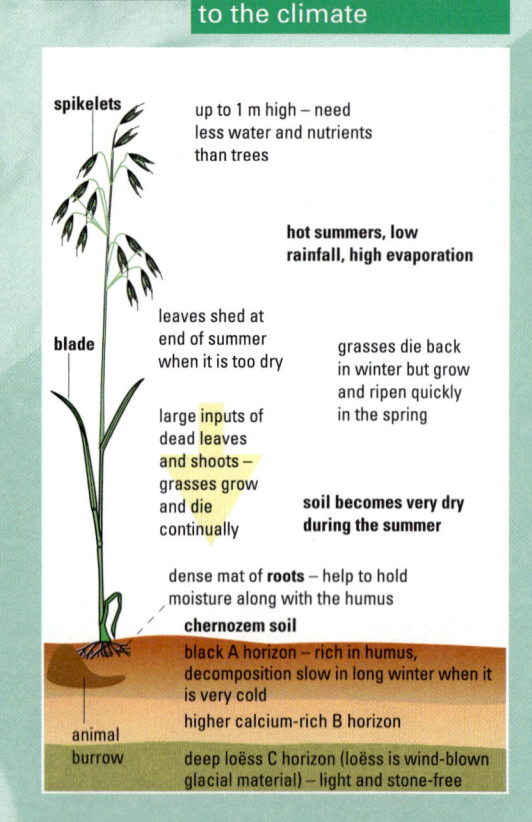

- spikelets
- up to 1 m high – need less water and nutrients than trees
- hot summers, low rainfall, high evaporation
- blade
- leaves shed at end of summer when it is too dry
- grasses die back in winter but grow and ripen quickly in the spring
- large inputs of dead leaves and shoots – grasses grow and die continually
- soil becomes very dry during the summer
- dense mat of roots – help to hold moisture along with the humus
- chernozem soil
- black A horizon – rich in humus, decomposition slow in long winter when it is very cold
- higher calcium-rich B horizon
- animal burrow
- deep loëss C horizon (loëss is wind-blown glacial material) – light and stone-free

How vegetation adapts
tropical rainforest in Brazil

5.12

Brazil is the largest country in South America. In the north, the climate is equatorial (page 86). The hot, wet greenhouse conditions produce very rapid growth of vegetation all year round. The tropical rainforest is the richest vegetation in the world. Study Source 1 and notice the five layers of vegetation and the large variety of different trees and plants. There are over 1000 different tree species, for example mahogany, teak and rosewood. Study Sources 2 and 3 to discover how very well adapted the vegetation is to the special conditions in the rainforest.

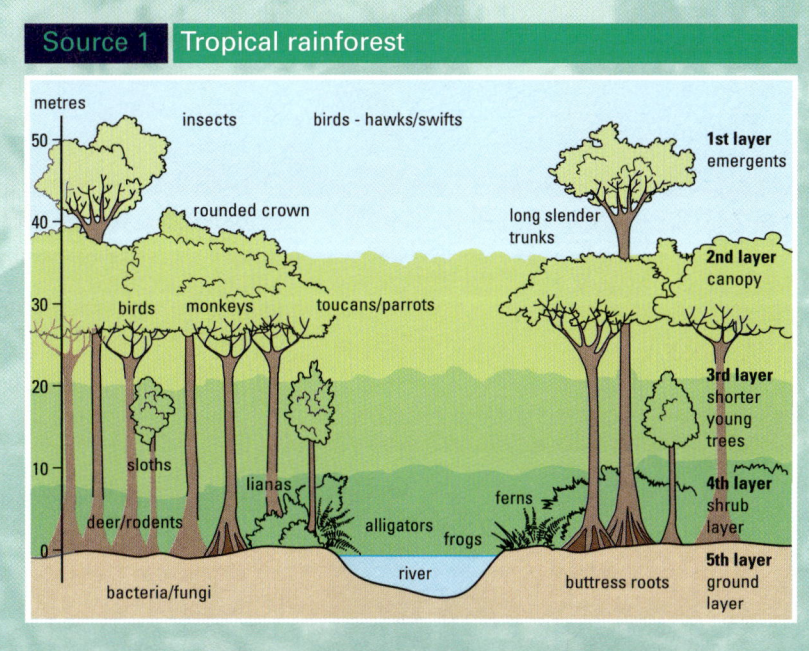

Source 1 Tropical rainforest

A fragile environment

The lush rainforest vegetation fools people into thinking the soils are fertile. But these tropical soils are infertile and heavy rainfall quickly leaches the minerals. About 90 per cent of all the nutrients in the rainforest are held in the trees. Cutting down the trees removes the nutrients and leaves the soil unprotected. The tropical rainforest ecosystem is very fragile and easily damaged.

What is sustainable development?

Today, people are supporting the idea of sustainable development. This is the ability of one generation to hand over to the next at least the same amount of resources it started with. It should also be development which helps all people, particularly the poorest. Sustainable development should:

- respect the environment and cultures
- use traditional skills and knowledge
- give people control over their land and lives
- use appropriate technology – machines and equipment that are cheap, easy to use and do not harm the environment
- generate income for communities.

Source 2 Buttress roots

The huge buttress roots at the base of the trees help to give the trees support and to take in the vast quantities of water and nutrients the trees need to survive.

Source 3 Drip tips

Some of the leaves have drip tips which act like the lip on a jug helping the leaves to shed water. This stops disease.

5.13 Deforestation
tropical rainforest in Brazil and Malaysia

Source 1: Peninsular Malaysia

Source 2: Jengka Triangle Project

For centuries the tropical rainforests have been inhabited by groups of Indians. The Indians hunt for animals, collect fruits and clear small patches of the forest to grow crops. This type of farming is called slash and burn. The clearing is small and after two or three years it is abandoned and the forest once again develops. The Indians do no long-term damage to the forest and their use of the forest's resources is sustainable.

Recent human activity in the rainforests has been much more devastating. Large-scale deforestation has taken place for a variety of reasons:

- mining, for example the iron ore mine at Carajas in the Amazon Basin
- plantations, for example rubber and oil palm in the Jengka Triangle Project in Malaysia
- road building, for example the Trans-Amazonian Highway in Brazil
- new settlement and small farms to house migrants from the cities, for example the transmigration projects in Indonesia and Brazil
- logging for timber exports, for example teak and mahogany in the Amazon Basin
- huge cattle ranches as in the Amazon Basin.

Source 3: Problems caused by deforestation: the problems affect the soil, vegetation, climate, rivers and local people – find an example for each one

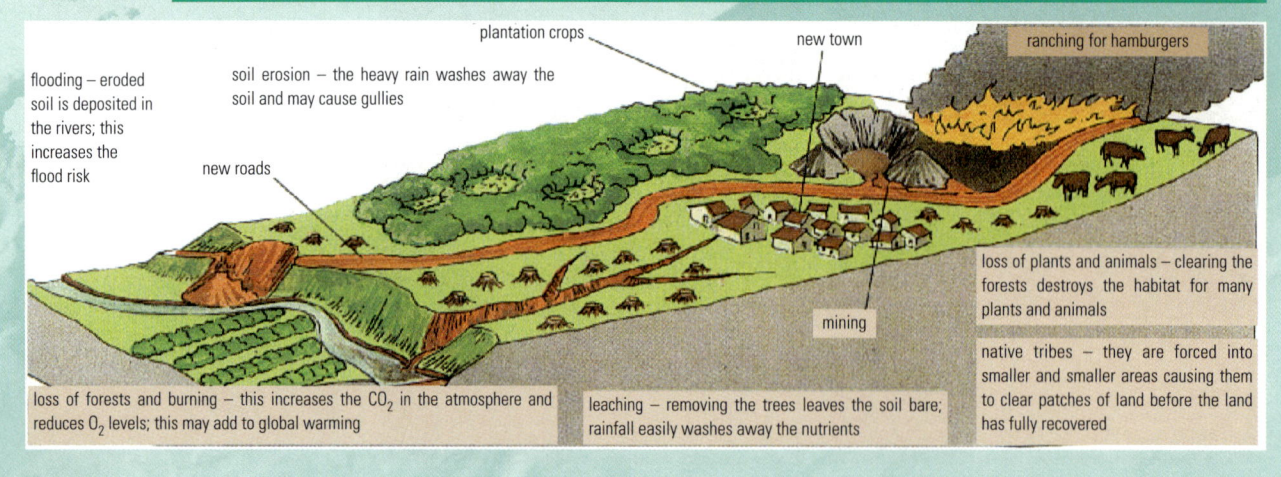

- flooding – eroded soil is deposited in the rivers; this increases the flood risk
- soil erosion – the heavy rain washes away the soil and may cause gullies
- plantation crops
- new roads
- new town
- ranching for hamburgers
- mining
- loss of plants and animals – clearing the forests destroys the habitat for many plants and animals
- native tribes – they are forced into smaller and smaller areas causing them to clear patches of land before the land has fully recovered
- loss of forests and burning – this increases the CO_2 in the atmosphere and reduces O_2 levels; this may add to global warming
- leaching – removing the trees leaves the soil bare; rainfall easily washes away the nutrients

Weather, climate and ecosystems

Governments have encouraged the clearing of the forests because:

- the revenue earned from selling timber, drugs and minerals helps to pay off debts and to develop their countries
- new land is needed to house and feed the growing populations in countries such as Brazil and Malaysia.

The Jengka Triangle Project

In Malaysia the FELDA (Federal Land Development Authority) has cleared forest for 307 development projects. The Jengka Triangle Project (Source 1) is one of these schemes. It involves:

- clearance of over 120 000 hectares of land (Source 2)
- the creation of 40 500 hectares of oil palm and rubber plantations
- housing for 9000 families.

Before the scheme began sawmills and roads were built to process the cut timber. The trees were felled using modern chainsaws and cranes. Huge tractors and lorries removed the logs and less valuable trees and plants were burned. The finished scheme has rubber and oil palm plantations, a good network of roads, processing factories for the rubber and oil palm, plywood factories, three new towns and many farms.

The management of forests

Today the scale of forest removal is huge in the tropical rainforests and the deforestation causes many problems. Study Source 3 to find out more.

The loss of forests not only in the tropics but all over the world is causing concern. Many governments and international organisations recognise the need to manage forests to ensure the resources are there for future generations. This is called sustainable development. But it is difficult for some governments, especially of the LEDCs, because they need the money the developments bring.

The sustainable management of forests can be achieved by:

- protection of forests - in some countries areas of forest are conserved and protected as National Parks where no development is allowed to take place
- carefully planned and controlled logging in forests
- selective logging of only those trees that are valuable leaving the rest of the forest untouched, for example in parts of Indonesia only 7 to 12 trees per hectare are allowed to be felled
- replanting of forested areas that have been felled
- restrictions on the number of logging licences that are allowed to reduce the amount of forest loss
- heli-logging, for example in Sarawak where helicopters are used to remove the logs because less damage is done to the remaining forest.
- developing alternative energy supplies, for example biogas, solar and wind power to reduce the amount of wood needed for fuel.

Source 4 Logging in Sarawak

5.14 Activities

1 Study the photograph on page 81. Are the following statements true or false? Try to explain each of your answers.
   a There is a lot of cloud over the Sahara desert.
   b There is a lot of cloud approaching the UK.
   c There is a lot of cloud over the equatorial area of West Africa.

2 a Name five elements of the weather.
   b Draw labelled sketches of the instruments used to measure temperature, rainfall, sunshine, humidity and pressure.
   c Write notes alongside each one to explain how it works.
   d Explain why you would not site a weather station close to some tall trees and buildings.

3 a Copy the diagrams and labels from page 84 to explain the effect of latitude, prevailing winds and altitude.
   b Complete a table like the one below to give the features of air masses affecting the UK. The table has been started for you.

Air mass	polar continental		tropical maritime	
Source region		North Africa		Arctic Ocean
Summer weather				
Winter weather				

4 a On a world map mark and label three climate zones.
   b Using the figures in Source 1 draw a climate graph.

Source 1 Climate figures

Months	J	F	M	A	M	J	J	A	S	O	N	D
Temperature °C	20	21	26	32	38	39	39	35	30	23	20	18
Rainfall mm	0	20	30	35	18	0	0	0	0	0	0	0

   c Describe the main features of the climate graph you have drawn. Include the maximum and minimum temperatures, the range of temperature, the rainfall total and any dry or wet seasons.
   d Using the information on pages 86–7 decide what type of climate you have described.

5 a Copy and complete the paragraph below.
   Scotland and the north of England are *(colder/warmer)* than the south of England in summer. This is because the south is *(further from/closer to)* the Equator. In winter, the east coast is *(colder/warmer)* than the west coast. This is because there are *(cold/warm)* winds from the north and east. Also the west coast is affected by the *(warm/cold)* ocean currents. The north and west of the UK receive *(more/less)* rainfall than the south and east. This is because the warm *(moist/dry)* winds come in from the west. The uplands are *(colder/warmer)* than the lowlands and receive *(more/less)* rain. This is because temperatures *(decrease/increase)* with height and there is relief rainfall.
   b For both depressions and anticyclones:
      i describe their characteristics
      ii describe and explain the weather they bring to Britain.

6 a Draw the section through a tropical storm on page 90.
  b Explain how a tropical storm forms.
  c List the effects of tropical storm Gordon in 1994.
  d Suggest how people can prevent or reduce the damage caused by tropical storms.

7 a What is an urban microclimate and urban heat island?
  b Give four reasons why urban areas are usually warmer than the surrounding countryside.

8 a List the five main ingredients of soils.
  b For each of the three soils on page 93 draw and label a soil profile diagram like that shown in Source 2 on page 92.
  c Explain how each soil type is formed.

9 a Write your own definition of an ecosystem.
  b Why is there so little natural vegetation left today?
  c What is a biome? Give two examples of biomes.

10 For the coniferous forest ecosystem:
  a Mark and label its distribution on a world map.
  b Describe the climate and soils.
  c Describe the features of the vegetation.
  d Explain how the vegetation is adapted to the climate.

11 a Draw and label a sketch map to show the location of the Sahel in Africa.
  b Describe the main features of the climate and vegetation in the Sahel.
  c Explain how the vegetation is adapted to the climate.
  d What is desertification?
  e Explain the human and physical causes of desertification in the Sahel.
  f Study sources 1 and 2 on page 97. Describe what has happened to the land in the photographs.

12 a Repeat the tasks in question 10 for the tropical rainforest.
  b What is sustainable development and what should it involve?
  c Why is the traditional use of the rainforests by the Indians a good example of sustainability?
  d List five causes of deforestation today.
  e Give two reasons why governments are encouraging deforestation.
  f Describe the Jengka Triangle Project as an example of deforestation.
  g Divide your class into four to represent each of the following groups of people:
   - the Malaysian government
   - an international logging company
   - a shifting cultivator
   - a conservation group like Greenpeace.

   In your chosen role write a report in favour of or against the development of the rainforest. Present your report to the class as a whole.
   Following your presentations decide which groups were in favour of conservation or development.
  h In your groups study the definition of sustainable development on page 99. Write your own definition for sustainable development based on the role that you have chosen.
  i Look again at the Jengka Triangle Project. Write two lists, one for the ways in which the project supports sustainable development and one for the ways in which it does not.
  j Try to produce some suggestions for the Malaysian government as to how it could improve its development projects in the future.

13 Study Source 3 on page 100.
  a Explain how removal of trees affects the soil, climate, vegetation, rivers and local people.
  b Describe three ways forests can be managed to ensure sustainability.

5.15 Sample examination questions

1 Study the diagram of a tropical rainforest in Source 1.

Source 1 A tropical rainforest

a How tall are the tallest trees? (1 mark)
b What is the correct name for the parts of the forest shown at A and B? (2 marks)
c Explain two ways the rainforest is adapted to the hot, wet tropical climate. (4 marks)
d List three causes of deforestation in the tropical rainforests. (3 marks)
(Total: 10 marks)

2 a Using the figures below draw a climate graph. (4 marks)

Months	J	F	M	A	M	J	J	A	S	O	N	D
Temperature (°C)	−20	−20	−16	−10	8	10	16	12	3	−8	−12	−18
Rainfall (mm)	10	8	8	12	10	60	80	75	50	25	20	18

b Describe the main features of the temperature and rainfall shown on the climate graph. (3 marks)
c Select from the following list the type of climate shown: Equatorial; Hot Desert; Cold Continental Interior. (1 mark)
d Give two reasons why few people live in areas with this climate. (2 marks)
(Total: 10 marks)

3 Study the chart below which shows the rates of deforestation of rainforest in selected areas of the world.

Country	Area of forest lost per year (1000s hectares)
Costa Rica	65
Malaysia	255
Philippines	91
Ivory Coast	290
Nigeria	300
Brazil	1480
Indonesia	600

a Show the figures on a bar graph. (4 marks)
b Give two reasons why forests need to be managed. (2 marks)
c Describe how forests can be managed to ensure sustainable development. (4 marks)
(Total: 10 marks)

UNIT 6

Population

Unit Contents

- Distribution and density
- Population change
- Migration
- Population structure
- Population distribution: the United Kingdom
- Internal migration: the United Kingdom
- Internal migration: Brazil
- An ageing population: France
- Population policy and population control: China
- Population contrasts: the USA and Mexico

People galore. Why is this a scene in a LEDC, not a MEDC?

6.1 Distribution and density

There are six billion people living in the world today. They are unevenly spread across the earth's surface.

Source 1 — The world distribution of people

Key
· 1 dot = 1 million people

A dot map as in Source 1 is used to show population distribution. One dot represents 1 million people. In some areas, without the natural resources to attract settlement, there are few people. This pattern or **distribution of population** can be seen in Source 1. The main problem for people living in the area marked A is that it is too dry. It is also very hot during the day. Therefore **climate** has discouraged people from living there (Source 2).

The area marked B in Source 1 is the Himalayas. These mountains include Mount Everest, the world's highest mountain, which rises to 8848 metres above sea level. These mountains are too high and too steep for many people to make a living there. **Relief** therefore has discouraged people from living in this area.

Source 2 — Why few people live in hot deserts

Climatic factors
- Under 250 mm precipitation per year
- High daytime temperatures above 30°C

↓

Problem: Shortage of water

↓

Farming is difficult if not impossible
- Little grass for grazing
- Crops will not grow without water

↓

Problem: Shortage of food

↓

Result: Few people live in hot desert regions

Population

Density of population is the number of people per square kilometre. It is worked out by using the following formula.

$$\frac{\text{number of people living in an area}}{\text{size of the area in which they live}} = \text{population density}$$

To explain why some areas of the world have high densities of population, more than one favourable factor is needed. The factors may be **physical,** such as climate, relief and soils. They may be **human**, such as economic, social and political. Source 3 shows farmers growing rice in the Ganges valley in India (marked C in Source 1). The labels in Source 3 show the favourable physical and human factors which help to explain why rural densities of population here are among the highest in the world. Different colours have been used to distinguish between the physical and human factors.

Source 3 Cultivating rice in the Ganges valley

- monsoon climate
- hot: about 27°C
- wet in summer (above 100 mm rain)
- people do the work
- flat land
- fertile silt soils
- large amount of rice grown to feed a lot of people
- irrigation water

Source 4 The World Trade Centre in New York

However, most of the areas of high density of population in the world are in urban areas. Letter D in Source 1 marks the east coast of the USA centred around New York. There is an almost continuous line of cities between Boston and Washington. The great variety and number of jobs make it possible for large numbers of people to make a living there. The list of city-based jobs is almost endless. There are jobs in factories (secondary) as well as in offices, transport, shops, cafés and hotels (tertiary). Source 4 shows a well-known New York landmark, the World Trade Centre. Each tower has over 100 storeys. Over 50 000 people work in these two towers alone.

107

6.2 Population change

Population change may mean an increase or a decrease in the number of people living in an area. It is natural to assume that it means population increase because the world's population is continuing to grow as Source 1 shows.

Birth rates

High **birth rates** contribute to population growth. Birth rate is the number of live births per 1000 people per year in a country or region. Source 2 shows the average birth rates for the different continents. Notice how much higher the average birth rate is in Africa, where there are many less economically developed countries (LEDCs), compared with Europe, where most of the countries are more economically developed (MEDCs). Some of the factors which help to explain these differences are given in Source 3.

In general it is true to say that birth rates in the world are declining as more and more people are practising birth control. Wealth and education are the best contraceptives: richer and better educated people have fewer children. Why, therefore, is world population continuing to increase? It is necessary to look at the other element in the formula – the **death rate**.

Death rates

Low death rates contribute to population growth. Death rate is the number of deaths per 1000 people per year in a country or region. Death rates are at an all time low (Source 2). Notice how much lower the death rates are than the birth rates. The reason for this is improved medical treatment and **primary health care,** which reduces the chances of a person becoming ill in the first place. Source 4 illustrates some of the ways in which this can be done. **Secondary health care** is more widely available. Particularly in the cities in LEDCs, there are hospitals to treat sick people, where modern medicines and drugs are available.

Source 1 World population growth 1950–2075

Source 2 Average birth and death rates

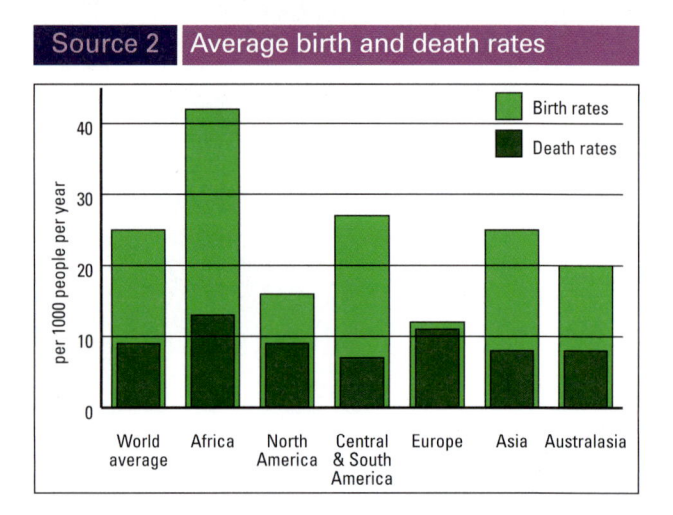

Source 3 Factors which affect the birth rate

Factor	High birth rates in LEDCs	Low birth rates in MEDCs
Economic	• Children can work on the farm or earn money begging or selling goods in the city. • Children support elderly parents.	• Children cost their parents a lot of money. • Pensions for the old.
Social	• Little use of birth control. • 6–10 children in a family is normal.	• Many methods of birth control are used. • 2–3 children are the norm.
Political	Governments in Muslim and Catholic countries will not always provide family planning education.	Government-financed family planning services.

| Source 4 | Ways to prevent illness and death |

Primary health care | Secondary health care

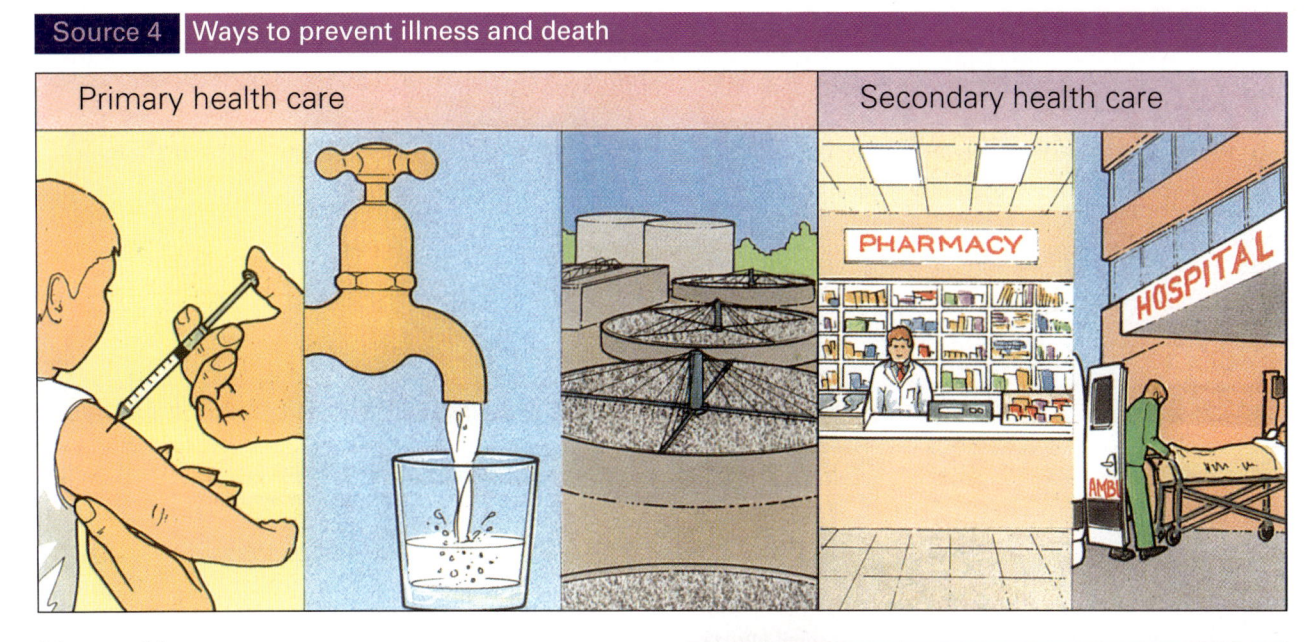

Natural increase

The rate of **natural increase** in a country or region is worked out by the following formula.

$$\frac{\text{birth rate}}{\text{death rate}} = \text{rate of natural increase}$$

Using the values from Source 2 the rates of natural increase for the continents can be worked out (Source 5).

A big difference between the birth rate and death rate, as there is for Africa (Source 5), means a high rate of natural increase and high population growth. The changing relationships between birth and death rates through time are shown on a graph called the demographic transition model (Source 6).

| Source 5 | Rates of natural increase |

Continent	Birth rate per 1000	Death rate per 1000	Rate of natural increase per 1000	per 100 (%)
Europe	12	11	1	0.1
Africa	42	13	29	2.9

What has really happened is that the death rate has fallen rapidly in the LEDCs in stages 2 and 3. It has fallen much more quickly than the birth rate. The big difference between the death rate and the birth rate has resulted in the high rate of population increase. Only in the MEDCs have birth rates fallen to the same level as death rates, so keeping the population increase low. Most European countries are in stage 4.

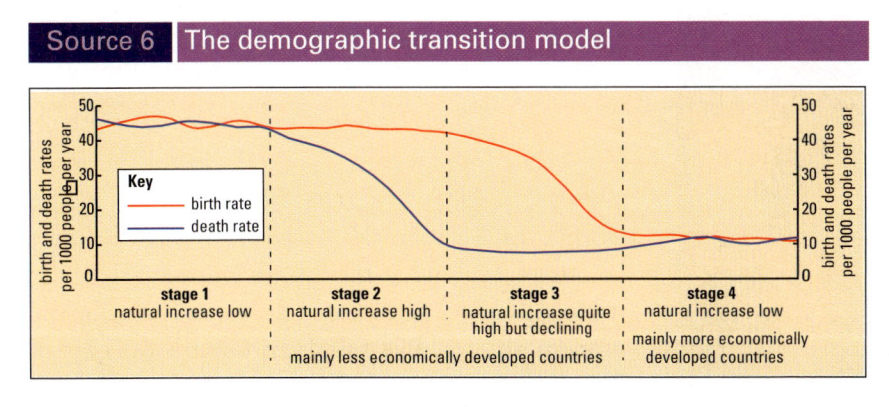

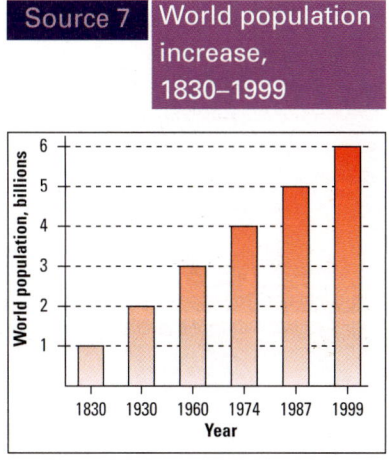

| Source 6 | The demographic transition model |

| Source 7 | World population increase, 1830–1999 |

6.3 Migration

Migration means the movement of people. What makes people move? Normally there are things they do not like about where they live. These are *push* factors. Usually there are things they like about the place they are moving to. These are called *pull* factors. Source 1 shows some of the main types of migration taking place in the world today. All these types of migration can be explained by referring to push and pull factors.

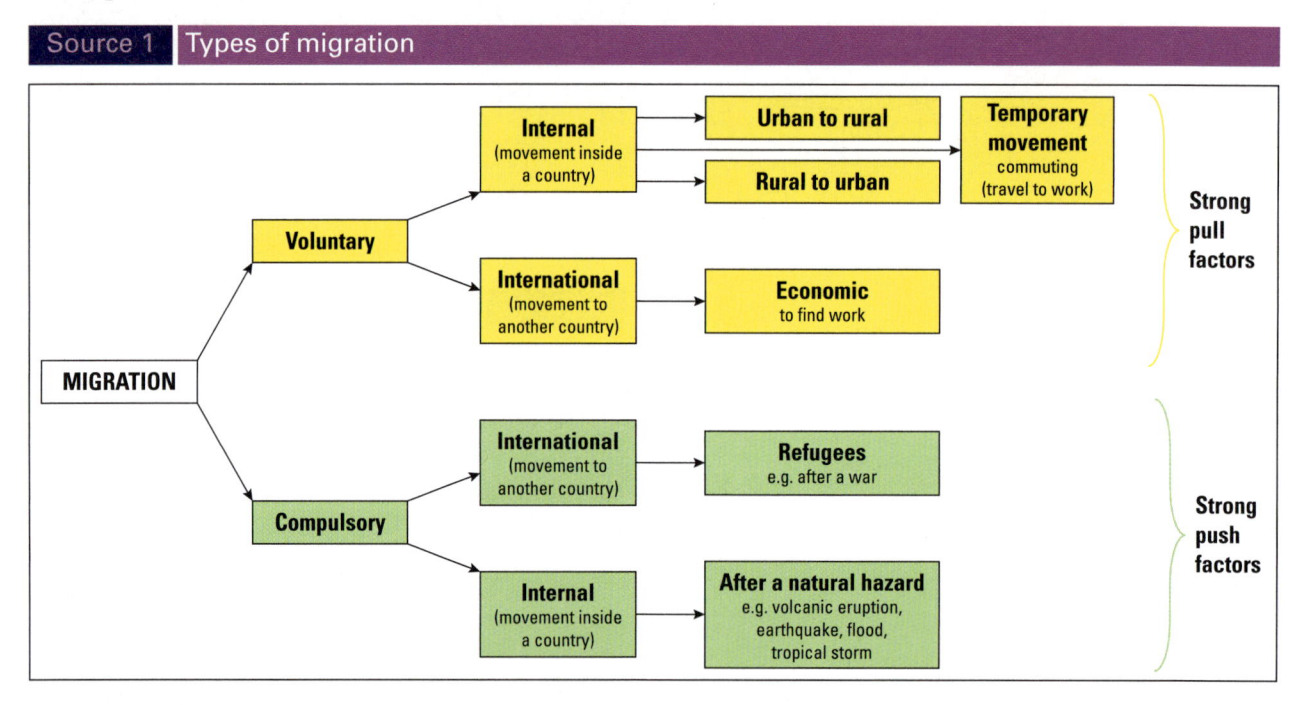

Source 1 — Types of migration

- MIGRATION
  - **Voluntary**
    - Internal (movement inside a country)
      - Urban to rural
      - Rural to urban
      - Temporary movement — commuting (travel to work)
    - International (movement to another country)
      - Economic — to find work
    - } Strong pull factors
  - **Compulsory**
    - International (movement to another country)
      - Refugees e.g. after a war
    - Internal (movement inside a country)
      - After a natural hazard e.g. volcanic eruption, earthquake, flood, tropical storm
    - } Strong push factors

Source 2 — A deserted Peruvian village

For some of the migrations the push factor is the most important. People may be forced out of a place by natural disasters or wars. They have to move whether they want to or not. They are called **refugees** if they have to flee to another country. In Peru, when a flood destroyed all the houses in a village and the farmland was covered by useless boulders (Source 2), the villagers were forced to move.

For other migrations, the pull factor is more powerful. People living in the rural areas in the world's less economically developed countries may be attracted by what they think are the chances of work and higher paid jobs in the cities. It may be the modern services that pull them towards the city: of great importance is electricity supply because they can watch the films, soaps and sport on TV – just as most people in the rich countries of the world do.

Population

Source 3 Reasons for rural to urban migration in LEDCs

rural areas — movement — urban areas

Source 4 Reasons for urban to rural migration in MEDCs

urban areas — movement — rural areas

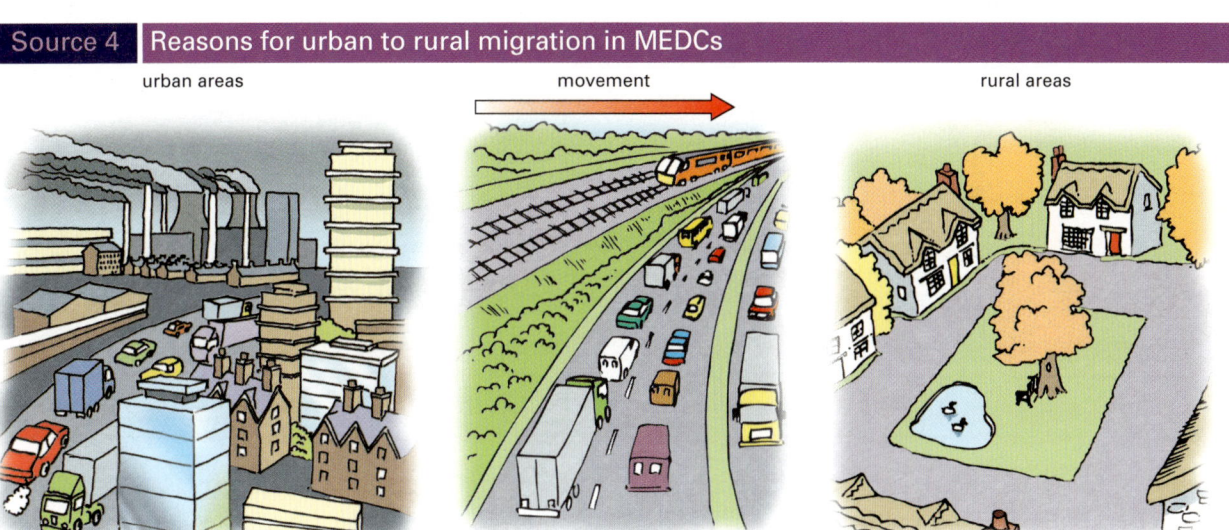

Source 3 shows the push and pull factors for **rural to urban migration,** which is the most common type of migration in LEDCs. Many people are leaving the countryside and flooding into the cities. They are making worse the already great problems in the cities but few want to go back. Life in the city is better than life in the countryside.

In contrast, in the more economically developed countries the exact opposite is happening. Some people here believe that the countryside is a better place to live than the city. Source 4 shows push and pull factors for **urban to rural migration**.

It is important to realise just how different living in the countryside is in the rich countries compared with the poor countries. In rich countries piped water and electricity exist in the countryside just as they do in the towns. Many people own cars, which means they have easy access to the shops, services and places of work in the towns.

However, there are many problems associated with both types of migration. Rural to urban migration causes population growth in the city which leads to urban problems, such as housing shortages, lack of essential services and unemployment. Urban to rural migration causes the growth of the village which leads to a change in its character. Conflicts often develop between old residents and newcomers, house prices increase and there is more traffic.

6.4 Population structure

Information about the characteristics of a population, such as age, sex and ethnic make-up, is recorded in a census. The age-sex composition of a population is known as the **population structure**. It is shown by a population pyramid. The percentage for each age group is plotted by horizontal bars for males and females. Source 1 shows the population pyramids for the Democratic Republic of the Congo (formerly Zaire) in Africa and the United Kingdom in Europe. The Congo is in stage 2 in the demographic transition model (see Source 6 on page 109) while the UK is in stage 4.

Source 1 — Population pyramids for the Democratic Republic of the Congo and the UK

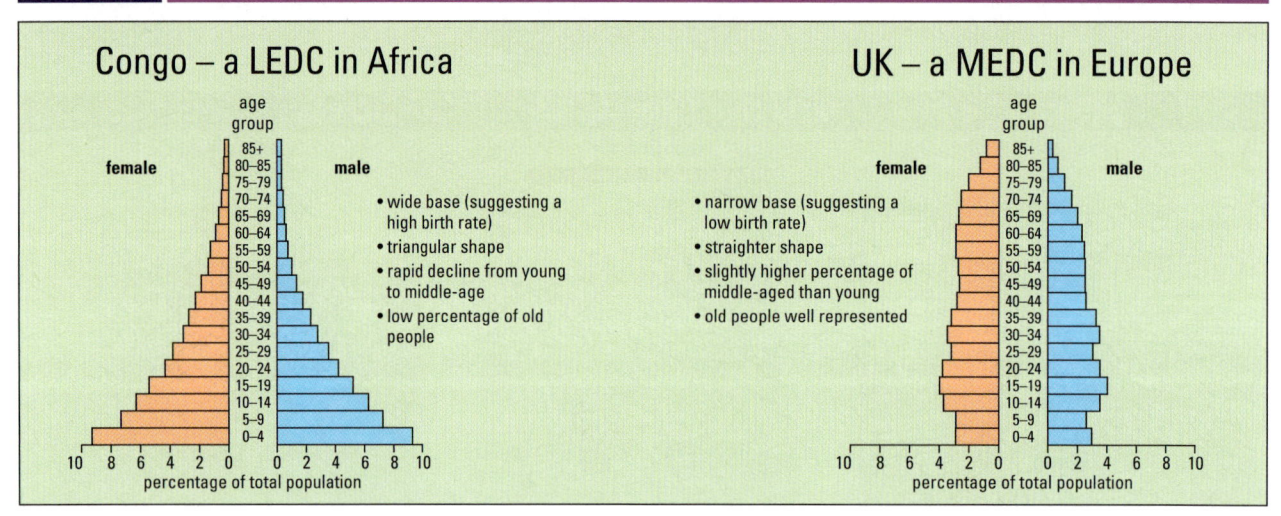

Congo – a LEDC in Africa
- wide base (suggesting a high birth rate)
- triangular shape
- rapid decline from young to middle-age
- low percentage of old people

UK – a MEDC in Europe
- narrow base (suggesting a low birth rate)
- straighter shape
- slightly higher percentage of middle-aged than young
- old people well represented

It is possible to use the population pyramids to work out the **dependency ratio**. Those over 65 and below 15 are regarded as **dependants**. Most of them do not work and so they need to rely upon some income from those in work. The dependency ratio can be worked out from the percentage values taken from the pyramids in Source 1.

Source 2 — There are plenty of young people in LEDCs

	Congo	UK
% under 15	= 46	= 18
% over 65	= 4	= 15
% dependants	= 50	= 33
Ratio dependant:worker	= 1:1	= 1:2

The dependency ratio is so high in the Congo because of the large numbers of young people (Source 2).

Population

Population problems
(i) LEDCs

It is very difficult for a poor country to provide the clean water, electricity, schools and all the other services that its young and growing population needs. Soon these young people will have families of their own. Even though many of these young people are better educated about birth control than were their parents, there are so many of them that, even with smaller families, the population will increase for many years to come. This has been described as a 'demographic time bomb'. A more basic question is, 'How is everyone going to be fed?' More food is needed from the land but can food be provided without further damage to the environment (Source 3)?

(ii) MEDCs

In countries such as the UK it is not the high dependency ratio, but the **ageing population** which is the 'demographic time bomb'. There is an increasing proportion of people over 65. For these countries one big cost is providing state pensions for an increasing number of people. Also the elderly need to use state medical services more frequently. The cost of care for the old in residential homes is already spiralling upwards (Source 4).

Source 3 Environmental damage from rapid population increase

large numbers of young people → rapid population increase → land must provide more food → possible environmental damage:
- soil erosion
- desertification
- loss of wildlife habitats
- global warming and climatic change

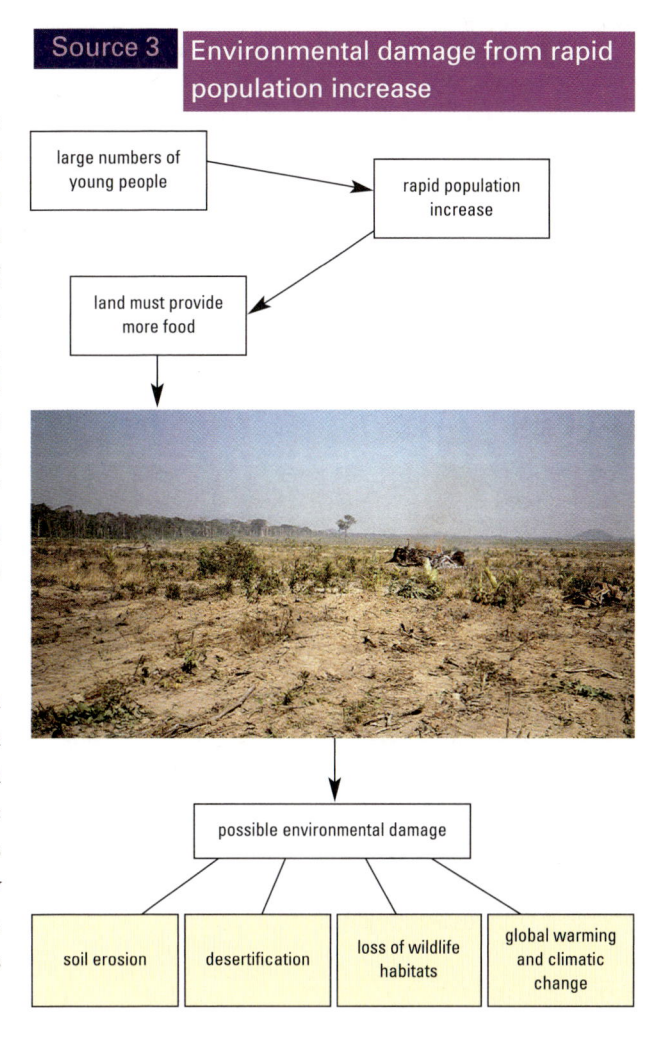

Source 4 Europe's population is growing old

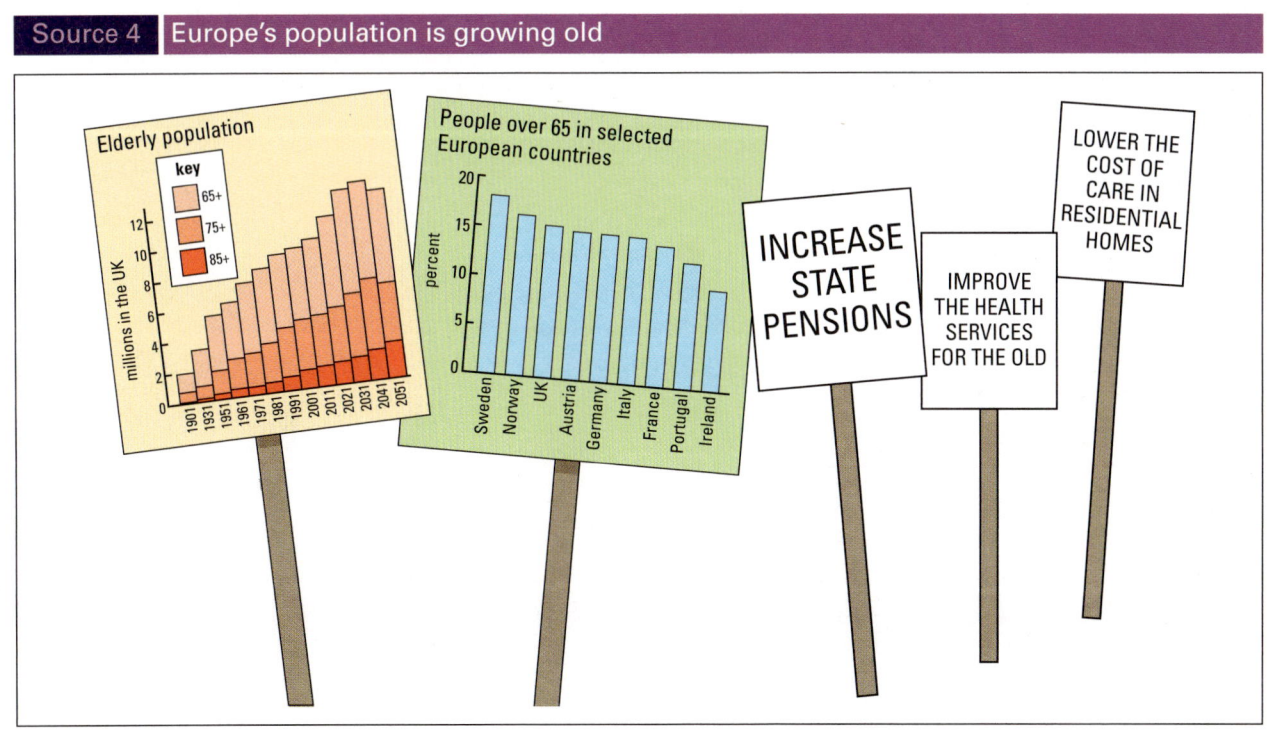

- Elderly population (millions in the UK, 1901–2051), key: 65+, 75+, 85+
- People over 65 in selected European countries (percent): Sweden, Norway, UK, Austria, Germany, Italy, France, Portugal, Ireland

Placards:
- INCREASE STATE PENSIONS
- IMPROVE THE HEALTH SERVICES FOR THE OLD
- LOWER THE COST OF CARE IN RESIDENTIAL HOMES

6.5 Population distribution
the United Kingdom

Source 1 shows variations in population density within the United Kingdom. The map suggests an uneven spread of people across the country.

High density
Certain areas of high density can be identified. Some of the largest areas of high density are associated with the seven **conurbations** named in Source 1. Conurbations are large, continuously built-up areas around a big city or cities. The most continuous area of high population density stretches from Greater London through the Midlands to the major conurbations in northern England around Liverpool (Merseyside), Manchester (Greater Manchester) and Leeds–Bradford (West Yorkshire).

Low density
Certain areas of low density are equally clear in Source 1. The most extensive areas with low population densities are upland areas, which are mainly located in the northern and western parts of the country. Areas of intermediate population density fill the lowland areas between the big cities. Lowland areas cover more of the land area in England than they do in Wales and Scotland.

Reasons for different densities
Why do some areas have higher population densities than others? It is always necessary to refer to several factors for a full explanation (Source 2).

Source 1 Density of population in the UK

Key
People per sq. km
- over 150 (high density)
- 11–150 (intermediate density)
- 0–10 (low density)

A–G: conurbations
- A Clydeside
- B Tyneside
- C West Yorkshire
- D Greater Manchester
- E Merseyside
- F West Midlands
- G Greater London

Population

Source 2 Reasons for different population densities

Highlands of Scotland
Reasons for the **low population density**:

Physical factors
A Climate – cool summers and high precipitation
B Relief – high land and steep slopes
C Soils – thin and acid soils and much of the land is bare rock

Economic factors
- remote position away from the markets
- poor communications with few railway lines and no motorways

Results
- there is a lot of unproductive land
- farming is difficult and cannot employ many people
- industry is not interested in locating here

Comment
This example is a reminder of the importance of physical factors for explaining low densities of population.

Greater London
Reasons for the **high population density**:

Historical factors
- the capital city with many Government departments
- long-established centre for business and trade in the City

Economic factors
It is an attractive location for industry and business because:
- of the large and wealthy market both in London and the South-East
- it is the centre for communications with fast rail services and good motorway links (such as the M1 to the North, M40 to the Midlands, M4 to South Wales)
- its position is close to Europe

Results
- no other part of the country can match the variety of work
- there is an enormous variety of jobs in the service sector – in government, in banks and offices, in transport, in shops and in serving visitors in hotels, and in places of entertainment

Comment
Human advantages are concentrated here in a way not found in any other part of the UK.

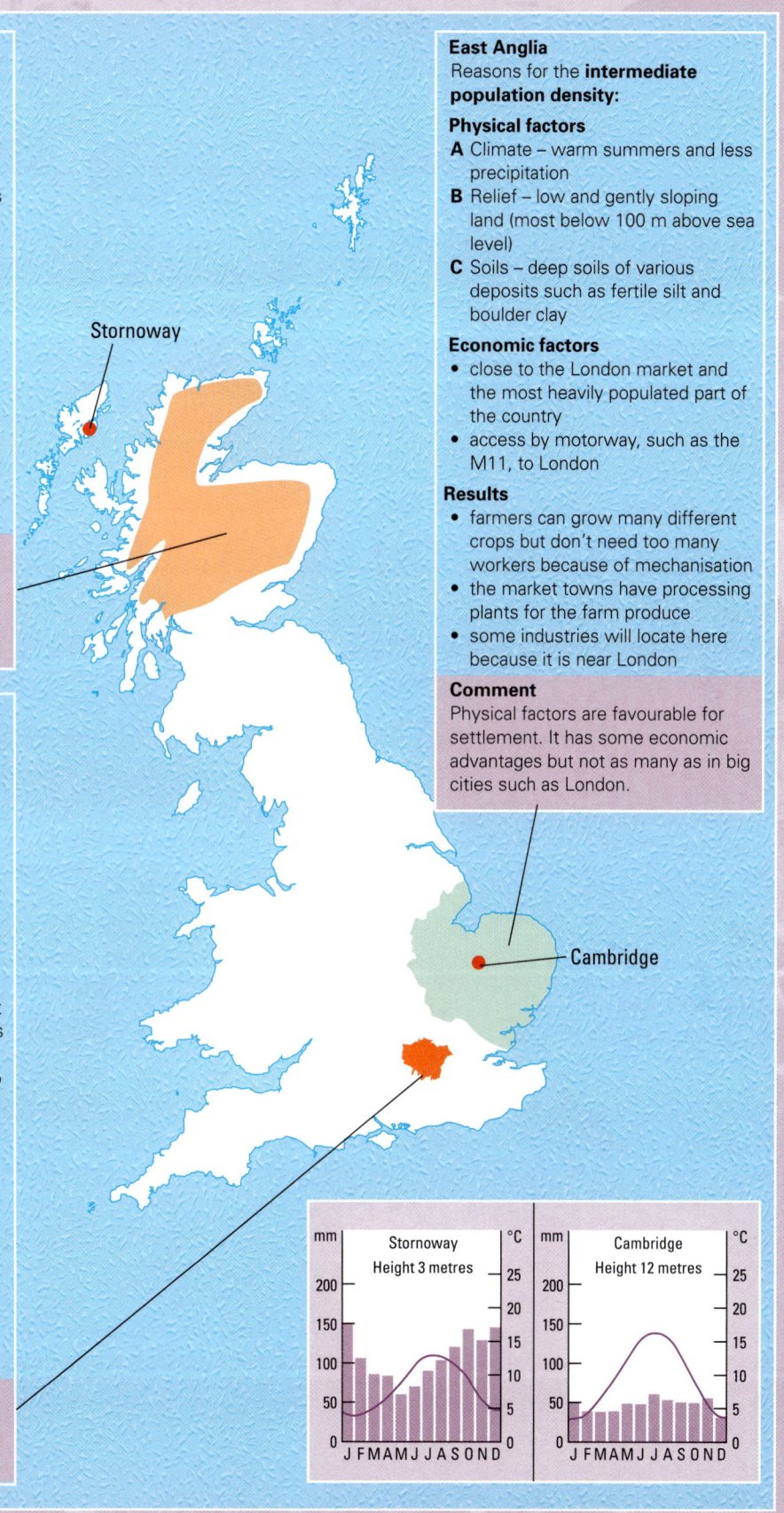

East Anglia
Reasons for the **intermediate population density**:

Physical factors
A Climate – warm summers and less precipitation
B Relief – low and gently sloping land (most below 100 m above sea level)
C Soils – deep soils of various deposits such as fertile silt and boulder clay

Economic factors
- close to the London market and the most heavily populated part of the country
- access by motorway, such as the M11, to London

Results
- farmers can grow many different crops but don't need too many workers because of mechanisation
- the market towns have processing plants for the farm produce
- some industries will locate here because it is near London

Comment
Physical factors are favourable for settlement. It has some economic advantages but not as many as in big cities such as London.

Stornoway

Cambridge

Stornoway Height 3 metres

Cambridge Height 12 metres

6.6 Internal migration
the United Kingdom

Source 1 shows the average population change for the different regions in Great Britain that was revealed by the census taken in 1991. Scotland and all the regions in the north of England lost people, while most regions in the south and east of England increased in population. This suggests that the long-established migration of people from the North to the South was still taking place (Source 2).

Source 1 | Population change 1981–91

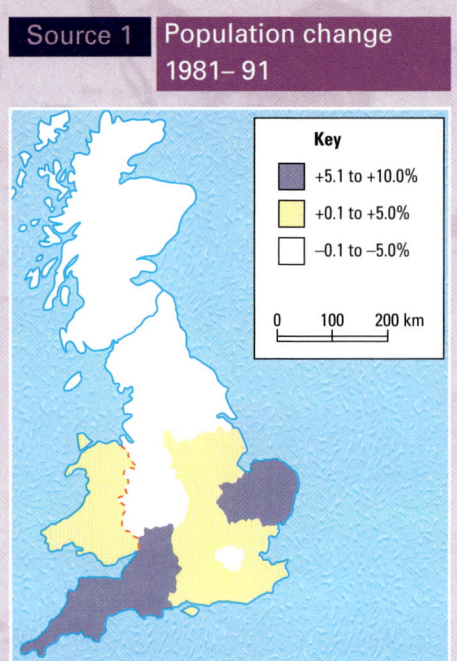

Key
- +5.1 to +10.0%
- +0.1 to +5.0%
- −0.1 to −5.0%

Source 2 | Migration movements

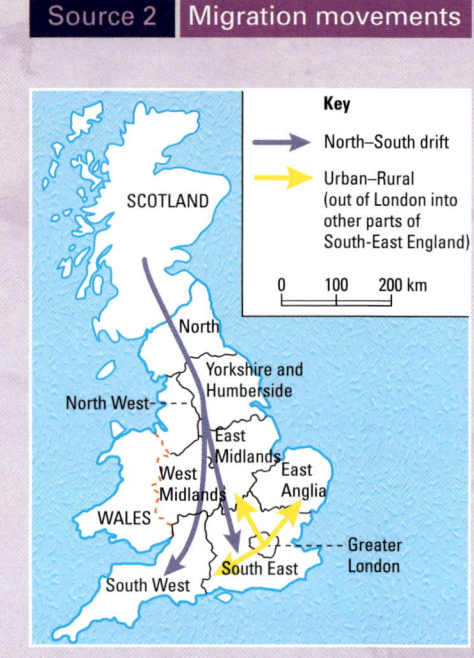

Key
- North–South drift
- Urban–Rural (out of London into other parts of South-East England)

Source 3 | Population change by county 1981–91

Key
- >10% increase
- 5–9.9% increase
- 0–4.9% increase
- 0–4.9% decrease

Source 4 | Job changes 1981–96

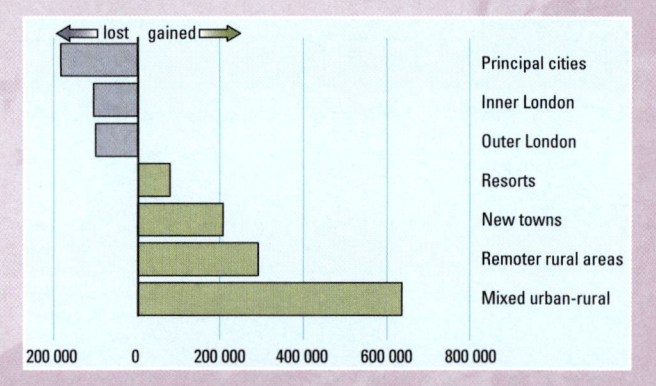

lost ← → gained
- Principal cities
- Inner London
- Outer London
- Resorts
- New towns
- Remoter rural areas
- Mixed urban-rural

The map in Source 3 gives more detail about population changes for southern England because it is based upon county statistics. This map highlights more clearly the way in which Greater London has lost population, while counties to the north and west of London have grown the most. This change in population can be explained by the process of **urban to rural migration**. The push and pull factors for this were given in Source 4 on page 111.

Many jobs have moved to the country (Source 4). Planners have also played their part in encouraging this movement. There are restrictions upon building new houses in the Green Belt which surrounds London. New towns, located outside London, were selected as growth points. Much of the population increase in Buckinghamshire is concentrated in the 'new town' of Milton Keynes.

Internal migration 6.7
Brazil

Although patterns of movement in a country are always complex, two main migrations are dominant in Brazil (Source 1).

The main migration is from north to south. People living in the largely rural North-East and North of Brazil are much poorer than those in the South-East and South. The index of human poverty is highest in the North-East at 46 per cent and lowest in the South-East at only 14 per cent (Source 2). Poverty in the North-East has both human and physical causes. Most of the people are landless peasants. The large landowners pay low wages, offer work only at certain times of the year, and drive peasants off any empty land that they try to cultivate. Fewer workers are needed as a result of mechanisation on the farms. At the same time high birth rates are increasing population pressure on the land and the need for essential services to be provided is greater than ever. From time to time the interior of the North-East suffers from catastrophic droughts. When the crops fail, people are driven to the cities and farms in the South-East and South of Brazil in even greater numbers. Job-hungry migrants from the North-East are found everywhere in Brazil where there is a chance of work.

The second movement is westwards, from the well-populated coastal region into the interior with its great empty spaces. Opening up the interior and tapping the wealth of mineral and timber resources of the Centre-West and North has been the dream of the Brazilian government for more than 50 years. The 'great march' westwards began with the creation of Brasilia as the capital in 1960. This was followed by a road building programme which is still continuing. Mining and logging companies moved in first, followed by cattle ranchers. Landless people, many of them from the North-East, followed in the hope of a fresh start. Amazon forest is still being cleared and new mineral finds are still being made. Several million Brazilians already live in the interior and more are moving there.

Source 1 Main directions of migration in Brazil

Key
- Boundaries of regions
- Roads
- Migration N to SE
- Migration from the east in to interior
- Cities

Source 2 Variations in poverty levels within Brazil – the higher the index, the greater the poverty (the index is based upon life expectancy, literacy and access to health care and safe water)

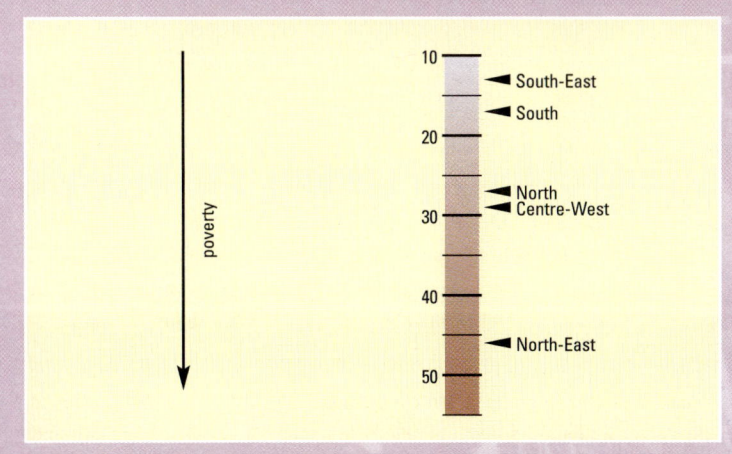

- South-East ~10
- South ~15
- North ~25
- Centre-West ~28
- North-East ~46

6.8 An ageing population
France

Source 1: Age dependency ratios for EU countries

Age dependency ratio		
persons 65 + as percentage of persons aged 15–64	1990	2040
Belgium	21.9	41.5
Denmark	22.2	43.4
France	21.9	39.2
Germany	23.7	47.1
Greece	20.5	41.7
Ireland	18.4	27.2
Italy	20.4	48.4
Luxembourg	20.4	41.2
Netherlands	17.4	48.5
Portugal	16.4	38.9
Spain	17.0	41.7
UK	23.5	39.1
EU	**21.4**	**42.8**

One population prediction that it is safe to make about EU countries is that their populations will grow much older over the next 40 years. Within the EU the number of people aged 65 and over is expected to rise from 50 to 75 million between 1990 and 2040. Also the percentage of persons aged 65 and over will increase relative to those of working age between 15 and 64 (Source 1).

As Source 1 shows, France is close to the EU averages. Further information about France is given in Source 2.

Source 2: France

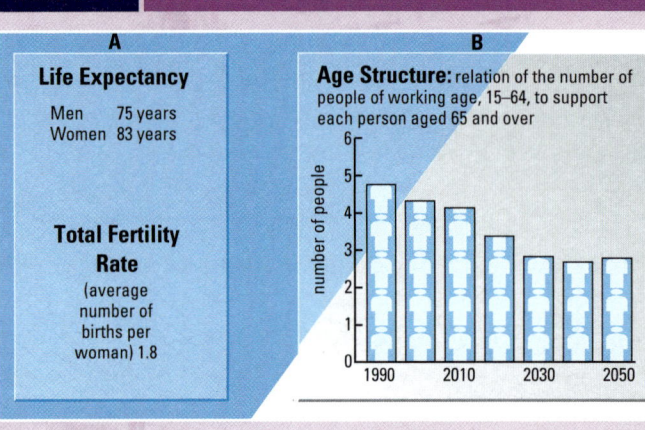

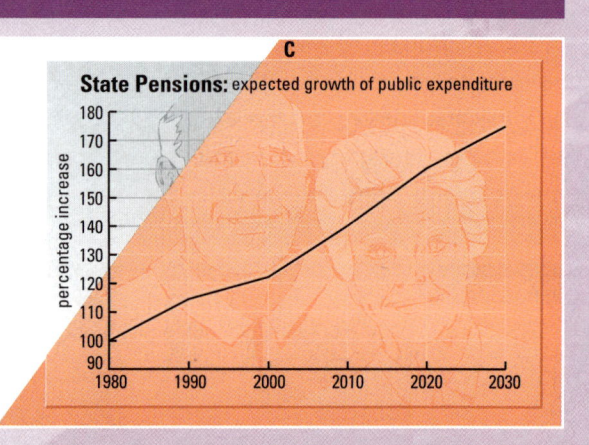

A — Life Expectancy
Men 75 years
Women 83 years

Total Fertility Rate (average number of births per woman) 1.8

B — Age Structure: relation of the number of people of working age, 15–64, to support each person aged 65 and over
(bar chart: number of people, years 1990, 2010, 2030, 2050)

C — State Pensions: expected growth of public expenditure
(line graph: percentage increase, years 1980–2030)

There are two reasons why France's population is ageing (Source 2A).

1. **Life expectancy** is high. People are living longer as medical technology improves.
2. **The fertility rate** is low. To replace the population, the fertility rate needs to be 2.1 births during the lifetime of a woman.

The result is that there are fewer people of working age to support the elderly. In 1990 there were almost five people of working age to support one retired person (Source 2B); by 2040 there will be under three.

A big increase in what the state pays out in pensions is expected (Source 2C). At the same time as fewer people are earning money by working, more people will be drawing a state pension. Those working will need to pay higher taxes to support the great army of over 65s. It is an increasing worry for the French government as to where the money will come from, just as it is for all the EU governments. But it is not all gloom. Parts of the economy will benefit. Surveys in France show that some old people are quite wealthy and keen to spend money on leisure, holidays and health care.

Population policy and population control
China

6.9

There are more people in China than in any other country, at least 1.25 billion out of the total world population of 6 billion. For years Chinese governments showed no concern at having such large numbers of people. Quite the reverse; many governments viewed their huge population as an asset. After all, a country with between one-fifth and one-quarter of the world's population cannot be ignored by other countries, even if by world standards it is quite a poor country.

However, in the 1970s the Chinese government was forced to change its policy because of the speed with which the population was rising. Falling death rates, mainly due to improved medical care, were not matched by falling birth rates. The result was a high rate of natural increase. Measures taken to reduce average family size gradually became stronger until the 'one child per family' policy was introduced in 1979. The government recognised that further population growth could be stopped only by reducing the number of children in most families to no more than one.

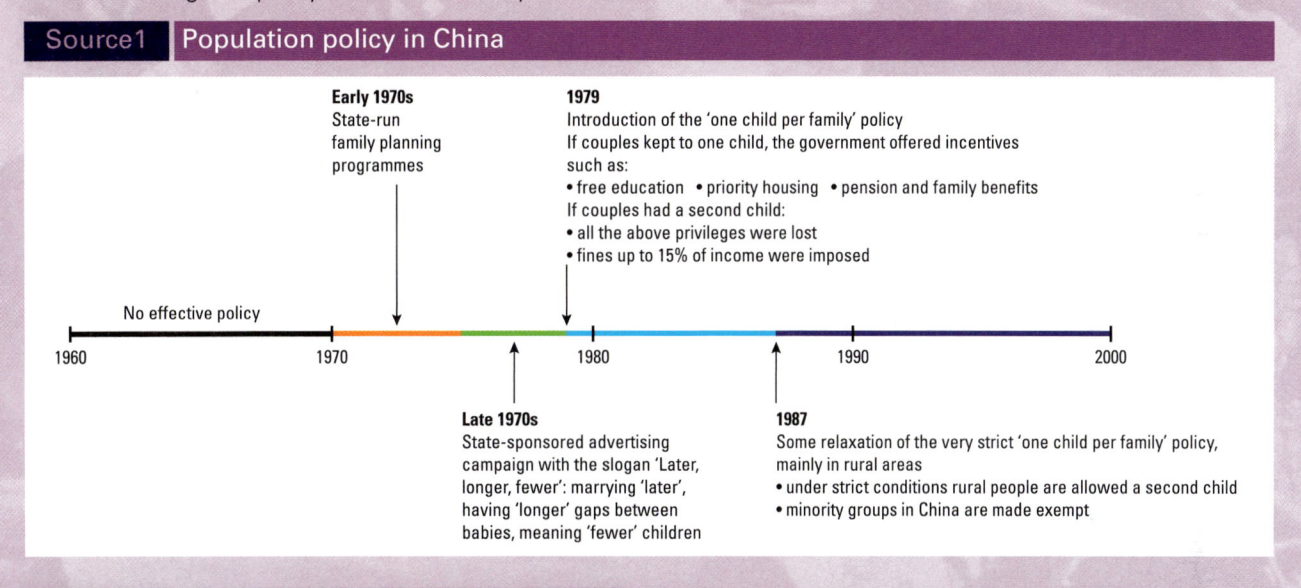

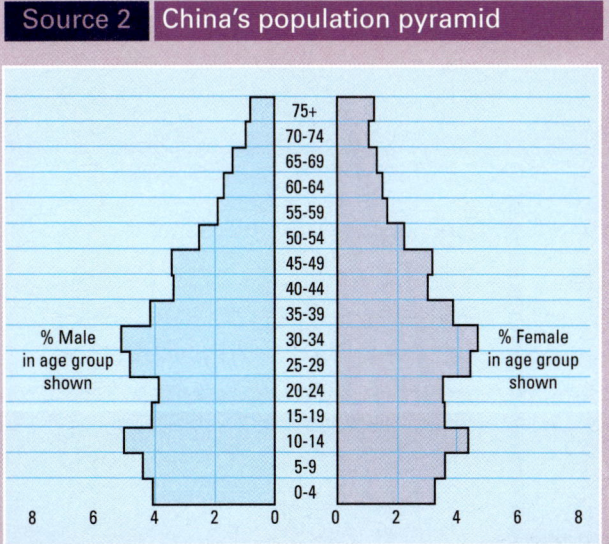

Source 1 Population policy in China

Early 1970s
State-run family planning programmes

1979
Introduction of the 'one child per family' policy
If couples kept to one child, the government offered incentives such as:
• free education • priority housing • pension and family benefits
If couples had a second child:
• all the above privileges were lost
• fines up to 15% of income were imposed

No effective policy
1960 — 1970 — 1980 — 1990 — 2000

Late 1970s
State-sponsored advertising campaign with the slogan 'Later, longer, fewer': marrying 'later', having 'longer' gaps between babies, meaning 'fewer' children

1987
Some relaxation of the very strict 'one child per family' policy, mainly in rural areas
• under strict conditions rural people are allowed a second child
• minority groups in China are made exempt

Source 2 China's population pyramid

% Male in age group shown | % Female in age group shown

Age groups: 0-4, 5-9, 10-14, 15-19, 20-24, 25-29, 30-34, 35-39, 40-44, 45-49, 50-54, 55-59, 60-64, 65-69, 70-74, 75+

8 6 4 2 0   0 2 4 6 8

The 'one child per family' policy is very unpopular with the Chinese people and has had some terrible side effects, such as baby girls being killed in rural areas because families wanted a boy to work on the farm. However, over the last thirty years the birth rate has fallen from 40 to 17 per 1000. The narrowing of China's population pyramid at its base illustrates this (Source 2).

6.10 Population contrasts
the USA and Mexico

It is interesting to compare the population characteristics and movements of countries with different levels of economic development. Here we look at Mexico and the USA. Source 1 examines the basic population data, while Source 2 shows the population structure. Source 3 looks at the economic and social data for each country.

Source 1 — Basic population data

	USA	Mexico
Birth rate (per 1000 per year)	16	28
Death rate (per 1000 per year)	9	6
Rate of natural increase (% per year)	0.7	2.2
Percentage of married women using birth control methods	74	53

Comment
USA – slow population growth; it will take 100 years for the population to double.
Mexico – fast population growth; it will take only 31 years for the population to double.

Source 2 — Population structure: population pyramids for the USA and Mexico

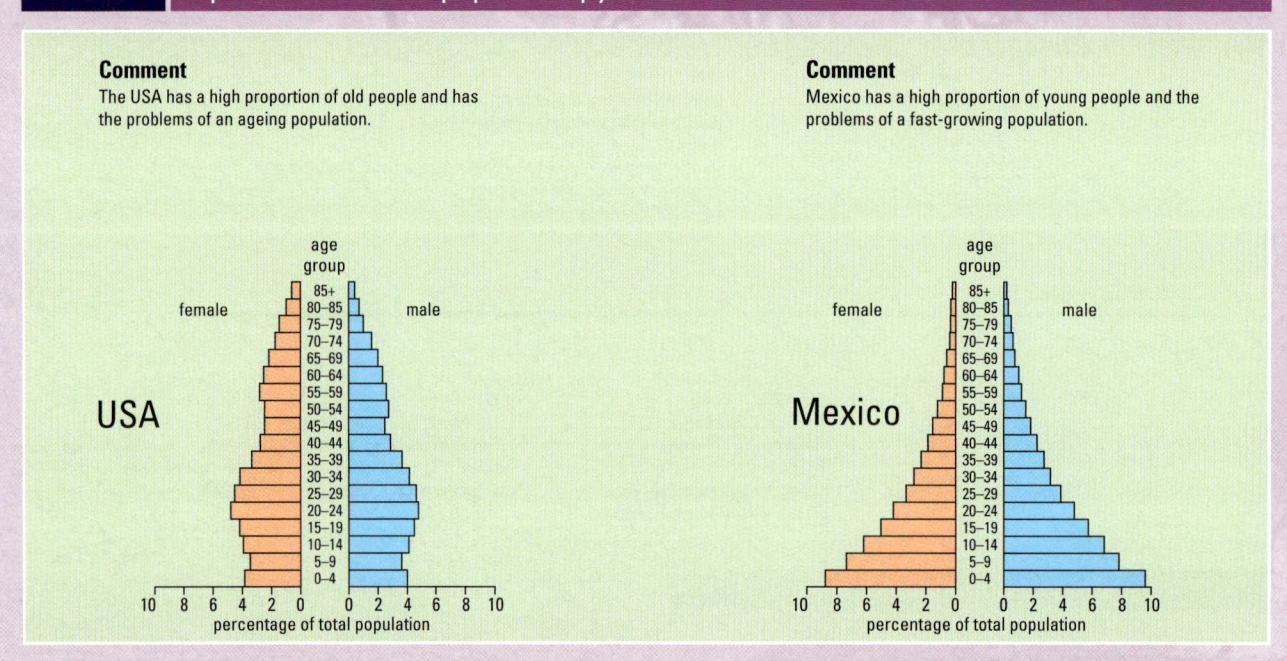

Comment
The USA has a high proportion of old people and has the problems of an ageing population.

Comment
Mexico has a high proportion of young people and the problems of a fast-growing population.

Source 3 — Economic and social data

Non-population data	USA	Mexico
GDP per head (in US$)	23 120	3470
Unemployment rate (%)	8	28
Number of people per doctor	500	2000
Life expectancy at birth	76	70
Infant mortality rate (per 1000)	8	35

Comment
These economic and social statistics confirm how much better developed economically the USA is than Mexico. The differences explain why so many Mexicans migrate to the USA.

Source 4 Present-day migrations in the USA

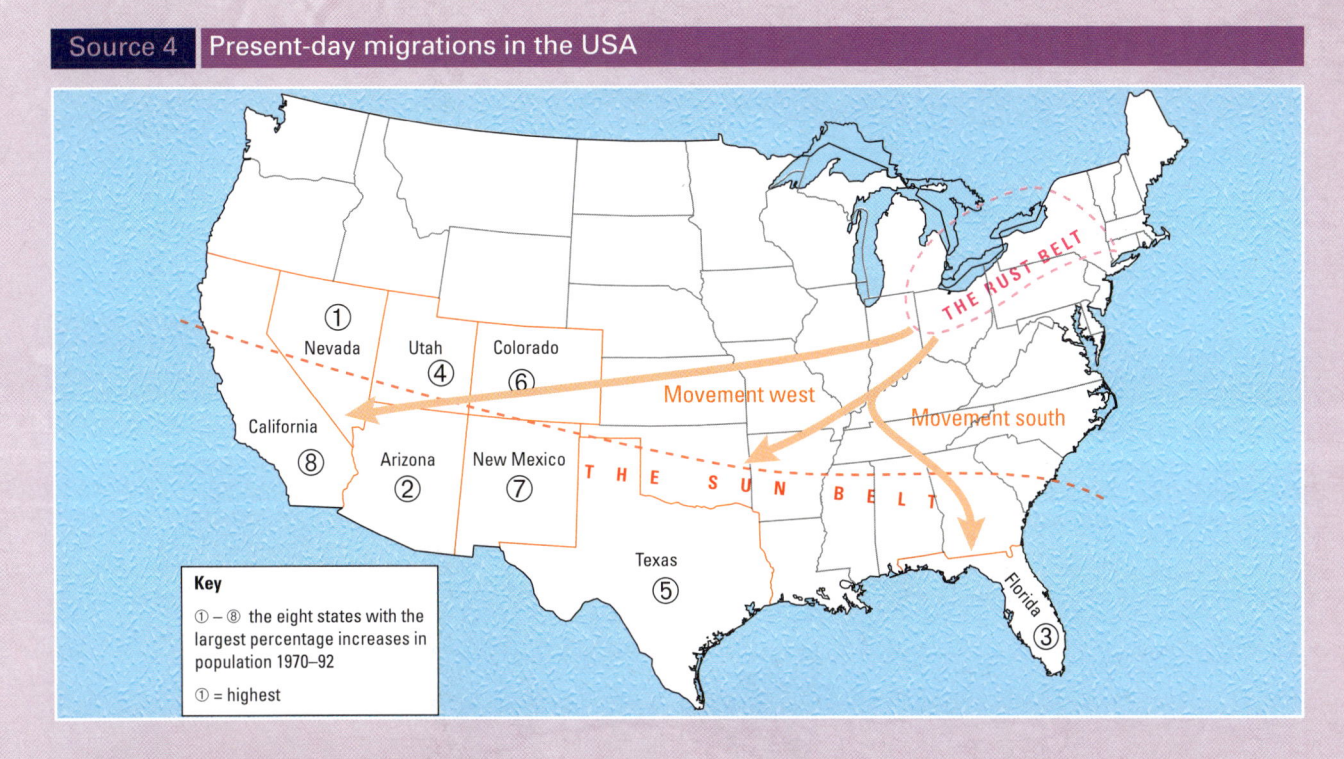

Key
①–⑧ the eight states with the largest percentage increases in population 1970–92
① = highest

(Map labels: Nevada ①, Utah ④, Colorado ⑥, California ⑧, Arizona ②, New Mexico ⑦, Texas ⑤, Florida ③; THE RUST BELT; THE SUN BELT; Movement west; Movement south)

Internal migration in the USA

There are two main migrations flows:
1 **Urban–rural** – out of the big cities and into the small towns and country areas around the cities.
2 **'Rust belt' to 'sun belt'** (Source 4) – the name 'rust belt' conveys the image of old factories being closed down, machinery being allowed to rust in the old steel and engineering works and resulting unemployment. In the 'sun belt' it is warm all year, and a different world in winter to the cold and snowy north-east. Many retired people have been attracted there. So too have high-technology companies, which have increased the number of jobs.

Source 5 On the border

Internal migration in Mexico

One type of migration dominates – rural to urban. All roads lead to Mexico City. It is the capital city. It has the head offices of the main Mexican companies. There are more industries here than in any other city. With a population of around 20 million, it is now ten times larger than the next largest city. This means that no other city can be as attractive for new economic development.

International migration

This is from Mexico to the USA. At least 2 million people, most of them illegal immigrants, are estimated to cross the land border which separates wealth and poverty every year. Most Mexicans in the USA only find unskilled work on farms, in the food processing factories, on the building sites and in the hotels and cafés. By American standards the work is low paid. By Mexican standards it is well paid, which is a good economic reason for Mexicans to carry on trying to beat the border patrols (Source 5).

6.11 Activities

1 a Give the differences between each of the following:
  i distribution and density of population
  ii physical and human factors.
 b Look at the world map (Source 1).

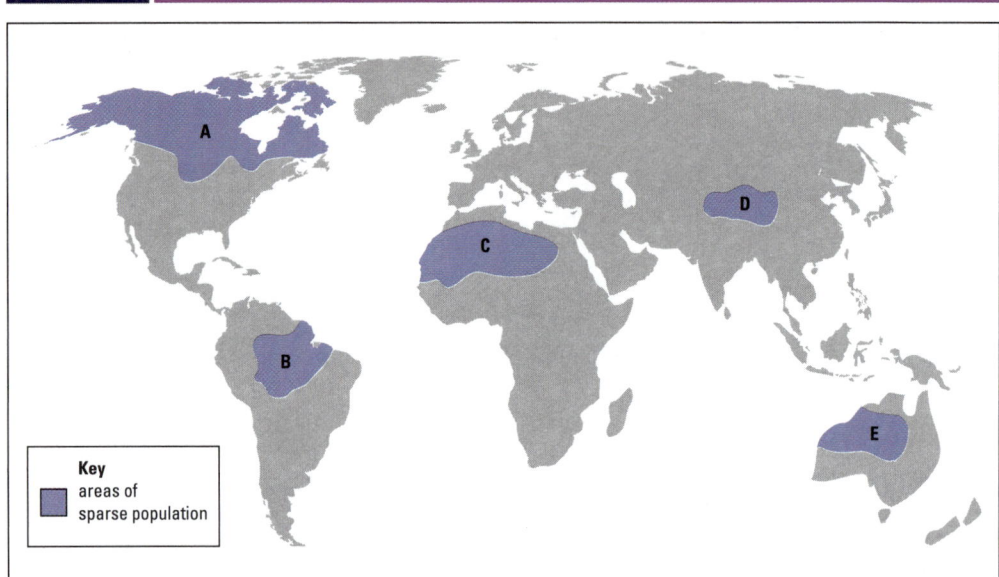

Source 1 World map

Key: areas of sparse population

  i Name the area labelled A.
  ii Describe the factors which help to explain why it is sparsely populated.
  iii Name the areas lettered C and E.
  iv What do they have in common to explain why they are sparsely populated?
  v For either area B or area D, find out the reasons why it is sparsely populated.

2 a Name the continent with:
  i the highest average birth rate
  ii the lowest average birth rate.
 b Suggest reasons for the difference in the size of the birth rate between them.
 c i Explain why death rates have declined everywhere in the world.
  ii How has this decline affected world population change?
 d From Source 2 on page 108 work out the rates of natural increase for Asia and North America. Show your working.
 e Explain why the photograph on page 105 was most likely to have been taken in a LEDC.

3 a Briefly explain the differences between the following types of migration:
  i compulsory and voluntary
  ii international and internal
  iii permanent and temporary.
 b i Name one natural hazard.
  ii Explain how this hazard might cause migration.
 c Illustrating your answers with labelled sketches:
  i give reasons for rural to urban migration in less economically developed countries
  ii explain why urban to rural migration is of greater importance in the more economically developed countries.

4 a State what is meant by each of the following; population structure; population pyramid; dependant; dependency ratio; ageing population.
 b i Draw a flow diagram to show how increases in population can lead to environmental damage.
  ii Explain what your diagram shows.

5 a i From the climate graphs in Source 2 on page 115, compare the climates of Stornoway and Cambridge using the following headings: Summer temperature; Winter temperature; Amount of precipitation.
  ii Give reasons why the climate of Cambridge has resulted in a higher density of population.
 b i From Source 1 on page 114, describe the distribution of areas with high densities of population.
  ii Choose one area of high density and explain why high densities are found there.

6 a i Give the reasons for urban to rural migration in the UK.
  ii Why is rural to urban migration more important in Brazil?
 b 'The main direction of internal migration in both the UK and Brazil is from north to south, but the reasons for the two migrations are very different.' Explain this statement.

7 a i State three different ways by which Chinese governments have attempted to limit population growth.
  ii The ways used have changed over time. Why?
  iii Describe and suggest reasons for the shape of the population pyramid of China shown in Source 2 on page 119.
 b i France has an ageing population. Outline two causes and two consequences of this.
  ii 'The "problem" of an ageing population is shared by all the other countries of the EU, but it is more of a problem in some countries than others.' Give the evidence from Source 1 on page 118 to support this statement.

8 Suggest reasons for the differences between the USA and Mexico using the following headings: Birth rates, Population increase, Population structure.

6.12 Sample examination questions

1 a i Draw a population pyramid for Nigeria using the following values:

Age group	Male (%)	Female (%)	Age group	Male (%)	Female (%)
0–9	14.6	14.2	40–49	3.6	3.6
10–19	12.6	12.4	50–59	1.7	1.7
20–29	10.7	10.5	60–69	0.8	0.8
30–39	5.6	5.4	70+	0.9	0.9

(4 marks)

ii State the characteristics of the pyramid which show that Nigeria is a LEDC.

(2 marks)

b i Draw a pictogram to show the total population of Nigeria for the four years given below.

Year	Estimated total population (millions)
1940	20
1960	45
1980	75
2000	120

(2 marks)

ii Describe the evidence for the lack of an effective population policy in Nigeria.

(2 marks)

(Total: 10 marks)

2 a Source 1 shows the population structure for Australia.

Source 1 Australia: population structure

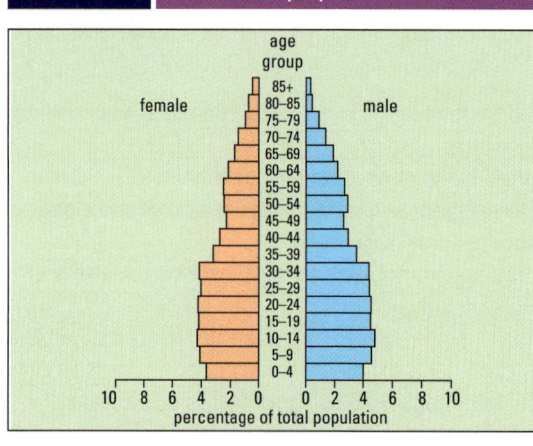

i From Source 1 state the percentage of the total population aged 0–4. (1 mark)

ii Describe two features of the pyramid which suggest that Australia is a MEDC. (4 marks)

b Outline the problems caused by ageing populations in MEDCs. (5 marks)

(Total: 10 marks)

3 a Look at the photograph in Source 2. Draw a labelled sketch to show the populated and non-populated areas on the photograph. (4 marks)

Source 2 Otz valley in Austria

b Choose one area of the world with a high density of population and one area with a low density. Give reasons for the differences in density of population between them. (6 marks)

(Total: 10 marks)

UNIT 7

Settlement

Unit Contents

- The nature and growth of settlements
- Patterns of land use
- Changing cities
- Changes around the city
- World urbanisation
- Urban growth in a MEDC: London and the South-East of England
- Out-of-town shopping centres: the United Kingdom
- An out-of-town shopping centre: the MetroCentre, Gateshead
- Urban growth in a LEDC: São Paulo
- Urban transect: Manchester
- Urban problems: LEDCs
- Shanty town improvement: Lima, Peru

Chicago, the home of the skyscraper. Which characteristics of a CBD are shown?

7.1 The nature and growth of settlements

A **settlement** is a place where people live and work. Settlements may be classified using different factors (Sources 1 and 2). When settlements are put into order of size and importance, a **hierarchy** of settlements is produced.

Source 1 — Classification of settlements

A Rural or urban	B Size	C Function	D Area served
capital city (URBAN)	above 2 million	Government, HQs of companies, big shops, finance, tourists	whole country
conurbation	500 000 – 2 million	industry, offices, shops	large area around it
regional centre	150 000 – 500 000	HQs of local companies, shops, offices, industry	its own region
industrial town	25 000 – 150 000	industry, shops	local area around it
market town (small town)	2 500 – 25 000	shops and local services	small local area
village (RURAL)	100 – 2 500	basic services e.g. pub, church, shop	only the farms outside the village
hamlet	10 – 100	no services	no services
isolated farm	less than 10 people	no services	no services

Settlements which are small and in the middle of countryside are **rural**. Those which are large and provide services for the areas around them are **urban**. The market town, which serves the rural area around it, is the smallest urban settlement.

There are thousands of small settlements in the United Kingdom such as farms, hamlets and villages, but there is only one capital city (Source 2). This is why Source 1 has the shape of a pyramid.

This is the purpose of a settlement – why it is there and what job it does. All settlements are places for people to live, but most settlements have other functions. The larger the settlement, the greater the number and the variety of its functions.

The area served by a settlement is called its **sphere of influence**. London's sphere of influence is the whole country. It has some functions, such as Government, which are not found in any other city. Outside London there are regional centres such as Norwich serving East Anglia and Plymouth serving South-West England.

Source 2 — The range of settlements in the UK – a farm in Upper Teesdale, and London

Location and change

The **site** of a settlement includes the features of its specific location. The **situation** of a settlement is its location in relation to its surrounding area. Settlements were originally located with great care (Source 3). The factors taken into consideration for selecting a settlement site in the UK included:

- water supply – access to a reliable source of fresh water, a wet point site
- drainage – freedom from flooding, a dry point site
- aspect – facing south for sun and warmth
- shelter – protected from cold or strong winds by high ground
- resources – next to good farmland or a mineral source such as coal
- special features – such as an easy bridging point across a river or a steep hill for defence.

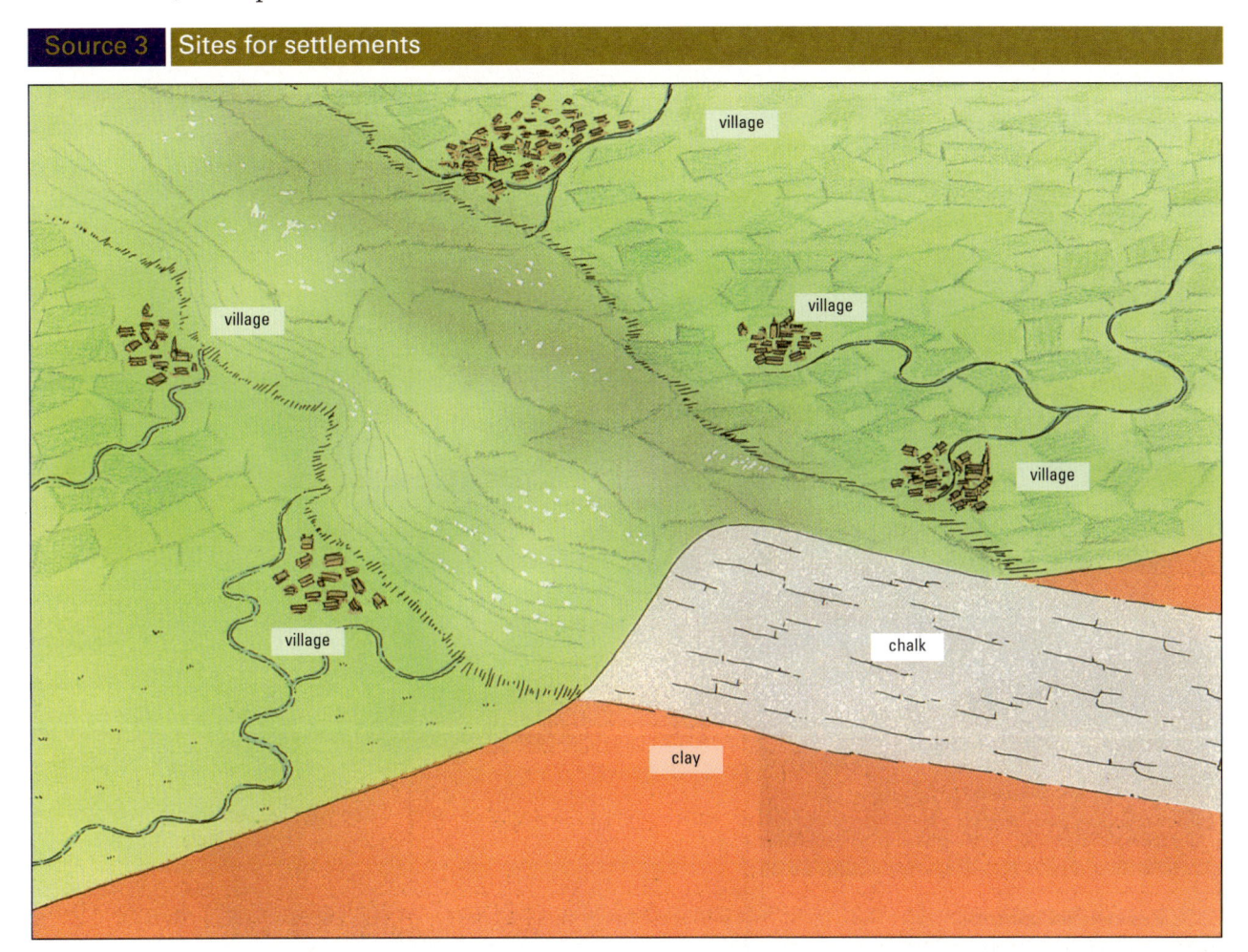

Source 3 | **Sites for settlements**

Many settlements have changed through time. Those with a favourable situation are likely to have grown and changed their function. For example, some villages favourably situated near the meeting point of roads grew to become market towns. Others situated next to coalfields became mining villages or even grew into industrial towns. Those settlements that have stayed as small villages may also have changed their function. No longer are the majority of people living in villages in the UK directly connected with farming. They are more likely to be **commuters**. This change in function from farming to commuting village may bring new problems and conflicts. Some villages in the UK have declined in population, notably those affected by closure of the coal mines.

7.2 Patterns of land use

Urban land uses include shops, offices, factories, transport, recreation and waste land. However, the land use which covers the largest amount of land is housing. The term **morphology** is used to describe the layout of an urban area and the way in which the land uses are arranged within it. In most British cities it is possible to recognise three **urban zones** based upon location and land uses (Source 1).

Source 1 Urban zones in British towns

Urban zone	Location and appearance	Land use characteristics
CBD (Central Business District)	• city centre • tall buildings including skyscrapers containing offices • high building density with little open space	• old buildings, e.g. cathedral, castle • many shops of different types including department stores • company offices, banks and building societies • places of entertainment such as theatres and night clubs
Inner city (also known as the twilight zone or the zone of transition)	• around the edge of the city centre • unattractive, run-down appearance with many old buildings, made worse by vandalism and graffiti	• factories and warehouses • residential – often terraced houses and high-rise flats • universities and hospitals • inner ring roads • small shopping centres selling everyday convenience goods
Residential suburbs	• all the outer areas up to the edge of the built-up area • generally smarter appearance in the outer suburbs • some areas of open space	• residential – with the houses increasing in size, becoming more recent, changing from terraced to semi-detached and detached towards the outskirts • small shopping centres selling everyday convenience goods

Urban models

Various **urban models** have been devised to show the general arrangement of land use zones in cities (Source 2).

The Burgess model (Model 1) shows a circular pattern of land uses around the CBD. This model uses five zones because the inner city and residential suburbs have each been subdivided into two. The Hoyt model (Model 2) uses the circles of the Burgess model as its base but then adds sectors to show that similar land uses are concentrated in certain parts of the urban area. For example, factories may be concentrated in one area to form a zone of industry. A sector containing many high-priced houses may follow the line of a main road resulting in the formation of a high-class residential area for the wealthy. The Burgess and Hoyt models had to be adapted to show the general land use patterns in cities in the less economically developed countries. Model 3 includes the inner city slums and shanty towns which house many people.

There are three explanations for these land use patterns.

1 Historical
The urban area expanded outwards from the original site which is where the city centre is found today.

2 Economic
Rents and rates in the CBD became too expensive for people. In the suburbs there was more land and it was cheaper. Only businesses could afford to stay in the CBD, but even they needed to make the most of expensive land by building upwards.

3 Concentrations of similar land uses
One part of the urban area may have all the advantages for industrial location so that a lot of factories want to locate there; but few people want to live next door to a factory, so the residential areas are located elsewhere. Planners also prefer this **segregation of land uses** into definite zones.

Source 2: Urban models for land use patterns

Model 1 (Burgess)

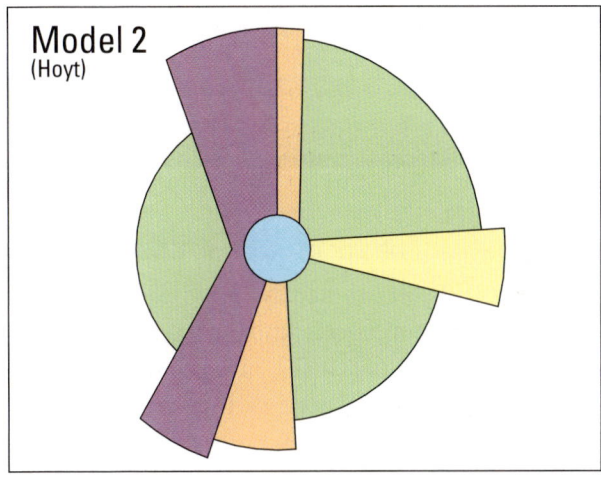

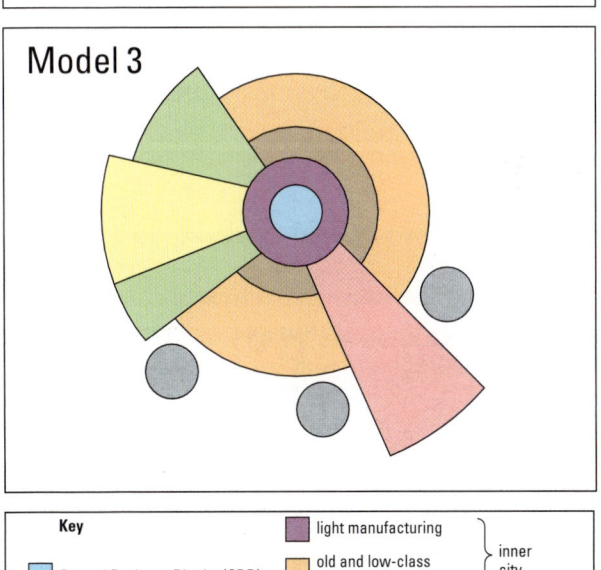

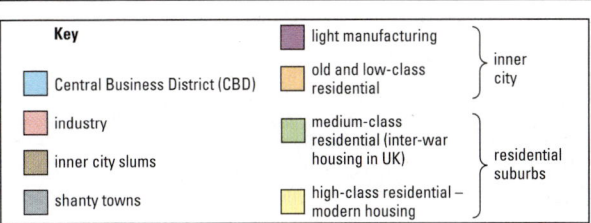

Model 2 (Hoyt)

Model 3

Key
- Central Business District (CBD)
- industry
- inner city slums
- shanty towns
- light manufacturing } inner city
- old and low-class residential } inner city
- medium-class residential (inter-war housing in UK) } residential suburbs
- high-class residential – modern housing } residential suburbs

7.3 Changing cities

Cities are dynamic places which are constantly changing. Some areas within them are growing or expanding. Others may be losing population.

Source 1 Changes in the city centre and the reasons for them

Change	Reason for change
skyscraper office blocks	shortage and high price of land
inner ring roads	traffic congestion
one-way streets	traffic congestion
improvements in public transport: bus lanes trams	too much use of the car for travelling to work and for shopping, parking problems
metro links between buses and cars park and ride schemes	air pollution: photochemical smog and low-level ozone
shopping streets pedestrianised indoor shopping centres	conflicts between shoppers and motorists

In the CBD

Visit the centre of any British city after a gap of a few years and you can hardly recognise it. Familiar old buildings have been knocked down to make room for skyscraper office developments. Main shopping streets have been pedestrianised. Indoor shopping centres have been built. Multi-storey car parks have been provided as part of city centre redevelopment schemes. New one-way street systems have changed traffic flows through the centre. You should be able to notice some of these changes in the city centre nearest to your home. What all these changes are designed to do is to overcome city centre problems (Source 1). There is more urgency than ever to improve city centres because many of the functions of the traditional city centre are being threatened by out-of-town developments for shopping and business (see page 133).

Source 2 The environment can be grim in the inner city

In the inner city

Many inner city areas are depressing places in which change has usually meant decline and decay (Source 2). City authorities and businesses have invested in the CBD. Much less has been spent in the inner city and here the environment is a growing problem. Large areas of waste land have become dumping grounds. Big factories are derelict monuments of the Industrial Revolution. Terraced houses, built for the better-off people in Victorian times, are now derelict and boarded up. Empty buildings are favourite targets for vandals and paint sprayers.

Settlement

Economic decline follows. Those who could afford it have moved out, leaving behind the unemployed and the unskilled on low wages. Crime rates are high. The social character of the area has changed. Concentrations of people from the ethnic minorities are found in many inner cities. The numbers of pensioners, one-parent families and students are also above average.

You may find it hard to believe that in the 1960s planners believed that moving residents into high-rise blocks of flats was the solution to the problem of slum housing. The people who were forced to live in these flats had very different views (Source 3)!

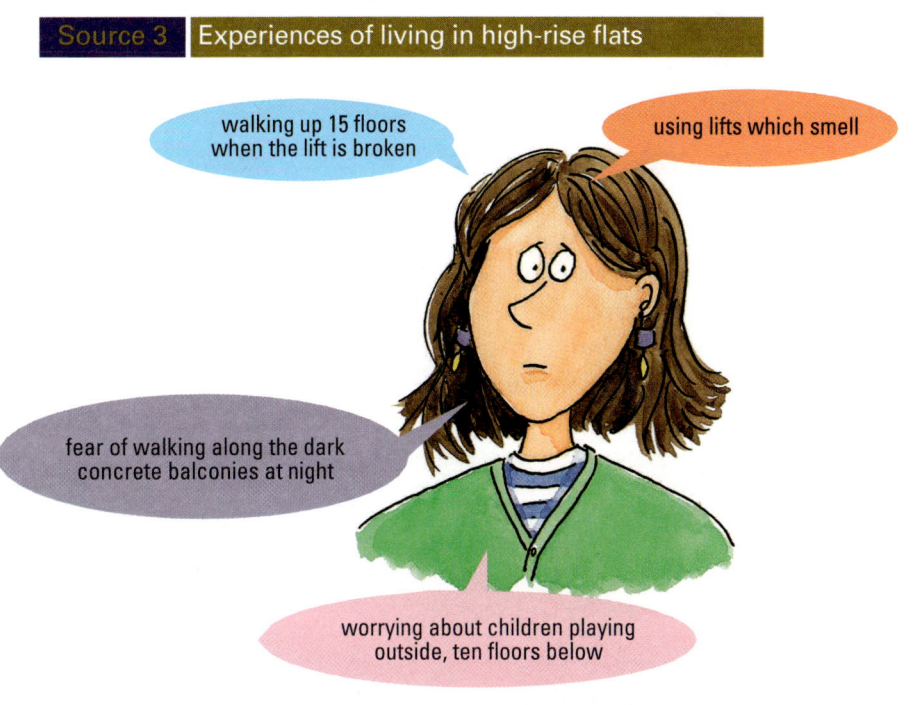

Source 3 Experiences of living in high-rise flats

- walking up 15 floors when the lift is broken
- using lifts which smell
- fear of walking along the dark concrete balconies at night
- worrying about children playing outside, ten floors below

Source 4 Salford Quays

There are many schemes for inner city renewal, such as the City Challenge in which local authorities work with other local interest groups, supported by government money, to build new houses and community facilities. The Enterprise Zone idea was used to attract investment into redevelopment of the Docklands in the East End of London. The old Manchester Dock basins were landscaped and luxury houses were built around them. Now their name is Salford Quays (Source 4). Improving housing in inner city areas to make it more attractive to richer people is called **gentrification**. The problem with this and with all the other schemes is that only a tiny proportion of inner city residents feel any benefits.

7.4 Changes around the city

The rural-urban fringe

The area around the edge of a city is known as the **rural-urban fringe**. It is where the green fields and open spaces of the countryside meet the continuously built-up areas of the city. Countryside has been lost by the continued outward growth of cities and their suburbs. The open land around the edge of a city is in great demand for housing, industry, shopping, recreation and the needs of the public utilities, such as reservoirs and sewerage works.

One reason for growth and change in the rural-urban fringe is a feeling of dissatisfaction with the city.

- Houses are close together with few open spaces.
- Air quality is poor.
- Companies find that there is a shortage of land for building new offices and factories.

These are all **push factors**. There are also **pull factors** on the city edge.

- Land is cheaper so houses are larger.
- Factories can be more spacious and have plenty of room for workers to park their cars.
- Closeness to the main roads and motorways allows for quicker and easier customer contacts.
- New developments on the outskirts of the city are favoured by the greater personal mobility allowed by the car.

Not everyone is happy with the continued loss of countryside around the cities. Many environmentalists are very concerned. There are often conflicts of interest, such as between farmers and developers (Source 1). People who have spent all their lives in villages resent the changes which they are faced with as villages grow into commuter settlements (Source 2).

Source 1 Conflicts of interest between farmers and developers

- People from the town trample on my crops.
- I have lost half of my farmland to builders.
- My farm is split into two parts by the motorway.
- The public want to shop in out of town centres where parking is free and easy.
- Businesses can make more profit if they are next to motorways.

Source 2 Changes in a village as it becomes a commuter settlement

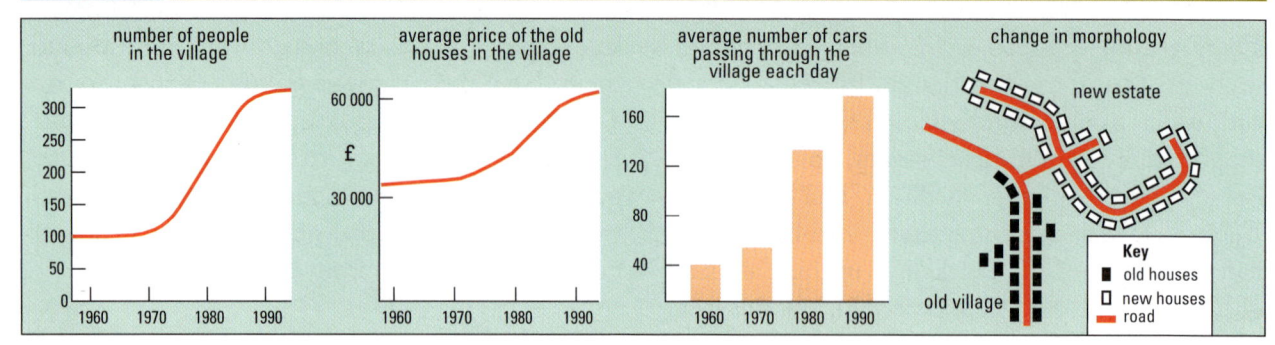

Retailing

In the more economically developed countries there has been a great increase in **out-of-town retailing**, with large purpose-built **superstores** and shopping centres located in the rural-urban fringe. The number of superstores has increased dramatically in the United Kingdom since 1980 (Source 3). It is easy to understand why. More people own their own cars. The large car parks are free. Access is easy because the shopping centres are located next to main roads and motorway junctions. In contrast, city centre shoppers face traffic congestion and expensive parking. Also the larger centres have shopping malls which are bright and modern with everything under one roof. Other facilities, such as multi-screen cinemas or bowling alleys, are often included within the shopping centre, or are located close by, so that there is something there for all the family (Source 4).

Source 3 Supermarket sweep

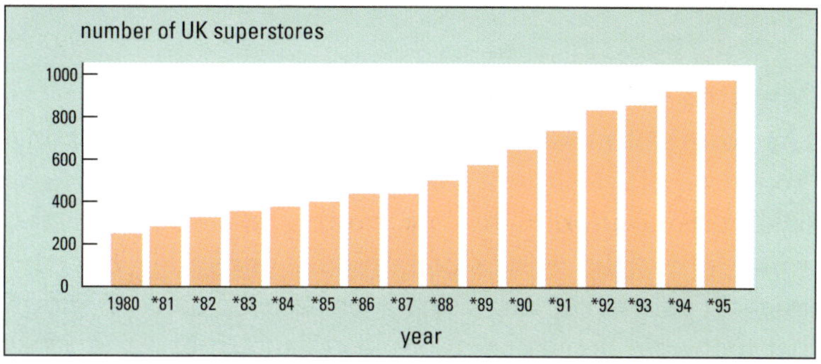
number of UK superstores
1000
800
600
400
200
0
1980 *81 *82 *83 *84 *85 *86 *87 *88 *89 *90 *91 *92 *93 *94 *95
year

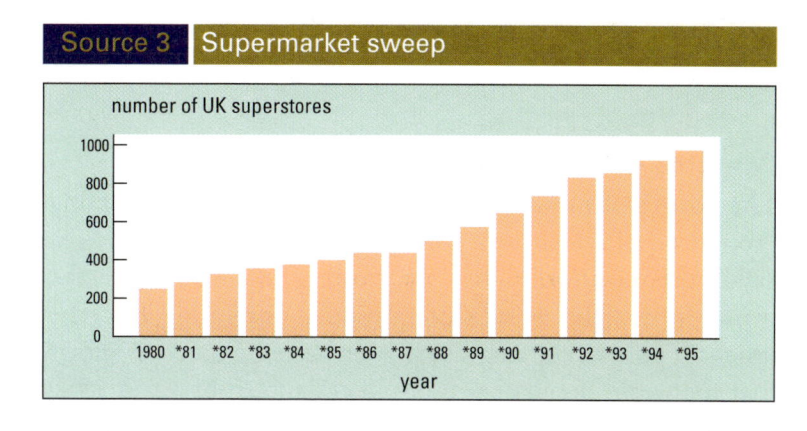

Source 4 Out-of-town shopping centre near Durham

KWIK SAVE
FOODSTORE
HALFORDS
SALE

Source 5 Shopping hierarchy

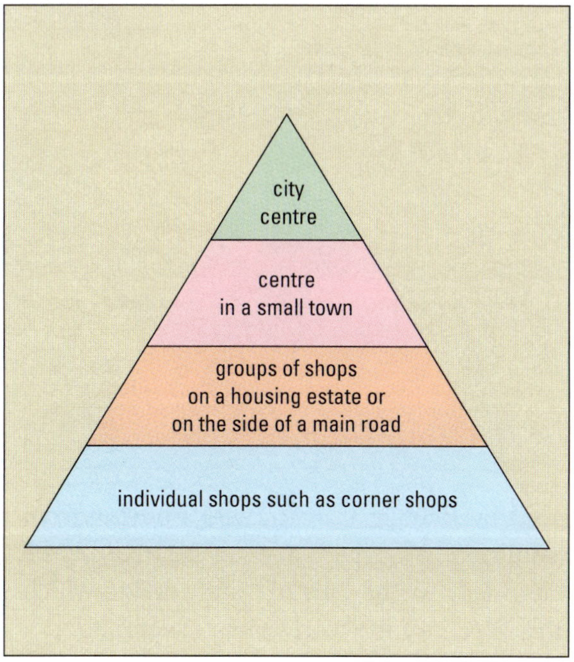
city centre
centre in a small town
groups of shops on a housing estate or on the side of a main road
individual shops such as corner shops

Out-of-town shopping centres do not fit the traditional **hierarchy** of shopping centres found in the UK (Source 5). At the bottom of the hierarchy is the corner shop, where everyday goods, such as milk, newspapers and sweets, known as **convenience goods**, are bought. These are **low-order goods**, used often, for which most people are prepared to travel only a short distance.

At the top of the hierarchy is the city centre. This is where people go to buy clothes or to have a look around department stores. Many of the goods sold in department stores, such as clothes, electrical items and furniture, are **comparison goods**. People buy these less often and are willing to travel further to buy them. The department store has a high **threshold**. A large number of people must shop there for the store to be profitable. It has a large **sphere of influence:** people travel from some distance away to shop there, helped by the fact that the city centre is the focus for the main roads and most bus and rail services.

7.5 World urbanisation

Features of urbanisation

The growth of towns and cities which leads to an increasing proportion of a country's population living in urban areas is called **urbanisation**. Cities are growing in size all over the world. While the world's population is increasing fast, the urban population is increasing even faster. Source 1 shows that the world population more than doubled between 1950 and 2000 but that the urban population more than trebled.

What is significant about present-day rates of urbanisation is the difference in the speed of growth between the cities in the more economically developed countries and those in the less economically developed countries. The rate of city growth is much higher in the LEDCs (Source 2) so that the number of urban dwellers is now greater than in the MEDCs. Present trends are expected to continue.

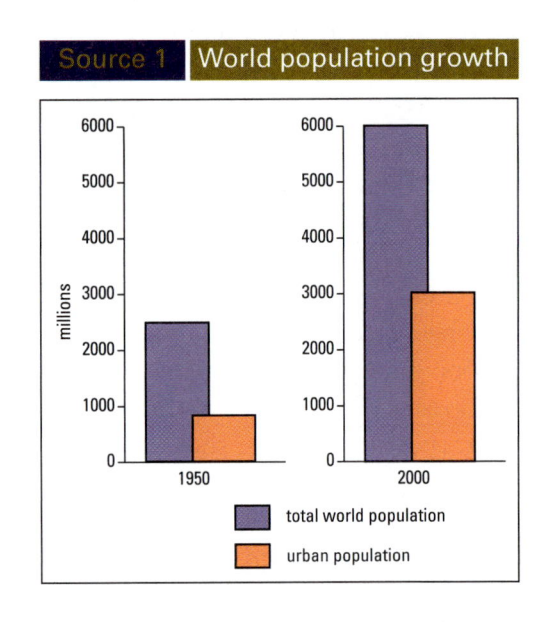

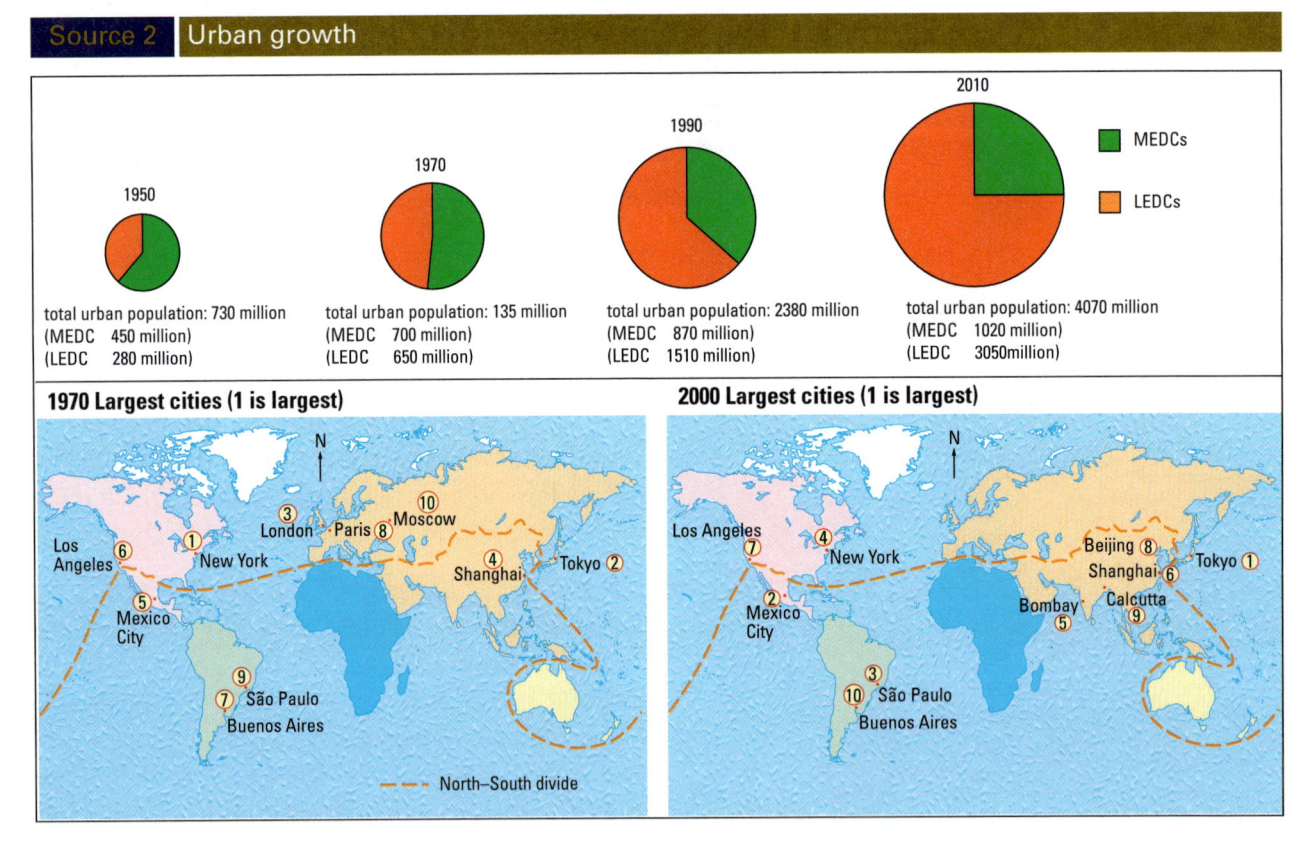

Source 1 — World population growth

Source 2 — Urban growth

1950 — total urban population: 730 million (MEDC 450 million) (LEDC 280 million)

1970 — total urban population: 135 million (MEDC 700 million) (LEDC 650 million)

1990 — total urban population: 2380 million (MEDC 870 million) (LEDC 1510 million)

2010 — total urban population: 4070 million (MEDC 1020 million) (LEDC 3050 million)

1970 Largest cities (1 is largest): Los Angeles (6), New York (1), London (3), Paris (8), Moscow (10), Shanghai (4), Tokyo (2), Mexico City (5), São Paulo (7), Buenos Aires (9)

2000 Largest cities (1 is largest): Los Angeles (4), New York (7), Beijing (8), Shanghai (6), Tokyo (1), Bombay (5), Calcutta (9), Mexico City (2), São Paulo (3), Buenos Aires (10)

– – – North–South divide

This means that the distribution of the world's big cities is changing. Source 2 shows the world's top ten cities by size for 1970 and 2000. Three have dropped out of the top ten – London, Paris and Moscow. All are in Europe. They have been replaced by Beijing, Calcutta and Bombay from the continent of Asia. They are located on the southern side of the North–South divide which roughly separates the world into rich and poor.

Settlement

The size of big cities is another feature of world urbanisation. For many years the **millionaire city** (a city of more than one million people) was considered a big city, especially since in 1900 there were only two – London and Paris. Now there are about 400 (Source 3).

Each of the top ten cities now has more than ten million people. The use of the term 'mega city' may be more appropriate. Mexico City is the world's second biggest city with a population of up to 20 million (Source 4). This one city has more people living in it than live in many of the countries of Central and South America!

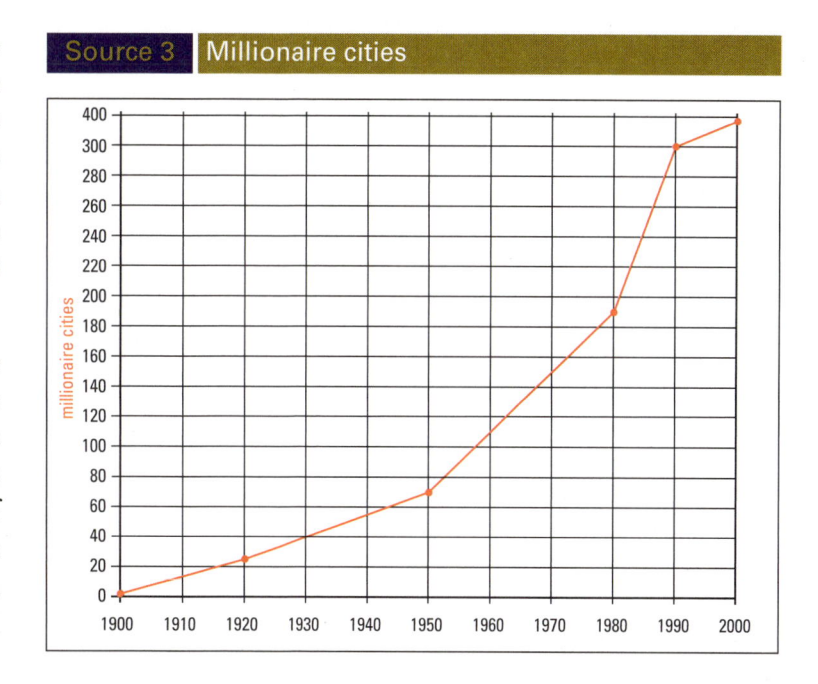

Source 3 Millionaire cities

Source 4 Mexico City, the largest city in a LEDC

Causes of urbanisation

Urban growth has always been associated with economic development. As a country increases in wealth, fewer people work in primary activities such as farming and forestry in the rural areas. Increasing numbers of people now work in secondary (manufacturing) and tertiary (service) occupations, which are overwhelmingly concentrated in urban areas.

High rates of urbanisation in LEDCs occur because:

- most new economic developments are concentrated in the big cities
- push and pull factors lead to high rates of rural to urban migration
- cities experience high rates of natural increase of population.

7.6 Urban growth in a MEDC
London and the South-East of England

Countryside in Britain has been lost to urban areas at an alarming rate since the 1930s. The outward growth of London has been on a different scale to that of other cities within the United Kingdom. As long ago as the late 1940s planners realised that something needed to be done to stop the continued growth of London. Two measures were tried (Source 1):

- declaring a **green belt** around London, within which most types of new development were forbidden.
- building **new towns** beyond the green belt.

As the slum properties in the inner city regions were cleared, people had to be rehoused somewhere. Eight new towns (named on Source 1) were originally planned as growth points with houses, shops, offices and factories. They were located far enough from London to stop the continuous **urban sprawl.** The intention was to make them as self-contained as possible, with their own places of work, to discourage residents from commuting into London. Milton Keynes is an example of a later and larger new town which has attracted people and companies.

Planning policies change over time. In recent years attempts have been made to renovate and to redevelop some of the inner city areas within London to make them more attractive places in which to live and work. This helps to reduce the pressure for growth around the edge of Greater London. Although the Docklands development in the East End is the largest example of this, in other inner city areas houses are being improved to increase their attractiveness as residential neighbourhoods (Source 2). Examples are Islington and Notting Hill, which have seen large increases in house prices. This is another example of the process of gentrification referred to on page 131.

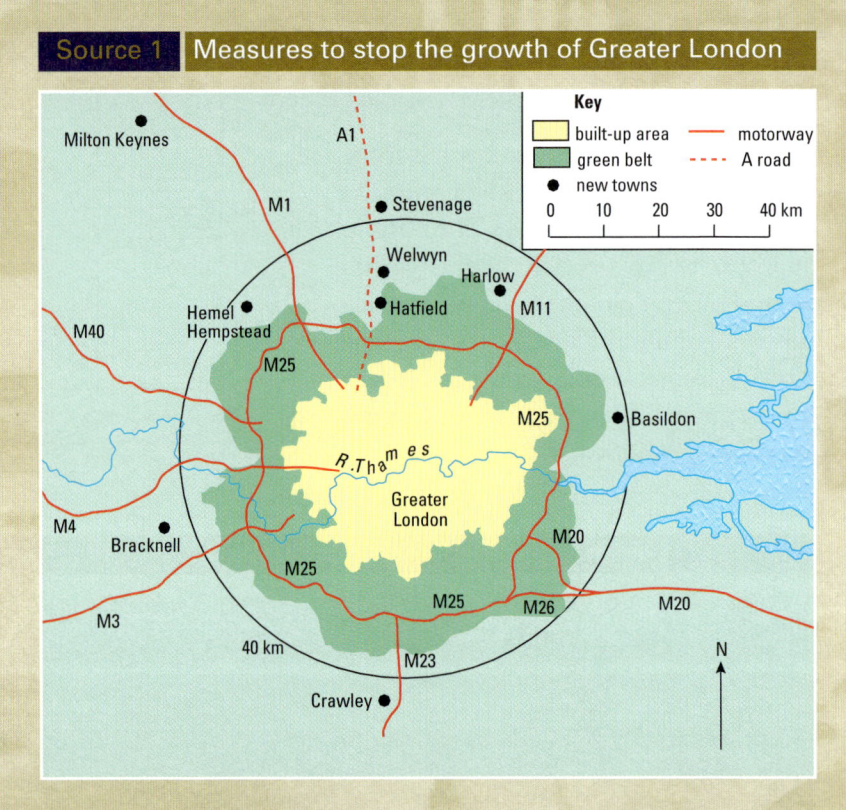

Source 1 Measures to stop the growth of Greater London

Source 2 Improved housing in London

The pressures for urban growth in London and South-East England have not gone away. Their causes are summarised in the flow chart in Source 3. Migration from north to south continues because there are more jobs with better rates of pay in London and the South-

Settlement

East. Growing companies in the profitable financial, high-tech and research sectors are often only willing to consider locations in this part of the UK. More space is needed for houses, offices and roads.

A report from government appointed inspectors was published in October 1999, which suggested that another 1.1 million homes will have to be built in the region by 2016 if growth needs are to be satisfied. It put forward four major areas for urban growth (Source 4).

Source 3 | Why more space for building is needed in London and the South-East

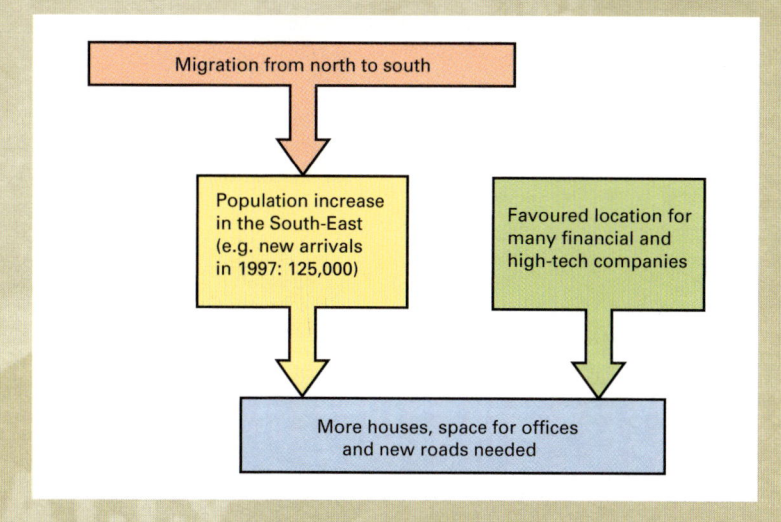

Migration from north to south → Population increase in the South-East (e.g. new arrivals in 1997: 125,000)

Favoured location for many financial and high-tech companies

→ More houses, space for offices and new roads needed

Source 4 | Proposed major growth areas

- Near Milton Keynes in Buckinghamshire – further growth of this
- Near Stansted in Essex – a new town on a greenfield site
- At Crawley in West Sussex – major expansion of this previous
- At Ashford in Kent – population growth

key: proposed major growth areas

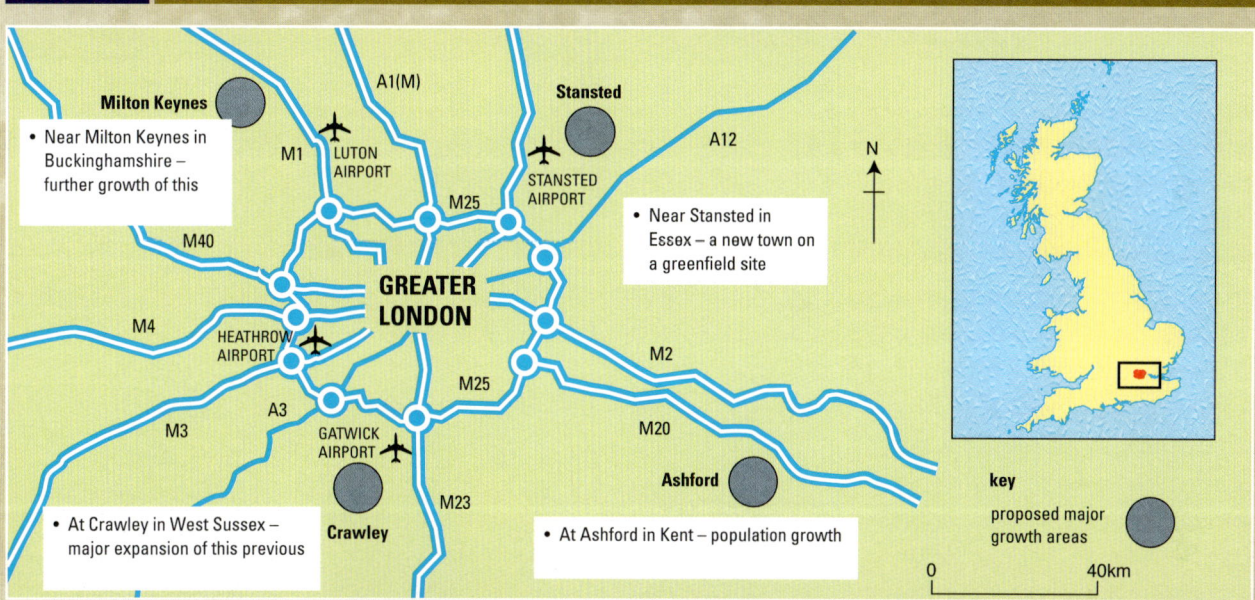

This report created an immediate reaction with hostile comments from local politicians both in the South-East and elsewhere in the UK (Source 5). However, it is highly likely that some growth will go ahead, even if it is not as much as the report suggested was needed.

Source 5 | Comments from the South-East

'You would be destroying the most beautiful part of Essex.'
'99% of people living here would oppose the scheme.'
'Great areas of countryside would be swallowed up.'
'The already great pressures on roads, schools and hospitals would increase.'
'More concrete jungles.'

Comments from other parts of the UK

'This would stop new investment in the North of England.'
'The North–South divide would increase.'
'Encouraging more people and companies into the South-East is just not sustainable.'

7.7 Out-of-town shopping centres
the United Kingdom

Although out-of-town supermarkets, superstores and small shopping centres are to be found around the edges of most large towns and cities in the UK, the big out-of-town centres are more narrowly distributed (Source 1). They are located close to very large centres of population, where there is good access, normally by motorway. The South-East of England is different in that there are two large centres close together, although they are situated on different sides of the River Thames. The presence of two reflects the size and wealth of the consumer market in London and the surrounding areas.

The success of out-of-town shopping centres has exceeded expectations. They are very popular with shoppers. Many are seeking planning permission to expand. Not everyone is in favour. Large out-of-town shopping centres are definitely not popular with local councils and high street shopkeepers from nearby towns, where shops close and 'For Sale' signs go up everywhere. The appearance of the high street deteriorates. Even fewer people want to go there. Council income from business rates goes down. A spiral of decline occurs. This happened in Dudley after Merry Hill opened. It only takes a few big names to abandon a town centre, such as Marks and Spencer and Sainsbury's, and many others follow. There are no longer sufficient shoppers for the larger shops to make a profit. Planners and environmental groups do not like the way greenfield sites are being swallowed up by out-of-town developments, which also encourage greater car use.

As a result, owners, developers and managers of the large centres are keen to drop the out-of-town label. They claim that they are becoming, or have already become, towns in their own right. At the MetroCentre people spend the same amount in a year as in a city the size of Oxford. The developers of Bluewater, opened in 1999, say that it may look like out-of-town in 2000; but with a planned 5000 houses to be built close by before 2010, they claim it will soon look like a new town.

Source 1 Location of large out-of-town shopping centres

Braehead
Renfrew, near Glasgow
Scotland's first big out-of-town centre
100 shops
66000m²

MetroCentre
Edge of Gateshead, Tyneside
320 shops
160000m²

Trafford Centre
Outskirts of Manchester
300+ shops
140000m²

Meadowhall
Outskirts of Sheffield
270 shops
130000m²

Merry Hill
Dudley, West Midlands
225 shops
200000m²

Lakeside
Thurrock, Essex
350 shops
140000m²

Cribbs Causeway
Near Bristol
140 shops
80000m²

Bluewater
Near Dartford, Kent
300+ shops
170000m²

An out-of-town shopping centre
the MetroCentre, Gateshead

7.8

The first of the big out-of-town shopping centres to be built in the United Kingdom was the MetroCentre near Gateshead (Source 1).

The MetroCentre is located within 6 km of the main shopping areas of Newcastle-upon-Tyne and Gateshead (Source 1). It occupies 50 hectares of what was largely waste and derelict land along the south bank of the River Tyne – land that was relatively cheap to buy.

The MetroCentre brought new ideas to UK retailing:

- It created an artificial indoor environment which brought new comforts to shoppers all year round.
- It provided the full range of types of retail outlet with everything from department stores such as Marks and Spencer to small specialist shops such as model shops.
- It included leisure facilities such as a multi-screen cinema and superbowl, as well as restaurants and street cafés.
- It is surrounded by open car parks and there are also multi-storey car parks.

The MetroCentre is now so large and so popular that there are direct bus services from most towns in the North of England. Its sphere of influence, therefore, now extends westwards across to Carlisle and southwards to Harrogate and York.

Source 1 The location of the MetroCentre

Fact File MetroCentre

- The MetroCentre opened in 1988.
- There are 335 shops under one roof.
- The MetroCentre has an 11-screen cinema, its own fun park, 28 lanes of tenpin bowling and more than 50 restaurants and cafés.
- The MetroCentre now includes a hotel and conference centre, exhibition centre and office block.
- There are more than half a million visitors each week.
- The MetroCentre is well placed next to the main A1 road.
- Almost 100 trains per day stop at the MetroCentre.
- The Centre's own bus station handles over 1000 bus movements a day.
- A £50 million expansion is under way, adding a further 27 shops to the complex.

139

7.9 Urban growth in a LEDC
São Paulo

Source 1 Aerial view of the central area of São Paulo

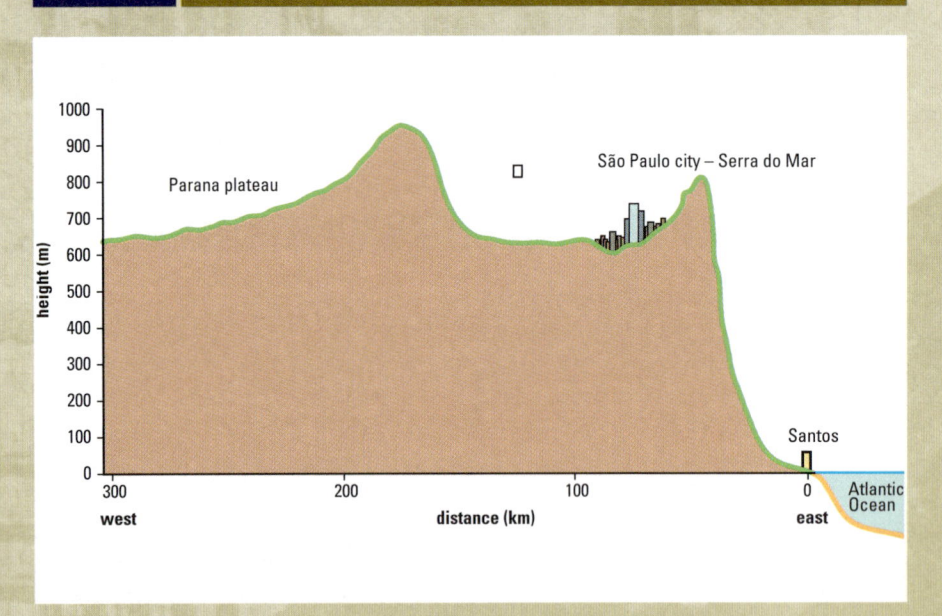

Source 2 The location of São Paulo

The built-up area of São Paulo houses about 17 million people making it the world's third largest urban area. From the air it does not have the appearance of a city in the less economically developed world (Source 1). Its skyscrapers and modern concrete and glass buildings make it look more like New York. Yet way back in the 1870s it was described as a 'sleepy, shabby little town'. However, that was before the coffee boom in the

140

interior of São Paulo state. The city's present size and appearance reflects its importance as the main industrial and business centre of Brazil. With a population of 165 million, there are more people in Brazil than there are in all the other South American countries added together.

The city is located on the plateau, not on the coast (Source 2). It was coffee growing on the Parana plateau inland from São Paulo which triggered its early growth. The flow chart in Source 3 illustrates how and why this happened. Profitability and growth led to more growth, a pattern which has continued to the present day.

During the 1950s and 1960s there was a burst of new economic growth in Brazil. Coffee remained important, but was left behind in the rush to industrialise. This industrial growth was driven by investments from multi-national companies, many with well-known names – VW and Ford, Philips and Sony. All chose to locate in São Paulo. Why? At that time São Paulo offered two main attractions as a location for manufacturing industry:

- Labour – an enterprising and hard-working labour force with some industrial skills.
- Energy – HEP, at first from stations at the base of the Serra do Mar, and later from dams along the big rivers on the plateau.

Source 3 — The early growth of São Paulo (1870–1950)

```
Coffee cultivation prospered on the
fertile red soils of the Parana plateau.
              ↓
The coffee was sent to
market in São Paulo.
              ↓
Out of their fabulous profits, coffee estate
owners built mansions and invested in the city.
              ↓
Manufacturing industries to process the farm
products were set up.
              ↓
Immigrants from Europe and Japan with
their different skills were attracted.
              ↓
Coffee and manufacturing industries yielded
big profits, some of which were reinvested.
```

Success bred success. The pool of skilled industrial workers grew. It is continuously topped up by the inflow of migrant workers from rural areas such as the North-East; although they need to be trained, migrants tend to have the most drive and energy. University and research establishments in and around the city generate new ideas. The largest market of consumers in the country is on the doorstep. In this region is the highest density of paved roads and highways in Brazil, along which manufactured goods can be distributed to all parts of the country as well as to the port of Santos for export.

The positive result is that 40 per cent of Brazil's manufacturing output comes from São Paulo and surrounding areas. Although best known for its car, electrical and electronic industries, a full range of manufactured goods, from satellite dishes to canned drinks, is produced. The headquarters of most major companies are located in or on the edge of São Paulo's CBD, as also are those of the banks and other financial institutions.

The negative result is that the city continues to attract more migrants than it has jobs. City authorities have been unable to keep pace with the increasing demands for housing and for access to public services such as a clean water supply, sewerage removal, schools and health care. Air, water and ground pollution are serious problems. Traffic is gridlocked for most of the day, which has led to a boom in helicopter use as the favoured means of transport for rich business people.

7.10 Urban transect
Manchester

In this unit we are going to follow a **transect** through Manchester to explore how land use changes. The transect runs north to south from Manchester city centre to the River Mersey along one of the main roads in and out of the city (Source 1).

Manchester's CBD shows up clearly on the map. It is where many main roads meet. The main railway and bus stations are found here, along with the city's main exhibition centre (G-MEX). The area is almost continuously built up with few open spaces.

The inner ring road which marks the southern boundary of Manchester's CBD is partly a motorway (in squares 8397 and 8497 on Source 1). The inner city begins to the south of this road. At first public buildings, particularly universities, hospitals and museums, take up a lot of the land, then residential land uses become more important from Moss Side and Rusholme southwards.

Source 1: Location of the transect

Source 2: Manchester city centre

Source 3: Rusholme shopping centre

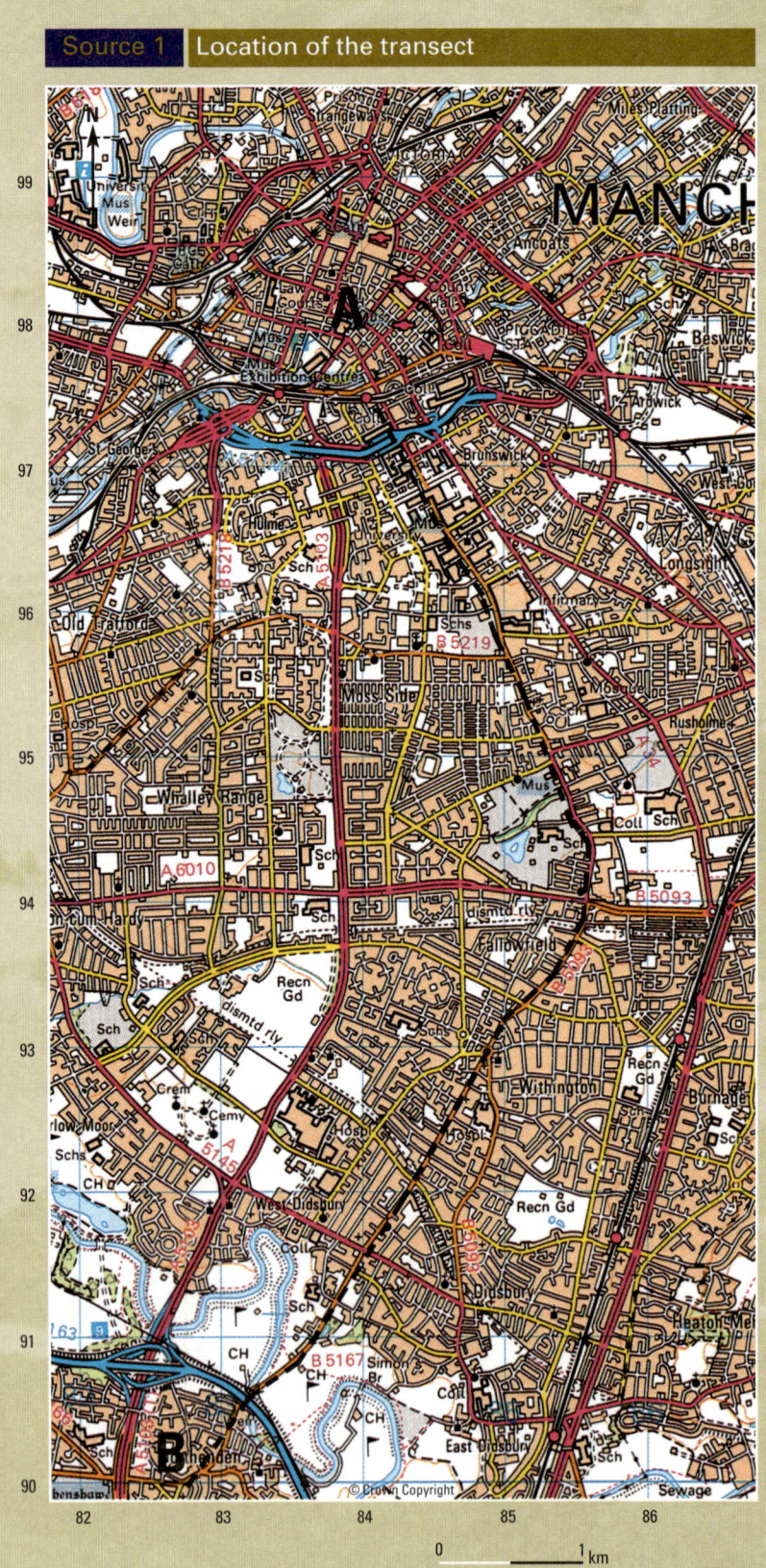

Settings

Source 4: Census information about Rusholme, Fallowfield, Withington and Didsbury

	RUSHOLME	FALLOWFIELD	WITHINGTON	DIDSBURY
Types of housing	Detached 2.3% Semi-detached 34.3% Terraced 34.3% Flats 29.2%	Detached 5% Semi-detached 43% Terraced 24.9% Flats 27.1%	Detached 2.6% Semi-detached 48.8% Terraced 19.3% Flats 29.3%	Detached 8.2% Semi-detached 50.6% Terraced 15.3% Flats 25.9%
Ethnic group of the inhabitants	White 68.8% Black 7.3% Asian 28.7% Other 4.2%	White 77.1% Black 6.7% Asian 13.0% Other 3.2%	White 87.2% Black 2.0% Asian 8.5% Other 2.4%	White 91.3% Black 1.0% Asian 5.9% Other 1.9%
Households without a car	56%	54%	42%	30%
Head of household working in a professional or managerial occupation	26%	22%	32%	44%
Out of work	22%	21%	13%	8%

Information about four of the wards along the transect route has been taken from the 1991 census (Source 4). It illustrates some of the ways in which the land uses and features of an urban area change between the city centre and the edge of the built-up area. Similar changes can be identified in most British cities.

What the information suggests is that Rusholme and Fallowfield have many of the features associated with the inner city. There are more terraced houses than further out in the suburbs of Manchester. Socially, there is a significant concentration of people from the ethnic minority groups, mainly Asian; some of the features of the local shopping centre reflect their presence (Source 3). Economically, people are less well off than those living in the suburbs. More are out of work and fewer have well-paid jobs. Lower rates of car ownership result from this.

Withington and Didsbury, on the other hand, show features which are associated with the residential suburbs. Didsbury is located nearer the edge of the city and is the wealthiest of the four wards. There is a significantly higher proportion of detached houses here.

7.11 Urban problems
LEDCs

In LEDCs, cities are seen as places of wealth and great opportunity, particularly when compared with living in the countryside. It is the speed at which the cities have grown that has led to many problems (Source 1). São Paulo in Brazil, for example, grew by half a million people per year in the 1970s and 1980s. It is impossible to plan and to provide for such rapid growth.

Source 1 | Urban problems

1 Housing
Poor housing is the biggest urban problem. Self-help is the only option for most migrants to the city because they have no money. They must collect whatever free 'building materials' are available and build a shack on any empty land. Empty land is usually located around the edge of the city, but sometimes it exists within the city, such as next to a river with a high flood risk or on land too steep for normal building. Large numbers of people building their own shacks leads to the growth of a shanty town.

2 Provision of essential public services
The supply and distribution of water and electricity require a great deal of planning and investment. Most governments don't have the kind of money needed. Large areas of cities are not connected up to mains services. Power failures are frequent.

3 Unemployment
Many people have no regular work. Instead they scratch a living from the informal sector by selling vegetables and cigarettes on the streets or by collecting papers and plastic for recycling.

4 Traffic and transport
Public transport is usually overcrowded to bursting point. City-centre roads are often heavily congested with traffic. Controls on exhaust emissions are either non-existent or not enforced; there is air pollution.

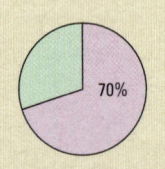

Casablanca, Morocco: 70%
Mexico City: 40%

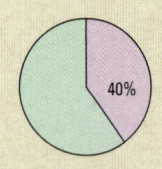

percentage in shanty towns

Shanty town improvement
Lima, Peru

7.12

Lima, in Peru, is in many ways a typical capital city of one of the world's less economically developed countries. It has grown fast (Source 1) and the growth shows no sign of stopping as the countryside empties its surplus people. An increasing proportion of Lima's residents live in shanty towns (Source 2). Such shanty towns in Lima are called **barriadas** (Source 4).

The city is located in a desert and surrounded on its northern and eastern sides by low hills. These drab dry hills around the city were not farmed, and so this empty land has been used for homes by the new migrants into the city. Surveys among residents in the barriadas indicate that most have work, but perhaps only 10 per cent are in full-time jobs (Source 3).

There are a few examples within Lima of shanty towns that have been improved over time to become proper residential areas. One example is the township of Santiago near to the centre of Lima. This changed from a squatter settlement on empty land on the dried-up bed of an old river, to a normal residential area with all the public services and shops you would expect in any residential area. Good organisation among the residents and government help were essential in achieving this transformation. While not all of Lima's shanty towns will be able to do the same, Santiago's development does offer them some hope.

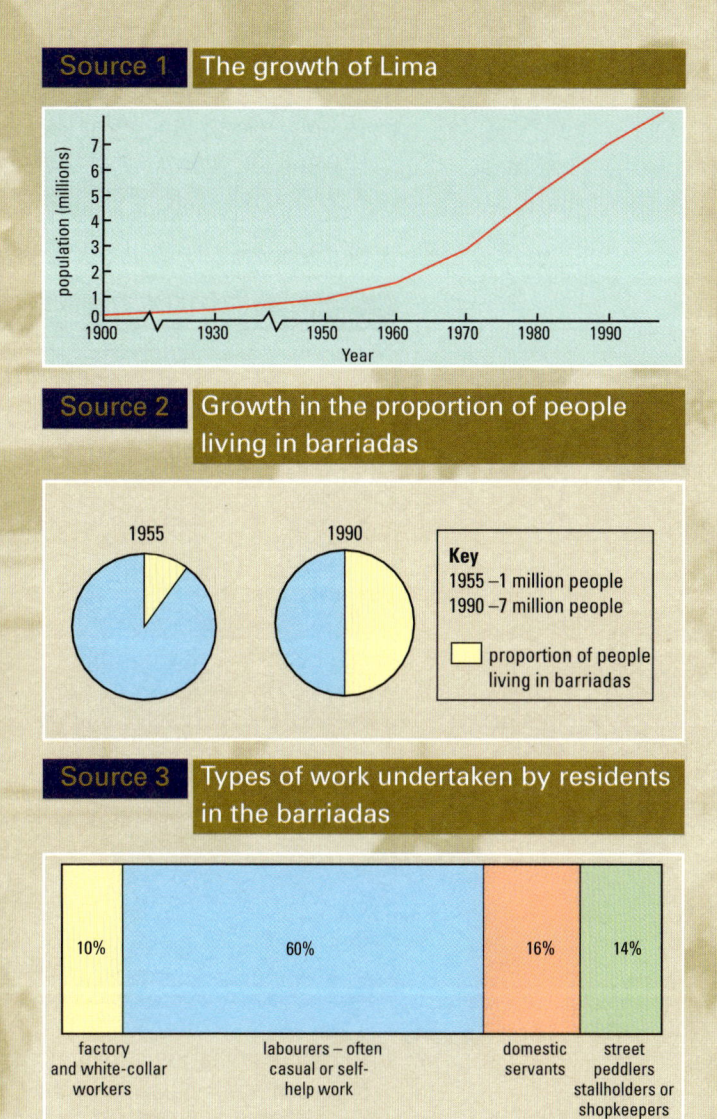

Source 1 The growth of Lima

Source 2 Growth in the proportion of people living in barriadas

Key
1955 – 1 million people
1990 – 7 million people

proportion of people living in barriadas

Source 3 Types of work undertaken by residents in the barriadas

10%	60%	16%	14%
factory and white-collar workers	labourers – often casual or self-help work	domestic servants	street peddlers stallholders or shopkeepers

Source 4 A barriada in Lima

7.13 Activities

1 a i Explain with the help of a diagram what is meant by a hierarchy of settlements.
  ii For the region in which you live, name examples of settlements for different levels in the hierarchy.
 b Give three differences between a village and a town.
 c The map below (Source 1) shows an English village. From the map:
  i name the services provided in the village
  ii describe the map evidence which suggests that the village should be free from the risk of being flooded
  iii give three other site advantages for this village.

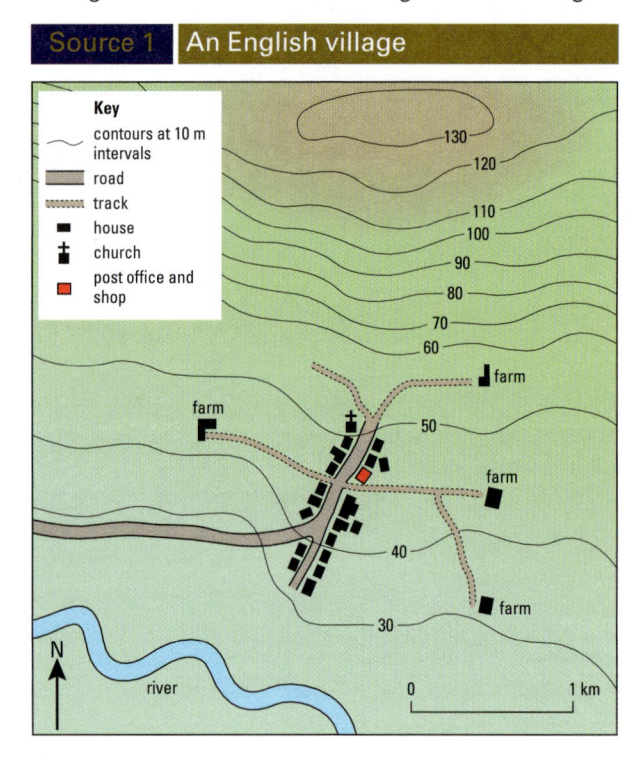

Source 1 An English village

Key
- contours at 10 m intervals
- road
- track
- house
- church
- post office and shop

2 a i Define the terms 'urban morphology' and 'urban zone'.
  ii Describe the features of the CBD which can be recognised on the photograph of Chicago (page 125).
  iii Why is the city centre called the central business district?
 b i What are skyscrapers?
  ii Why are they built and who uses them?
 c i Describe the differences in types of housing between the inner city and residential suburbs.
  ii Give two reasons for the differences you have described in **c (i)**.

3 a i Describe the changes which have occurred in recent years, or are still occurring, in the centre of the city nearest to your home.
  ii Explain why these changes have occurred.
 b i Describe what makes the environment look so unattractive in the inner city areas.
  ii Why do some people refer to high-rise flats as a 'planning disaster'?
 c i What is meant by 'gentrification'?
  ii Why is it not a solution to the problems of every inner city area?

4 a Describe what is meant by the 'rural-urban fringe'.
  b Explain why it has become an attractive location for out-of-town shopping centres and business parks.
  c write a speech for either an environmentalist or a developer. Use in a public meeting which has been called to discuss the proposals for building an out-of-town shopping centre in the rural-urban fringe.

5 a Give as many different pieces of evidence as you can find which show that cities are growing fast in the less economically developed countries of the world.
  b With the help of information from other units in this book, explain as fully as you can the reasons why cities in LEDCs are growing so quickly today.

6 a Give details about the attempts that have been made to stop the outward sprawl of London.
  b Why have they not been totally successful?
  c i What do the locations of the four proposed major growth areas have in common?
    ii Choose three different comments from Source 5 on page 137. Suggest why they were made.

7 a i Describe the distribution of large out-of-town shopping centres in the UK.
    ii Give reasons for their distribution.
    iii Choose one of them as a case study. Make case study notes using the following headings: Site and situation; How the centre is reached; Shops, services and facilities; Future plans.
  b Why are all these shopping centres keen to lose the out-of-town label as quickly as possible?

8 a Describe the main features of the central area of São Paulo shown in Source 1 on page 140.
  b i Name the manufacturing industries present in São Paulo.
    ii Describe three factors that explain the huge growth of manufacturing industry in São Paulo.
  c Make a chart showing the costs and benefits for the inhabitants of São Paulo of the presence of a large amount of manufacturing industry.

9 a Draw a line down the page the same length as the transect line from A to B in Source 1 on page 142.
    Along or next to the line, shade in and label:
    • the CBD of Manchester
    • an area with many public buildings (schools, colleges and hospitals)
    • a (likely) area of terraced housing
    • a (likely) area of semi-detached housing
    • open space that could be 'green belt'.
  b From Source 1, describe the main changes along the transect from A to B.
  c i Draw labelled diagrams to show the differences between Rusholme and Didsbury as housing areas.
    ii Into which two zones of the Burgess model (see page 129) would Rusholme and Didsbury fit? Explain your answers.

10 a Make brief notes about the urban problems of cities in less economically developed countries.
  b Explain why slums and shanty towns in LEDCs may be:
    i places of despair
    ii places of hope.
  c Draw a pie chart to show the information in Source 3 on page 145.

7.14 Sample examination questions

1 a i Using the data below draw a line graph to show the changes in the percentage of people living in urban areas in Brazil from 1940 to 2000.

Year	Percentage living in urban areas
1940	31
1950	36
1960	45
1970	55
1980	66
1990	76
2000	81

(4 marks)

    ii Describe what the data shows. (2 marks)
b i What is meant by urbanisation? (1 marks)
    ii State three causes of urbanisation. (3 marks)

(Total: 10 marks)

2 a Look at Source 1 which shows the Moss Side area of Manchester.

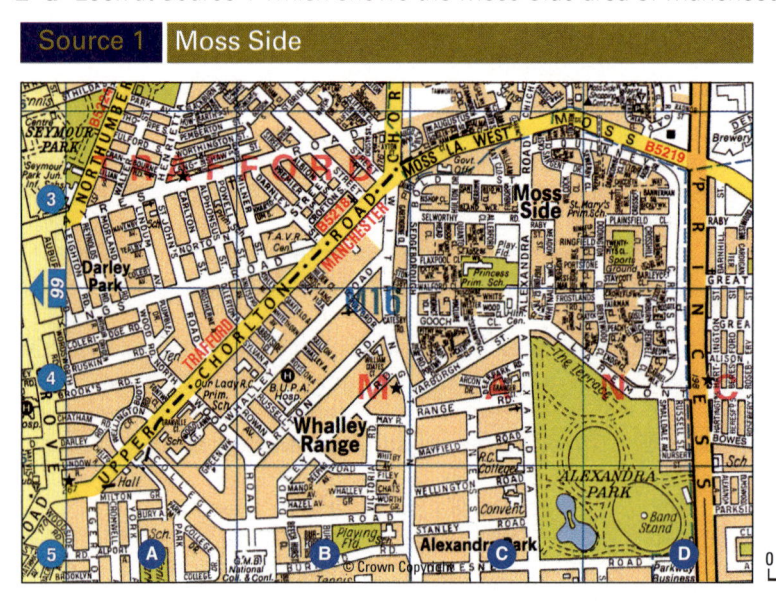

Source 1 Moss Side

This is an inner city area with mixed land uses. Describe the evidence from Source 1 that there are mixed land uses in this area. (3 marks)
b Some inner city areas in the UK have been gentrified.
   i Name one example of a gentrified area from within a UK city. (1 mark)
   ii Describe some of the changes associated with gentrification in inner city areas. (4 marks)
   iii Suggest why there are many inner city areas, such as Moss Side, that have not been gentrified. (2 marks)

(Total: 10 marks)

3 Choose one large city in a less economically developed country (LEDC). For your named city:
a give details about the nature and causes of the main urban problems (6 marks)
b explain why finding solutions to these urban problems is difficult. (4 marks)

(Total: 10 marks)

UNIT 8

Industry

Unit Contents

- Types of work
- Industrial location
- Industrial change
- Global industry: multi-nationals
- Industrial change: South Wales
- A multi-national corporation: Nike
- A newly industrialising country (NIC): Malaysia
- Industry in a LEDC: India
- Industry in the EU

What are the advantages and disadvantages of using robots in factories?

8.1 Types of work

The word 'industry' covers a range of activities which may involve making, supplying or delivering goods and services to a number of people.

Industries can be classified according to the types of jobs which people do; this is called **employment structure**. There are three main types, although with changes in technology a fourth one can now be added (Source 1).

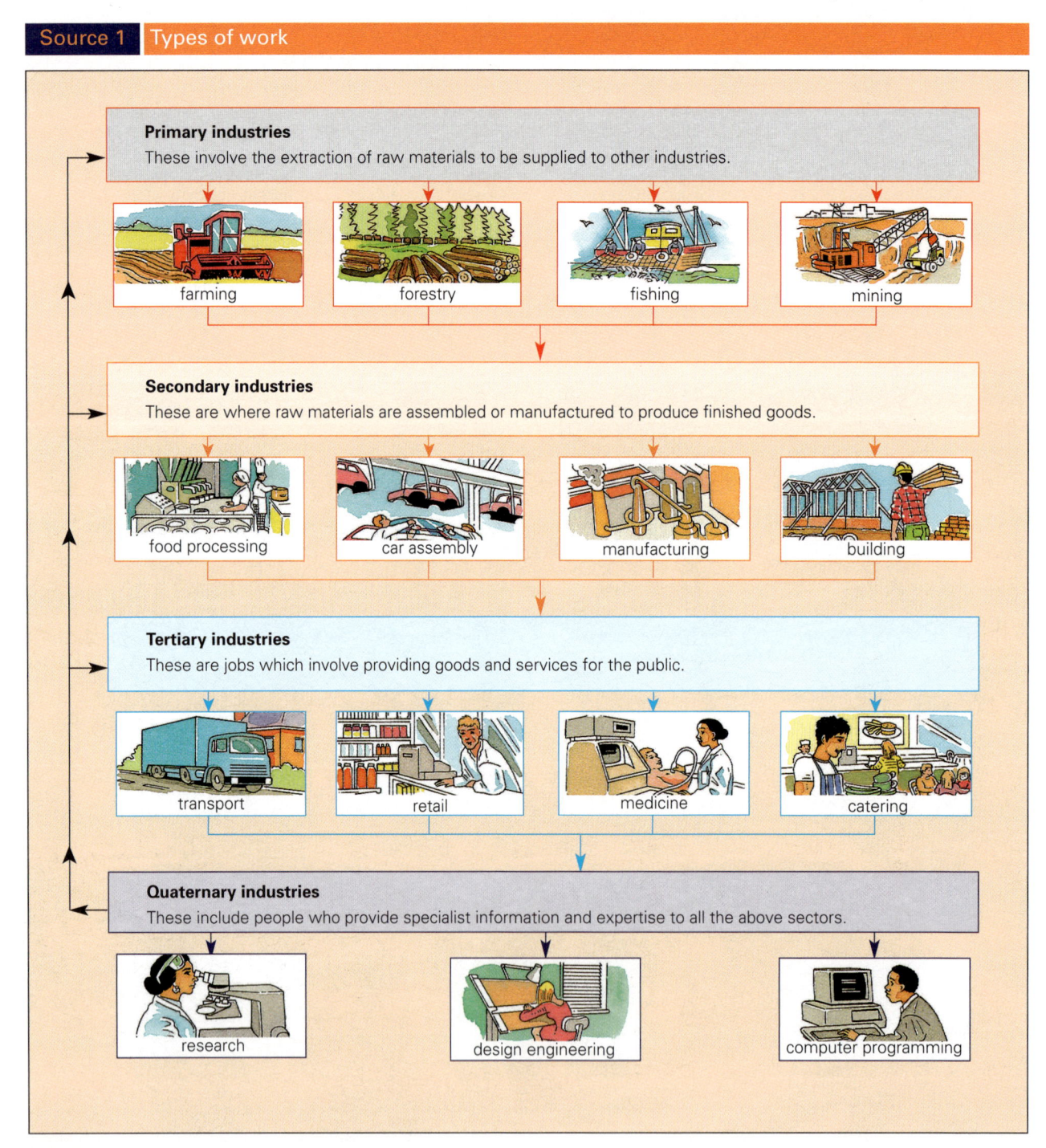

Source 1 Types of work

Primary industries
These involve the extraction of raw materials to be supplied to other industries.

- farming
- forestry
- fishing
- mining

Secondary industries
These are where raw materials are assembled or manufactured to produce finished goods.

- food processing
- car assembly
- manufacturing
- building

Tertiary industries
These are jobs which involve providing goods and services for the public.

- transport
- retail
- medicine
- catering

Quaternary industries
These include people who provide specialist information and expertise to all the above sectors.

- research
- design engineering
- computer programming

Comparing employment structures

Employment structure can change over time and it also differs from country to country. The pie charts in Source 2 show the proportion of people working in three different sectors in the UK and Bangladesh. This information can also be used to compare levels of development between countries. The pie chart for Bangladesh shows that a higher proportion of the population work in primary industries like farming. By contrast a more economically developed country (MEDC) like the UK has a high proportion of people working in the tertiary sector.

Source 2 Percentages of people working in the different sectors in the UK and Bangladesh

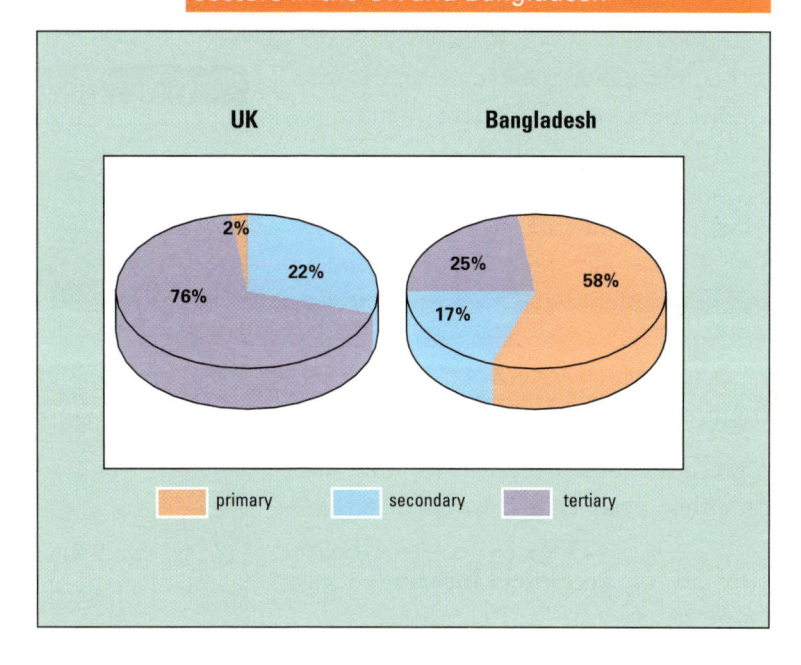

UK: 2% primary, 22% secondary, 76% tertiary
Bangladesh: 58% primary, 17% secondary, 25% tertiary

Industry as a system

One way of describing how the manufacturing industry works is to view it as a system. A system is a way of organising an activity. It is made up of inputs, processes and outputs.

- **inputs** these are the raw materials that go into making a product
- **processes** these are the jobs or activities that take place in a factory
- **outputs** these are often the finished goods, which are sold to make a profit for the company.

The flow diagram below (Source 3) shows what the system might look like for a car factory. The feedback loop shows how some of the profits are reinvested in the business, ensuring that the industry continues to make money.

Source 3 A car factory system

Inputs: Steel, Glass, Rubber, Paint, Plastics, Textiles, Tin, Iron ore

Processes: At the final stages the engine is placed in the car

Outputs → Profits

151

8.2 Industrial location

Economic activities are not evenly spread around the United Kingdom. Some areas have high concentrations of industry – for example, the Midlands remains an important industrial region (Source 1). Other areas, like the Scottish Highlands for example, have few industries. Different industries have specific needs or factors which influence their location. Some of these factors are outlined below.

Flat land Some industries, like car factories, need large areas of flat land. Often the cheapest and most suitable sites are on **greenfield locations** away from the city.

Raw materials Manufacturing industries like steelmaking rely on bulky raw materials, for example coal and limestone, which are expensive to transport. As a result many traditional **heavy industries** are located close to their raw materials.

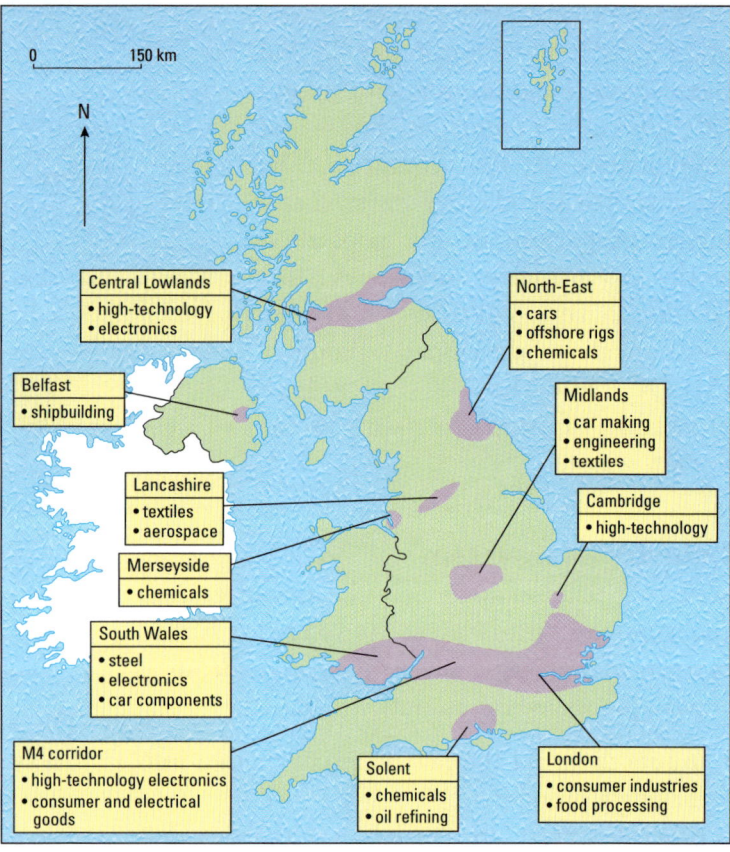

Energy In the past it was important for factories to be close to power supplies, for example textile mills were built close to supplies of fast-flowing water. Today the widespread availability of electricity makes this less important.

Source 1 Industrial areas in the UK

- **Central Lowlands**: high-technology, electronics
- **Belfast**: shipbuilding
- **Lancashire**: textiles, aerospace
- **Merseyside**: chemicals
- **South Wales**: steel, electronics, car components
- **M4 corridor**: high-technology electronics, consumer and electrical goods
- **North-East**: cars, offshore rigs, chemicals
- **Midlands**: car making, engineering, textiles
- **Cambridge**: high-technology
- **Solent**: chemicals, oil refining
- **London**: consumer industries, food processing

Source 2 An inner city clothing factory

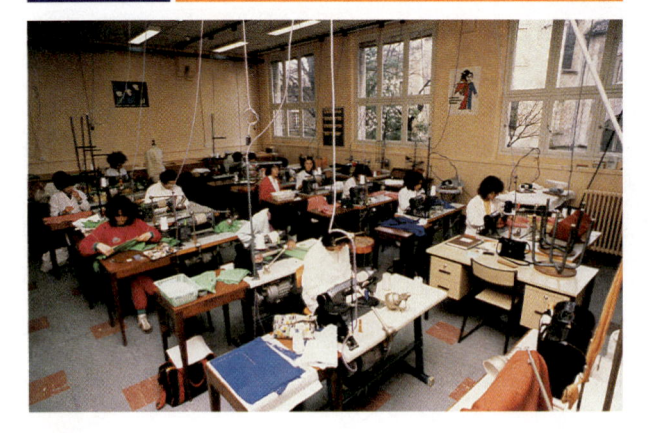

Labour force Industries that rely on a large workforce, like car production, tend to be found close to or within easy reach of cities where many of their workers and customers live. Source 2 shows another example of a **labour-intensive** factory: clothing factories are often found in inner cities.

Markets Manufacturers do not like to be far from their markets as this increases costs. One reason why Sony decided to make televisions in Britain was to be nearer to its European markets. The EU is a market of nearly 350 million, mainly wealthy, people.

Transport links Factories need to be located close to good transport links to ensure that the raw materials they need and the finished products they manufacture are moved with ease. Many prefer to locate near to motorway junctions.

Industry

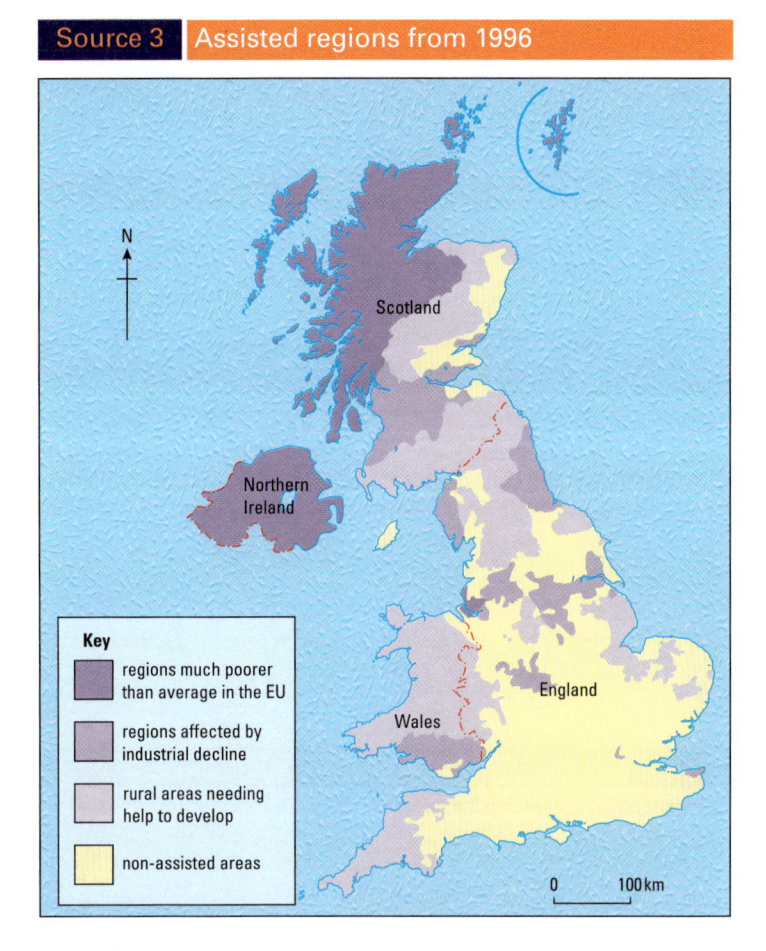

Source 3 Assisted regions from 1996

Key:
- regions much poorer than average in the EU
- regions affected by industrial decline
- rural areas needing help to develop
- non-assisted areas

Source 4 Industrial estate

Labels: close to city for workers; purpose-built buildings; car parks; cheap land; close to roads

What can governments do?

Where regions have lost industries or unemployment is high, then governments may provide money or other forms of help to attract new investment. The EU has a regional policy to promote new development in its less wealthy regions (Source 3). Help may come in the form of:

- giving businesses rent-free periods, grants and loans
- infrastructure: building new roads, water supplies and electricity
- retraining workers – to provide labour with relevant skills
- providing sites for business parks and new start-ups.

New jobs in new places

Some secondary activities can be grouped according to their location.

Heavy industries rely on bulky raw materials and tend to be found close to them, to reduce transport costs.

Light or **footloose industries** can locate almost anywhere, provided that communications are good. In the past, manufacturing industries were found close to their raw materials. Now, with developments in transport, industries do not have to be tied to a certain location. They can be footloose. Today many products are made on industrial estates (Source 4) located close to cities. Offices are attracted to business parks, usually in out-of-town locations.

Highly specialised quaternary activities like research take place in **science parks** (see page 159).

The widespread use of computers, modems and the Internet will probably allow more people to work from home in the future or in small communities known as **tele-cottages**, such as those already in existence in rural areas of South Wales.

153

8.3 Industrial change

Workplaces rarely stay the same. The way goods and services are produced and delivered has changed dramatically over the last century. This has had a huge impact on people's lives and on the location of work in the United Kingdom.

One of the biggest changes has been the loss of jobs in the primary and secondary sectors (Source 1). Since the Second World War (1939–45) there has been a decline in the number of people working in mining and manufacturing. Some reasons for this include the following:

- Mechanisation and **automation** meant that fewer people were needed in factories.
- Many firms did not spend enough money on updating their factories.
- Competition from certain newly industrialised countries like South Korea and Taiwan, who can manufacture products more cheaply and efficiently.

As thousands of jobs disappeared it was the regions of traditional heavy industry, such as the North-East, that suffered the most, as Source 2 shows.

The impact of change

Unemployment can have a devastating effect upon individuals, families and society at large. It can result in:

- high levels of poverty
- increased levels of crime and vandalism
- low educational achievement and expectations

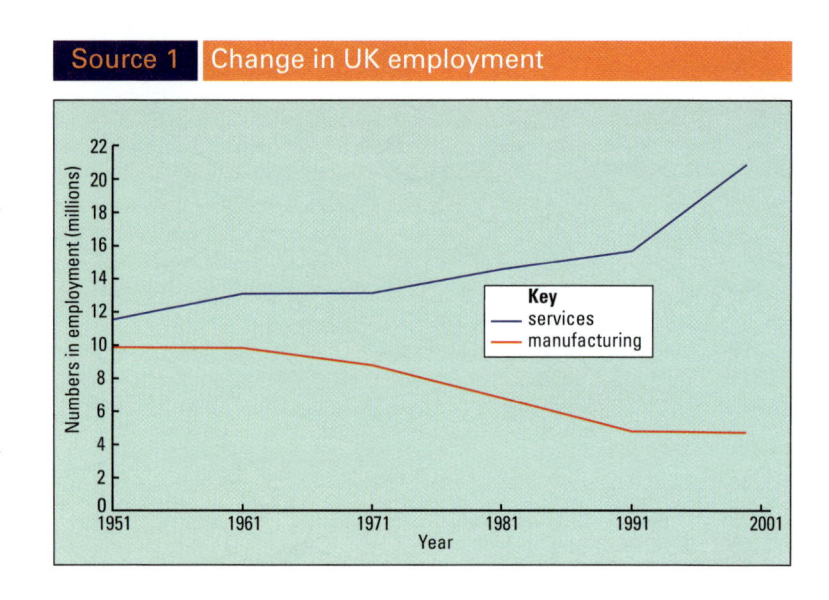

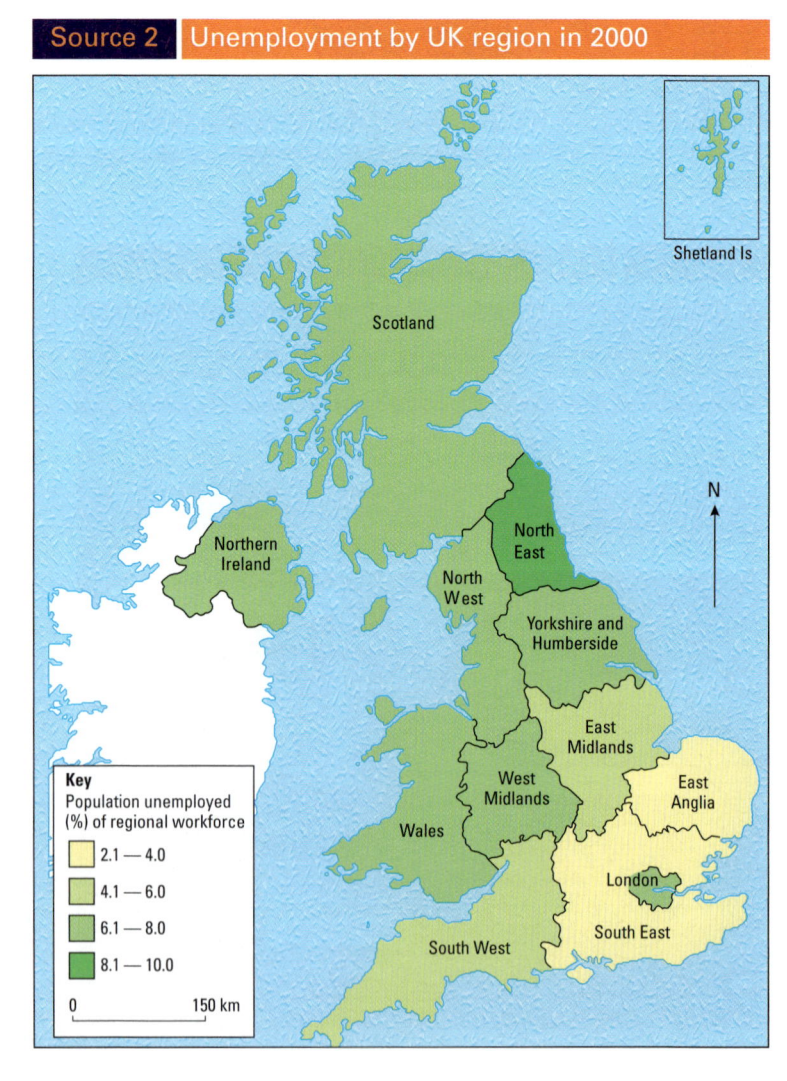

Source 1 Change in UK employment

Source 2 Unemployment by UK region in 2000

Key
Population unemployed (%) of regional workforce
- 2.1 — 4.0
- 4.1 — 6.0
- 6.1 — 8.0
- 8.1 — 10.0

Other effects of industrial decline are that:

• people may lose their homes
• local shops close because people can't afford to use them
• families may break up.

Service industries

Not all areas of industry have been in decline over the last 100 years, for example many new jobs have been created in **service industries**. Service industries include activities as diverse as tourism, banking and transport. Much of the growth has been concentrated in urban areas, especially in southern Britain. Here, the importance of London as a financial centre has played an important role in attracting new jobs. Economic decline in the north and west and growth in the south have led to **regional inequalities**. However, in the late 1980s the technological revolution began to affect service industries and many jobs have been lost in sectors like banking as cash machines have replaced bank clerks (Source 4).

New jobs for old?

Areas affected by industrial decline were given EU and government assistance (see page 153) to attract new industry. This has led to a steady stream of inward investment by companies from the Far East like Sony and Toyota. The head of a Taiwanese firm opening a new TV factory in Scotland said his company was attracted to Britain for the following reasons:

• low labour costs
• there are few strikes – so industrial relations are good
• government help in the form of grants
• to be close to their European markets.

One drawback of the new jobs created is that many of the long-term unemployed do not have the skills to work in the new industries. While some people have been retrained, this has not been possible for all workers.

There has also been an increase in the number of **part-time jobs** which has attracted women into the workforce (Source 5). Part-time work often pays less and is less secure than full-time work. In future it is thought that people will no longer have a job for life. They will need to train and retrain throughout their careers, to keep pace with changes in the workplace.

Source 3 A new service industry – the call centre: this one is located on an out-of-town business park

Source 4 Machines like this cost jobs

Source 5 Women play an active role in the workforce

8.4 Global industry: multi-nationals

One of the biggest changes in industry in the last 50 years has been the way the provision of many goods and services has become increasingly concentrated in the hands of a few large companies. Source 1 names a number of famous companies. What they all have in common is that they are all multi-national corporations. Another name for them is **transnational corporations** (TNCs).

A multi-national corporation is a large company which has factories, branch plants or offices in a number of different countries. Many are involved in a range of different economic activities. Unilever is a good example of this type of company. Its headquarters are in Rotterdam in the Netherlands and in London in the UK. These are the places where the most important decisions about the company are made. However, Unilever, which owns many brand names from Bird's Eye fish fingers to Persil washing powder, operates in many countries (Source 2).

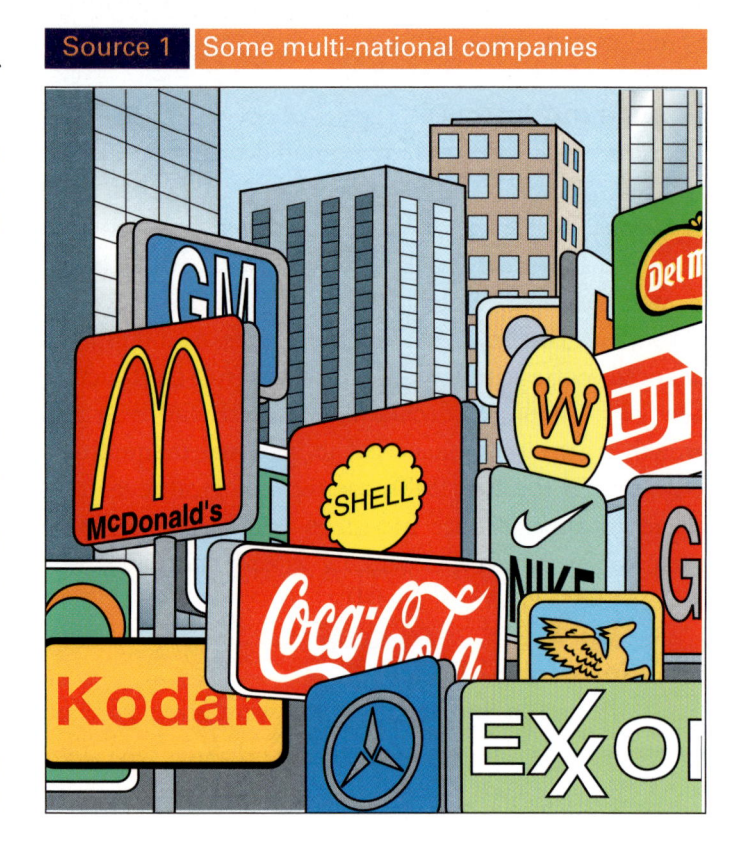

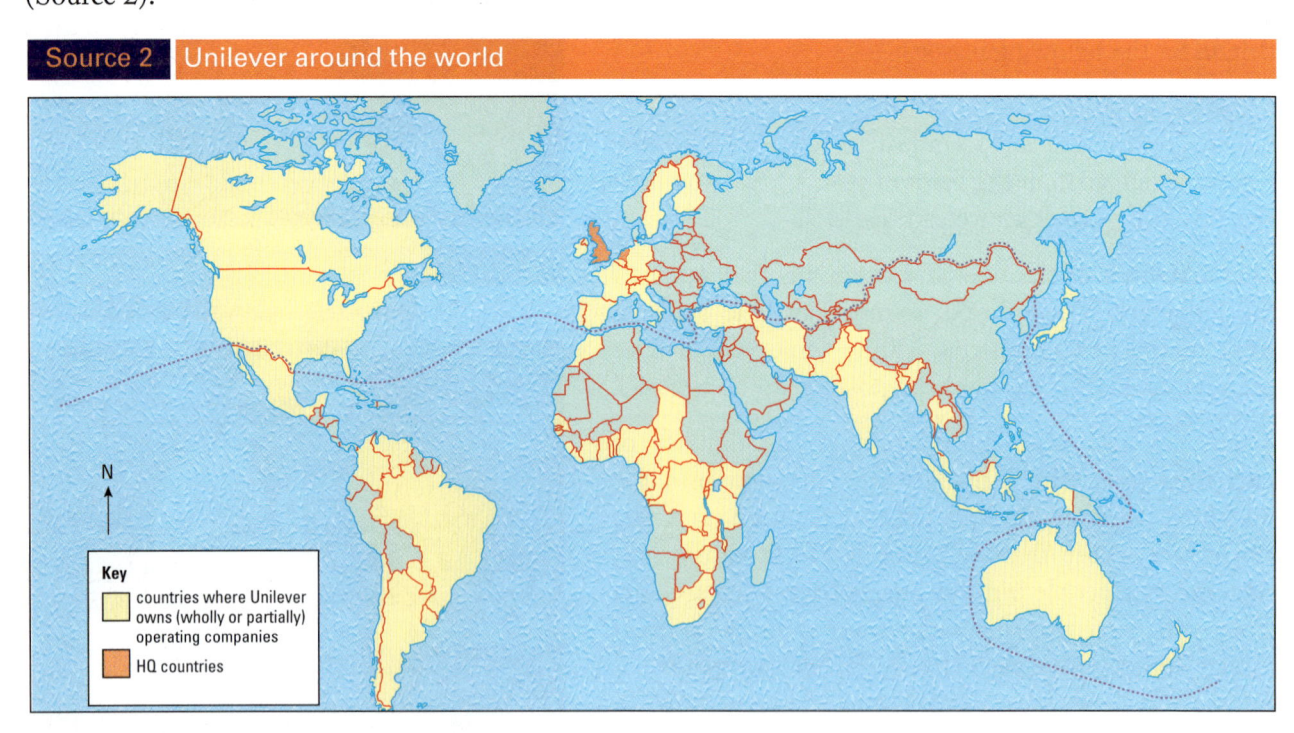

Source 1 Some multi-national companies

Source 2 Unilever around the world

Key
- countries where Unilever owns (wholly or partially) operating companies
- HQ countries

Industry

Many multi-nationals control the whole production process, from raw materials to the finished product. For example, where a product like a car is assembled or put together in a factory, many of the raw materials will have been gathered together from all over the world.

Source 3 — The advantages and disadvantages of multi-nationals

Advantages	Disadvantages
develop trade links with other countries	often have no regard for the local environment
provide jobs in mines, factories and plantations	profits may leave the country
develop infrastructure, like roads and railways	may use cheap unskilled labour
earn the host country foreign currency when goods are sold abroad	may close factories and move to somewhere more profitable
bring in professional skills	may produce goods which are not appropriate to local needs
invest in new technology	use of technology may increase unemployment

As a result, multi-national companies are extremely powerful. Some multi-nationals have higher turnovers than some LEDCs. It is not surprising that many poor countries are keen to attract investment from these corporations, but there are advantages and disadvantages which need to be weighed up carefully (Source 3).

Among LEDCs, some countries have attracted more investment than others. Those in the Far East, such as Taiwan, South Korea, Thailand and Malaysia (page 161), are now described as NICs (newly industrialising countries) after much investment by multi-nationals. Companies making clothes, shoes, electrical and electronic goods are attracted mainly by their reliable and well-trained workforces, willing to work for low wages. Countries with large populations, such as Brazil and Mexico in Latin America, attract investment because of the great size of their domestic markets as well.

Globalisation

Globalisation is a word which is now used frequently to describe the way in which more and more companies are operating in an increasingly international manner. Company decisions are taken in one country which affect what happens in many other countries. For example, when General Motors took the decision to stop car production in their factory in Luton in early 2001, this decision was made in their headquarters in Detroit in the USA. When someone buys a new car from a multi-national company such as Ford, it is difficult to know where it was made. The car itself could have been assembled in one of a number of different European countries, while the parts will have been made in many different countries.

Source 4 — A multi-national in Malaysia

Source 5 — Benetton in Namibia

One indication of the power of multi-nationals is the way people from many different countries buy and consume the same products. Levis are worn, Ford Mondeos are driven and McDonald's burgers are eaten by people in many different places worldwide. Benetton's 'United Colours' advertising theme supports the idea that we are all global consumers as well as producers (Source 5).

8.5 Industrial change
South Wales

There was a time when the industrial landscape of Wales was littered with chimney stacks and smoke, signs that the region was dominated by heavy industry.

During the 1920s there were over a quarter of a million coal miners in South Wales. The number of miners and collieries declined dramatically, as Source 1 shows. Coal was a major source of fuel and helped provide the power needed for the Industrial Revolution. South Wales also had the raw materials needed to make steel: limestone, iron ore and coal (Source 1). Coal and steel were the two biggest industries in the region and part of their success was due to the fact that Britain still had an empire, which was a ready market for coal and steel.

Source 1 — The decline in coal-mining in South Wales

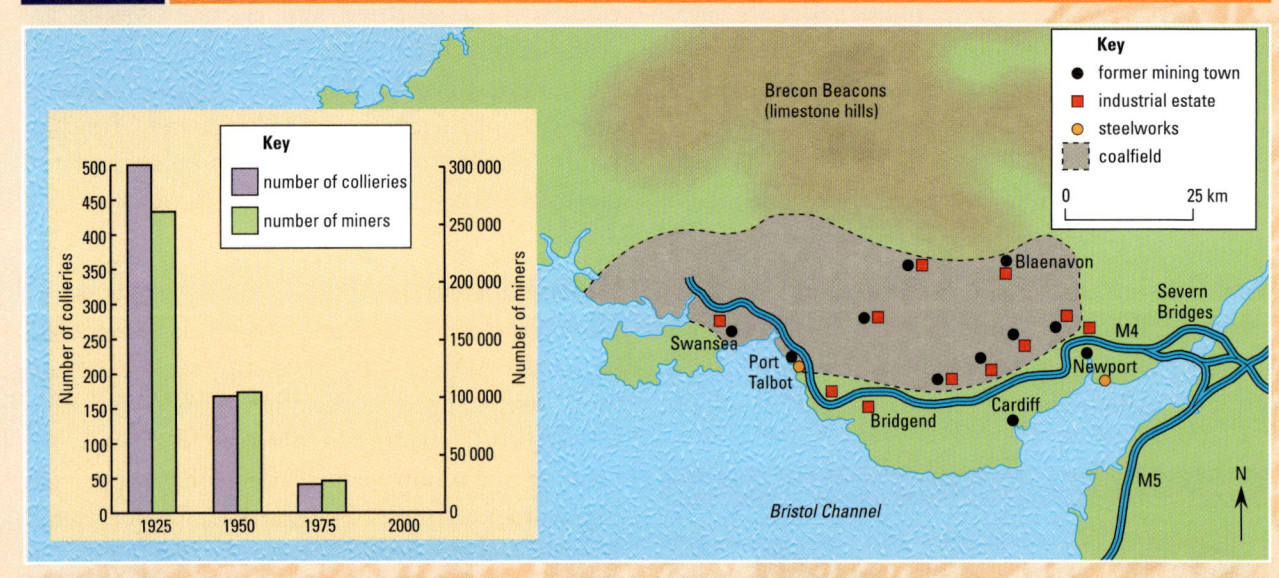

Source 2 — Big Pit in Blaenavon

Today coal mines are more likely to be tourist attractions, such as Big Pit in Blaenavon (Source 2), on the northern edge of the old coal field. The last British Coal owned mine closed in 1994, although a small number of privately run mines still operate. The steelworks that remain are found on the coast because they now rely on imported coal and iron ore.

Reasons for the decline in coal-mining included:

- the UK lost many of its markets for coal
- competition from Japan and South Korea destroyed the coal-using industries
- all the easily worked coal seams were exhausted
- natural gas is now a major source of fuel so demand for coal has fallen.

Unemployment in South Wales was above the national average for many years. This had a huge impact on smaller mining communities where the local pit would have been the only source of work.

Industry

Regenerating South Wales

In recent years, however, unemployment has fallen and South Wales has succeeded in **diversifying** by attracting a range of different industries. The Welsh Development Agency (WDA) was set up to help attract new investment into Wales. Parts of South Wales were given Enterprise Zone status. This meant that new companies locating in the area did not have to pay local taxes, and received help with planning. The work of the Welsh Development Agency and the Enterprise Zone have helped to change the industrial scene in South Wales.

As a result, many large industrial estates have emerged on the southern edge of the old coalfield where the road links are better. Grants and loans were given to new companies. This, combined with a pool of skilled workers, acted as a magnet for foreign firms like Sony, Bosch and Toyota, who have all set up factories in South Wales.

Source 3 — Imperial Park, South Wales

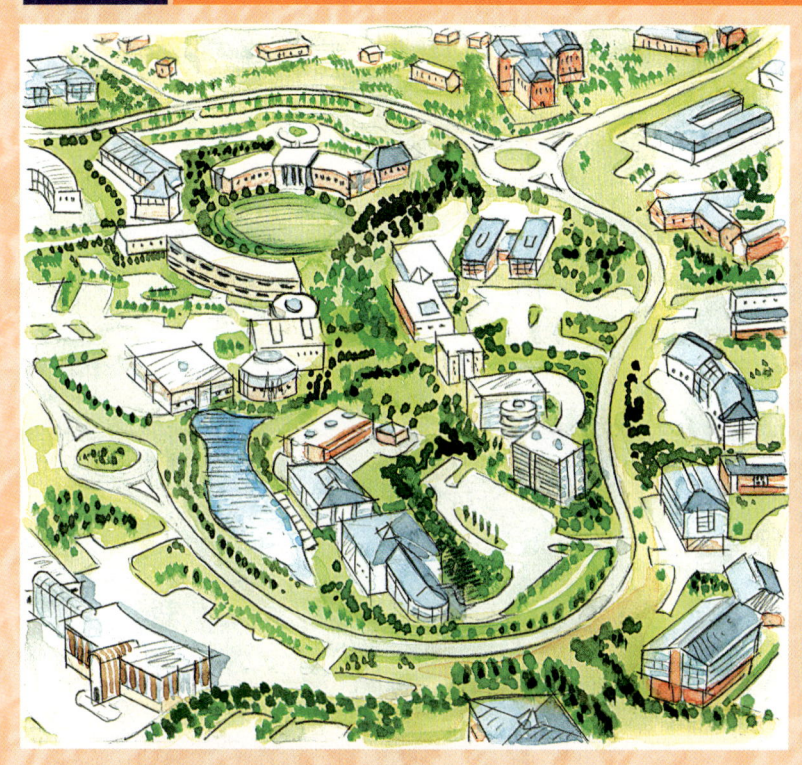

- excellent road and rail links
- spacious parkland setting
- 9140m^2 office space available
- close ties with Imperial College of Science and Technology
- future links with Cardiff University planned
- purpose-built accommodation
- support from Newport Borough Council and the Welsh Development Agency

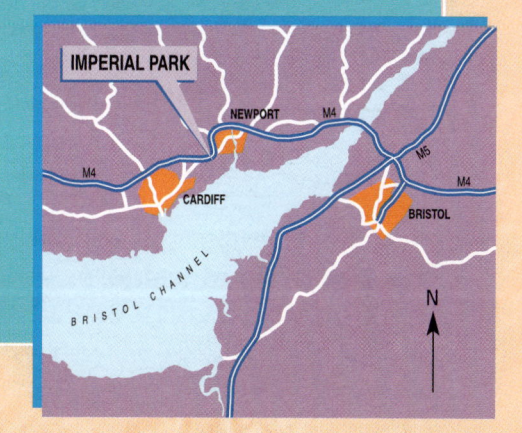

A science park: Imperial Park, Newport

In Newport in South Wales the WDA together with Newport Council have been keen to encourage the development of high-technology based industries. They achieved this by creating a science park named Imperial Park. This opened in 1994. Source 3 shows what it offers.

Here, good access, a scenic location and links with local universities are important locational factors. By 1996, there were eight companies operating in Imperial Park, specialising in food testing and software design. Imperial Park prides itself on being an extension of the M4 corridor, which is home to many science parks and hi-tech industries.

South Wales is a clear example of how a region which for so long specialised in a few industries can diversify. Today it plays host to manufacturing, service, high-technology and the tourist industry, with the signs of heavy industry fading fast. The latest to suffer is the steelworks at Llanwern.

8.6 A multi-national corporation
Nike

Nike trainers (Source 1) are sold and worn throughout the world. Nike is a typical transnational corporation (TNC). Its headquarters are in the USA, where all the major decisions and research take place, yet its sports shoes are manufactured in many countries around the world.

Like many TNCs, Nike **subcontracts** or uses independently owned factories in different countries to produce its trainers. Often this takes place in less economically developed countries (LEDCs) where labour costs are low.

Nike's main activities are in South-East Asia, and up until recently it manufactured many of its trainers in South Korea. In the late 1980s labour costs in South Korea rose, so Nike decided to move production to Indonesia where costs were lower.

Source 1 Where your money goes

cost to you £53.00

Where does the £26.00 go?
Transport £16.00
Materials £6.50
Administration £1.60
Labour £1.10
Sub-contractors' profit £0.80

wholesale price £26.00

Source 2 Nike offices on a business park near Sunderland

The true price of trainers

Many of the workers in the Indonesian factories come from the surrounding countryside where they live in poverty. The conditions they move to are better, but not much. Some of the problems they face are:

- low wages and long hours
- industrial accidents
- no workers' rights – trade unions are illegal in Indonesia.

Where workers do complain or protest they can lose their jobs.

The contractors say they cannot afford to pay the workers more and Nike says that it is difficult to control what is happening in individual factories. This means that in a nation where unemployment is high and employees can be easily replaced, workers will continue to be open to **exploitation** (Source 3).

Source 3 Workers can be exploited

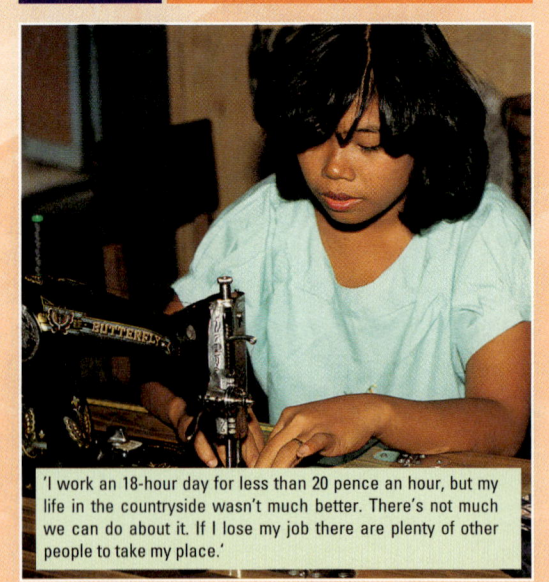

'I work an 18-hour day for less than 20 pence an hour, but my life in the countryside wasn't much better. There's not much we can do about it. If I lose my job there are plenty of other people to take my place.'

A newly industrialising country (NIC)
Malaysia

8.7

Many of the countries in South-East Asia named in Source 1 have fast-growing economies. Much of this growth is due to industrialisation. China and India have their own huge populations which provide a ready market. South Korea, Taiwan, Hong Kong and Singapore are known as the 'Tiger economies' because of the speed with which they have industrialised and developed over the last 50 years. Industry has grown, and continues to grow, in other countries of the Far East, such as Malaysia, which is why 'newly industrialising countries' is a good label for them.

Source 2 shows how the type of goods exported from Malaysia has changed greatly over the past 30 years. In 1970 exports were dominated by primary products such as rubber and tin. By 1997 the three main primary products made up less than 15 per cent of Malaysia's exports, which are now dominated by manufactured goods.

Why the big change? Several reasons help to explain why Malaysia industrialised so quickly.

- The government was stable and wanted industrialisation.
- Multi-national companies were encouraged to invest.
- Malaysia offered plenty of labour, well educated compared with many other LEDCs.
- Wage rates were much lower than in MEDCs.
- Access to ports and the main shipping routes was easy for exporting goods to MEDCs.

Industrial areas were set aside for factories. One example is the Bayan Lepas Industrial Park (BLIP) in Penang. Some of the world's best-known multi-national companies are located in Penang (Source 3). Some make clothing, but many make goods and software for the high-technology sector such as semi-conductors, disk drives, computers and keyboards. Malaysia also has its own car company, Proton, which exports worldwide.

Source 1 NICs in South-East Asia

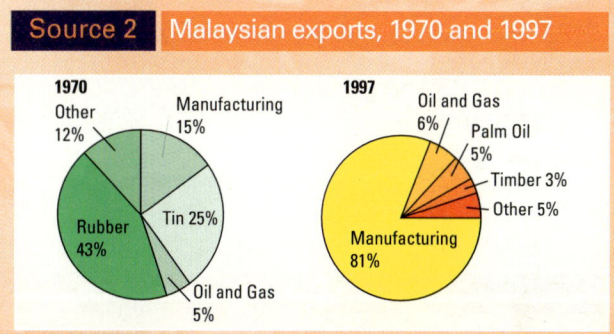

Source 2 Malaysian exports, 1970 and 1997

1970: Other 12%, Manufacturing 15%, Tin 25%, Rubber 43%, Oil and Gas 5%

1997: Oil and Gas 6%, Palm Oil 5%, Timber 3%, Other 5%, Manufacturing 81%

Source 3 Multi-nationals in Malaysia – how many have you heard of?

8.8 Industry in a LEDC
India

Despite a population of 1 billion people and a wealth of natural resources, India remains one of the world's poorest nations.

Source 1 compares India with the UK. Despite its poverty, the Indian government has invested vast amounts of money trying to **industrialise** the country.

Planning for growth

After independence from Britain in 1947 India put into action a series of five-year plans. These were based on a communist model of development, called **import substitution**. This is where a country tries to produce all the goods it needs so it does not have to import products from other countries. Source 2 summarises what the plans tried to achieve.

Source 1 India compared with the UK

	UK	India
Area (in km²)	241 595	3 287 590
Population (in millions)	59.2	1000
Population density (per km²)	241	280
Natural increase (%)	0.2	1.7
Life expectancy (years)	76	61
GNP per capita (US $)	18 620	1348

Source 2 India's five-year plans

Plan	1–3	4	5–9
Years	1951–66	1969–74	1979–1990
Aims	Develop heavy industry	Develop rural area	Develop infrastructure
Example	Damodar Valley natural resources like coal, ore and bauxite used to develop heavy industry	the green revolution investment in high yielding seeds	increase power supplies improve irrigation new roads and railways

Source 3 India's main industrial regions

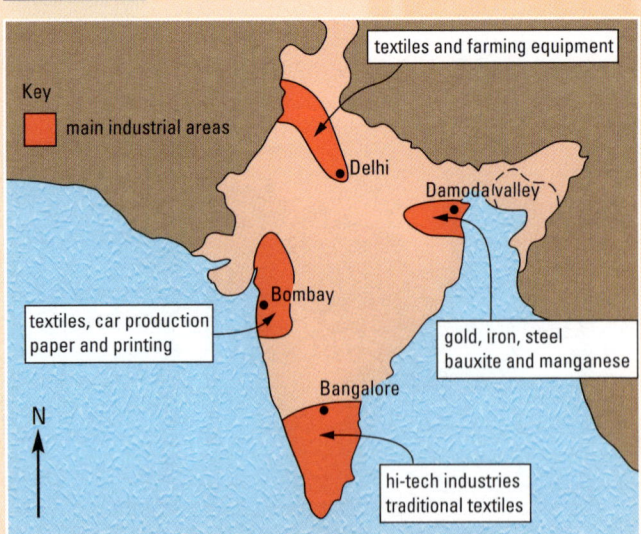

Key: main industrial areas

- textiles and farming equipment (Delhi)
- Damodar Valley
- textiles, car production paper and printing (Bombay)
- gold, iron, steel bauxite and manganese
- hi-tech industries traditional textiles (Bangalore)

A great deal of money was spent on developing manufacturing industries. Source 3 shows some of the main regions which emerged. While heavy industry was concentrated in the north-east in the Damodar Valley, newer hi-tech industries were being encouraged in cities like Bangalore further south. Despite these plans, Indian industries continued to face a number of problems.

- Many areas suffered power shortages.
- India continued to import more than it exported – this led to **trade deficits**. India especially relied on oil. When prices rose rapidly in the 1970s this had a serious effect on Indian industry.
- Poor transport links made it hard to develop industry in more remote regions.
- Corruption and inefficiency led to waste.

Industry

For almost 50 years the Indian government supported and developed large-scale manufacturing. However, smaller, privately run firms are found across India, producing goods for a local market, but many of them are limited in what they can sell because people are too poor to afford consumer goods.

The informal sector

Unemployment is a huge problem in India, so people will turn their hand to a variety of activities in order to make a living. These might range from shoeshining to selling scrap metal. These are all examples of work in the informal sector. This type of work is characterised by insecurity, no taxes are paid and often workers receive 'cash in hand' payment. It is difficult to estimate how many people work in this sector because informal activities are illegal (Source 4).

Source 4 — Children often work in the informal sector

A new future

Since the early 1990s the Indian government's approach to industry has changed. It is now keen to encourage foreign companies to open factories in India. It especially wants to develop hi-tech industries. One way forward is to create technology or science parks (Source 5).

The Indian economy is growing rapidly by more than 6 per cent per year. There is great potential for further growth because of the size of the home market. India is the world's second most populous country. However, major transport problems have yet to be solved. Indian industrialists regularly complain that their businesses are being held back by the need to move goods along pot-holed and congested roads. The passage of goods through overcrowded ports and airports is slow. The price of moving a container 1200 km by road from New Delhi to Bombay costs half as much again as to send it by sea to Europe. Jams on the information super-highway are frequent; using it at the best of times is not helped by the erratic nature of much of the country's electricity supply.

Source 5 — Information Technology Park, Bangalore

The main features of the Information Technology Park are the following.
- Space for offices, shops, luxury homes and parks.
- It is 18 km east of Bangalore and 20 minutes away from the airport.
- State-of-the-art modern buildings, power supply and communications.
- It is designed for technology-oriented companies.
- A landscaped park-like environment.
- It is India's first science park.

8.9 Industry in the EU

The M4 corridor in the UK

The M4 corridor is a zone of mainly footloose industries which stretches from London westwards to Bristol, following the course of the M4. The greatest concentration of industries is in the section between London and Reading, but towns further west such as Swindon and Bristol have a long history of manufacturing. There are many food and drink companies. Electrical and household goods are assembled and packed for distribution. Honda cars are made in Swindon. Over the past twenty years many high-tech companies have arrived. Oracle and NEC in Reading are just two examples. Many are engaged in research and development in the quaternary sector, as well as making telecommunications equipment, micro-electronics and computers.

Source 1 — The M4 corridor

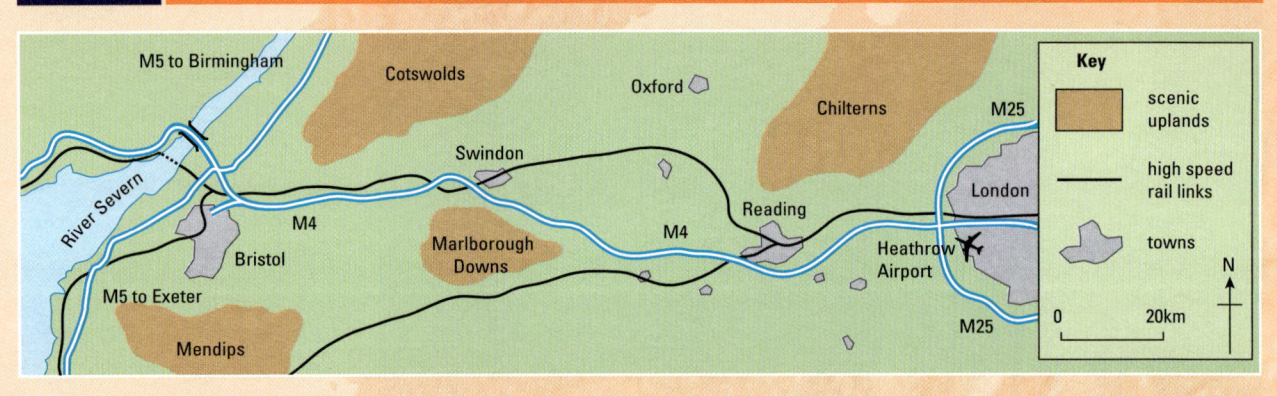

The footloose industries are mainly light or high-tech industries which have considerable freedom in location. This means that most have chosen to locate in the M4 corridor. They have studied its advantages and decided it is the best place for their company to be located. What attracts industries to the M4 corridor? The favourable factors can be arranged under three main headings.

- **Transport:** This is the most important factor for many industries. The M4 links into the UK's other major motorways allowing easy assembly of raw materials and distribution of finished products. The high speed rail link from London to South Wales runs through the middle of the corridor. Heathrow Airport lies between Reading and London allowing international contacts. Eurostar links to the Channel Tunnel and the rest of the EU.

- **Market:** The wealthiest market in the country is concentrated in London and the South-East. Motorways give access to markets elsewhere in the UK. To the east of London there are motorway and

Source 2 — Examples of companies which have chosen to locate in the M4 corridor

164

Industry

- **Labour:** High-tech companies in particular need skilled scientists and engineers. There are many places of research in the M4 corridor producing trained people. These include universities in Bristol, Oxford and Reading. These people are often happy to live in this region because of the nearness of London and its facilities, and because the corridor is surrounded by some scenic uplands such as the South Downs and Cotswolds. There is good countryside for recreation at weekends and in holidays.

The Rhine–Ruhr region in Germany

The Rhine is Western Europe's largest river. The Ruhr is Western Europe's largest coalfield. It is not surprising therefore that where they meet is the largest region of manufacturing industry in the EU. There are many large, well-known industrial towns. Cologne and Düsseldorf are located on the banks of the Rhine; others such as Dortmund and Essen are on the coalfield north of the Ruhr valley (Source 3).

For many years the region was dominated by heavy industries such as iron and steel, engineering, metal smelting and chemicals, just the same as in South Wales or North-East England. The original reasons for growth were also the same. Local coal provided the large amounts of power heavy industries needed. However, because the Ruhr coalfield was larger and contained higher quality coal, the amount of industry that grew here was greater than elsewhere and it has survived longer. Also having the River Rhine passing through the area was a big advantage. It is navigable by 2000-tonne barges. This allows bulky raw materials to be brought in using cheap water transport.

The River Rhine remains a major asset. It is a busy water highway with links northwards to the North Sea shipping lanes and southwards into the heart of Europe. As a cheaper way of transporting raw materials, fuels and large manufactured goods than road or rail, it allows the region to overcome the disadvantage of its inland location.

In other ways its inland location is a great advantage because the Rhine–Ruhr is in the middle of the richest part of the EU. It is in the centre of the EU with more than 350 million consumers. There is a high density of motorways and high speed railways, and many regional airports. Nowhere in Europe is better placed to take advantage of the increasing market as the EU grows.

As a result, there are no longer just the old heavy and textile industries in the region. Cars are made near Cologne and Bochum. Hundreds of smaller companies make parts for them. There are high-tech companies specialising in electronics and telecommunications equipment. Many food and drink manufacturers are here, as well as the logistics firms which arrange their distribution. Cologne has become the region's administrative and service centre with numerous banks and offices; it has been helped by its pleasant location on the banks of the Rhine.

Source 3 The Rhine–Ruhr industrial region

Source 4 Cologne, the largest city in the Rhine–Ruhr region

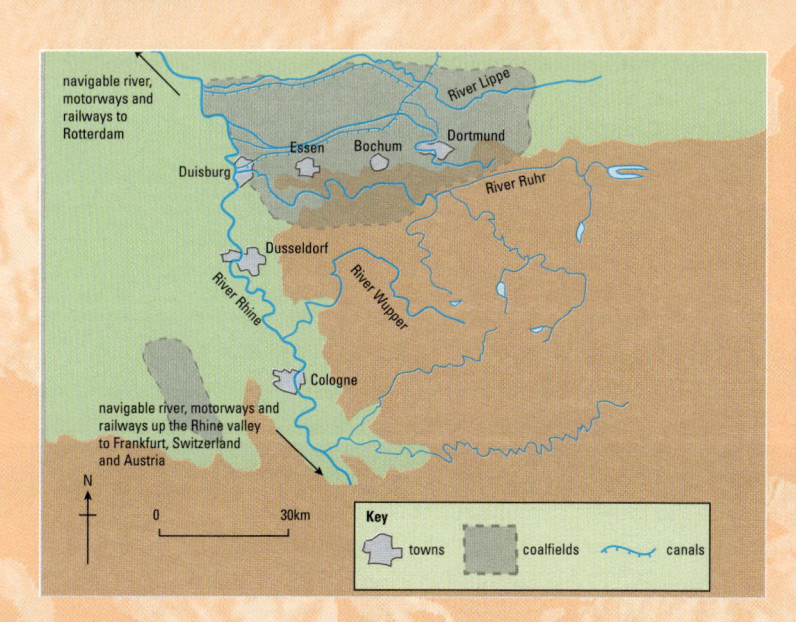

8.10 Activities

1 a Make a copy of the table below and name three examples of jobs in each of the sectors named.

Primary	Secondary	Tertiary	Quaternary
1	1	1	1
2	2	2	2
3	3	3	3

   b Write out and complete each of the following sentences to give definitions for the four sectors of economic activity.
   - **i** Primary industries involve …
   - **ii** Secondary industries involve …
   - **iii** Tertiary industries involve …
   - **iv** Quaternary industries involve …

   c The employment structure for Brazil is given below.
   Primary 20%   Secondary 25%   Tertiary 55%
   - **i** Draw a pie graph to show employment structure in Brazil.
   - **ii** Describe the differences between the employment structure in Brazil and the employment structures in Bangladesh and the UK.
   - **iii** Suggest reasons for the differences you have described in (**ii**).

   d i Draw a diagram to show a car factory as a system.
     ii Make two columns down the page. List the advantages and disadvantages of using robots in car factories.

2 a i From Source 1 on page 152, name two heavy industries.
     ii Explain why heavy industries are more likely to be located near to raw materials and energy supplies than light industries.

   b Look at Source 2 on page 152. Why is the clothing industry described as labour intensive?

   c Look at Source 3 on page 153.
   - **i** Describe where many of the non-assisted areas are located in the UK.
   - **ii** Name one non-assisted area and suggest why government assistance is not needed.
   - **iii** Outline the ways in which the UK government tries to encourage new economic growth in some parts of the country.

   d Name and give brief details about four factors which affect the location of manufacturing industry.

   e For one manufacturing industry located in (or close to) the area where you live:
   - **i** name the industry
   - **ii** state where it is located
   - **iii** outline the reasons why it has located there.

3 a i Describe what Source 1 on page 154 shows about changes in employment in the UK.
     ii Give two reasons for these changes.

   b Look at Source 2 on page 154.
   - **i** Name the region with the highest percentage of unemployed.
   - **ii** Name the regions with the lowest percentage of unemployed.
   - **iii** State the percentage of unemployed in the region where you live.

   c Outline reasons why there is an increasing number of (**i**) female workers, (**ii**) part-time workers and (**iii**) workers in call centres in the UK.

4 a State two characteristics of multi-national companies.
  b Make a table like the one below and fill it in for five multi-national companies.

Name of multi-national company	What it makes or does

  c Many multi-national companies have set up factories in LEDCs. State three advantages of this for LEDCs.
  d Multi-national companies are said to operate globally. Give as many examples as you can to show how they operate in a global way.

5 a Use Source 1 on page 158.
   i State the number of collieries (mines) in Wales that were working in 1925, 1950, 1975 and 2000.
   ii Draw a pictogram to show how the number of miners in South Wales has gone down.
  b Explain why coal mining declined in South Wales.
  c i What is meant by a region diversifying?
   ii Give three reasons why new industries have been attracted to South Wales.
   iii Describe the location and main features of Imperial Park.

6 a Draw a divided bar graph to show how the £53 that it costs to buy a pair of trainers is made up. Show four different costs – transport, materials, shopkeeper's share and other costs (total £3.50). Shade in and add a key for the four parts of the graph.
  b Why are many of the trainers bought in the UK made in LEDCs, such as those in Asia?
  c i What do the letters NIC stand for?
   ii Make notes on Malaysia as a case study of a NIC. Use the following headings:
    • Location
    • Types of industries
    • Growth of exports of manufactured goods
    • Reasons for the growth of industries.

7 a From Source 1 on page 162, state the evidence for each of the following.
   i India is less wealthy than the UK.
   ii India's population is increasing more quickly.
   iii People in India have a lower quality of life than people in the UK.
  b Draw a labelled sketch map to show the location and different types of industry in India.
  c An American multi-national company is investigating whether or not to open a factory in India for the first time. Write a report stating:
    • the advantages of locating a factory in India
    • the likely disadvantages
    • whether or not you would advise them to go ahead, giving your reasons.

8 a Name examples of (**i**) secondary, (**ii**) tertiary and (**iii**) quaternary industries which are present in the M4 corridor.
  b Good transport links are important for all of these industries. Draw a large labelled sketch map to show the good transport links in the M4 corridor.
  c Explain why the greatest concentration of industries is in the part of the M4 corridor between London and Reading.
  d i In what ways is the Rhine–Ruhr region in Germany a similar industrial region to South Wales?
   ii How is the Rhine–Ruhr region diversifying?
   iii Give the reasons why the Rhine–Ruhr region is an attractive location to new industries.

8.11 Sample examination questions

1. The values below show the percentages employed in different economic sectors for Malaysia in 1960 and 2000.

	Primary	Secondary	Tertiary
1960	60	15	25
2000	20	25	55

   a i Draw two pie graphs to show the percentages for 1960 and 2000.
         Shade in the sectors and add a key. *(5 marks)*
      ii In which sector was there the greatest change in percentage
         between 1960 and 2000? *(1 mark)*
   b Explain how the changes in percentages between 1960 and 2000 show that:
      i Malaysia is a newly industrialising country
         (2 marks)
      ii large numbers of Malaysians migrated from rural to urban areas from
         1960 to 2000. *(2 marks)*
   (Total: *10 marks*)

2. Source 1 below shows a factory system.

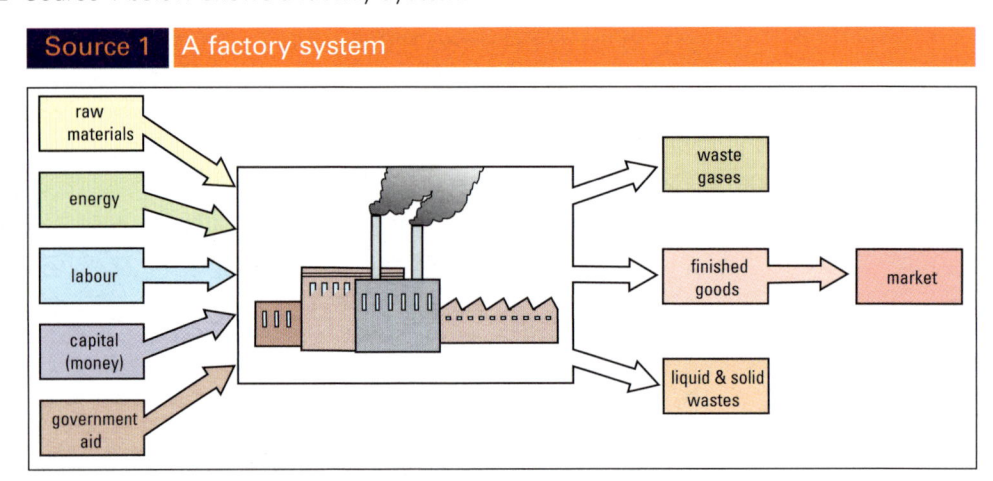

   Source 1 — A factory system

   [Diagram: Inputs (raw materials, energy, labour, capital (money), government aid) → Factory → Outputs (waste gases, finished goods → market, liquid & solid wastes)]

   a i   Name two types of energy inputs used in factories. *(2 marks)*
      ii How many other different inputs are shown in Source 1?
          (1 mark)
      iii Name the output shown in Source 1 from which the factory makes its
          profits. *(1 mark)*
   b State the evidence from Source 1 that factories can cause pollution. *(2 marks)*
   c Describe how raw materials are changed into finished goods in factories,
      such as for making cars. *(4 marks)*
   (Total: *10 marks*)

3. a Outline the different types of transport that the factory shown in
     Source 1 may use for both its inputs and outputs. *(5 marks)*
   b Describe the different ways in which governments in both MEDCs and
     LEDCs may encourage the growth of industries. *(5 marks)*
   (Total: *10 marks*)

UNIT 9

Farming

Unit Contents

- Types of farming
- Farming in rich and poor countries
- Soil erosion – a worldwide problem
- Farming in Britain
- Lowland and upland farming in Britain
- The changing face of farming
- Farming and famine
- Rice for subsistence: the Indian subcontinent
- Commercial coffee growing in Tanzania: Mahoma village
- Shifting cultivation in Papua New Guinea
- Intensive market gardening: the Netherlands
- Appropriate technology: farming in Peru
- Large-scale technology: irrigated farming in California

Intensive market gardening in southern Spain helps feed the large and growing markets of Western Europe

9.1 Types of farming

Commercial farming is the growing of crops (arable) and rearing of animals (pastoral) for sale at markets. This is the main type of farming in MEDCs.

Subsistence farming is the growing of just sufficient crops and the rearing of just enough animals to feed a family. This is the main type of farming in LEDCs.

Intensive farming uses a small amount of land from which high yields are obtained. One example of this in a MEDC is the kind of market gardening shown in the photograph on page 169. An example from a LEDC is rice growing in India (Source 3).

Extensive farming uses large areas of land from which lower yields are obtained. An example in a MEDC is shown in Source 1 where highly advanced machinery is reaping vast areas of wheat, with hardly a worker in sight. In LEDCs this farming is restricted mainly to animal herding.

| Source 1 | Mechanised wheat farming in Canada – commercial extensive farming |

| Source 3 | Rice cultivation in India – subsistence farmers use little machinery |

| Source 2 | A simple classification of farming |

Type	Commercial	Subsistence
Arable	Extensive cereal cultivation	Intensive rice cultivation to feed family, e.g. India
Pastoral	Ranching of cattle and sheep, e.g. cattle ranching in USA	Herding of cattle and sheep to provide food and hides to feed family or tribe

Farming in rich and poor countries   9.2

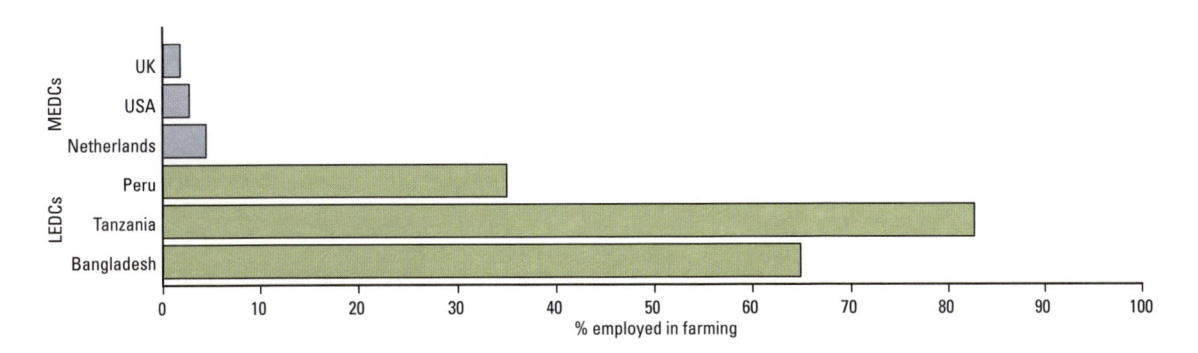

Source 1 — Dependence on farming in LEDCs and MEDCs

MEDCs: UK, USA, Netherlands
LEDCs: Peru, Tanzania, Bangladesh
% employed in farming (0–100)

In LEDCs most people work in the fields to provide enough food for themselves. If there are any crops left over, the smallholders take them to the local markets for sale. Source 2 is a bustling smallholders' market near Arusha in Tanzania.

In contrast, Source 3 shows the more common sight of a superstore selling fresh fruit and vegetables in the UK, a MEDC. Most of this food is produced under intensive commercial conditions in Europe.

Source 2 — Duluthi market, Arusha, Tanzania

Source 3 — Superstore products in the UK

9.3 Soil erosion – a worldwide problem

There are three main types of soil erosion. In parts of the world where there is enough rainfall, exposed soil will be removed down slopes as a mass movement – **sheet erosion**. Source 1 shows a scar of sheet erosion on a hill slope in eastern Brazil caused by removal of the forest to create a coffee and orange plantation.

Source 1 Sheet soil erosion

In some places where rain falls as heavy storms between drier times, soil will be removed in great gulleys – **gulley erosion** (Source 2).

In dry parts of the world, often on the edges of deserts, the loose, dry soil will be blown away by the wind – **wind erosion** (Source 3).

As populations increase in both LEDCs and MEDCs, so the pressure on the land increases.

Source 2 Gulley soil erosion in norther Tanzania

If there is too much pressure the land suffers.

The two main causes of soil erosion are deforestation and over-grazing (Source 6).

Source 3 Wind soil erosion

Farming in Britain 9.4

Over the centuries British farming has been influenced by different physical factors. Generally, pastoral farming has dominated the north and west; arable farming the south and east. Source 1 shows this pattern and suggests reasons why it has developed.

Source 2 shows how relief, rainfall and the number of sunshine hours vary from one place to another. There is clearly a link between farming type and physical factors.

Each of the maps in Source 2 has an imaginary line drawn between the mouth of the River Exe in the south-west and the mouth of the River Tees in the north-east. This 'Exe–Tees line' clearly divides the different kinds of farming in Britain.

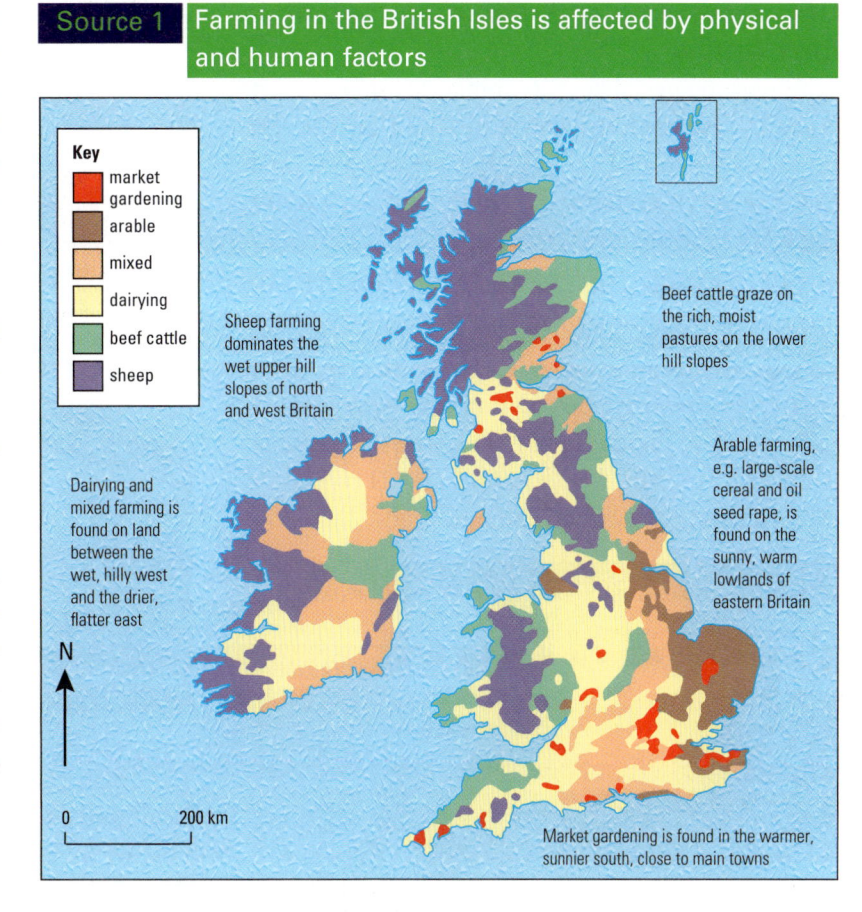

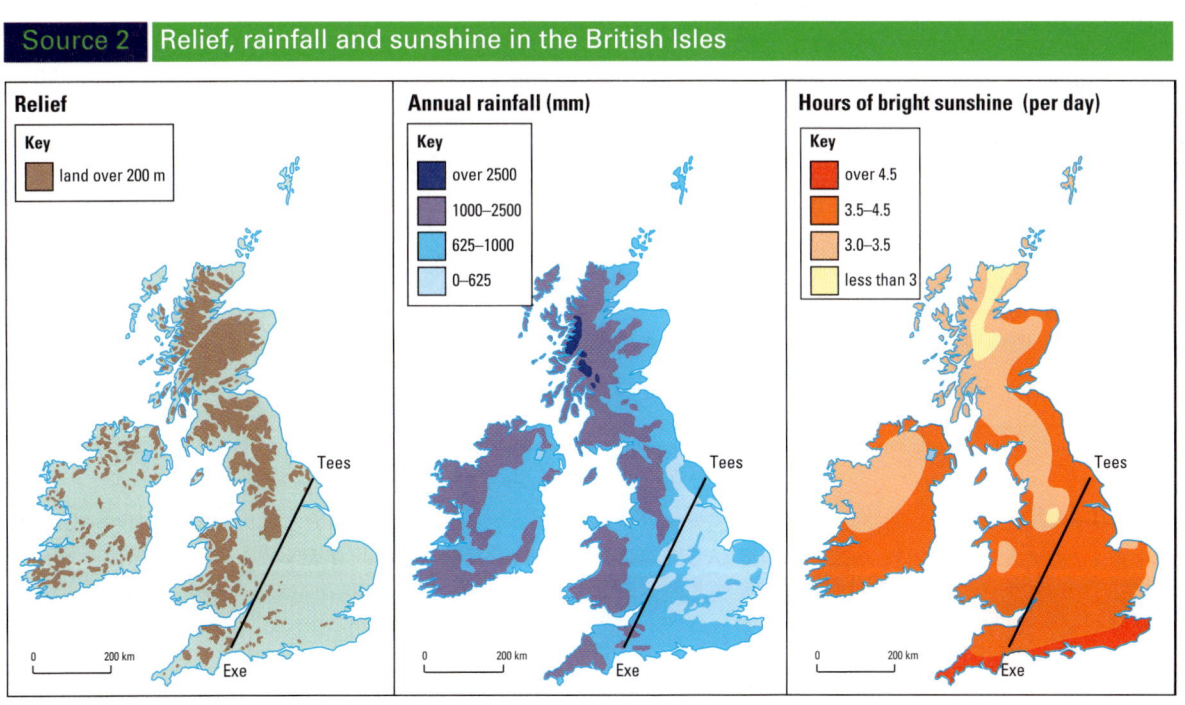

Source 1 Farming in the British Isles is affected by physical and human factors

Key:
- market gardening
- arable
- mixed
- dairying
- beef cattle
- sheep

Sheep farming dominates the wet upper hill slopes of north and west Britain

Beef cattle graze on the rich, moist pastures on the lower hill slopes

Dairying and mixed farming is found on land between the wet, hilly west and the drier, flatter east

Arable farming, e.g. large-scale cereal and oil seed rape, is found on the sunny, warm lowlands of eastern Britain

Market gardening is found in the warmer, sunnier south, close to main towns

Source 2 Relief, rainfall and sunshine in the British Isles

Relief
Key: land over 200 m

Annual rainfall (mm)
Key:
- over 2500
- 1000–2500
- 625–1000
- 0–625

Hours of bright sunshine (per day)
Key:
- over 4.5
- 3.5–4.5
- 3.0–3.5
- less than 3

9.5 Lowland and upland farming in Britain

Cereal growing and market gardening in East Anglia

One region specialising in arable farming is East Anglia. The Ryston Farm is situated on the flat **fenlands** north of Ely. The Fens are areas of land that have been **reclaimed** from the sea. As a result the soils are deep and fertile.

The dry climate, with less than 650 millimetres of rainfall per year, and warm summers, with an average temperature of 21°C, make this an ideal region for growing crops. During the winter, frosts help to kill off disease and break up the soil, making it easier to plough. The Ryston Farm is typical of many farms in this region (Sources 1 and 2).

Source 2 Ryston Estate

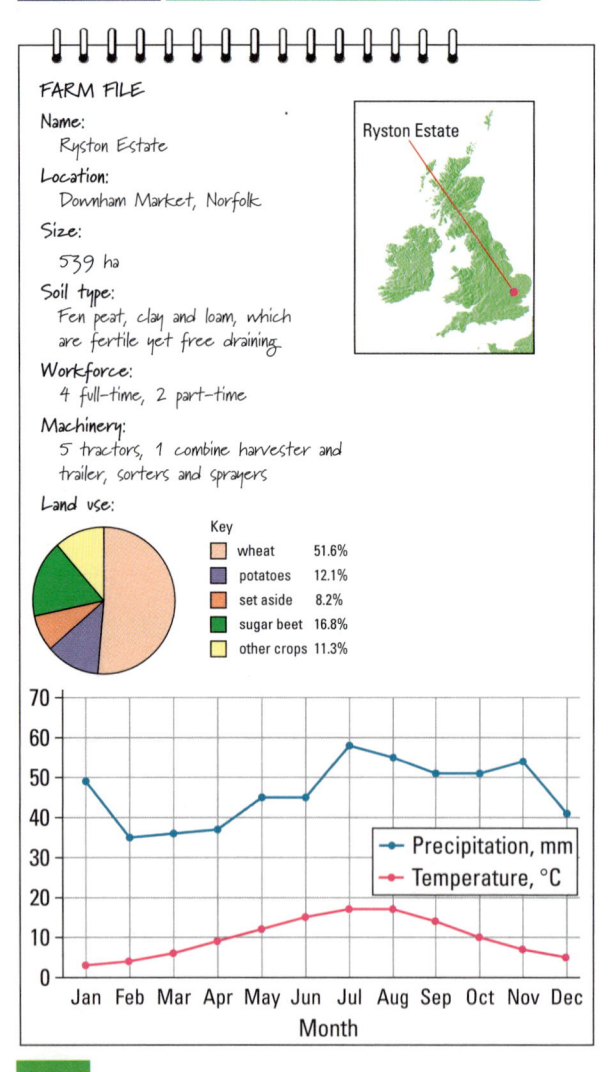

FARM FILE
Name: Ryston Estate
Location: Downham Market, Norfolk
Size: 539 ha
Soil type: Fen peat, clay and loam, which are fertile yet free draining
Workforce: 4 full-time, 2 part-time
Machinery: 5 tractors, 1 combine harvester and trailer, sorters and sprayers
Land use:
- wheat 51.6%
- potatoes 12.1%
- set aside 8.2%
- sugar beet 16.8%
- other crops 11.3%

Source 1 Ryston Estate

The main crop is wheat, which is sold directly to local mills to make animal feed. Sugar beet is another major source of income and is sold to the Wissington sugar beet factory. The linseed, beans and potatoes go to the local market.

The farm also receives **subsidies** from the European Union, without which the farm would not make a profit. In recent years the farmer has been encouraged to set aside some of his land and he currently receives a subsidy of £11 000 not to use 32 hectares of land.

East Anglia has two great advantages for food production:

- The flat landscape and suitable climate encourage extensive cereal farming as well as sugar beet and potato growing.
- Market garden produce, pigs and poultry can be sold to the rich markets of London and exported to the markets of Western Europe through the East Anglian ports of Felixstowe and Great Yarmouth.

Farming

Hill farming in the Lake District

Source 3 | Hill farming in the Lake District

Source 4 | A hill farmer in Cumbria

Source 5 | Fact file of the Lowther Estate

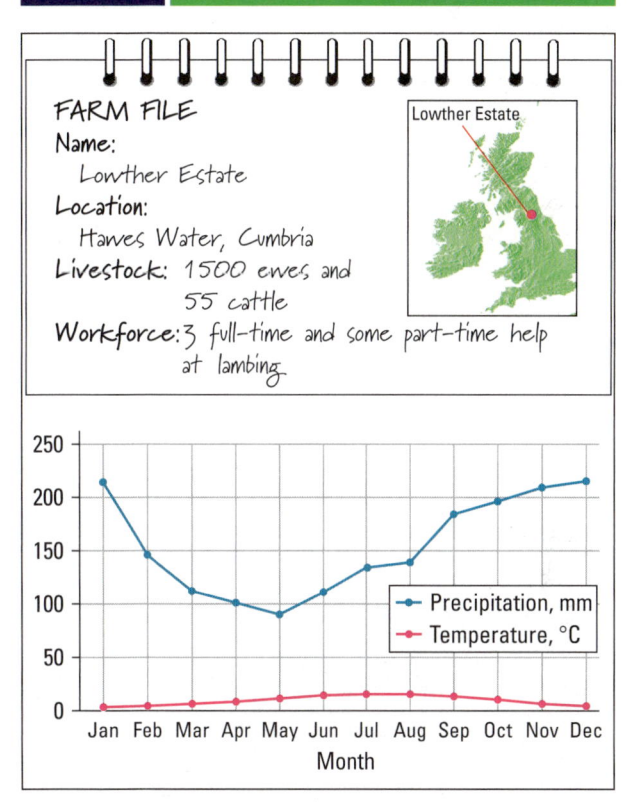

FARM FILE
Name: Lowther Estate
Location: Hawes Water, Cumbria
Livestock: 1500 ewes and 55 cattle
Workforce: 3 full-time and some part-time help at lambing

There are a number of differences between the Lake District and East Anglia. These are shown in Source 2 on page 173. The Lake District lies to the north and west of the Exe–Tees line. Here the hill slopes rise to over 800 metres, there is a great deal of rain (snow in winter), and there is not much sunshine.

The soils are thin and acid which, combined with the steep slopes, makes it very difficult to grow crops. Farmers came here to raise livestock. Sheep are grazed on the higher, poorer grasslands and beef cattle on the lower slopes.

This is called **hill farming**. Hill farmers make a living by selling wool and selling some of their livestock for meat. In the United Kingdom most hill farming takes place in the highlands of the north and west. Hill farms cover large areas of land and need little machinery or labour. This makes hill farming one of the most extensive forms of farming in Britain.

In recent years hill farmers have faced many problems, and in the Lake District alone almost a third of all farmers left the land in the 1980s to look for jobs elsewhere. It is difficult to make a living from hill farming as the price of sheep and their fleeces has fallen, while costs have risen. Even though hill farmers receive **subsidies** from the government, it is often not enough to make their work profitable. Some farmers in Cumbria believe they will be the last generation of hill farmers. Those hill farms which remain have had to diversify, and in the Lake District many of them have turned to tourism. Some now offer bed and breakfast facilities, farm tours and pony trekking in addition to their farming work. The income from tourists helps to keep the farms going.

175

9.6 The changing face of farming

British farming developed over centuries. The pattern of farming shown in Source 1 on page 173 is still to be seen. However, modern British farming is changing. As technology has improved the physical factors have become less important; more important are the commercial factors. Where to sell the product is a far greater influence than where to grow it.

The typical farm in Britain today employs far fewer workers than in the past and is much more mechanised.

It is now much larger and more specialised than in the past. As mechanisation and the demand for food increased, so farmers were encouraged to join up (amalgamate) their farms. As they did so, many hedgerows were ripped out – a serious loss to the natural wildlife which used them as their habitats.

Farmers were encouraged to sign contracts with major supermarkets and freezing and canning plants. The use of chemical fertilisers and pesticides increased in order to improve yields. This use of chemicals has also had an effect on wildlife and on the water quality of the rivers flowing through the farms.

Modern farming is changing fast. As farming has modernised in the MEDCs the application of technology has produced great improvements, as well as some dangers.

Source 1 Job losses on British farms

Source 2 The two pictures below show the same farm in 1963 and in 1991

European Union and the Common Agricultural Policy (CAP)

The European Union has encouraged farmers to use their land more intensively. It bought up surplus produce when farmers could not sell their crops. This led to the creation of huge food mountains. This food was going to waste and costs of storing it were high, so the CAP was reformed. From 1992 farmers who received grants from the EU had to take up to 20 per cent of their arable land out of production: this is called **set aside**.

The farming industry has been hard hit by these changes and many farmers have had to **diversify**. It is estimated that in 1991 almost 40 per cent of farmers were partly reliant on non-agricultural activities. These include the following:

- **Leisure** Farms with good access to urban areas have found it profitable to open their farms to the public. Some have applied for golf courses to be developed on their land.
- **Tourism** Farms in scenic locations such as the Lake District are increasingly offering bed and breakfast accommodation to tourists.
- **Conifer plantations** Under the Farm Woodland Scheme farmers receive a grant to plant conifers. The growing number of conifers is matched by a huge loss of broad-leaved woodlands.
- **Conservation** Farmers have been encouraged to protect their environment by agreeing to register their land as **Environmentally Sensitive Areas (ESAs)**. Under this scheme farmers receive a payment if they agree to:
  - limit their use of fertilisers
  - restore drystone walls
  - reduce the number of animals they keep.

Beef in crisis

There are fewer cattle on British farms than twenty years ago. As farmers tried to improve the yield of beef and milk, they used feed stuffs containing contaminated products. The result was 'mad cow disease' which was soon recognised as the source of a similar human disease. The effects on British farming were devastating. Foot-and-mouth disease in spring and summer 2001 also caused the slaughter of millions of sheep and cattle.

Source 3 Beef in crisis

Genetically modified (GM) crops

Scientists can now change the genetic make-up of crops. In doing so they are able to make them resistant to diseases or pests. This will avoid the need to use pesticides and fungicides. It will also enable plants to produce much higher yields.

Not everyone is happy. There are many consumers who fear that GM crops may be dangerous to eat. Planting such crops may damage the environment. If the crops are bred to resist certain insects, for example, the birds which live on the insects will disappear as their food supply disappears.

Organic farming

The beef crisis (Source 3) was one reason why consumers looked more carefully at the ways in which their food was produced. More people now refuse to buy products which have been produced using chemical fertilisers, pesticides, fungicides or antibiotics.

9.7 Farming and famine

Food is an essential resource, yet we live in a world where many people do not have enough to eat. Source 1 shows the parts of the world at risk from **famine**. All the areas shown are in less economically developed countries (LEDCs).

Source 1 Famine areas of the world – almost all countries most at risk are to be found as LEDCs in the tropics

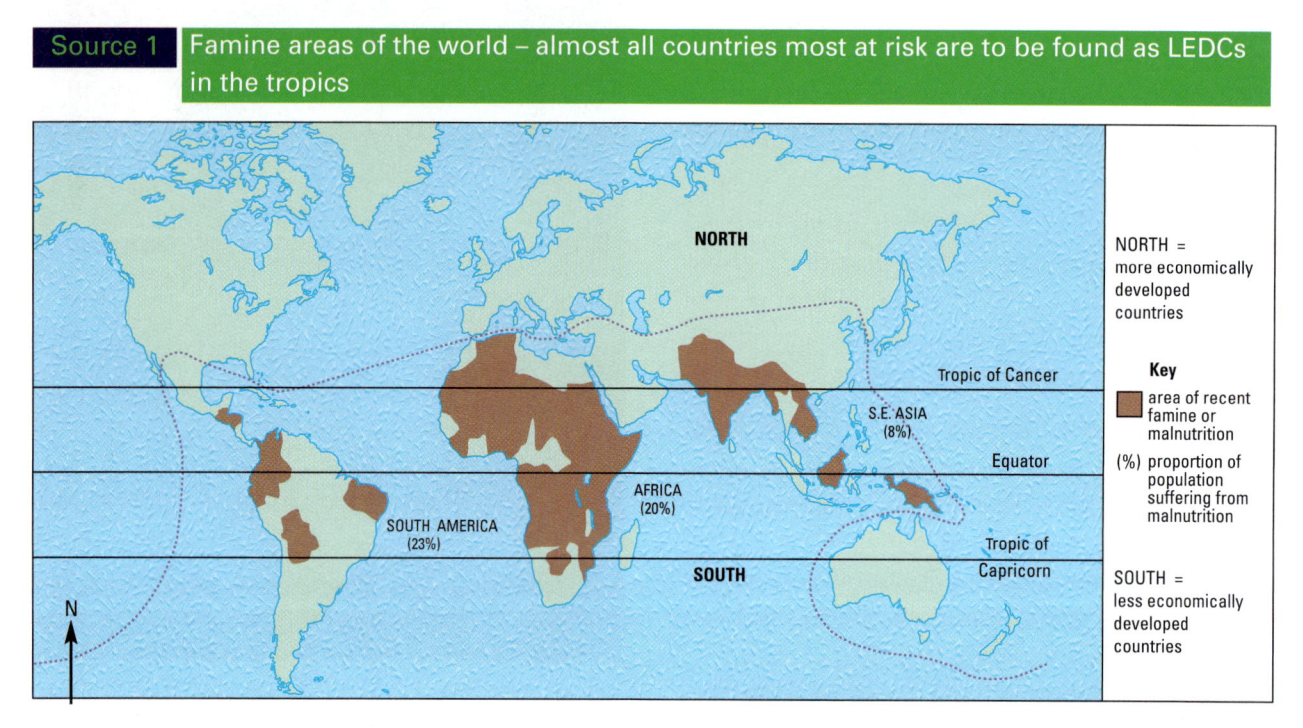

NORTH = more economically developed countries

Key
- area of recent famine or malnutrition
- (%) proportion of population suffering from malnutrition

SOUTH = less economically developed countries

S.E. ASIA (8%)
AFRICA (20%)
SOUTH AMERICA (23%)

It is estimated that on average an adult needs a balanced diet providing about 2300 calories per day. In the more economically developed countries (MEDCs), calorie consumption is high and the number of overweight people is increasing. This can lead to heart disease and strokes. By contrast, in many African nations people only manage to consume 80 per cent of this amount (Source 2). A lack of calories and the right vitamins can cause **malnutrition**, making people weak and sick.

Source 2 Daily calorie supply (% of requirements): UK, Brazil, Rwanda, Ethiopia

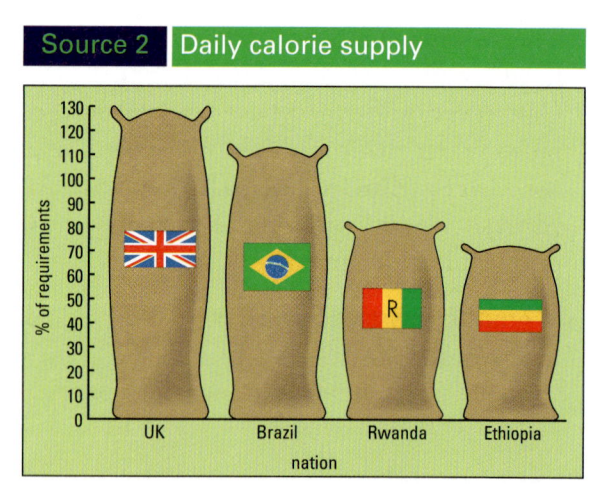

Source 3 The circle of hunger

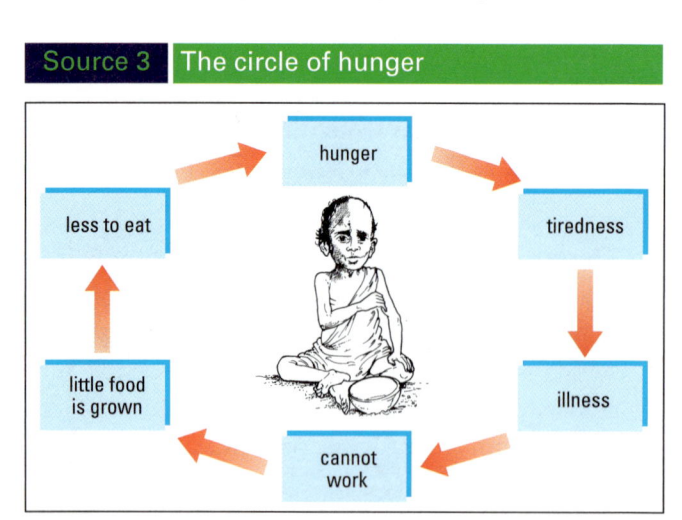

hunger → tiredness → illness → cannot work → little food is grown → less to eat → hunger

The result of many illnesses is that people become too weak to work. This contributes to the 'circle of hunger' (Source 3), from which it is difficult to escape.

Farming

The causes of famine

Some people believe that famines are a result of people's laziness or ignorance. The fact is that the causes are complex and can include any one or more of the following:

Drought When the rains fail, harvests can be destroyed and farmers are left without food.

Desertification The removal of trees (deforestation) and overgrazing result in land that is easily eroded and so turns to desert and becomes unproductive.

War Wars can destroy farming as people leave the land to fight or escape, and money is spent on weapons rather than on agriculture. Source 4 tells what happened to one family during the war in Somalia in 1992.

Poverty Landless people do not have land to farm on.

Trade LEDCs get poor prices for the cash crops which they export, yet they pay a high price for manufactured goods which they import from the developed world.

International debt LEDCs owe money to the MEDCs. Many countries have such a huge debt that most of their income goes towards paying off interest on their loans. This leaves little to spend on farming.

Source 4 Famine as a result of war

Famine in Somalia

The drought affected Abdi Husein's farm near Bardera in Somalia. When it passed he was able to grow corn, tomatoes and olives. But then war reached his village and things got worse.

'I had plenty stored, but they grabbed all my food and took all my animals and personal belongings,' said Husein from his hospital bed.

With his wife, daughter and six sons, Husein made his way to Doblei, the nearest town, eating wild fruits and leaves and gnawing on animal skins. The children died, some from gunfire during the battle, some from hunger.

In Doblei, Husein became more ill, before they heard a rumour that emergency food supplies were on their way.

What can be done?

Source 5 shows some of the ways in which the MEDCs can help the poorer world. Recently there have been moves by Britain, among others, to 'write off' some or all of the international debt, perhaps one of the most important recent moves to help the poor world.

Source 5 'Fairtrade' means a fairer price

- We could give aid, but this might only help people in the short term. People might become too dependent on aid in the long term.

- We need to improve the way food is produced. Farmers ought to use more intensive methods such as machinery, fertilisers and pesticides.

- Farmers should be given their own land. Small loans would help them buy inexpensive tools, allowing them to use their own knowledge and skills.

- Farmers should be given a fair price for their crops. Some companies that do this use the 'Fairtrade' mark. Maya Gold, which is an organic chocolate from Belize, tries to guarantee that peasant farmers are not exploited.

Fairtrade — Guarantees a better deal for Third World Producers

GREEN & BLACK'S MAYA GOLD ORGANIC DARK CHOCOLATE
From cocoa beans *forest-grown* in the Maya Mountains of Belize – with orange and spice.
20g 0.70Z

9.8 Rice for subsistence
the Indian subcontinent

Source 1 Rice-growing areas of the Indian subcontinent – high temperatures and heavy monsoon rains provide ideal growing conditions

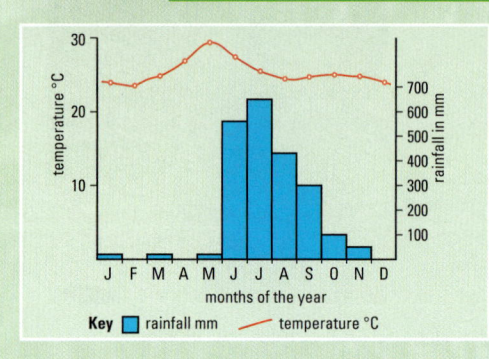

There can be no doubt that rice is a major crop, given that it feeds one-third of the world's population. The main rice-growing areas of the world are the nations of South-East Asia, including India. Here, rice is grown mainly for subsistence and what little is left is sold.

The main growing areas of India offer the perfect type of climate for rice as temperatures do not fall below 21°C throughout the year (Source 1) and there is a long wet season, called the **monsoon**. The monsoon arrives in May and ends in November. The monsoon winds pick up their moisture over the oceans. The monsoon is then followed by a dry spell which allows the rice to ripen and harvesting to take place (Source 2).

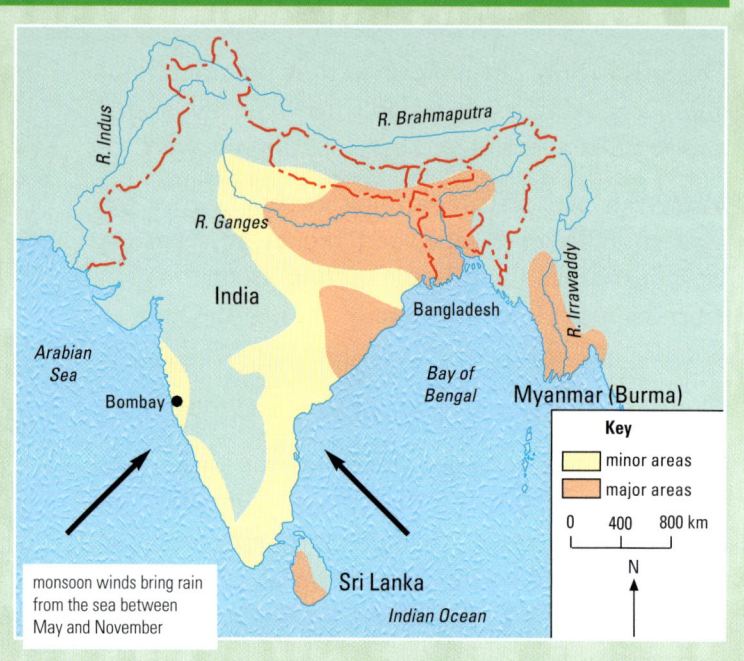

Rice is grown in flooded fields called **padi fields** (Source 3). Where the slopes are too steep, **terraces** are cut into the hillsides. Rice requires a great deal of the farmer's time and attention and it can be grown on small plots of land. This makes rice growing an intensive form of farming.

Source 2 The rice farmer's year – how does it respond to the climate?

Months	Farming activities
January	Farmer ploughs lowland fields. Plants peas, beans and lentils
February	Tends crops, weeds fields
March	Harvests crops
April	Non-farming jobs completed
May	Prepares rice seed bed, weeds, adds ash and manure to the fields. Waits for the rains, then sows seeds
June	Weeds fields
July	Ploughs in manure
August	Rice plants are moved to another field and are planted 25 cm apart
September	Continues to weed and add manure
October	Plants begin to flower
November	Rice ripens
December	Harvesting and threshing

Farming

Source 3 | **A padi field in India**

Many people work in the fields – a labour-intensive farming system

Flooded fields provide ideal growing conditions

Sowing the seeds of change

Traditional varieties of rice meant that there simply was not enough food to go around. As the population of the south-east Asian countries grew rapidly, food could not be grown fast enough. In 1959 the International Rice Research Institute (IRRI) was set up in the Philippines to look at how rice yields could be increased.

Researchers cross-bred two plants: a semi-dwarf plant from China with a strong, tall Indonesian plant. The result was a sturdy, short plant called IR8. How it compared with the traditional variety is shown in Source 4.

Source 4 | **Comparing old and new rice plants**

Old plant	New plant
grows rapidly	shorter, stronger plant
tall plant, can fall over easily	can be planted close together, needs little space
needs to be planted far apart	needs fertiliser and pesticides
5 months' growing season	4 months' growing season
average yield 1.5 tonnes per ha	average yield 5.0 tonnes per ha

New plants like IR8 proved to be a success because much more food could be produced. However, they made many demands on farmers. Expensive fertilisers and pesticides were needed and they required much more irrigation. Large-scale irrigation projects meant many small farmers lost their homes. The result has been that the rich have benefited while poor farmers could not afford to grow the new crop.

Plants like IR8 also attracted far more pests than the traditional varieties, and despite the many changes that have been made to IR8, this still remains a problem. The development of GM crops (see Unit 9.6) may revolutionise farming in the LEDCs, producing high-yield plants without the problems of IR8.

9.9 Commercial coffee growing in Tanzania
Mahoma village

On the lower slopes of Mount Kilimanjaro, Walter Semali Lyatuu grows coffee. The village in which his small farm stands, Mahoma, is just a few kilometres from the coffee-processing town of Moshi in northern Tanzania, East Africa (Source 1).

Mount Kilimanjaro is the highest peak in Africa, rising to 5896 metres. It is a volcanic mountain. Three-quarters of a million years ago the eruptions began, lasting for 300 000 years. The lava that flowed down its sides built up the mountain (see Unit 1.2). Since that time the lava has weathered to form fertile soils, ideal for the growing of coffee.

The climate, too, is good for growing crops such as coffee. Throughout the year temperatures rarely fall below 28° to 30°C. Rainfall is ample with over 800 mm per year, the main rainy months being April to July and October to November.

Coffee grows best in shady conditions. Throughout the year there is plenty of cloud cover. The plants are grown with other tree crops, especially bananas (Source 3), which provide shade for the coffee bushes in sunnier months.

Source 1 Location of Walter's farm

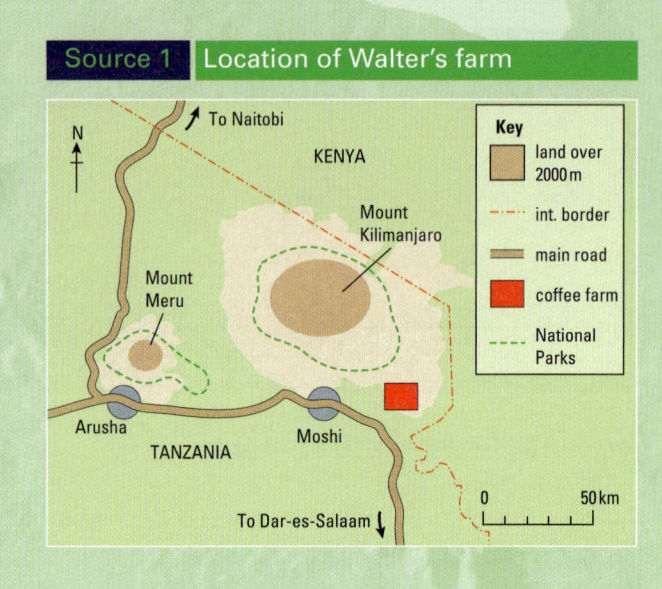

Source 2 Land use on Walter's farm

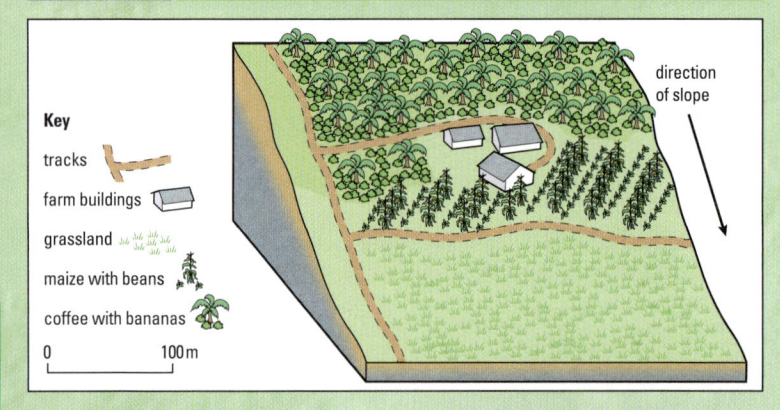

Source 3 Walter shows how banana trees (A) shade coffee plants (B) on his farm

Source 4 Grace, a local wildlife guide, displays the drying coffee beans outside Walter's house

Farming

Walter's family help on the farm. The annual cycle of work is shown in Source 5. Weeding and pruning follow the summer rains. In the drier months between January and March, chemical insecticides and fungicides and natural cow manure are applied. After that each coffee bush produces its beans and they are harvested.

Walter has done well. He now has 700 coffee bushes. In 1994 there were only 80 bushes on his farm.

The costs of producing coffee beans on Walter's farm are mainly the insecticides/fungicides ($192 per year) and cow manure ($106 per year). As the family works the farm, Walter does not need to pay for labour (Source 6).

From 1997 to 1999 the farm produced an average of 300 kilos of coffee beans each year. The price which Walter gets for the beans fell from $1.6 per kilo in 1998 to only 80 cents in 1999. His income from coffee fell from $480 in 1997 to only $200 in 1999.

When the beans are harvested the family remove the husks, put them in barrels to ferment to get rid of excess sugar, wash and dry them and pack them into sacks to send to the local Cooperative Society factory in Moshi (Source 7).

The impurities in the beans are removed by curing in the factory and then they are ready to be placed into sacks and sent to many different countries in the world.

Tanzania is a poor country. The average GDP (Gross Domestic Product) per person is only $730. Walter makes much less than this from coffee for his whole family. Today 60 per cent of Tanzania's GDP comes from agriculture, which occupies 90 per cent of the workforce. It is the government's plan to double the production of coffee by 2010. If this is to make a big difference to the country's income, the price which farmers like Walter get for their crop must stop falling.

Coffee could become an important part of the **sustainable development** of Tanzania. It will be necessary to improve the land. The way in which Walter 'inter-crops' coffee with bananas and other tree crops will help protect the wet mountain slopes on which coffee is grown. Growing trees on slopes prevents soil erosion. Trees can also give much-needed added income to the farmers. Fruits can be marketed locally.

Source 5 | The annual cycle on the farm

January	Weeding, pruning, applying insecticides
February	Pruning, applying fungicides
March	Applying fertiliser bought from Moshi
April–September	Harvesting in rotation
October–November	Flowering of plants – general maintenance
December	Beans begin to grow

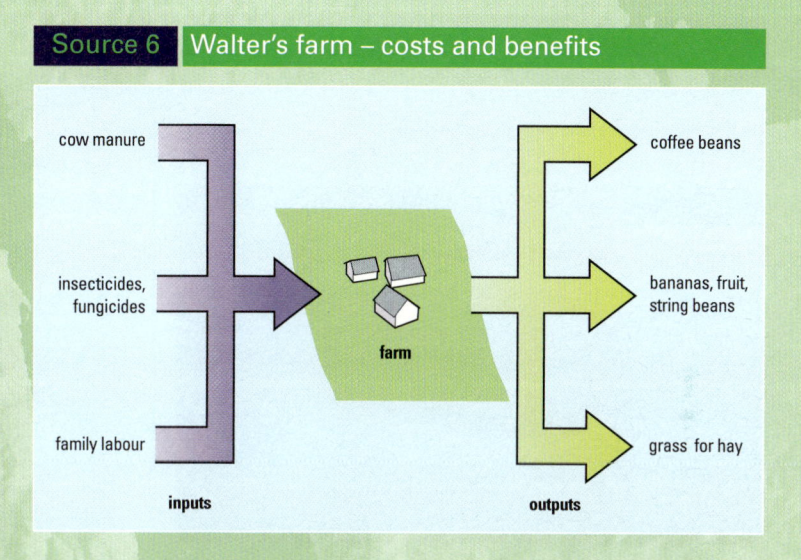

Source 6 Walter's farm – costs and benefits

Source 7 The Cooperative Society coffee factory in Moshi

9.10 Shifting cultivation in Papua New Guinea

The Bismarck mountain range lies in Papua New Guinea. It reaches up to 4500 metres high and lies just 5° south of the Equator. This is an area of steep slopes, heavy rainfall and thick rain forest (Source 1). It is the home of the Maring shifting cultivators (Source 2).

The Maring men clear an area of forest (Source 3), after which it is cultivated by the women. Cultivation of bananas, sweet potatoes and yams continues until the soil is exhausted. After this the village group will move on to clear another patch of forest.

Source 1 The Bismarck rainforest of Papua New Guinea

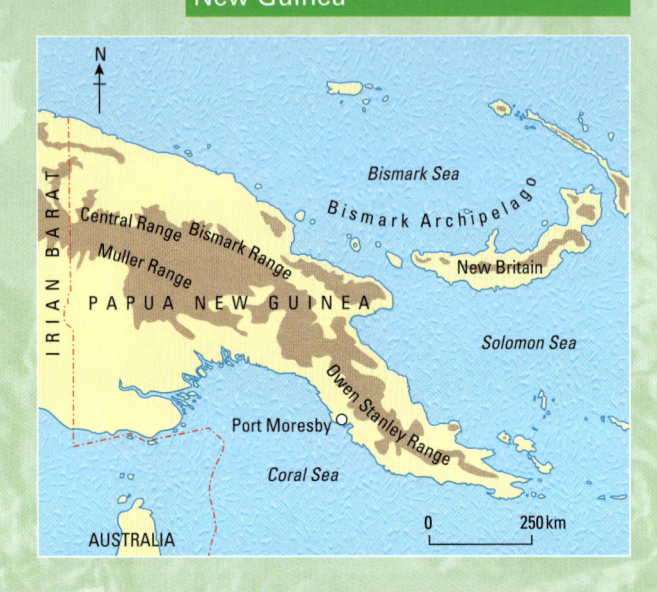

Source 2 Typical village location in the Bismarck range

Source 3 Forest being cleared prior to cultivation

Source 4 Women cultivating a cleared site

For many years the Maring system of shifting cultivation was a good example of how people can use resources without damaging the environment. After they cleared the land it would take anything from eight to forty years for the forest to regrow. Since there was no population pressure, there was no need for the Maring to use the same patch of land during this time. This was a good example of sustainable farming.

Today a different picture emerges. Increased population has led to over-use of the land. When forest regrows, it is first colonised by 'secondary forest' (saplings and small trees). During the cultivation and pre-secondary forest phase, heavy rain falling on the unprotected soil causes the nutrients to be washed down to the sub-soil (**leaching**) or washed away down the slope (**soil erosion**). If the land is cleared in this state the soil is poor. There has not been enough time for the nutrients to return to the soil. This leads to unsustainable farming and the environment is seriously damaged.

Intensive market gardening the Netherlands

9.11

Market gardening or **horticulture** involves the cultivation of fruit, vegetables and flowers on small plots of land. It is one of the most **intensive** forms of farming. Traditionally market gardens were found close to urban areas where produce could be sold as fresh as possible. Today, with improvements in transport, a market location is less important. The ideal climate for horticulture is a Mediterranean one – a mild winter and an early spring. However, these conditions can be created artificially in glasshouses. The Netherlands has become a specialist region: the coastal area of Westland is called 'the city of glass'.

The Netherlands devotes 27 per cent of its land to farming, with whole areas dedicated to producing fruit, vegetables or flowers (Source 1). There are several reasons for this.

- Almost 50 per cent of the land has been reclaimed from the sea. The new areas of land are called the Polders and have a fertile, peat and clay soil.
- Much of the land is flat, and there are plenty of waterways providing irrigation.
- Dutch farmers have access to cheap natural gas, which is used to heat the glasshouses.
- A good transport network makes it easier to reach the local markets of Amsterdam, Rotterdam and the Hague, and more distant places.
- The European Union has helped the Netherlands to expand its market throughout Western Europe.

What makes market gardening intensive? One farmer in Westland, south of the Hague, described what made his farm intensive. 'The Polder lands are very expensive, so the land has to be used almost continuously, using crop rotation, to keep the soil fertile. My farm is 2.25 hectares, which is more than twice the average size. Market gardening is labour-intensive, so we need plenty of people to work on the farms especially at harvest time. It is a costly business, and we can only sell produce which will give us a high price, if we are to make a profit.'

Source 1 Market gardening in the Netherlands

Source 2 Intensive market gardening produces a pattern of colour

9.12 Appropriate technology farming in Peru

Small-scale farming projects can often cause less damage to the environment than large-scale activities and yet be just as effective. **Appropriate technology** uses the skills of local people to find the best ways of improving their farming.

Intermediate Technology is an international development agency which works with people in rural communities in Kenya, Sudan, Zimbabwe, Sri Lanka, Bangladesh and Peru. It works with peasant farmers called *campesinos* in Peru.

Farmers in the highly populated, dry, western area of Peru are dependent on irrigation to grow crops. In recent years poor rains in the sierra mountains have reduced irrigation and water flows, leading to poor harvests. In the Ica Valley (Source 1) this situation is made worse by rapid population growth caused by the migration of people from the drought-stricken sierra. Farmers in the valley depend on irrigation and draw their water either from the River Ica or the Choclocaya Dam in the upper reaches of the river, by way of La Archivana irrigation canal.

However, the way water has been managed favours richer farmers who produce cash crops for export, leaving the *campesinos* with little water for their land.

The aim of Intermediate Technology is to help organise the small farmers so that they can have a fair share of the water:

- farmers now have better access to information about their water rights and are helped to defend their interests through improved organisation
- technical support is also given and the *campesinos* are being helped to rebuild some of their traditional technologies, such as the wooden irrigation gates shown in Source 2.

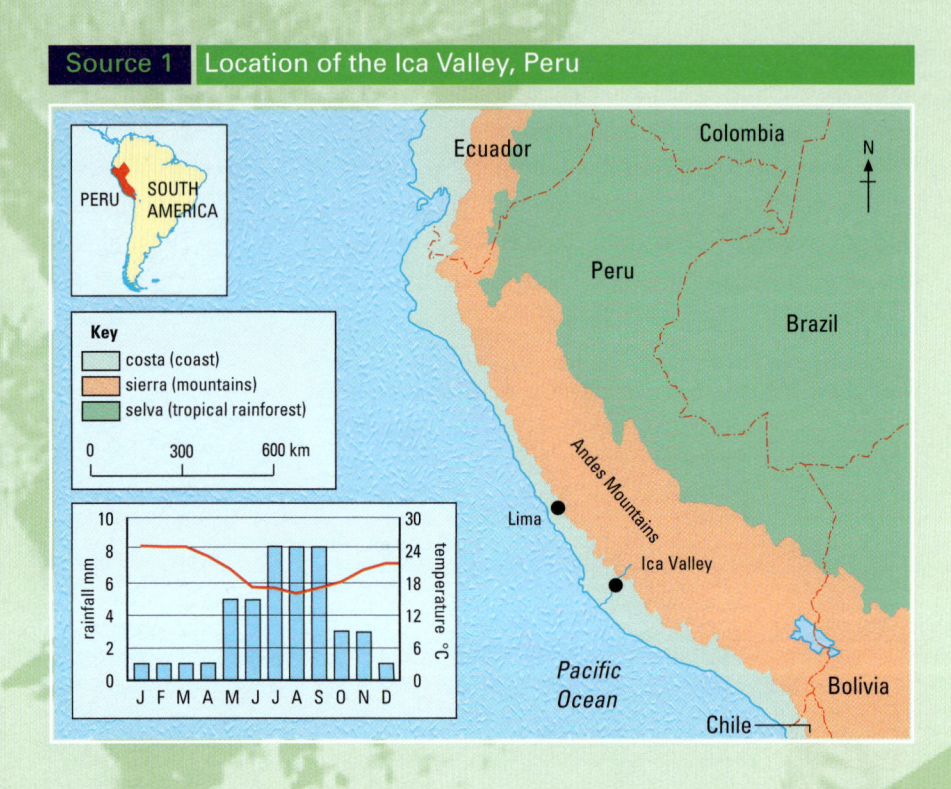

Source 1 Location of the Ica Valley, Peru

Source 2 Traditional methods of irrigation in the Ica Valley

Note very dry fields – crops cannot survive without irrigation

Primitive well-based irrigation system

Large-scale technology
irrigated farming in California

9.13

In contrast to the small-scale technology in Peru (LEDC), the irrigation farming of California (MEDC) is based on capital-intensive, large-scale technology.

It is hard to imagine how a desert can be one of the most productive areas of the USA. However, with money and technology the Central Valley desert in California is now a fertile agricultural region.

Much of California has a Mediterranean climate and, as Source 1 shows, this means there is a long summer drought during which little can grow. Farmers in the region faced two specific problems.

1. The Rivers Sacramento and San Joaquin did not supply enough water to **irrigate** the land.
2. Most of the rain fell in the northern part of the valley, yet the most fertile land was in the south.

The Central Valley Project was developed to help distribute water in California more effectively. It is a large irrigation project. Source 1 shows how dams were built in the upper reaches of the main rivers to store water. A series of canals connect these dams (Source 2) to the dry valleys 500 km further south. Water is then brought to the fields by a network of pipelines, sprays and sprinklers.

The cost of the scheme was so high that the land has to be farmed intensively. Only crops which have a high yield and value are grown, such as vines, vegetables and citrus fruits (oranges and lemons). Large-scale intensive commercial farming of this type is called **agribusiness**.

Large schemes like the Central Valley Project are controversial. They have advantages and disadvantages as the table below shows.

Advantages	Disadvantages
Crops can be grown.	Cost – farmers pay a high price for the water. This benefits rich Californian farmers.
Dams can be used for tourism.	
Dams can provide hydro-electric power.	Salts are left behind when water evaporates. This poisons the land.
Industry is attracted to cheap sources of power.	Dams will silt up in time.

Source 1 Irrigation of the San Joaquin Valley

key
— main rivers
→ major canals
▧ irrigated land – 8500 sq km

high rainfall, coast ranges, Shasta Dam, Sacramento River, Folsom Dam, Sierra Nevada, San Francisco Bay, delta, coast ranges, San Joaquin River, Fresno Dam, Fresno, San Luis Dam, low rainfall

Key: temperature, rainfall

Source 2 The Shasta Dam

Streams from surrounding hills feed the dam

HEP generated from the dam as diverted water turns turbines

The multi-purpose irrigation and power schemes of California are in marked contrast to the small-scale, single-purpose individual projects in Peru.

9.14 Activities

1 a Explain the difference between:
  i commercial and subsistence farming
  ii intensive and extensive farming
  iii arable and pastoral farming.
  b Explain why more people work in agriculture in LEDCs than in MEDCs.
  c Compare how farmers market their crops in LEDCs with farmers in MEDCs.

2 a In your own words explain the differences between sheet, gulley and wind soil erosion.
  b Look at Source 3 on page 172. Explain why this is an area likely to be affected by soil erosion.

3 a Construct a simple map of farming in Britain.
  b Describe how physical factors have helped produce the pattern shown on your map.

4 a On a simple map of Britain put in the Exe–Tees line and the location of Ryston Farm and the Lowther Estate (see pages 174–5).
  b Describe the main differences in rainfall and temperature between the two farms.
  c Explain the reasons why the two farms produce very different products.

5 a Suggest reasons why employment on British farms is in decline.
  b In what ways has the Common Agricultural Policy affected the type of farming in Britain?
  c Describe what is meant by organic farming and GM crops.

6 a In what parts of the world is famine most common?
  b Describe the main causes of famine.
  c How can the rest of the world best help those countries suffering from famine?

7 a Describe the conditions which best suit wet rice cultivation in India.
  b Explain how the rice farmer's year is adapted to the physical conditions in India.
  c In what ways can rice and other crops be improved to produce higher yields? What dangers may lie in plant technology?

8 a Describe the physical conditions which have helped coffee growing on the slopes of Mount Kilimanjaro.
  b Using Source 6 on page 183 describe the input costs and output benefits of Walter's farm.
  c Explain the importance of sustainable development to Tanzania.

9 a Summarise the main differences between the shifting cultivation of the Maring and the intensive market gardening in the Netherlands.
  b How do the Maring overcome physical obstacles to grow their crops?
  c How have the Dutch overcome the climatic problems to produce crops?

10 a What do you understand by the terms 'appropriate technology' and 'capital-intensive technology'?
   b Describe the ways in which irrigation has helped farmers in the Ica Valley in Peru.
   c Describe the cost and benefits of dam building in the San Joaquin Valley of California.

11 Use your local library, encyclopaedia or CD-Rom to produce a Farm File on any one or more of the following farming types:
   - plantations
   - shifting cultivation
   - rice cultivation
   - dairy farming
   - arable farming

   Your File should include information on:
   - the location of the farming type
   - the farming system – the inputs, processes and outputs of the farming type.

   Where appropriate, try to describe:
   - changes to the farming type
   - advantages and disadvantages of the farming type you have chosen.

12 Look at Sources 1 and 2 below.

| Source 1 | A city of glass in the Netherlands |
| Source 2 | Nomads in the Sahara Desert |

   a Describe the farming shown in each photograph.
   b State the main differences between them.
   c Suggest reasons why the farming is so different in the two areas shown.

9.15 Sample examination questions

1. **a** Define the following terms: intensive farming; commercial farming; organic farming. *(3 marks)*
   b The two photographs in Source 1 show a marketplace in Tanzania and a superstore in Europe. Describe the differences between these two scenes under the headings: Types of products, Quality of products, Methods of buying and selling. *(3 marks)*

   Source 1   A Tanzanian marketplace and a European superstore

   c Describe the type of farming found in one LEDC you have studied. *(4 marks)*
   (Total: *10 marks*)

2. **a** Study the map in Source 2.
   i Describe the main differences in the farming types on either side of the line joining the mouth of the River Exe with the mouth of the River Tees. *(2 marks)*
   ii Explain how physical factors have helped cause these differences in farming types. *(3 marks)*
   b Select one farm or farming area in Britain which you have studied.
   i Draw a simple sketch map to show its location in Britain. *(2 marks)*
   ii Describe the main products of the farm and explain why these are produced. *(3 marks)*
   (Total: *10 marks*)

   Source 2   Types of farming in the UK

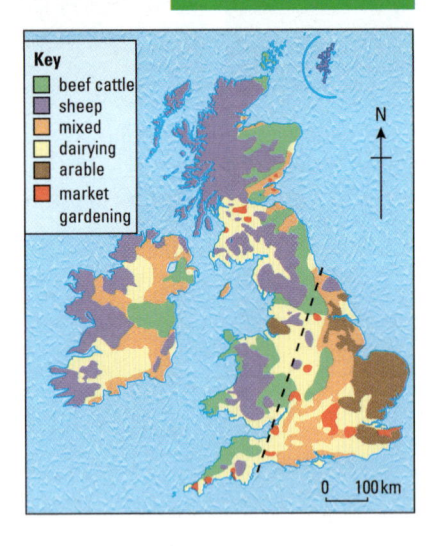

   Key:
   - beef cattle
   - sheep
   - mixed
   - dairying
   - arable
   - market gardening

3. **a** Using named examples, compare shifting cultivation in LEDCs with intensive market gardening in MEDCs under the headings: Location, Cultivation methods, Environmental effects. *(5 marks)*
   b Using named examples, explain why some LEDCs are facing famine. *(5 marks)*
   (Total: *10 marks*)

UNIT 10

World development

Unit Contents

- Measuring development
- World trade
- Global citizenship
- Development project in a LEDC: improving the water supply in Moyamba, Sierra Leone
- The benefits and problems of aid
- Countries with different levels of development: Brazil and Italy
- Contrasts in development within countries: Italy and Brazil
- A trading nation: Japan
- Primary product dependency: Dominica
- Assisting development: British overseas aid in Bangladesh

Rich and poor – where do you think these photographs were taken? The left one shows part of a ghetto in Harlem in New York City and right is a view of the impressive CBD skyline in São Paulo in Brazil. How typical of each country are these two scenes?

10.1 Measuring development

The photographs on page 191 are not typical images of Brazil and the USA. Source 1 shows just how different the two countries are and how much more developed the USA is compared to Brazil. But what is development? Development refers to the stage a country has reached economically, culturally and socially. It is not only about how rich it is in money but also about how well the people are fed, clothed and educated; how many doctors there are per person, and the quality of farming, industry and transport. Sometimes important development factors are difficult to measure and are ignored. These are qualities such as happiness, contentment and freedom from persecution.

The level of development of a country can be measured. The most common measure is the **Gross National Product** (GNP) per person. This measures the wealth of a country. Source 1 gives you some values for different countries. It is a useful measure but it does have limitations. Some countries have a high GNP per person because they are rich in oil and their population is very small. The wealth may be owned by just a few rich people.

In most countries, wealth is not shared equally and so the GNP figure hides great differences in wealth within countries. Source 2 shows how the world can be divided up using GNP.

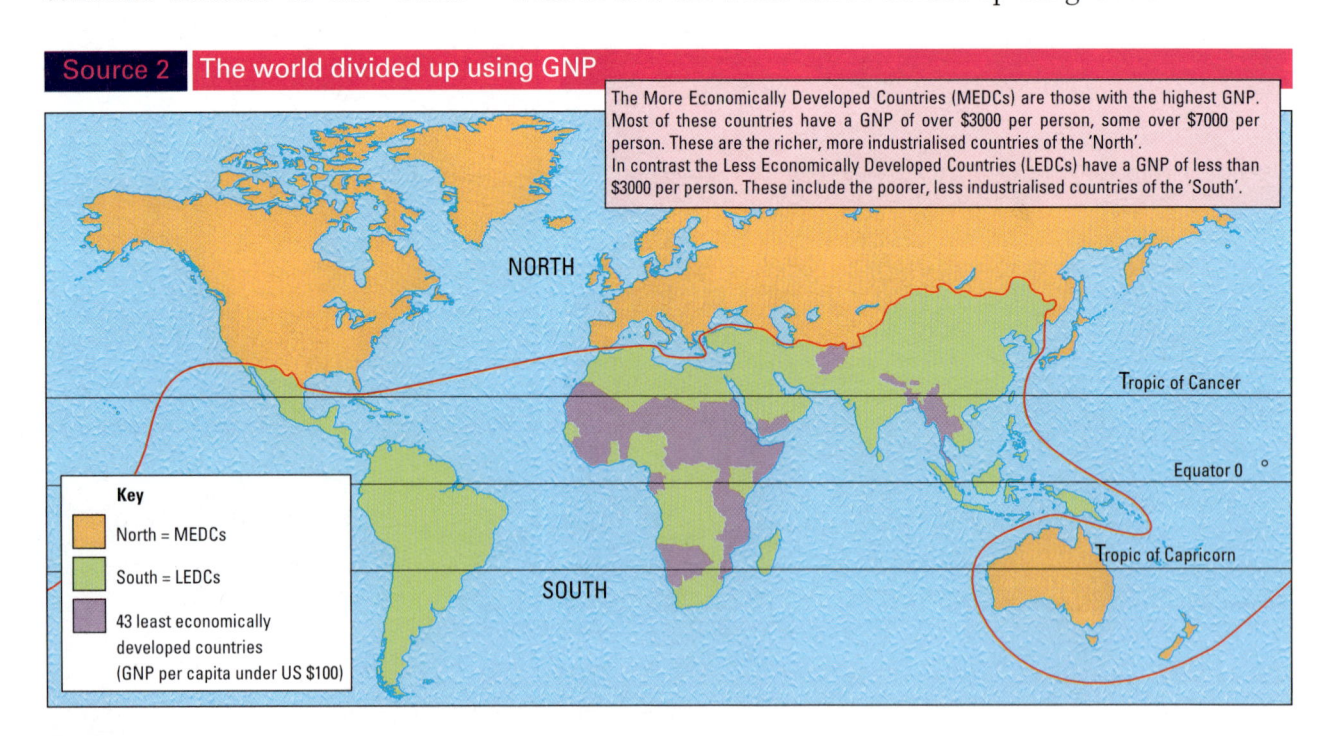

Source 1 — Gross National Product for different countries

Gross National Product per capita (per person) is the total value of all of the goods and services produced in a country in one year divided by the number of people. It is measured in US dollars ($) and includes the net income from overseas.

Country	GNP US $ per person	Birth rate per 1000	Death rate per 1000	Adult literacy %	Life expectancy years	Calorie intake per day	% of labour force in agriculture	Population per doctor	Infant mortality per 1000
Japan	31 450	10	7	100	79	2822	3	613	4
Sweden	24 830	13	12	100	78	3031	3	322	5
USA	24 750	15	9	96	76	3644	2	408	8
Kuwait	23 350	25	2	73	74	3127	1	739	12
UK	17 970	13	11	100	76	3259	2	623	7
Libya	6500	42	8	64	63	3393	13	862	68
Brazil	3020	25	8	82	66	2703	23	729	58
Bolivia	770	36	10	78	56	2096	40	2331	71
Bangladesh	220	36	12	35	53	1925	67	6615	108
Ethiopia	100	46	16	5	47	1715	73	41 075	120

Source 2 — The world divided up using GNP

The More Economically Developed Countries (MEDCs) are those with the highest GNP. Most of these countries have a GNP of over $3000 per person, some over $7000 per person. These are the richer, more industrialised countries of the 'North'.
In contrast the Less Economically Developed Countries (LEDCs) have a GNP of less than $3000 per person. These include the poorer, less industrialised countries of the 'South'.

Key
- North = MEDCs
- South = LEDCs
- 43 least economically developed countries (GNP per capita under US $100)

World development

Indicators of development

For a long time people used GNP alone to measure the level of development of a country. Today the meaning of development has been widened. Other indicators, many of them linked to the quality of life in countries, are now used to measure development (Source 3).

These measures are then used to classify countries as LEDCs (Less Economically Developed Countries) and MEDCs (More Economically Developed Countries). Sometimes people also refer to Middle Income Countries. The map in Source 2 includes a line – called the Brandt line – that divides the world into the MEDCs to the north and the LEDCs to the south. But how relevant and accurate is this in the 21st century? Kuwait, for example, is one of the richest countries in the world yet is shown as being one of the LEDCs.

Source 3 Indicators of development

Development indicator	LEDCs	MEDCs
Jobs	High % work in farming, e.g. Bangladesh 67%. Low % work in industry and services	Low % of work in farming, e.g. in the UK 2%. Higher % work in industry and services.
Housing	Poor quality often with no water supply, sewage systems, toilets or electricity as in some shanty towns.	Higher standards, most with all the services.
Diet	Low calorie intake, average 2000 per day. Often rely on one main food, e.g. rice, potatoes, which has little protein.	High calorie intake, average 3600 per day. Variety of foods high in protein.
Health Life expectancy is the average number of years people live. Infant mortality is the number of children per 1000 who die before they are 1 year old.	High rates of infant mortality – can be over 30%. Low life expectancy, as low as 45–50 years. Shortage of doctors and hospital beds. More diseases which spread rapidly, e.g. cholera, malaria.	Low rates of infant mortality and higher life expectancy – over 70 years. More doctors and hospital beds per person. Less disease.
Education Literacy is the % of adults who can read and write.	Literacy can be under 50%. Many only have primary education in makeshift schools. Little education for women.	Literacy 100% in many countries. Compulsory primary and secondary education.
Population Death rate is the number of deaths per 1000 of the population. Birth rate is the number of births per 1000 of the population.	High growth rates, large % children so pressure on resources, e.g. food, schools, hospitals. High BR, falling DR	Low growth rates, lower % children. Higher % old people. Less pressure on resources. Low BRs & DRs
Trade	Rely on export of foods and raw materials, i.e. primary products. Most are low in value and prices fluctuate. Import costly manufactured goods. Often a trade deficit.	Buy cheaper raw materials from LEDCs. High % of manufacturing, sold at higher prices to rest of the world.

10.2 World trade

Trade is the flow of goods and services between people. There are many different types of trade, as Source 1 shows. International trade involves selling goods to other countries (**exports**) and buying goods from other countries (**imports**). Trade is essential and Source 2 shows why countries need to trade.

Source 1 | Types of trade

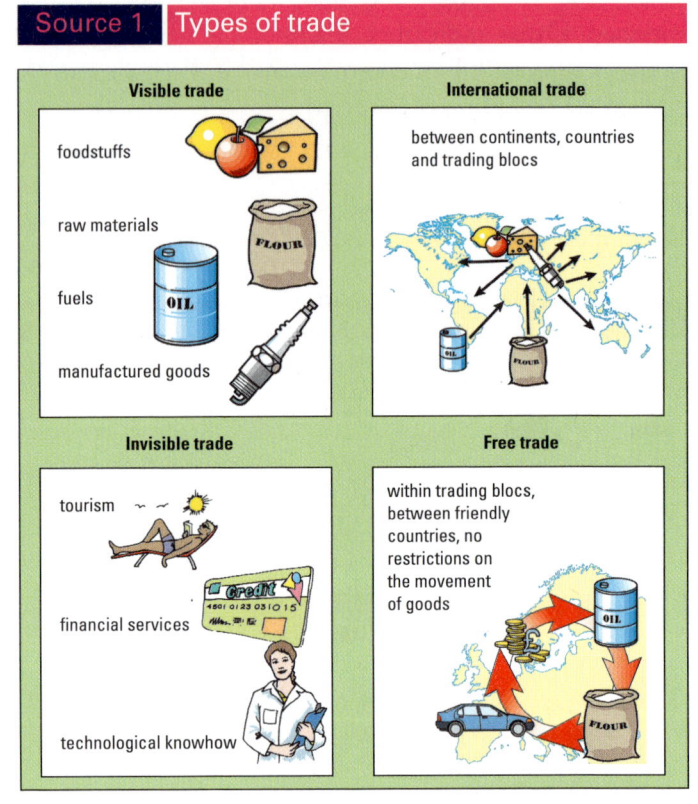

Visible trade
- foodstuffs
- raw materials
- fuels
- manufactured goods

International trade
- between continents, countries and trading blocs

Invisible trade
- tourism
- financial services
- technological knowhow

Free trade
- within trading blocs, between friendly countries, no restrictions on the movement of goods

Source 2 | Why do we trade?

"We are not self-sufficient in grain or oil supplies. We need to import these."

"We need to export more goods abroad to pay for all our imports."

Trade groupings

Some countries have grouped together to form **trading blocs** (Source 3). The European Union is one example. Trading blocs allow member countries to buy and sell goods often with no tariffs (taxes) being charged, so goods traded inside the bloc are cheaper. The countries can sometimes negotiate lower prices for imported goods because the countries act together. The richer countries of the North can often dictate the price they will pay for goods from the LEDCs.

Source 3 | Some trading blocs

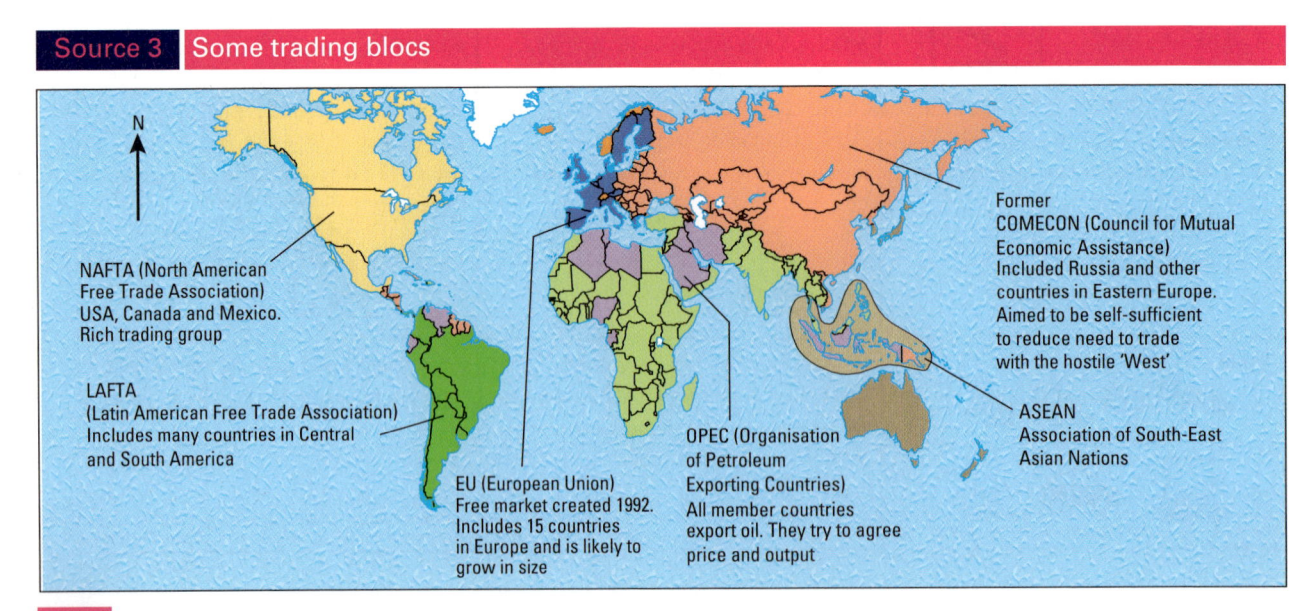

NAFTA (North American Free Trade Association) USA, Canada and Mexico. Rich trading group

LAFTA (Latin American Free Trade Association) Includes many countries in Central and South America

EU (European Union) Free market created 1992. Includes 15 countries in Europe and is likely to grow in size

OPEC (Organisation of Petroleum Exporting Countries) All member countries export oil. They try to agree price and output

Former COMECON (Council for Mutual Economic Assistance) Included Russia and other countries in Eastern Europe. Aimed to be self-sufficient to reduce need to trade with the hostile 'West'

ASEAN Association of South-East Asian Nations

World development

The balance of trade

The **balance of trade** is the difference between the costs of imports and the value of exports. Some countries earn vast profits from their exports and need to import very little. These countries have a trade surplus. They become richer and more developed. Other countries earn much less from their exports, and imports cost much more. These countries have a trade deficit and they become poorer.

The world pattern of trade

The pattern of trade is different for the MEDCs and the LEDCs (Source 3). Most trade is between the richer countries such as Japan, USA and the members of the European Union (EU). The MEDCs have a greater volume of trade and their goods are higher in value. The LEDCs have little to export and their products are relatively low in value as they are usually raw materials or commodities, to which little value has yet been added. Many LEDCs rely on just one or two export products.

The MEDCs rely upon foods, fuels and minerals from the LEDCs. The LEDCs use the money from exports to buy machinery and technology from the MEDCs. This helps the LEDCs to develop. However, the trade is not balanced because:

- the primary products, i.e. fuels, minerals and food, mostly produced by LEDCs, are low in value
- the prices of primary products fluctuate on the world market and are often controlled by the demand from MEDCs
- the value of primary products has not risen at the same rate as the value of manufactured goods
- tariff barriers act against the LEDCs.

In general, MEDCs have a trade surplus. They earn more from their exports than the cost of their imports. However, most LEDCs have a trade deficit. The costs of their imports are greater than what they earn from their exports. This means that many LEDCs have needed to borrow money, usually from the World Bank, to cover the shortfall. Some LEDCs have huge debts and in recent years many have been unable to repay the interest charges, let alone the borrowed money.

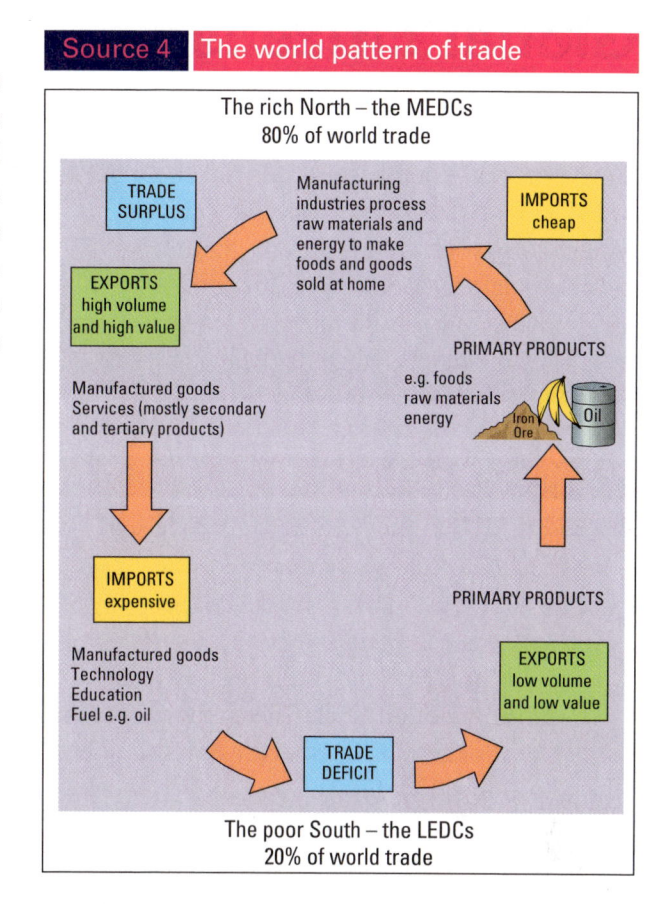

Source 4 | **The world pattern of trade**

Source 5 | **The trade trap**

195

10.3 Global citizenship

Many of the poorer countries in the world are in debt as a result of trade deficits. They also suffer from natural disasters such as floods, drought, famine and tropical storms. This has led to several campaigns being launched to promote global citizenship by:

- reducing or writing off the debts of the LEDCs
- promoting fair and free trade where the MEDCs pay a proper price for the goods they buy from the LEDCs or reduce the tariffs they charge on imports
- increasing the amount of aid to countries with no strings attached: it has been suggested that 1 per cent of the GNP of every MEDC should be given as aid from the year 2000 – Source 1 shows that this is not being achieved.

Source 1 The world's best donors of aid in the 1990s

Donor country	Aid in billions of dollars	% of GNP
Netherlands	2.6	0.94*
France	9.4	0.79*
Canada	2.5	0.44
Germany	6.3	0.42
Italy	3.4	0.32
Japan	9.1	0.31
UK	2.6	0.28
USA	17.4	0.21
Others	7.1	0.51

*above the recommended level of 0.7% GNP in the 1990s.

Source 2 Kayapo villages in the Amazon Basin

Source 3 Kayapo Indians extracting oil from the Brazil nuts

The Body Shop and the Kayapo Indians

One company that has been involved in fair trade is the Body Shop. Since 1991 the Body Shop has been trading with the Kayapo Indians in the Para region (Source 2) of the Amazon Basin in Brazil. The Kayapo wanted to trade rainforest products in order to buy fishing lines, outboard motors and medicines to cure western diseases brought in by white people. The Body Shop buys Brazil nut oil from the Indians and manufactures it into a hair conditioner. The Indians collect the nuts between January and March and extract the oil using a hand-operated press bought with a loan from the Body Shop (Source 3). The Indians get a higher price for the extracted oil than they would for simply exporting the Brazil nuts. The trade is also sustainable and does not lead to the loss of resources or damage to the environment.

Fair and free trade has many advantages:

- it gives the local people a proper and fair price for their products
- it helps the people to develop by increasing their skills and use of technology
- it helps the people to develop by increasing their skills and use of technology
- it increases trade for the country
- it is a fairer and more equitable system of trade
- it means increased earnings from partly processed products.

However, fair trade may lead to more expensive products in the MEDCs and to job losses as more of the processing takes place in the LEDCs.

World development

Aid

Aid is the transfer of money, goods and expertise to assist the development of the world's poorest countries (Source 4).

Source 4: Types of aid

Official Development Aid (DFID)
This includes bilateral grants, loans and technical assistance. This is the aid which goes from government to government. The LEDC designs the development scheme.

Voluntary aid
This is given by individuals rather than governments to national and international charities, for example Oxfam, Red Cross.

Multilateral aid
A country provides aid through a third party such as the United Nations, the World Bank or the IMF (International Monetary Fund). This is a growing source of aid and is not tied to any one country.

Emergency short-term aid
This is aid in the form of food, shelter, medical supplies and water that is sent to countries following a natural disaster.

Aid can come from two main sources:

1 Governments Governments are involved in two types of aid. The first is **bilateral aid** where the government of the country gives the aid directly to the government of the receiving country. The aid may include grants, loans and technical assistance.

The second main source is **multilateral aid** where a government donates aid to large international institutions such as the World Bank or the United Nations. These institutions then send the aid to the countries in need.

Some governments give aid with strings attached. This is called tied or conditional aid because the donor countries look for something in return, perhaps a military base, the purchase of weapons or a trade agreement. For example, the USA gave Peru large amounts of aid to search for oil. In return Peru purchased jet aircraft from the USA and allowed fishing boats from the USA into their waters.

2 Non-governmental organisations (NGOs) NGOs are charitable organisations such as Oxfam, the Red Cross (Source 5) and Save the Children. They rely on donations and fund-raising events to pay for projects in poorer countries. It is sometimes called **voluntary aid** because the money is given by individuals. Projects tend to be on a smaller scale but have more of a direct effect on the lives of the local people in the LEDCs.

As well as long-term development projects, short-term **emergency aid** (food, shelter, medical supplies etc.) is given following a natural disaster. Mozambique, for example, received emergency aid during the floods in 2000.

Source 5: The Red Cross giving out emergency aid

10.4 Development project in a LEDC

improving the water supply in Moyamba, Sierra Leone

In many LEDCs the water supply is not adequate for the local people in terms of both quality and quantity. Often the water supply is not clean and may be used by both people and animals for drinking and bathing and by people for washing and cooking. There may be no sewage systems so the water can be polluted. Pests and diseases caused by hookworms and the guinea worm make some supplies unsafe.

Moyamba is an isolated rural area in southern Sierra Leone (Source 1) which is home to 250 000 people. Most of the people are very poor subsistence farmers growing food only to feed themselves. Until 1980 few villages had safe drinking water. They relied on streams and pools that became polluted, causing water-borne diseases and poor health.

Source 1 Location of Moyamba, Sierra Leone

Since 1980 a UK-funded project has paid for 200 hand-dug wells (Source 2) to be completed. At first the schemes were not successful. The wells became polluted because there were no proper sewage systems or health education. Later projects also involved the building of pit latrines and health education for the people. The water supplies are now much cleaner and safer. The people's health has improved and diarrhoea and hookworm infections have reduced.

Source 2 Cross-section of a hand-dug well in Moyamba

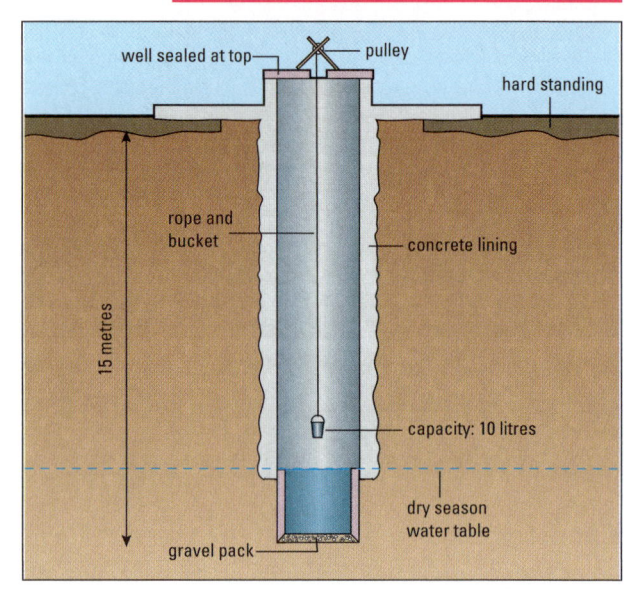

The scheme used local labour, local skills and simple technology that does not need expensive parts or maintenance. The scheme has directly benefited the local people and is a good example of appropriate technology.

Source 3 Improved water supply in Moyamba

The benefits and problems of aid 10.5

Giving aid has both advantages and disadvantages for the receiving countries.

Benefits to the receiving country

Well-planned medium- and long-term aid programmes help a country to develop and to become less dependent on aid. For example, schemes in Ethiopia are helping the people become less dependent on emergency aid when a drought occurs. The schemes also:

- improve the education and skills of the people
- increase crop yields to feed the local population rather than growing crops for export
- encourage small-scale industries to be set up
- improve water supplies and health care.

When a natural disaster strikes such as a flood or hurricane the short-term emergency aid, including food, shelters, medical equipment and clothing, is often essential in saving lives.

Problems for the receiving country

Poorly-planned aid often makes a country more, not less, dependent on others. The large prestigious schemes such as the Itaipu HEP scheme in Brazil or the Aswan High Dam in Egypt often have more disadvantages than advantages for the local people who:

- lose their farm land and have to buy food
- need expensive pumps and irrigation systems to access the water
- have to purchase fertilisers instead of being able to rely on natural flooding
- need to purchase expensive equipment, fuel and spare parts from MEDCs.

Small-scale technology that used local resources and was in keeping with the skills, education and financial resources of the local people would have been more appropriate.

Look at the schemes in Sources 1 and 2. Which scheme do you think benefited the local people most?

Source 1 | A small-scale well system

Source 2 | Aswan High Dam

Some countries give tied aid and expect something in return for the aid that is given such as trade agreements or military bases. Sometimes the aid is not free and has to be paid back as a loan, pushing the LEDCs into more debt.

Some aid does not reach the poorest people in a country due to poor transport arrangements or corrupt governments who may spend the money on the armed forces, on cities or on tourism. As a result the rich get richer and the poor get poorer.

In recent years the MEDCs have suffered a series of recessions and have given less money towards aid projects.

10.6 Countries with different levels of development
Brazil and Italy

Can you name any wealthy and poor areas within your local area? Differences in development can be seen within a single city, between regions in a country and between countries. Remember how the photographs on page 191 were the opposite of what we might have expected. Here we compare Brazil and Italy. A variety of indicators are used to measure the level of development:

- economic indicators, for example GNP, trade and aid
- social indicators, for example health care and education.

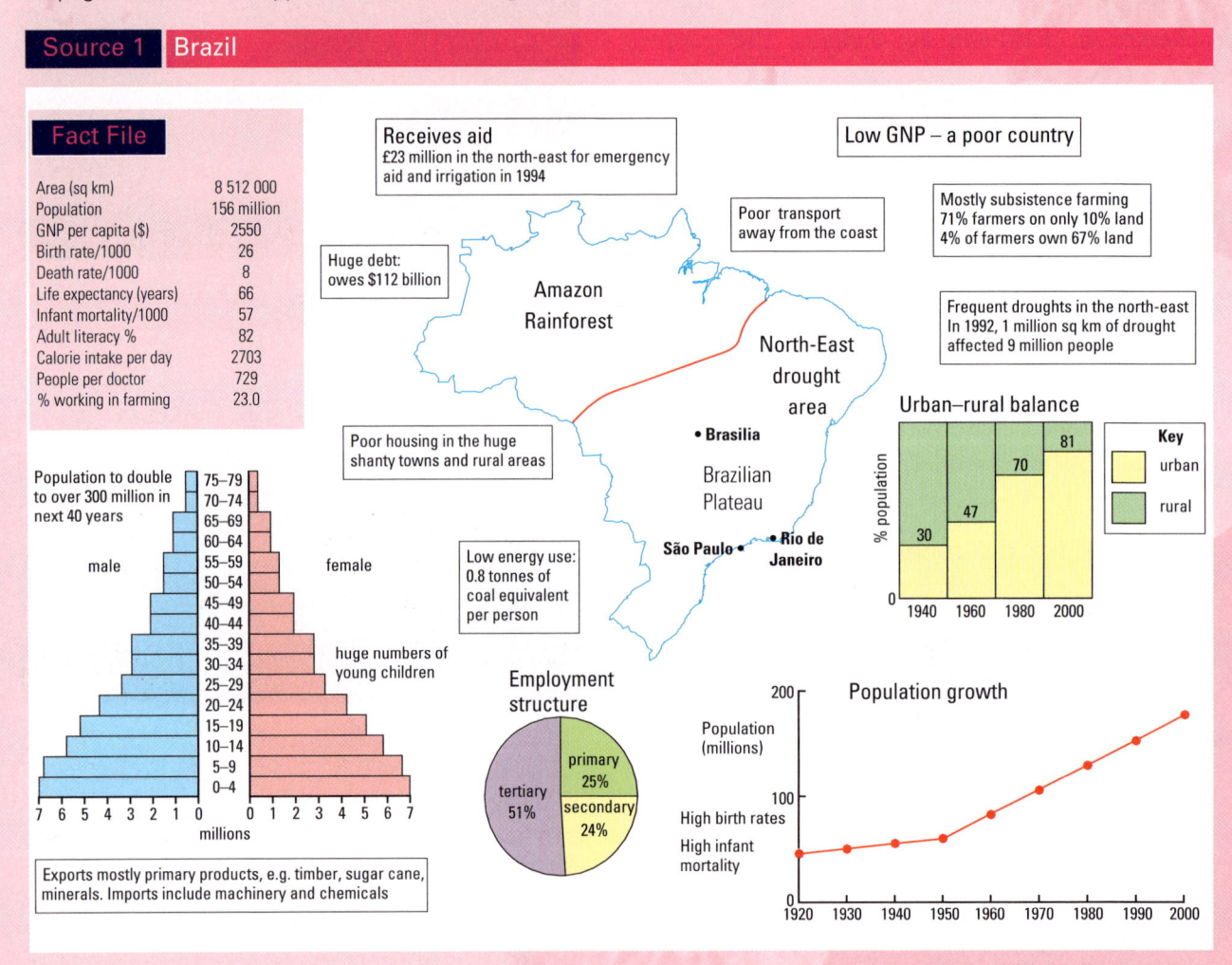

Source 1 — Brazil

Fact File

Area (sq km)	8 512 000
Population	156 million
GNP per capita ($)	2550
Birth rate/1000	26
Death rate/1000	8
Life expectancy (years)	66
Infant mortality/1000	57
Adult literacy %	82
Calorie intake per day	2703
People per doctor	729
% working in farming	23.0

Receives aid: £23 million in the north-east for emergency aid and irrigation in 1994

Low GNP – a poor country

Huge debt: owes $112 billion

Poor transport away from the coast

Mostly subsistence farming 71% farmers on only 10% land, 4% of farmers own 67% land

Frequent droughts in the north-east In 1992, 1 million sq km of drought affected 9 million people

Poor housing in the huge shanty towns and rural areas

Low energy use: 0.8 tonnes of coal equivalent per person

Map labels: Amazon Rainforest, North-East drought area, Brasilia, Brazilian Plateau, São Paulo, Rio de Janeiro

Urban–rural balance (% population): 1940: 30 urban; 1960: 47; 1980: 70; 2000: 81
Key: urban / rural

Population pyramid — Population to double to over 300 million in next 40 years. Age groups 0–4 to 75–79, male/female, in millions. Huge numbers of young children.

Employment structure: primary 25%, secondary 24%, tertiary 51%

Population growth (millions), 1920–2000: High birth rates, High infant mortality. Rises from ~30 million in 1920 to ~170 million by 2000.

Exports mostly primary products, e.g. timber, sugar cane, minerals. Imports include machinery and chemicals.

Brazil: summary

Brazil is one of the world's less economically developed countries (LEDCs). The figures for birth rate, energy consumption and infant mortality support this. Brazil also has some characteristics expected of the MEDCs. These include the low death rate, the percentage of people living in urban areas and a trade surplus.

Since the 1960s, there has been an economic miracle in Brazil. Large-scale industries have developed, raw materials and energy resources have been exploited and the GNP has risen. However, much of the country remains poor and undeveloped, especially the north-east where there are frequent droughts. The government also borrowed heavily to pay for these developments.

World development

Source 2 — Italy

Fact File

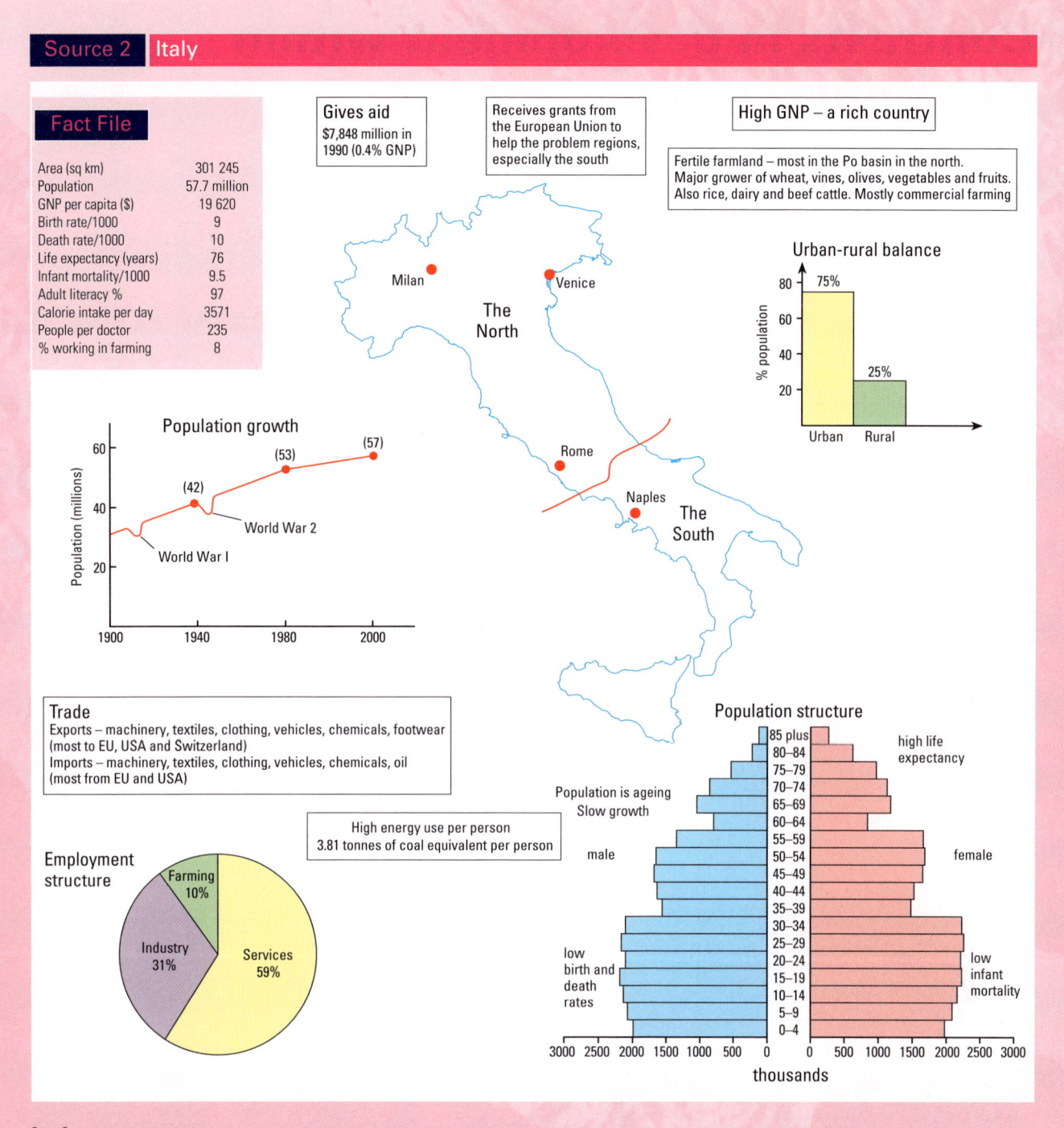

Area (sq km)	301 245
Population	57.7 million
GNP per capita ($)	19 620
Birth rate/1000	9
Death rate/1000	10
Life expectancy (years)	76
Infant mortality/1000	9.5
Adult literacy %	97
Calorie intake per day	3571
People per doctor	235
% working in farming	8

Gives aid
$7,848 million in 1990 (0.4% GNP)

Receives grants from the European Union to help the problem regions, especially the south

High GNP – a rich country
Fertile farmland – most in the Po basin in the north. Major grower of wheat, vines, olives, vegetables and fruits. Also rice, dairy and beef cattle. Mostly commercial farming.

Map labels: Milan, Venice, The North, Rome, Naples, The South

Urban-rural balance: Urban 75%, Rural 25%

Population growth (millions): 1900 ~30, 1940 (42), 1980 (53), 2000 (57); dips at World War I and World War 2

Trade
Exports – machinery, textiles, clothing, vehicles, chemicals, footwear (most to EU, USA and Switzerland)
Imports – machinery, textiles, clothing, vehicles, chemicals, oil (most from EU and USA)

High energy use per person 3.81 tonnes of coal equivalent per person

Employment structure: Farming 10%, Industry 31%, Services 59%

Population structure: high life expectancy, low infant mortality, low birth and death rates, Population is ageing, Slow growth — male/female pyramid in 5-year bands from 0–4 to 85 plus, thousands.

Italy: summary

Italy is one of the world's more economically developed countries (MEDCs). It has none of the characteristics of a LEDC except a small trade deficit. Italy has generally high living standards, low population growth and a high GNP. Poorer Italians are supported by welfare payments.

The country has a variety of landscapes and climates. There are large areas of fertile farmland which are used intensively to grow arable crops, vines and vegetables. The country can afford to import oil and has supplies of gas, oil and HEP (hydro-electric power). There is a long history of manufacturing and there are many different industries.

Italy also has problems. There are summer droughts and several volcanoes in the south, and there may be avalanches and the occasional earthquake in the Alps. The world recession has caused a trade deficit in recent years. Congestion and pollution are growing problems in large cities such as Milan, Venice and Rome. Perhaps Italy's greatest problems lie in the south of the country which remains quite undeveloped in many areas.

10.7 Contrasts in development within countries
Italy and Brazil

Wealth is not shared evenly within a single country. It is often concentrated in just one favoured region called the **core**, leaving other regions quite poor in comparison. These poorer regions are called the **periphery**.

Italy

Italy is a country with a north–south divide (Source 1). The north, especially the Po basin, is the core region and is wealthier and more developed than the south. The south of Italy, called the *Mezzogiorno,* is the periphery.

Source 1 Italy's north–south divide

Advantages of the north:
- supplies of natural gas in the Po basin and HEP from the Alps
- more jobs in industry and services
- fertile lowland with irrigation water available
- large cities, for example Milan, Turin and Genoa connected by an efficient transport system
- close to large European markets
- better-quality housing and services and higher standard of living

Disadvantages of the south:
- mountainous relief makes communications difficult
- the climate is hot and dry in summer with a few months' drought
- heavy winter rainfall causes soil erosion and flooding
- the rocks are mostly limestone and form thin soils
- low yields of wheat, olives and vines
- poor-quality grazing for sheep and goats
- poor transport, little industry, emigration

Since 1950 the Italian government has invested money to try to improve the south. In recent years the EU has also provided grants and loans. In the south:

- some new *autostradi* (motorways) have been built
- new irrigation schemes allow tomatoes, citrus fruits and vegetables to be grown
- some large-scale industry, such as iron and steel, and car manufacture, has located in the South.

However, the north–south divide remains and the gap is widening.

	North Italy	South Italy
Area %	60	40
Population %	63	37
Birth rate per 1000	11	17
Death rate per 1000	10	8
Income per person (million lira)	>2500	<1600
% farm production	65	35
% share of hospital beds	74	26
% unemployment	8	22

World development

Brazil

Brazil's core region is the south-east of the country. The north and north-east form the periphery (Source 2).

Source 2 Brazil's south-east–north-east divide

Prosperity and urban growth in the south-east of Brazil

The north-east

The north-east forms part of the periphery in Brazil. It is poorly developed and has many problems.

- The region suffers frequent droughts. In 1992 the drought affected 9 million people.
- Most farmers are subsistence farmers.
- The land is poor with infertile and eroded soils.
- Crop yields are low but the birth rate is high – there is not enough food to feed the population.
- The best land is used for plantations, often owned by **transnationals**. The crops are for export.
- The region has poor housing and services.
- Thousands of people have migrated from the area.

The south-east

Early growth was linked to coffee-growing near São Paulo. Coffee, gold and diamonds were exported. Later, rapid growth began with the mining of iron ore, the making of steel and the manufacture of cars and ships. Services were provided for the growing number of **migrants** from the rural areas.

Why is the south-east the core region?

- It is the centre of commerce, industry, education, transport and culture.
- The region has the highest standard of living in Brazil and contributes most to GNP.

However, many people live in shanty towns and there is major congestion and pollution in the cities.

	South-East Brazil	North-East Brazil
Population %	42	30
Birth rate per 1000	22	48
Infant mortality per 1000	49	109
Life expectancy (years)	63	48
Adult literacy %	72	39
% share of national wealth	64	14
% employed in industry	70	10
% with clean water	64	23

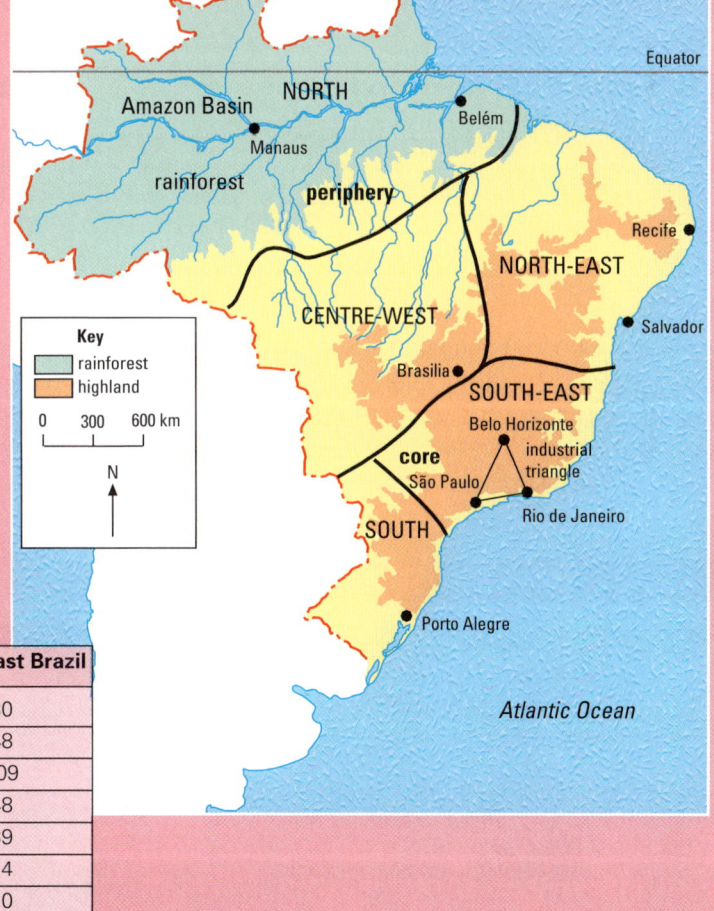

10.8 A trading nation
Japan

Before 1945 Japan was very isolated from the rest of the world. Few foreigners were allowed entry and there was little trade. Since 1945 there has been an economic miracle. The GNP has risen greatly and in 1989 Japan replaced the USA as the world's richest nation despite having very few natural resources. Trade and industry have developed for the following reasons:

- Japan has no oil or iron ore, very little coal or other raw materials, and needs to import these items
- Japan has to export to pay for the imports. Steel, chemicals, cars and ships were sold abroad. Since the 1970s these industries have declined. They have been replaced by a growth in the electronics industry and in services
- The Japanese have developed and manufactured many new products, for example computers, video recorders, compact disc players and video cameras. Source 1 shows the main imports and exports of Japan today.

The reasons for Japan's economic miracle are as follows.

Economic
- modern machines and methods of working
- profits used in research to develop new products
- large home market which has become richer

Social
- well-educated workforce
- the workforce operates well in teams and are prepared to work long hours
- workers have a high degree of loyalty to their employers

Political
- strong government support for industry
- political stability

Japan has been so successful that every year there is a huge trade surplus. It was $135 billion in 1995. The country is very dependent upon the rest of the world to supply the raw materials that its industry needs, and to provide the market for the goods it makes. Japan is **interdependent** with many countries.

Japan's success has also brought some problems. Japan has been in trouble in the world over its trading policies. Japan has the benefit of free trade in many areas of the world yet charges high tariffs on goods entering Japan.

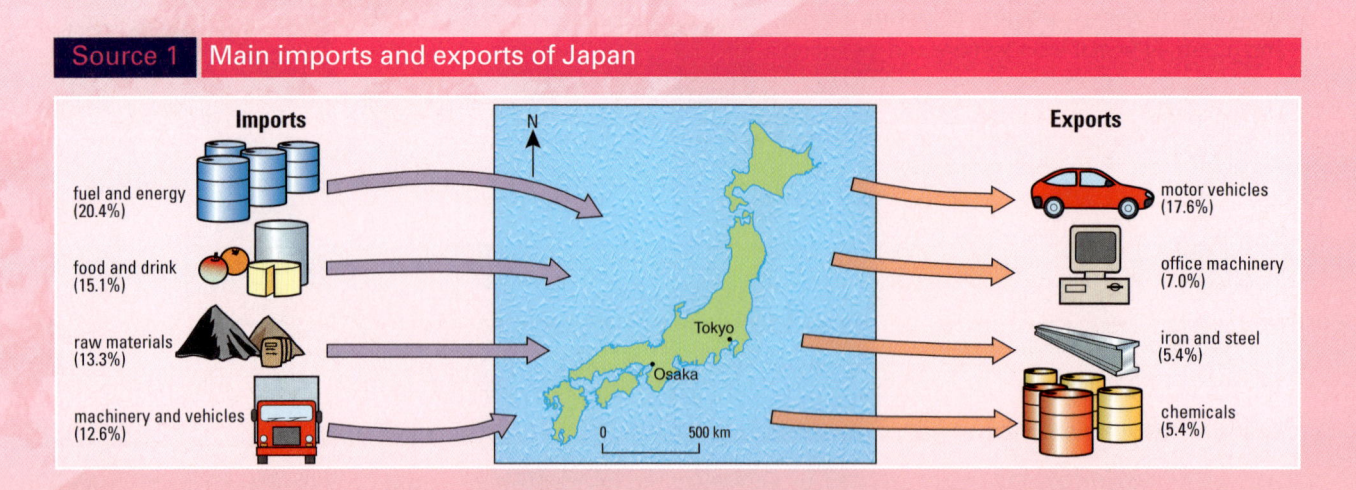

Source 1 Main imports and exports of Japan

Imports
- fuel and energy (20.4%)
- food and drink (15.1%)
- raw materials (13.3%)
- machinery and vehicles (12.6%)

Exports
- motor vehicles (17.6%)
- office machinery (7.0%)
- iron and steel (5.4%)
- chemicals (5.4%)

Primary product dependency

10.9 Dominica

Dominica is one of the Windward Islands in the Caribbean (Source 1). Today the islands are mostly dependent upon a single crop – bananas. This is called **primary product dependency**.

The banana industry employs over 15 000 people out of a population of 88 000. The family-run farms are small – about five acres. Vegetables to feed the family are grown on one acre and bananas grow on the other four acres. The bananas have to be perfect or they will not sell in Europe.

Dominica is a poor country, its GNP is only $2570 per person. Growing bananas is not a very profitable activity and 50 per cent of the turnover goes on fertilisers, pesticides, blue plastic sheets to protect the crop from insects and the cardboard boxes used to pack the bananas (Source 2).

Source 1 The Windward Islands

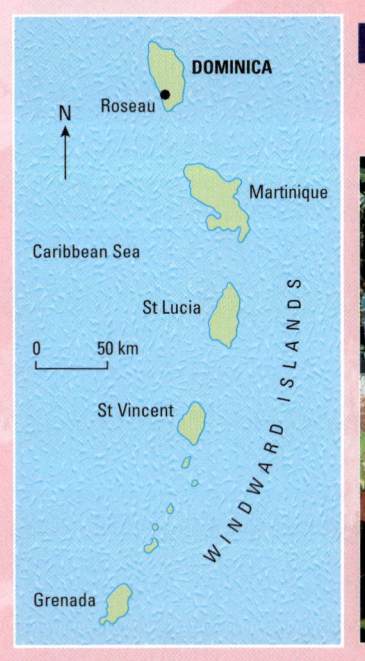

Source 2 Bananas being packed in Dominica

Source 3 Problems in Dominica

Tragedy for Dominica if Geest pulls out
Geest (established banana traders since colonial times) are threatening to pull out of the banana industry in Dominica. Two out of every three bananas produced are eaten in the UK. Talks to negotiate a new contract with Geest and the EU are taking place.

Hurricane David destroys banana crop

Dominica on a loser
Recent reports show that only 25 per cent of the money earned from bananas ends up in Dominica.

Dominica is dependent on bananas because:

- the British influence in colonial times means each person in the UK still eats an average of 8.2 kilos of bananas a year
- the climate and relief are suitable for bananas but little else grows well
- there are few raw materials or energy supplies to develop other industries
- there are few natural attractions to bring in many tourists (other Caribbean islands have developed because of tourism).

Look at Source 3 to discover some of the problems facing the banana growers.

SPAT, the Small Projects Assistance Team in Dominica, is working to:

- rebuild plantations after the hurricanes
- develop livestock farming, e.g. pigs
- diversify crops, e.g. root crops, herbal medicines
- negotiate new contracts with the EU.

Dominica needs to reduce its dependency on bananas in order to develop in the future.

10.10 Assisting development
British overseas aid in Bangladesh

Britain is one of the wealthy countries of the world and a major aid donor. Britain gives over £1500 million a year, but it is still not up to the 1 per cent of GNP expected by the United Nations from 2000. Britain gives aid to help poorer countries to:

- raise their standard of living
- make better use of land and resources
- preserve the environment
- improve health and education
- cope with natural disasters.

Britain's official aid programme is managed by the Department For International Development (DFID). The DFID is part of the Foreign and Commonwealth Office. Over 50 per cent of Britain's aid is spent on bilateral aid, which is paid directly to the governments of individual countries.

Partners in development: Britain and Bangladesh

Britain has a special relationship with Bangladesh. The country has received over £700 million in aid since 1971 when Bangladesh gained independence. Britain gives Bangladesh different types of aid.

- **Bilateral aid**, since 1974, has been in the form of grants. This money does not have to be repaid and there are no interest charges.
- **Multilateral aid** is given through contributions to the World Bank, the European Union, the Asian Development Bank and the World Food Programme.
- **Non-governmental organisations** include Oxfam, CARE, Christian Aid, Save the Children and the British Red Cross. They work at the grass-roots level in communities (Source 2).

Britain works with Bangladesh to support the Five-Year Development Plan which aims to tackle the country's most serious problems (Source1). Source 3 shows more about British aid in Bangladesh.

Source 1 — British aid in Bangladesh

Problems of Bangladesh
- lack of natural resources, e.g. minerals, energy
- high dependence on agriculture
- floods and hurricanes
- low literacy rates
- poor communications
- huge population and high population growth

The Five-Year Development Plan
- reduce population growth
- expand employment
- primary education for all
- improve technology
- self-sufficiency in food
- greater economic growth
- improve standards of living and health care

Aims of British aid
- to reach the poorest people
- to give priority to women's development
- to involve British goods and services
- to focus on agriculture, energy, transport, health, family planning and education

Source 2 — Health care in the community – notice how it is targeting women

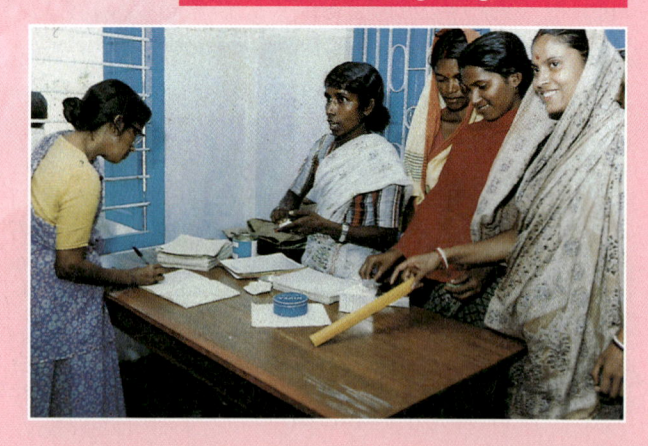

206

World development

Source 3 — Aid to Bangladesh

Agriculture

The Deep Tubewell Project aims to increase food production. It will allow the farmers to grow rice in the dry season. Britain has given £17 million towards building 4000 wells. The wells will irrigate 130 000 hectares of land. The money provides consultants as well as diesel engines, electric pumps, well casings and computer equipment. Other agricultural schemes include:

- deep-water rice research project to increase yields, develop new varieties, and improve methods of pest control
- tea project to improve quality and output
- improving cattle health
- developing fish hatcheries.

Power and energy

Greater Dhaka, the region around the capital of Bangladesh, has a population of over 20 million. It uses one-third of the country's power and demand is rising. Britain began giving aid for a power project in the region in 1974. Since then £63 million has been spent on over 2500 km of transmission cables and 14 new substations.

Britain has also given aid for a gas-fired power station at Ashuganj in Bangladesh and for the development of gas fields. This will reduce the need for Bangladesh to import fuels.

Emergency aid

The British government often sends emergency aid for refugees and disaster relief. In the last decade Britain has given large amounts of food aid to Bangladesh. In several years the crops have failed because of natural disasters. The aid is provided as wheat and it often totals over 100 000 tonnes in a year.

Non-governmental organisations

Other work in Bangladesh is carried out by NGOs (or charities) such as Oxfam, the Red Cross and Save the Children. The National Lottery now provides some funding and the British government also supports NGOs. The amount of government funding has increased in recent years because of the huge floods.

In 1985 Christian Aid established the Nari Kendra, a women's centre near Dhaka. It trains women in health care, literacy, numeracy and other skills. The DFID gave £55 000 to support the project.

Multilateral aid

About 40 per cent of the British government's aid is paid to large international agencies such as the World Bank, the European Union and the United Nations. Bangladesh has received over $520 million of multilateral aid. The money is used in a range of projects to improve agriculture, power and social conditions.

10.11 Activities

1 a Study the photographs on page 191. Write down five differences in the quality of life that the photographs suggest.
  b What do the photographs tell you about the level of development in the USA and Brazil?
  c Use Source 1 on page 192 to give four examples of development indicators that show the USA is more developed than Brazil.

2 a What does GNP stand for? What does it measure?
  b Use the GNP data in Source 1 on page 192 for this exercise.
    List those countries with a GNP per capita (**i**) above $20 000 and (**ii**) below $10 000.
  c Using the two lists from (**b**), say which list is made up of MEDCs and which is made up of LEDCs.
  d Give two reasons why GNP is not always a good indicator of development.

3 a Scattergraphs can show whether there is a link between GNP and the other indicators of development. Draw scattergraphs between GNP and some of the other indicators shown in Source 1 on page 192. Source 1 below shows the example of GNP and birth rate. Write a sentence below each of your graphs to say what it shows.

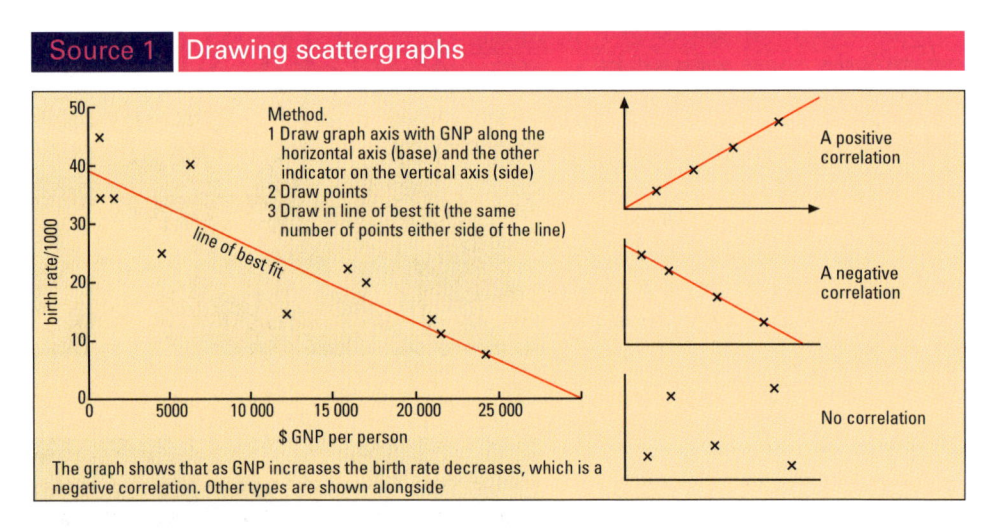

Source 1 | Drawing scattergraphs

Method.
1 Draw graph axis with GNP along the horizontal axis (base) and the other indicator on the vertical axis (side)
2 Draw points
3 Draw in line of best fit (the same number of points either side of the line)

The graph shows that as GNP increases the birth rate decreases, which is a negative correlation. Other types are shown alongside

A positive correlation
A negative correlation
No correlation

  b What is development?
  c What sort of development indicators are not used and why?

4 a Define the following terms: trade; international trade; exports; imports; balance of trade; trade deficit; trade surplus.
  b Give three reasons why countries need to trade.
  c Give three reasons why there is a trade gap and trade is unfair between the MEDCs and LEDCs.

5 a Suggest three ways global citizenship could be improved.
  b Draw a sketch map to show the location of the Kayapo villages in Brazil.
  c Explain why the Kayapo people wanted to trade.
  d Describe the scheme that has been set up with the Body Shop.
  e Why is it a good example of fair trade and trade that is sustainable?

World development

6 a What is aid and why do the LEDCs need it?
  b According to the UN, how much aid should each MEDC give?
  c Name the four types of aid and write a sentence to say what each one means.

7 a Give three problems of water supply in many LEDCs.
  b Draw a labelled sketch map to show the location of Moyamba in Sierra Leone.
  c Describe the UK scheme that has improved the water supply in the area.

8 Draw up a table like the one below to show some of the benefits and problems of aid.

Benefits of aid	Problems of aid

9 a Produce a table in summary form to show the differences between Brazil and Italy. Use the following headings as a guide: Population characteristics; Employment (farming, industry and services); Trade; Urban rural balance; Energy use; Food intake; Aid; Problems; GNP; Literacy.
  b In what ways is Brazil as developed as Italy?
  c In what ways is Italy like a less economically developed country?

10 Italy and Brazil both have differences in development within their countries. You could use these questions for one or both countries.
  a What do you understand by the core and periphery in a country?
  b Draw a sketch map and label some of the main features of the country.
  c On your sketch map clearly mark the core and periphery.
  d Quote three statistics that show the differences between the two regions.

11 a Find out some of the indicators of development for Dominica. Is the country a MEDC or a LEDC? Explain your answer.
  b Give four reasons why Dominica is dependent on the banana trade.
  c What are the problems caused by having only one main source of income?
  d How can Dominica solve its problems?

12 a Give three reasons why Britain gives aid to the LEDCs.
  b For each of the aims of British aid say which problem it helps to solve for Bangladesh.
  c Describe the three types of aid Britain gives to Bangladesh.
  d Choose one of the types of aid from page 206. Describe the main features of your chosen project. What advantages does the project have for Bangladesh?

13 Hold a class discussion about world trade and aid. Prepare some ideas on the following:
- To what extent do you think world trade is fair and why?
- What should happen to tariff boundaries?
- Should there be more fair trade and why?
- What sort of aid is best for the LEDCs?
- What sort of aid should be avoided?
- How effective is trade and aid in closing the poverty gap between rich and poor countries?
- What would a fairer system look like?
- Do you think it will ever be achieved and why?

10.12 Sample examination questions

1 Study Source 1 which shows information about the UK compared with two countries in Central America.
   a Which indicator best shows the level of education? (1 mark)
   b Give two indicators that show the level of health care. (2 marks)
   c What does the term gross national product (GNP) per capita mean? (2 marks)
   d What is the relationship between GNP per capita and life expectancy in Source 1? (2 marks)
   e What are the advantages and disadvantages of using GNP per capita as a development indicator? (3 marks)

Source 1: Honduras, Nicaragua and the UK

Indicators	Honduras	Nicaragua	UK
Population	5.8 million	4.1 million	58.9 million
GNP per capita	$600	$380	$18.342
Life expectancy	69 years	68 years	76 years
Access to safe water	87%	58%	100%
One doctor for every	1266 people	2000 people	850 people
Infant mortality	47 per 1000	51 per 1000	6 per 1000
Literacy	73%	66%	99%

(Total: 10 marks)

2 Study Source 2 which gives information about the coffee trade.

Source 2: The change in coffee prices 1975–1995

Year	Price (US cents/kg)	Year	Price (US cents/kg)
1975	158	1986	376
1976	312	1987	237
1977	504	1988	255
1978	341	1989	202
1979	373	1990	157
1980	331	1991	147
1981	254	1992	117
1982	275	1993	136
1983	282	1994	296
1984	311	1995	305
1985	293		

   a Draw a line graph to show how the price of coffee has changed. (4 marks)
   b Coffee is a primary product. What does this mean? (1 mark)
   c Why do so many LEDCs rely on primary products such as coffee for trade? (1 mark)
   d Describe the advantages to MEDCs and the disadvantages to LEDCs of trade in primary products? (4 marks)

(Total: 10 marks)

3 Study the cartoon about aid being given to LEDCs.

Source 3: What price development?

   a What aid has the farmer received? (1 mark)
   b Suggest two disadvantages of this type of aid to poor farmers in LEDCs. (2 marks)
   c Using a case study, describe an aid project that would be more helpful to a LEDC. (6 marks)
   d Give one reason why it is a more helpful project. (1 mark)

(Total: 10 marks)

UNIT 11

Energy

Unit Contents

- World energy resources
- Non-renewable energy
- Renewable energy
- The changing demand for energy in the UK
- Wind power: Haverigg Wind Farm, Cumbria
- Energy in Africa: fuelwood
- Hydro-electric power: the Three Gorges Dam in China
- Nuclear energy

An oil rig in the North Sea. What do you think it is like living and working on this oil rig?

11.1 World energy resources

Energy is one of the most important of all the world's resources. We need energy to keep us warm and to cook with. It gives us light and drives machinery for transport and industry. Fortunately our natural environment provides us with a wide range of energy sources. **Fossil fuels** are coal, oil and natural gas. Fuelwood, uranium, flowing water, the wind and the sun can be used to produce energy. Source 1 shows the relative importance of each of these in 2000.

Energy sources such as fossil fuels are classed as **non-renewable** – once used up they cannot be replaced. Newer energy sources are often **renewable**, for example solar and wind power – they can be used again and again. These are often **sustainable**, and are likely to play an increasingly important role in the future.

Source 1 | World energy sources

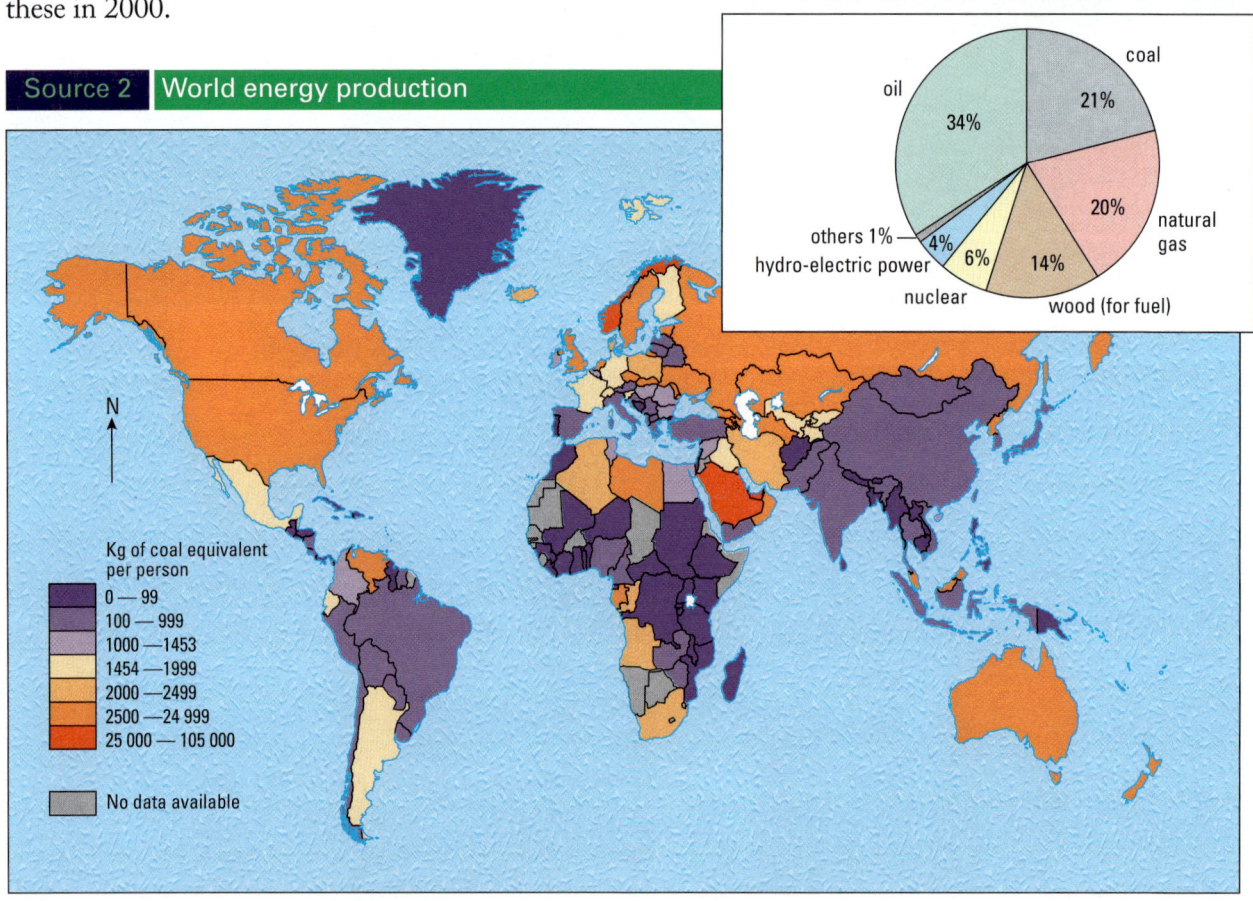

- oil 34%
- coal 21%
- natural gas 20%
- wood (for fuel) 14%
- nuclear 6%
- hydro-electric power 4%
- others 1%

Source 2 | World energy production

Kg of coal equivalent per person
- 0 — 99
- 100 — 999
- 1000 — 1453
- 1454 — 1999
- 2000 — 2499
- 2500 — 24 999
- 25 000 — 105 000
- No data available

Who supplies the world's energy?

Seventy-five per cent of the world's energy comes from fossil fuels. Source 2 shows that these are not very evenly distributed across the world. The USA, Canada, former USSR, Western Europe, Australia, China and the Middle East contain most of the world's coal, oil and natural gas. Western Europe and North America were the first regions to become industrialised. Their early industrial development was helped by the abundance of fossil fuels, particularly coal. Many of the world's MEDCs are found here today.

Source 2 does not take into account the use of wood and **biomass** fuels (fuels made from burning or rotting plants and vegetation). Many people in LEDCs rely on these to supply their energy needs.

Who uses the world's energy?

Europe and North America use 70 per cent of the world's energy (Source 3), although only 20 per cent of the world's population live there. These regions developed their industries quickly using fossil fuels. Today, with many of their own reserves falling or exhausted, they need to import energy to meet demands, especially oil.

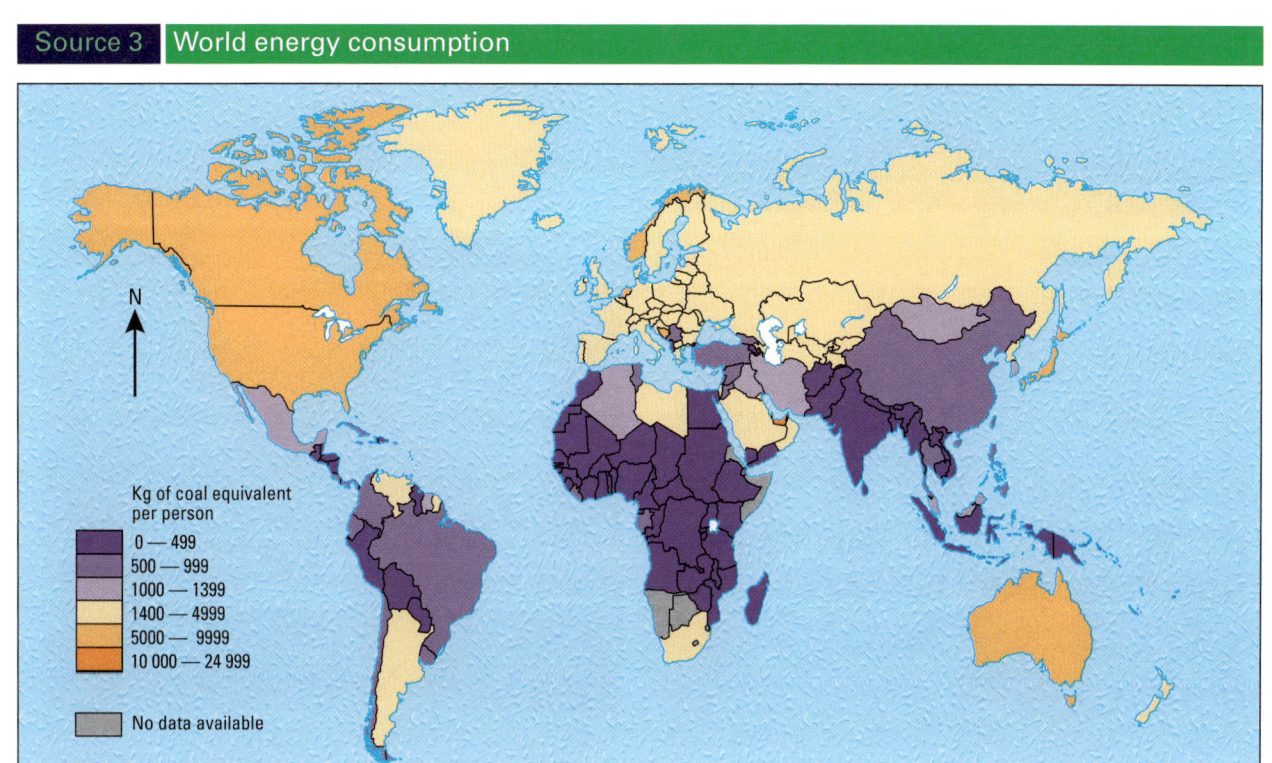

Source 3: World energy consumption

Kg of coal equivalent per person
- 0 — 499
- 500 — 999
- 1000 — 1399
- 1400 — 4999
- 5000 — 9999
- 10 000 — 24 999
- No data available

Source 4: Energy in the city

A comparison of Sources 2 and 3 shows quite clearly that the world's major producers of energy are also the major consumers. The amount of energy a country uses is a good indicator of its stage of development (Source 4). The presence of energy resources has obviously been a major factor in the industrial development of some countries. Many of today's MEDCs have substantial fossil fuel deposits – or have had them in the past. The main exception is Japan, whose industry has developed despite a lack of energy resources. Even so, Japan is looking to nuclear power in the future, rather than continuing to rely on importing oil.

As fossil fuels start to run out and countries become more aware of the environmental problems caused by their use, the relative importance of different types of energy seems likely to change.

11.2 Non-renewable energy

The world's energy resources can be divided into non-renewable and renewable resources. Non-renewable resources are finite – once they are used up they cannot be replaced because they take too long to form or regrow. They include the major fossil fuels formed over tens of thousands of years – coal, oil and natural gas, plus uranium (used in nuclear power stations) and fuelwood.

Fact File | Coal

Status non-renewable fossil fuel

Description formed underground from decaying plant matter

Lifespan 230 years

% share of world energy consumption 21

Main producers USA, China, Australia, India, South Africa, Russian Federation

Energy uses electricity, heating, coke

✓ **advantages** high world reserves; newer mines are highly mechanised

✗ **disadvantages** pollution – CO_2, the major greenhouse gas responsible for global warming; SO_2, the main gas responsible for acid rain; mining can be difficult and dangerous; opencast pits destroy land; heavy/bulky to transport

Fact File | Oil

Status non-renewable fossil fuel

Description formed underground from decaying animal/plant matter

Lifespan 41 years

% share of world energy consumption 34

Main producers Saudi Arabia, USA, Russian Federation, Iran, Mexico, Venezuela, China

Energy uses electricity, petroleum, diesel, fuel oils, liquid petroleum gas, coke and many non-energy uses, e.g. plastics, medicines, fertilisers

✓ **advantages** variety of uses; fairly easy to transport; efficient; less pollution than coal

✗ **disadvantages** low reserves; some air pollution; danger of spills (especially at sea) and explosions

Energy

Fact File: Natural gas

Status non-renewable fossil fuel

Description formed underground from decaying animal/plant matter; often found with oil

Lifespan 62 years

% share of world energy consumption 20

Main producers Russian Federation, USA, Canada, UK, Algeria

Energy uses electricity, cooking, heating

✓ **advantages** efficient; clean – least polluting of the fossil fuels; easy to transport

✗ **disadvantages** explosions; some air pollution

Fact File: Fuelwood

Status non-renewable fossil fuel

Description trees, usually in natural environment, not grown specifically for fuel

Lifespan variable within each country, but declining

% share of world energy consumption 14

Main producers of energy LEDCs, especially in Africa and Asia

Energy uses heating, cooking (also used for building homes and fences)

✓ **advantages** easily available, collected daily by local people; free; replanting possible

✗ **disadvantages** trees quickly used; time-consuming – wood collected daily; deforestation leading to other problems (soil erosion, desertification); replanting cannot keep pace with consumption

Fact File: Nuclear

Status non-renewable

Description heavy metal (uranium) element found naturally in rock deposits

Lifespan unknown

% share of world energy consumption 6

Main producers of energy USA, France, Japan, Germany, Russian Federation

Energy uses used in a chain reaction to produce heat for electricity

✓ **advantages** clean; fewer greenhouse gases; efficient; uses very small amounts of raw materials; small amounts of waste

✗ **disadvantages** dangers of radiation; high cost of building and decommissioning power stations; problems over disposal of waste; accident at Chernobyl raised public fears; Sellafield (Cumbria) has had a number of minor leaks

11.3 Renewable energy

Fossil fuels are non-renewable energy sources. However, there are many sources which can be classed as renewable sources. These include the use of water – hydro-electric power, tidal and wave; the wind; the sun; geothermal and biomass/biogas.

Renewable resources are generally cleaner than non-renewable sources, but as yet produce only 6 per cent of the world's energy needs. Solar, tidal, wave, geothermal and biomass/biogas are often called 'alternative' energies.

Fact File | Hydro-electric power

Status renewable

Description good, regular supply of water needed; water held in a reservoir, channelled through pipes to a turbine

% share of world energy consumption 4

Main producers Canada, USA, Brazil, China, Russian Federation

Energy uses electricity

✓ **advantages** very clean; reservoirs/dams can also control flooding/provide water in times of shortage; often in remote, mountainous, sparsely populated areas

✗ **disadvantages** large areas of land flooded; silt trapped behind dam; lake silts up; visual pollution from pylons and dam

Fact File | Tidal

Status renewable

Description tidal water drives turbines

% share of world energy consumption insignificant

Main producers France, Russian Federation

Energy uses electricity

✓ **advantages** large schemes could produce a lot of electricity; clean; barrage can protect coasts from erosion

✗ **disadvantages** very expensive to build; few suitable sites; disrupts coastal ecosystems and shipping

Energy

Fact File — Solar

Status renewable

Description solar panels or photovoltaic cells using sunlight

% share of world energy consumption less than 1

Main producers USA, India

Energy uses direct heating, electricity

✓ **advantages** could be used in most parts of the world – unlimited supplies; clean; can be built in to new buildings; efficient

✗ **disadvantages** expensive: needs sunlight – cloud/night = no energy; large amounts of energy require technological development and reduction in costs of PVs (photovoltaic cells)

Fact File — Wind

Status renewable

Description wind drives blades to turn turbines

% share of world energy consumption less than 1

Main producers Denmark, California USA

Energy uses electricity

✓ **advantages** very clean; no air pollution; small-scale and large-scale schemes possible; cheap to run

✗ **disadvantages** winds are unpredictable and not constant; visual and noise pollution in quiet, rural areas; many turbines needed to produce sufficient energy

Fact File — Geothermal

Status renewable

Description boreholes can be drilled below ground to use the earth's natural heat; cold water is pumped down, hot water/steam channelled back

% share of world energy consumption less than 1

Main producers Japan, New Zealand, Russian Federation, Iceland, Hungary

Energy uses electricity, direct heating

✓ **advantages** many potential sites, but most are in volcanic areas at the moment

✗ **disadvantages** sulphuric gases; expensive to develop; very high temperature can create maintenance problems

Fact File — Biogas/biomass

Status renewable

Description fermented animal or plant waste or crops (e.g. sugar cane); refuse incineration

% share of world energy consumption less than 1

Main producers Brazil, Japan, Germany, Denmark, India

Energy uses ethanol, methane, electricity, heating

✓ **advantages** widely available, especially in LEDCs; uses waste products; can be used at a local level

✗ **disadvantages** can be expensive to set up; waste cannot be used in other ways, e.g. fertilisers; some pollution

11.4 The changing demand for energy in the UK

The 1980s and 1990s saw great changes in the UK's energy demand. The greatest changes were in the electricity industry. No longer is the UK so heavily dependent on electricity generated in coal-fired power stations, like the one shown in Source 1. Source 2 shows that many of the country's coal-burning power stations are located in the Midlands and the North, close to the coalfields.

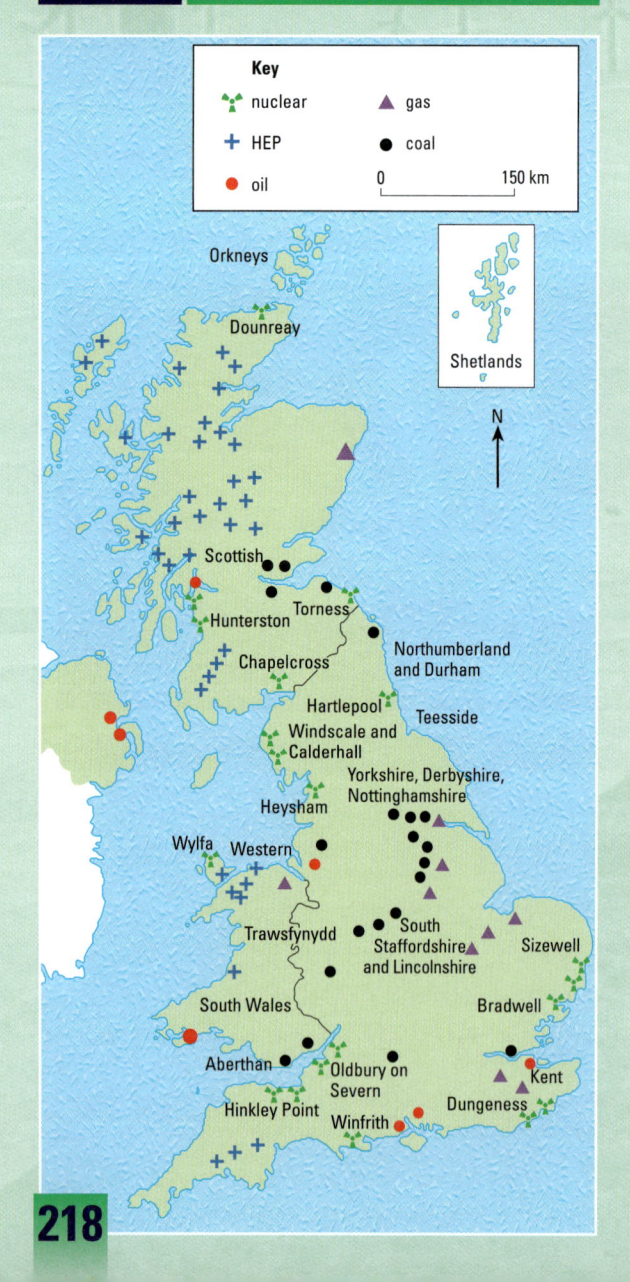

Source 1 Coal-fired power station

Source 2 UK power stations

Key:
- nuclear
- HEP
- oil
- gas
- coal

Locations shown: Orkneys, Dounreay, Shetlands, Scottish, Hunterston, Torness, Chapelcross, Northumberland and Durham, Hartlepool, Windscale and Calderhall, Teesside, Yorkshire, Derbyshire, Nottinghamshire, Heysham, Wylfa, Western, Trawsfynydd, South Staffordshire and Lincolnshire, Sizewell, South Wales, Bradwell, Aberthan, Oldbury on Severn, Kent, Hinkley Point, Winfrith, Dungeness

Source 3 UK energy generation

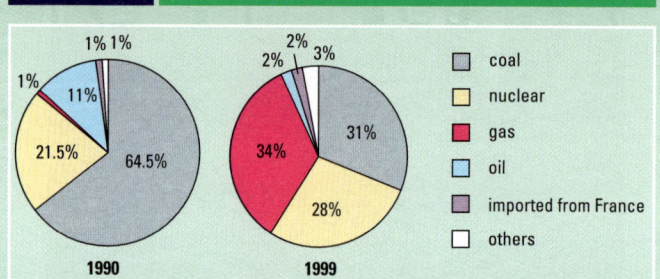

1990: coal 64.5%, nuclear 21.5%, oil 11%, others 1%, imported from France 1%, gas 1%

1999: coal 31%, nuclear 28%, gas 34%, oil 2%, imported from France 2%, others 3%

However, Source 3 shows how much the pattern of energy sources used to generate electricity in the UK has changed in ten years. Coal has suffered a great decline in relative importance, whereas natural gas has seen a massive increase in its importance. This has been called the 'dash for gas' to generate electricity. Nuclear power has risen as well, but by a much smaller percentage. Included in the 'others' category are renewable energy sources such as HEP and wind power. As you can see from Source 3, these still contribute only a small amount to the total electricity output of the UK, although future contributions are expected to be greater.

Source 4 Decline in coal in the UK

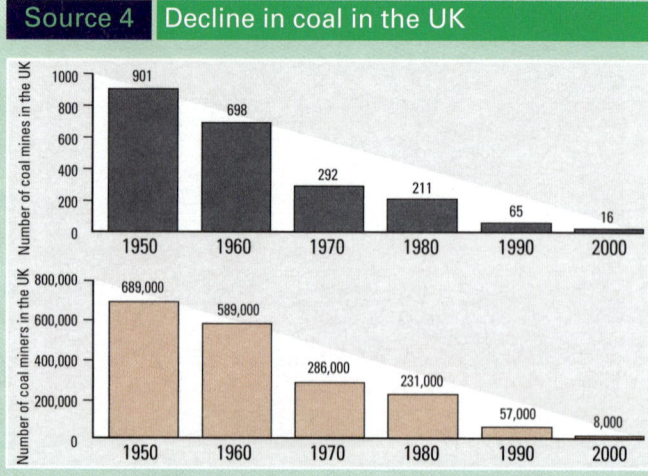

Number of coal mines in the UK:
- 1950: 901
- 1960: 698
- 1970: 292
- 1980: 211
- 1990: 65
- 2000: 16

Number of coal miners in the UK:
- 1950: 689,000
- 1960: 589,000
- 1970: 286,000
- 1980: 231,000
- 1990: 57,000
- 2000: 8,000

Energy

Decline in coal

Source 4 shows just how fast and dramatic the decline in coal mines and miners has been in the UK since 1950. There are a number of reasons for this decline. In many mines the seams of coal were narrow and expensive to work. In more modern mines, where coal seams were thicker, mechanisation meant that fewer men were needed to mine the same amount of coal. In many years it was cheaper to import coal from overseas. Burning coal releases more gases into the atmosphere than the other fossil fuels. Coal-fired power stations are a major cause of acid rain. Coal is dirty, bulky and expensive to transport compared with oil and gas. Only 16 deep mines were still working in the UK in 2000. Closing the mines caused many problems in the mining villages and towns. The number one problem was unemployment.

The dash for gas

Natural gas is a cleaner fuel than coal. When it burns, much less carbon dioxide is emitted. The UK has its own gas fields in the North Sea and off the west coast, for example in Morecambe Bay. In fact, the UK is the world's fourth largest producer of natural gas. Once a gas field is in production, little labour is needed and gas is much cheaper to obtain than coal. It is easy to pipe the gas onshore and then distribute it cheaply through the network of pipelines to homes, factories and power stations. Governments have encouraged electricity companies to change to gas to generate electricity, because it is helping them to meet their targets for reduced emissions of carbon dioxide into the atmosphere.

Little change in nuclear power

Sizewell B is the UK's only pressurised water reactor. It cost £2 billion to build and was opened in 1975 after many years of delay. There is now so much opposition to nuclear power from environmental groups and from the general public that the old Magnox reactors, which are coming to the end of their useful lives, will not be replaced. Therefore the percentage of electricity from nuclear power stations will soon start to go down. Greater interest is being shown in newer, renewable alternative sources, especially wind power.

Source 5 Sizewell B nuclear power station in Suffolk

11.5 Wind power
Haverigg Wind Farm, Cumbria

At present less than 1% of the UK's energy is produced by alternative sources, such as wind and solar power. Recent government legislation requires the industry to develop these sources through NFFO (Non Fossil Fuel Obligations).

Sixty wind projects have been approved in the UK. Electricity is generated by two or three-bladed **turbines**, usually built in groups of ten to a hundred creating **wind farms**. An average wind speed of at least 5 metres per second is needed. The map (Source 1) shows where such conditions are found in the UK. In future up to 10 per cent of the UK's electricity could be generated this way.

Ideal sites for wind farms are often in rural areas. Wind power is clean, but electricity cannot be generated when the wind stops. People are concerned about the noise of the turbines and the visual pollution spoiling large areas of countryside. In 2000 the first two offshore wind turbines started to produce electricity in the North Sea near Blyth in Northumberland.

Haverigg Wind Farm, Cumbria

The Haverigg Wind Farm (Source 2) is built on a disused airfield at a cost of £1 million. Five separate three-bladed wind turbines have been built facing the coast, using the prevailing south-westerly winds. The turbines are each 120 m apart and 30 m high. Computers control each turbine, turning the blades to catch the wind.

The wind farm took two months to build – access roads were not needed but concrete bases were needed for the turbines. Haverigg began electricity generation in August 1993.

Source 1 Wind farms and possible sites

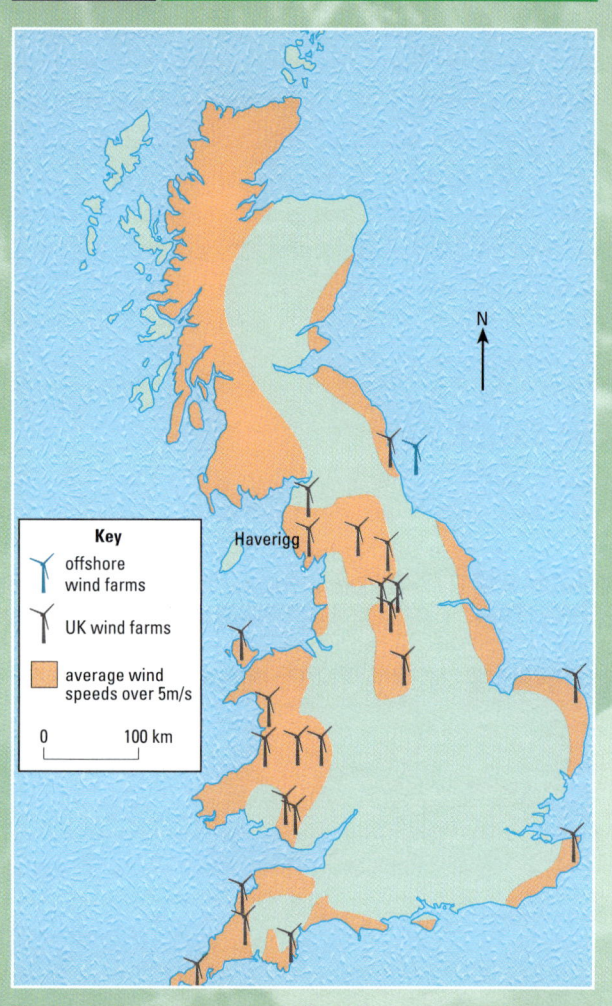

Key:
- offshore wind farms
- UK wind farms
- average wind speeds over 5m/s

The benefits of Haverigg Wind Farm are as follows:

- the site is a disused airfield; turbines are unlikely to cause objections on the grounds of noise or visual pollution
- a full EIA (Environmental Impact Assessment) was carried out; planning authorities and local people were consulted
- enough electricity is generated per year (3 Gwh) to meet the needs of 500 homes
- local firms were used for construction work, bringing income to the area
- the surrounding farmland can remain in use
- the electricity produced is clean and renewable.

Source 2 Haverigg Wind Farm

Energy in Africa 11.6
fuelwood

Whilst the world's MEDCs are looking to develop alternative energy sources to replace oil, coal and gas, many of the world's LEDCs are suffering from a fuel crisis of their own. Fifty per cent of the world's population use wood as their only source of fuel for cooking and heating (Source 1).

The **fuelwood** crisis is especially acute in African countries like Niger and Burkina Faso, south of the Sahara desert in a region known as the Sahel (Source 2). As the population has grown, so has the need to use more wood for cooking. Wood is also cut down to create farmland. As a result, people have to walk further and further from their homes to collect fuelwood as trees close to home have been cut down (Source 3). Trees are being used at such a rate that even replanting programmes cannot keep pace. People often cannot find enough wood and have to find money to buy it. As it becomes even more scarce, prices get higher.

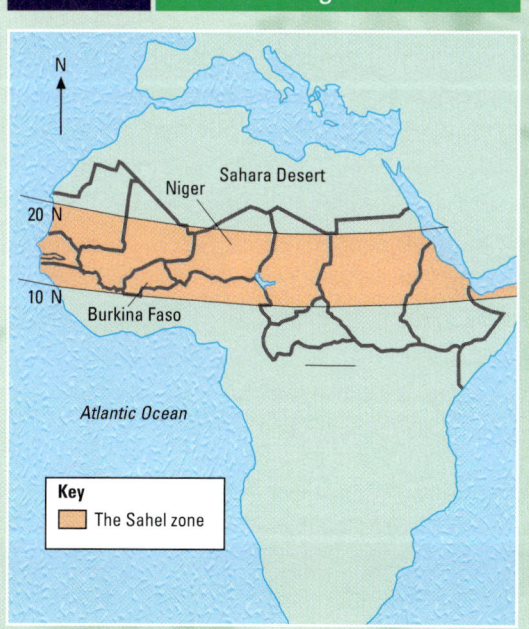

Source 1 Fuelwood is gathered on a daily basis

What can be done?

- More efficient ways of using and managing existing resources are necessary. Improved cooking stoves or ovens, not open fires, would use far less fuel and lose far less heat.
- Woodland needs to be managed carefully, with new trees replanted to replace those used up.
- If wood is an essential fuel, its other uses, e.g. fencing and building, need to be met by using alternative materials, e.g. wire, bricks etc. Once woodland is removed, bare soil may be lost through erosion and land becomes unproductive.

Source 2 The Sahel region

Source 3 Replanting fuelwood cannot keep pace with consumption

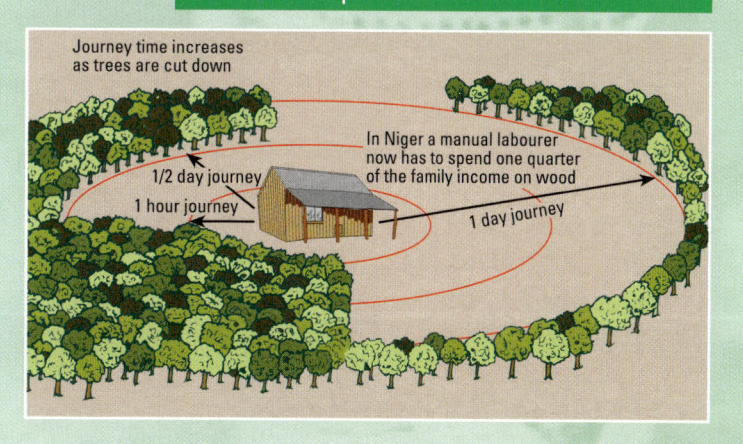

Journey time increases as trees are cut down

1/2 day journey
1 hour journey
1 day journey

In Niger a manual labourer now has to spend one quarter of the family income on wood

11.7 Hydro-electric power
the Three Gorges Dam in China

Most large dams are multi-purpose; there is more than one reason for building them. As they are so expensive to build, the cost can only be justified if several advantages result from their construction. The following are some of the advantages of building large dams:

- electricity production and power supply
- water supply for irrigation, homes and factories
- flood control
- improving navigation.

The Three Gorges Dam is being built mainly for electricity production and flood control.

Source 1 shows the location of the Three Gorges Dam, in the centre of China along the country's largest river, the Yangtze. Damming of the river began in 1997. When finished in about 2010, the dam will be the largest in the world. It will be 185 metres high and almost 2 kilometres wide. The lake, which will become the reservoir behind the dam, is expected to be up to 600 kilometres long. The plan is to build 26 generators producing over 18 000 megawatts of electricity, about 10 per cent of China's present energy needs. The electricity will be distributed over a wide area in central China. It is more than enough for the energy needs of ten big cities.

The major disadvantage of building such a massive reservoir is that the homes of more than 1 million people will have to be flooded by the rising waters behind the dam. These people need to be resettled. When a valley floor is flooded, the best and most fertile farmland is lost. The original plan was to rebuild villages and towns further up the valley sides. Here the slopes are steeper and without a covering of fertile silt.

Source 1 The Three Gorges Dam

There are great differences of opinion about whether the Three Gorges Dam Scheme should have gone ahead. The government of China sees it as an important symbol of China's modernisation. It is helping to reduce global pollution by cutting down on the burning of dirty coal in favour of clean and environmentally-friendly HEP. There is international pressure for China to reduce its emissions of greenhouse gases. It is the world's second largest burner of coal after the USA. At the same time, millions of Chinese will be protected from the risk of future floods from the Yangtze river.

Energy

| Source 2 | The Chinese government viewpoint |

- The scheme is vital for national needs.
- China cannot hope to industrialise further without HEP power from this dam.
- Coal burning in China will be reduced by 40 million tonnes a year.
- Emissions of carbon dioxide into the atmosphere will fall by 120 million tonnes each year.

| Source 3 | Landscape in the Yangtze valley near to where the Three Gorges Dam is being built |

Environmentalists argue that a series of smaller hydro-electric dams on the Yangtze tributaries would have been a more efficient way of generating power and managing the flood-prone river. They say that silt will be trapped behind the dam, making farmland lower down the Yangtze less fertile over time. Tonnes of industrial and human waste could be trapped behind the dam. Millions will die if the dam collapses. It is located in an area that has suffered earthquakes reaching 6 on the Richter Scale. Resettling people on steeper and poorer land will increase the dangers of soil erosion.

China is keen to develop economically. More energy is needed. Electricity from water power is much cleaner than that made from fossil fuels such as coal and oil. However, smaller HEP schemes cause less environmental damage. The Chinese government has been forced to admit that the resettlement schemes have not gone as well as they had hoped. Many people already resettled have been unable to find employment in the new towns to which they have been moved. People living next to a dam are not the ones who usually benefit from the electricity it produces.

| Source 4 | An artist's impression of the Three Gorges Dam when finished |

11.8 Nuclear energy

At one time nuclear energy was seen as the big hope for reducing the world's dependence upon fossil fuels, with their limited life expectancy (Source 1). Supporters of nuclear energy point out the big advantage it has over fossil fuels – no air pollution. Nuclear power stations do not emit greenhouse gases. They are not responsible for global warming. They generate electricity relatively cheaply. However, after the huge costs of building the power station are taken into account, electricity from nuclear power stations is usually more expensive than that from thermal power stations.

Source 1 The life expectancy of fossil fuels in 2000

Fossil fuel	Number of years
Coal	230
Oil	41
Natural gas	62

The top ten world producers of nuclear energy are listed in Source 2. Notice that most of them are MEDCs. A high level of technology is needed, as also is a large amount of capital investment, which most LEDCs do not have. What is remarkable is how few new nuclear reactors are being built. Why?

Source 2 Information about nuclear power (late 1990s)

Country	Total electricity output from nuclear power stations (in thousands of megawatts)	Number of nuclear reactors in use	Number of nuclear reactors being built
1 USA	106	110	0
2 France	61	56	4
3 Japan	43	53	3
4 Germany	23	20	0
5 Russian Federation	22	36	3
6 Canada	16	22	0
7 UK	14	35	0
8 Ukraine	14	15	4
9 Sweden	10	12	0
10 South Korea	9	11	5

Nuclear reactors produce radioactivity, which is dangerous to people and animal life. High levels of radioactivity cause cancers and death. Whilst safety standards are usually very high, there are occasional leaks, which worry people living close by. Much more dangerous and frightening was the explosion at the Chernobyl power station in the Ukraine in 1986; its cloud of radioactive dust was carried for thousands of kilometres by the wind and reached as far west as the UK. Levels of radioactivity in waste from nuclear power stations take hundreds, or even thousands, of years to fall to levels that cannot damage people. As one member of Greenpeace said: 'The nuclear industry is unable to deal with the waste it has already created, let alone the waste it will create in the future.'

These reasons help to explain why it took so many years for planning permission to be given for Sizewell B, the last nuclear power station to be built in the UK. No new nuclear plants are planned. Instead, research and investment is directed towards alternative sources, such as wind and solar power.

Energy

A nuclear nation – Japan

Japan has become one of the world's most important industrial nations despite lacking its own energy resources. Although Japan has small amounts of coal, oil and gas, most fossil fuels have to be imported. World oil crises in the 1970s led to sharp price rises. The Japanese are worried about their dependence on other countries – over 99 per cent of their oil is imported. Nuclear power is seen as a cheaper and cleaner alternative to the import and burning of fossil fuels.

Japan's first two reactors were built at the end of the 1960s. By 1980 there were 13 reactors. This had risen to 41 by the end of 1991 and to 53 by 2000. Source 3 shows the increasing importance of nuclear energy in Japan's energy consumption.

Japan has a variety of different types of reactor, but is also experimenting with the newer **fast breeder reactors** (FBRs). This type of reactor uses reprocessed nuclear fuel. This saves on imports since fuel (uranium) used in other Japanese reactors can then be reused. Japan already has a new uranium-enrichment plant and is building a new fuel reprocessing plant.

Source 3 Japan's energy consumption

1990:
- solar (1.5%)
- geothermal (0.5%)
- HEP (4%)
- nuclear (9%)
- gas (10%)
- coal (17%)
- oil (58%)

2010 (est):
- HEP (3.5%)
- geothermal (1%)
- solar (5%)
- gas (12%)
- coal (15.5%)
- nuclear (17%)
- oil (46%)

Source 4 Nuclear reactors at Wakasa Bay, Japan

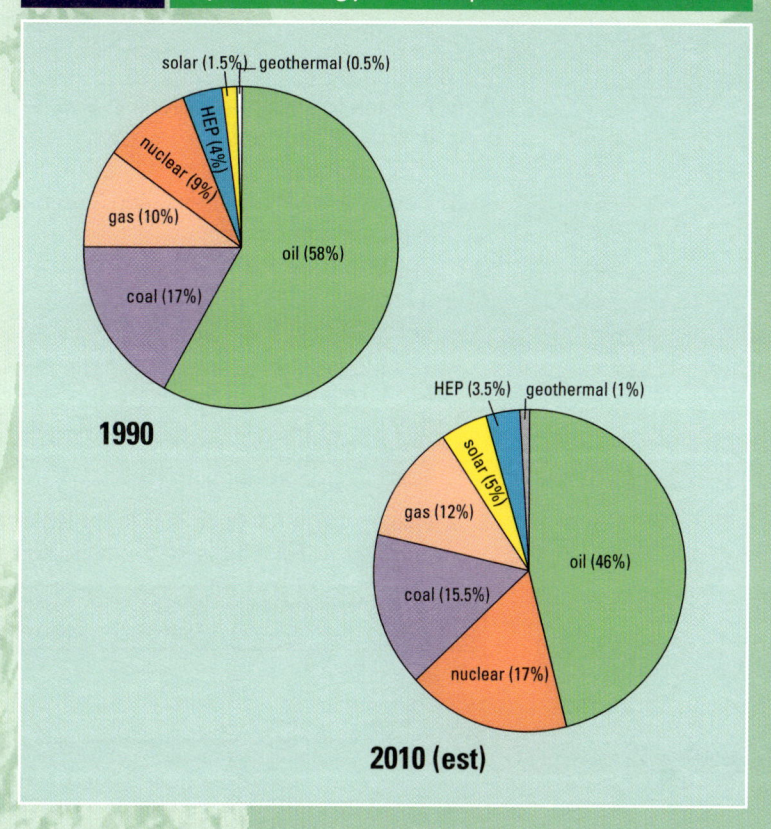

Good sites for nuclear power stations are in short supply. Flat land and a large water supply are needed. Another important consideration is the stability of the land. Japan experiences over 7000 earthquakes every year and so nuclear power stations must be located in areas safe from potential earthquakes. Pressure on available land has meant that several reactors are often built on the same site. Wakasa Bay has 15 separate reactors around it (Source 4).

Despite government enthusiasm, there is increasing opposition to the growth of nuclear power in Japan. A number of pressure groups actively oppose the nuclear programme. Some, like the CNIC (Citizens' Nuclear Information Centre), regularly publish anti-nuclear information. Protests are becoming more common. Concern centres on possible **radiation** leaks and the disposal of nuclear waste. Much of this waste is sent to the UK and France, but Japan is building its own waste plant in the north of Honshu.

11.9 Activities

1 a i Rank the energy sources in Source 1 on page 212 from highest to lowest.
   ii Explain how Source 1 shows that 75 per cent of the world's energy comes from fossil fuels.
 b Describe what Sources 2 and 3 on pages 212 and 213 show about energy production and consumption in:
   i North America
   ii Africa
   iii the Middle East.
 c The photograph in Source 4 on page 213 was taken in New York.
   i Make a list of all the different ways in which energy is being used.
   ii Why do people living in MEDCs, such as the USA, use much more energy than people in LEDCs?

2 a Make a large full-page summary table for non-renewable sources of energy, like the one below. Fill it in using the headings given.

Energy source	Description	Lifespan in years	% of world energy consumption	Uses	Benefits	Disadvantages

 b 'Most non-renewable sources of energy cause major environmental problems.'
 Write a short report either supporting or disagreeing with this statement.

3 a Make another large full-page summary table, like the one in question 2. This time fill it in with information for renewable sources of energy.

Energy source	Description	Lifespan in years	% of world energy consumption	Uses	Benefits	Disadvantages

 b 'Most renewable sources of energy are clean and environmentally friendly.'
 Write a short report either supporting or disagreeing with this statement.

4 a i Using Source 2 on page 218, describe where the following types of power stations are mainly located in the UK:
   A Coal-fired   B Gas-fired   C Nuclear   D HEP
   ii Give reasons why different types of power stations are located in different parts of the UK.
 b i Look at Source 3 on page 218. Make two columns, one for 1990 and the second for 1999. List the sources of electricity in their order of importance for the two dates.
   ii Explain why some sources increased in importance between 1990 and 1999 while others declined.

Energy

5 a Look at Source 1.
  i Identify the type of energy which the photograph shows.
  ii Is this energy renewable or non-renewable?
  iii What is the energy being used for in the photograph?
  iv List two advantages and two disadvantages of the type of energy shown.

Source 1 | **Energy in Cyprus**

b i Use Source 1 on page 220 to make a list of the areas of the UK most suited to the location of new wind farms.
  ii Using Source 2 on page 220, make a simple line drawing of a wind turbine. Add labels explaining how it works.
c i State the two main uses of fuelwood by people in African countries.
  ii Why do these people rely on fuelwood rather than oil or coal?
  iii Explain why people are finding it more and more difficult to collect enough fuelwood for their needs in many African countries.

6 a i Draw a sketch map of China to show the location of the Three Gorges Dam Scheme.
  ii Why is it a good place for building a dam and a hydro-electric power station?
  iii State three pieces of information about the Three Gorges Dam which indicate its great size.
b i Divide the page into two columns. At the top of the columns put the headings 'Costs' and 'Benefits'. Write down the costs (disadvantages) and benefits (advantages) of the Three Gorges Dam.
  ii Do you agree with the view held by some people that it should never have been started? Explain what you think.

7 a i Either draw a diagram or make a poster to show the information in Source 1 on page 224.
  ii On a bar graph, plot the electricity output for the ten countries named in Source 2 on page 224.
b i In 1995 the UK abandoned plans to build any more nuclear power stations. Give three reasons for this decision.
  ii The Japanese continued to build new nuclear power stations during the 1990s. Explain why Japan made a different decision to the UK.
c Nuclear power is controversial. Organisations like British Energy and BNFL support its use. Pressure groups like Greenpeace and Friends of the Earth are opposed to it. Work in groups and write down the arguments that both sides could use in a debate about nuclear power.

11.10 Sample examination questions

1 a **Source 1** Total world consumption of energy

Year	million tonnes of oil equivalent	Year	million tonnes of oil equivalent
1974	5600	1989	7800
1979	6600	1994	8000
1984	6800	1999	8500

  i Draw a graph to show the data in Source 1. *(3 marks)*
  ii How many more million tonnes of energy were consumed in 1999 than in 1974? *(1 mark)*
  iii State two reasons for the increase in world energy consumption between 1974 and 1999. *(2 marks)*
 b The percentages contributed by different energy sources in Europe in 1999 were: oil 42% coal 22% natural gas 25% nuclear 8% HEP 3%.
  i Draw a divided bar graph to show these percentages. *(3 marks)*
  ii What percentage in Europe was from fossil fuels? *(1 mark)*
  (Total: *10 marks*)

2 a Describe three features of the North Sea oil rig shown in the photograph on page 211. *(3 marks)*
 b State two reasons why many industries prefer to use oil instead of coal. *(2 marks)*
 c What is the difference between coal and fuelwood? *(2 marks)*
 d i Name one area of the world where many people use fuelwood as their main energy supply. *(1 mark)*
  ii Explain why people in the area you have named rely upon fuelwood. *(2 marks)*
  (Total: *10 marks*)

3 Look at Source 2. Some possible sites for wind turbines are marked by the letters A–D. Some possible sites for a HEP station are marked by the letters X–Z.

Source 2 Siting a wind turbine or HEP station

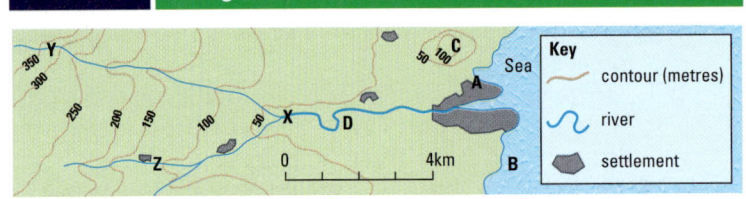

 a State two features that wind power and HEP have in common as sources of energy. *(2 marks)*
 b i Which one of the four sites A–D do you consider to be the best for erecting wind turbines?
  ii Explain why your chosen site is considered to be better than the other three. *(4 marks)*
 c i Which one of the three sites X–Z do you consider to be the best site for the location of a HEP station? *(1 mark)*
  ii Give one reason for your choice of site. *(1 mark)*
  iii What other information would you need to know about the area before you could be sure that it would be suitable for building HEP stations? *(2 marks)*
  (Total: *10 marks*)

UNIT 12

Managing environments

Unit Contents

- The global environment
- Global problems and pressures
- Transport development: road building in the UK
- New road schemes: the Newbury bypass
- Marine pollution: Europe
- Oil spills: the *Sea Empress* disaster
- Farming leading to desertification: Namibia
- Sustainable and non-sustainable development
- A National Park in the UK: the Lake District
- A National Park in a LEDC: Etosha National Park, Namibia
- Protecting a fragile environment: Antarctica

Antarctica. What features show that it is still a wilderness?

12.1 The global environment

The satellite image in Source 1 shows our planet. The newspaper headlines from 2000 identify a range of problems affecting environments at both local and global levels. Although natural hazards such as earthquakes, volcanoes and typhoons can cause major damage, it is the action of people that has led to widespread destruction of natural environments.

Many problems which may appear to be local often contribute to more widespread problems. Traffic in towns causes congestion and pollution. Building new roads to solve these problems creates others – destruction of rural environments and increases in traffic. This in turn leads to acid rain, the production of **greenhouse gases** and **global warming**.

Human and industrial waste pours into our seas and oceans. This may be accidental, or deliberate. Oil spillages resulting from tanker accidents, and the dumping of sewage, toxic chemicals and other rubbish cause widespread marine pollution.

Large areas of land on the edges of existing deserts are turning into deserts. Overgrazing, the removal of trees, **soil erosion** and decreasing rainfall are all to blame as land which was once useful to farmers becomes useless. The **exploitation** of natural resources in the world's rainforests leads to deforestation and the destruction of these important ecosystems.

As land becomes more and more precious, the pressure on the land which remains undeveloped increases. We want to **conserve** and protect the great variety of plants and animals which live on our planet, but in our eagerness to see and enjoy this diversity we are in danger of destroying it. Vast numbers of people are now frequent tourists – visiting National Parks and beaches as well as historic cities. Now the last untouched continent, Antarctica, is suffering from our actions, and is seriously threatened by damage to the ozone layer and the prospect of global warming melting the ice.

If the diversity of life and environments on our planet is to survive, careful management is necessary. Pollution and conservation know no national boundaries. Decisions made at local level often have far more wide-reaching effects. International co-operation and legislation may be the only solution.

Source 1 Satellite image of the earth

GALAPAGOS OIL CATASTROPHE
Leaking oil from stricken tanker threatens unique wildlife

TREELESS HILLS SEND TORRENTS INTO INDIA
More than 100 killed and 2 million left homeless by floods and landslides in NE India

ANTARCTIC FISH IN TROUBLED WATER
Ozone depletion could destroy one of the world's last great stocks of fish

Managing environments

INDIAN DROUGHT
Protest riots as 50 million Indians face famine

POLAR BEARS RISK EXTINCTION
Arctic ice is thinner than ever from global warming

1000 FLEE AS SEA BEGINS TO SWALLOW UP PACIFIC ISLANDS
Inhabitants on coral atolls off Papua New Guinea are the latest victims of rising sea levels

BYPASS ROW SPARKS NEW BATTLE OF HASTINGS

MELTING PERMAFROST THREATENS ALPS
Alpine communities face devastating landslides from unstable mountain ranges

DEATH SENTENCE FOR THE AMAZON
$40 billion project set to destroy 95% of rainforest by 2020

231

12.2 Global problems and pressures

While damage and pollution of water and land are widespread, atmospheric pollution probably has the most far-reaching global effects.

The main sources of atmospheric pollution are:

- the production of **greenhouse gases** leading to global warming
- **acid rain** causing damage to lakes, forests and buildings
- the use of **CFCs** leading to the depletion of the **ozone layer**.

Greenhouse gases and global warming

In a greenhouse, sun shines through the glass warming up the plants inside. When the sun stops shining, the heat does not disappear, it is trapped inside the greenhouse. In the same way, heat is trapped in the earth's atmosphere. During the day, radiation from the sun heats the earth. At night, clouds often trap this heat as it radiates back out. Gases in the atmosphere also trap this heat. In recent years, the amount of these greenhouse gases has greatly increased. The main gases and their causes are shown in Source 1.

Source 1: Greenhouse gases

Gas	Causes
Carbon dioxide (CO_2)	Release of carbon from fossil fuels in power stations and through vehicle exhausts. Burning of wood. Deforestation – trees use up CO_2 from the atmosphere; without them CO_2 remains.
Methane (CH_4)	Decay of organic matter – waste in landfill sites, animal manure, large areas of crops, e.g. rice.
Nitrous oxides (NO_2)	Burning fossil fuels – car exhausts and power stations. Use of fertilisers.
CFCs	Gas released via aerosols, coolants in fridges, freezers and air conditioning systems, certain packaging and insulation.

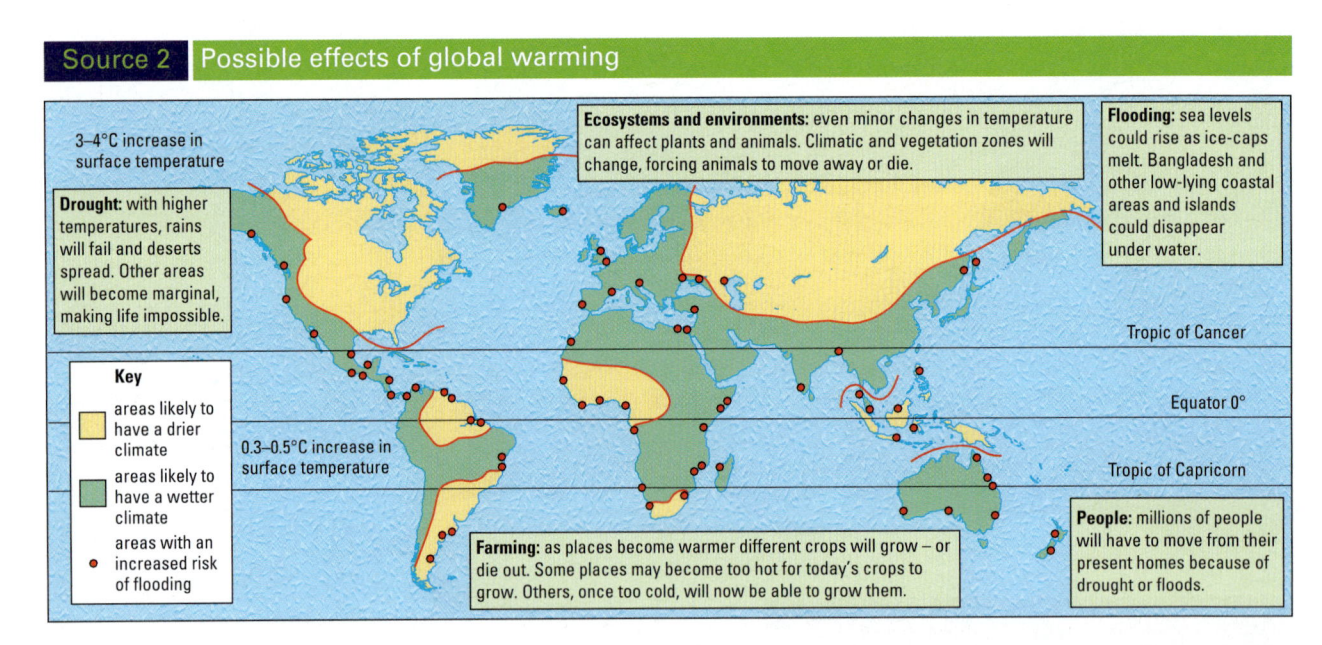

Source 2: Possible effects of global warming

- 3–4°C increase in surface temperature
- **Drought:** with higher temperatures, rains will fail and deserts spread. Other areas will become marginal, making life impossible.
- **Ecosystems and environments:** even minor changes in temperature can affect plants and animals. Climatic and vegetation zones will change, forcing animals to move away or die.
- **Flooding:** sea levels could rise as ice-caps melt. Bangladesh and other low-lying coastal areas and islands could disappear under water.
- 0.3–0.5°C increase in surface temperature
- **Farming:** as places become warmer different crops will grow – or die out. Some places may become too hot for today's crops to grow. Others, once too cold, will now be able to grow them.
- **People:** millions of people will have to move from their present homes because of drought or floods.

Key:
- areas likely to have a drier climate
- areas likely to have a wetter climate
- areas with an increased risk of flooding

The build-up of greenhouse gases is the main cause of the gradual increase in world temperatures known as global warming. Measurements over the past 100 years have shown a rise of 0.5°C. If the rise in CO_2 levels continues to increase at current levels, it could cause temperatures to rise by between 2°C and 5°C over the next 50 years. Source 2 shows the possible results of such rises.

Managing environments

Acid rain

Two of the main causes of greenhouse gases – the burning of **fossil fuels** in power stations and car exhaust emissions – are also the main causes of acid rain. They release sulphur dioxide and nitrous oxides into the atmosphere which are then deposited in either dry or wet form. Dry deposition occurs as tiny solid particles or as a gas. Wet deposition is known as acid rain. Gases react with water vapour and the sun causing rain to become acidic.

Winds can carry acid rain almost 1000 km away from its source. It damages buildings through **corrosion**, destroys forests and can build up in water killing fish and other wildlife. The loss of forests (Source 3) and acidification of lakes are particularly bad in Scandinavia.

Source 3 Scandinavian trees dying from the effects of acid rain

Source 4 How the ozone layer is damaged

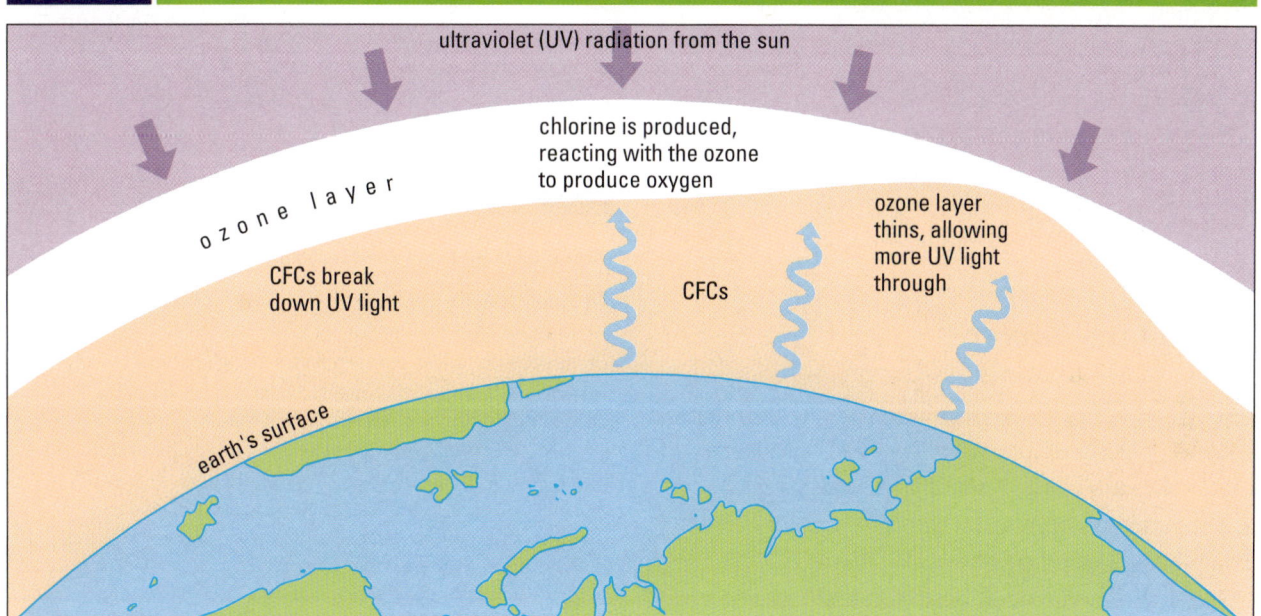

- ultraviolet (UV) radiation from the sun
- ozone layer
- CFCs break down UV light
- chlorine is produced, reacting with the ozone to produce oxygen
- CFCs
- ozone layer thins, allowing more UV light through
- earth's surface

The use of CFCs and the ozone layer

Ozone is one of the layers which make up the atmosphere. It protects the earth from UV (ultraviolet) radiation which can cause skin cancer and destroy organisms such as plankton at the base of the food chain. In the early 1970s British scientists discovered a hole in this layer above Antarctica. This hole has continued to increase in size. It is caused by the release of CFCs (chlorofluorocarbons) into the atmosphere (Source 4). CFCs, often used as coolants, are found in a range of products (Source 1).

Many countries are worried by ozone depletion. The Montreal Protocol of 1987 aimed to reduce the use of CFCs worldwide. It has been more successful than most other international agreements.

12.3 Transport development
road building in the UK

One of today's most controversial environmental issues concerns the growth of road transport. For example, in the UK today:

- there are five times as many cars (25 million) as 30 years ago
- there are four times as many lorries (3 million) as 30 years ago
- three out of every four households own a car
- over 80 per cent of the UK's freight is carried by road.

As a result, towns and cities have become congested with traffic and polluted by noise and exhaust fumes. Longer journeys cost money in terms of wasted time and larger fuel bills.

This huge growth in traffic has happened at the same time that the UK motorway network developed. The first motorway, the M1, opened in 1958. Since then the network has spread across the country. Motorways were built to speed up traffic and avoid congestion in town centres. Today many people argue that building new roads has encouraged the growth of even more traffic.

What of the future?

No new motorways are planned at present and several new bypasses have attracted opposition, with delays costing millions of pounds. However, many existing motorways are being widened and repairs (and delays) are common on others. Some of the problem areas in South-East England are shown in Source 1.

There are arguments both for and against road building (Source 2). Do new roads relieve congestion, or merely increase traffic? Should we be looking for alternatives to road transport? As the new century arrives, planners will have to make important decisions about the future, balancing the need to move goods and people with the needs of the environment.

Source 1 Motorway trouble spots in South-East England

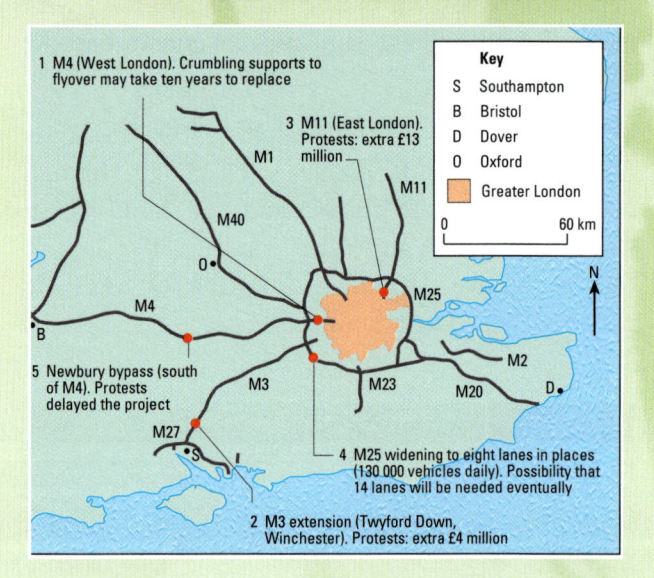

1. M4 (West London). Crumbling supports to flyover may take ten years to replace
2. M3 extension (Twyford Down, Winchester). Protests: extra £4 million
3. M11 (East London). Protests: extra £13 million
4. M25 widening to eight lanes in places (130 000 vehicles daily). Possibility that 14 lanes will be needed eventually
5. Newbury bypass (south of M4). Protests delayed the project

Key
S Southampton
B Bristol
D Dover
O Oxford

Source 2 The debate about road building

Arguments for more road building:
- helps to relieve congestion
- reduces road accidents
- speeds up traffic, saves industry money in both time and fuel
- pollution and noise are reduced in towns
- new cars are cleaner (due to catalytic converters and unleaded petrol)
- car ownership gives freedom and independence
- new superstores are built on out-of-town sites with easy road access and parking

Arguments against more road building:
- exhaust fumes produce greenhouse gases and acid rain
- new roads don't relieve congestion; they create more traffic
- even more land is destroyed and polluted by new roads
- cars should be discouraged; public transport is more efficient and less harmful and damaging
- important wildlife sites and habitats which should be protected are being destroyed
- tunnels are better than bypasses, but they are more expensive so few are built
- cars use up valuable and irreplaceable resources

New road schemes 12.4
the Newbury bypass

At the start of 1996 work began on a two and a half year project to build a 13 km long bypass to the A34 west of Newbury in Berkshire. The route (see Source 1) will cut through three Sites of Special Scientific Interest and the valleys of the Rivers Kennet and Lambourn. It will pass close to the sites of the two historic Battles of Newbury which took place during the English Civil War.

As contractors arrived, campaigners from the group the 'Third Battle of Newbury', backed by Friends of the Earth, set up camp in the woodland areas due to be cleared. Despite the hundreds of security guards on duty, work was delayed or stopped many times (Source 2). Surrounding Source 2 are some of the main arguments between those who support the building of the bypass and those against it. This is just one example of an issue which is becoming increasingly important as people become more environmentally aware.

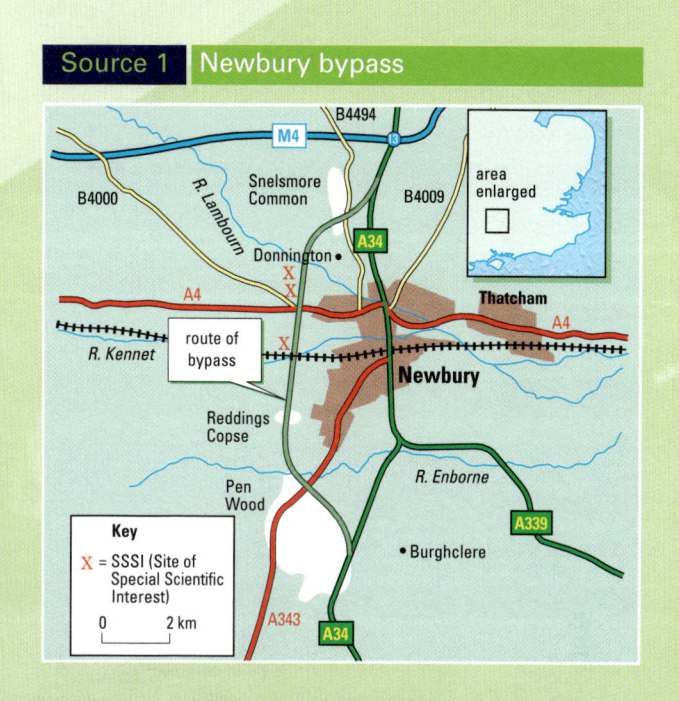

Source 1 Newbury bypass

Source 2 Newbury bypass protesters

> We have to drive through Newbury to get to the coast. Delays are frequent and we often miss ferries to the continent.

> Apart from Friends of the Earth other environmental bodies worried about the scheme include Greenpeace, the RSPB, the WWF and the Wildlife Trust. They are all campaigning against it.

> This will not solve Newbury's traffic problem – it will just create more traffic and ruin more land.

> Although some environmental damage will occur west of Newbury, most local people want the bypass to be built. It will help get rid of the traffic and pollution spoiling our town.

> My daughter is asthmatic. The traffic fumes are so bad I have to take her by car to school under a mile away. The journey takes 25 minutes, traffic is so bad. When the bypass is built she will be able to walk to school.

Newbury bypass 2000
The £74 million bypass was the longest running road dispute of the 1990s, destroying several protected sites and costing up to £50 million to guard. It was opened in 1998 and has taken the large lorries out of the town centre and reduced off-peak traffic. But traffic is said to be just as congested at peak times, and the level of bypass traffic is believed to be higher than expected.

12.5 Marine pollution
Europe

Most of the UK and Western Europe is close to the sea. Yet few people are aware that they are responsible for causing coastal pollution (Source 1). Seas and oceans seem to be treated like giant drains or sewers. Daily we pour waste into rivers which carry it to the sea, relying on tides to flush it away. Waste in rivers, seas and oceans can be moved vast distances by tides and currents.

Source 1 | Sewage outfall pipe

Source 2 shows the various causes of marine pollution. Sewage and industrial waste has always been discharged into rivers and seas, and large quantities can be broken down by natural processes. However, we are now producing so much waste that these processes are slowing down. Marine ecosystems are also suffering because much of this waste is toxic or so rich in **nutrients** that **algae** grow quickly, blocking out sunlight and reducing oxygen levels in the water (see page 61). The Mediterranean (which is not tidal) has seen great masses of algae in recent years. Swimmers and surfers increasingly suffer viruses and skin complaints through contact with contaminated water.

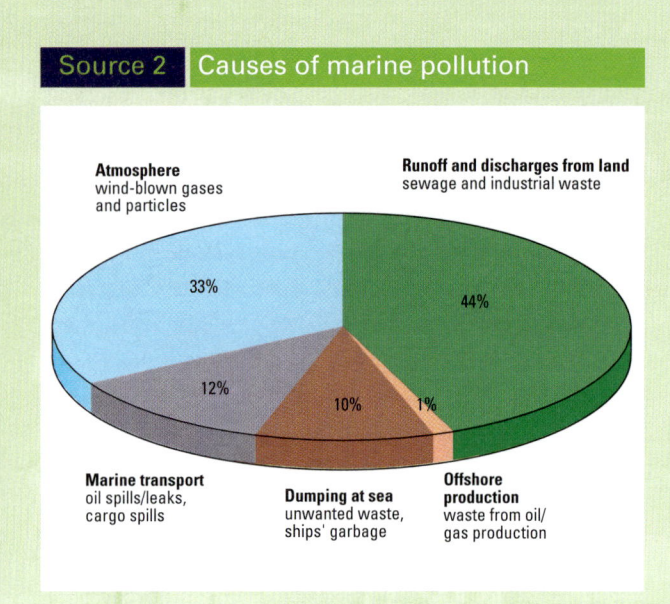

Source 2 | Causes of marine pollution

- Atmosphere – wind-blown gases and particles: 33%
- Runoff and discharges from land – sewage and industrial waste: 44%
- Marine transport – oil spills/leaks, cargo spills: 12%
- Dumping at sea – unwanted waste, ships' garbage: 10%
- Offshore production – waste from oil/gas production: 1%

The worst areas of marine pollution are found along the North Sea and Mediterranean coasts (Source 3).

While discharge of waste is constant, but often undetected, dumping from ships causes 10 per cent of marine pollution. Plastics account for half of this total. Plastic crates, bottles and packaging are often **non-biodegradable**, and so are a serious threat to marine life. Much of this waste is thrown overboard from ships despite laws banning it.

Source 3 | Areas of marine pollution

Oil spills 12.6
the *Sea Empress* disaster

Oil spills are often the most dramatic and widely reported forms of marine pollution. Even small spillages can have long-lasting effects.

One of the worst oil spills to affect the UK in recent years happened in February 1996. The 147 000 tonne oil tanker, the *Sea Empress*, hit rocks off St Ann's Head on the South Wales coast as it approached the oil refinery at Milford Haven (Source 1). Millions watched on television as attempts were made to rescue the tanker over a period of seven days (Sources 2 and 3).

Source 1 *The Sea Empress*

Source 2 Diary of a disaster

15 February	Tanker hit sand banks and rocks *en route* to Milford Haven oil refinery. Oil spilt into sea.
16 February	Tanker refloated. Russian crew of 28 and salvage experts on board.
17 February	Salvage delayed – gale force 8 winds.
18 February	Gales increased. Lines holding tanker to salvage tugs broke. Tanker's anchor chains snapped.
19 February	Salvage crew taken off tanker in gale force 9 winds. Ship drifting along the rocky coast.
20 February	Salvage team back on board.
21 February	Tugs finally pull tanker off the rocks at 7.15pm. Tanker towed to dry dock.

Effects of the spill

- over 70 000 tonnes of light crude oil were spilt
- damage and compensation claims could reach £160 million
- local fishermen were banned from fishing in the large affected area (8 km off the coast over a distance of 160 km)
- local salmon and trout rivers were polluted; inland fishing was banned over a wide area
- oil was washed onto beaches for 55 km around the area from an oil slick which was almost 100 km in length
- up to 50 000 seabirds were killed or injured
- unknown long-term damage to environment/local ecosystems.

Like many oil refineries, Milford Haven is located in an area of outstanding natural beauty and the risk of future spills remains.

Source 3 The effects of the *Sea Empress* disaster

12.7 Farming leading to desertification
Namibia

Namibia, on Africa's west coast, is the world's driest country outside the Sahara and Sahel regions of northern Africa (Source 1). Along Namibia's Atlantic coast stretches the Namib, the world's oldest desert. To the east is the start of another major desert, the Kalahari. In between these arid regions a constant struggle takes place to make marginal land productive, but the fear of drought and **desertification** is ever present. Despite the harsh conditions, over 70 per cent of Namibia's people rely directly on the land to survive.

Source 1 Location of Namibia

In northern Namibia, the land which is used for grazing cattle, sheep and goats is communally owned and run. There are many pressures which increase the need for communal land to be ever more productive. Rural populations in the north of Namibia are growing quickly, putting pressure on resources. Soil and grass are overused; trees are cut down for fuel, and to build homes and fencing. Lack of water leads to drought. Drought relief itself often causes long-term problems. The siting of emergency boreholes to supply water is haphazard, leading to overgrazing in the areas close by (Source 3).

Land ownership is a major problem in Namibia. In the past, land was taken away by partition as the country was divided up between different ethnic groups. Today ownership rights are complex. Communal farmers are less likely to care for land that they do not own. Some larger herd owners have started to enclose land for themselves. Overgrazing often results and the land suffers.

Source 2 Bush encroachment in Namibia

The effects of overgrazing are:

- **deforestation** – trees are cut down for fuel, fencing and building
- local resources become exhausted, poorer people have no alternatives, rural poverty increases
- cattle have to be taken away from villages to graze; land becomes less fertile without animal manure; crops decline; food output falls
- soil unprotected by trees is eroded more quickly.

Source 3 Cattle around a borehole, Namibia

Sustainable and non-sustainable development 12.8

Sustainable development is achieved when people meet their own needs without damaging the environment. By looking after the earth now, future generations will also be able to meet their own needs for food, shelter, clothing and recreation.

So far in this unit many signs of non-sustainable development in the natural world, caused by humans, have been mentioned. These and other natural signs of non-sustainability are given in Source 1.

Source 1 | Natural signs of non-sustainable development in the world

Changes
- Global warming
- Hole in the ozone layer
- Accumulations of radioactive, nuclear waste

Declining renewable resources
- Soil erosion
- Spreading desertification
- Water shortages
- Decline in ocean fish stocks

Threats to living things
- Deforestation
- Loss of wildlife habitats
- Loss of biodiversity
- Destruction of coral reefs

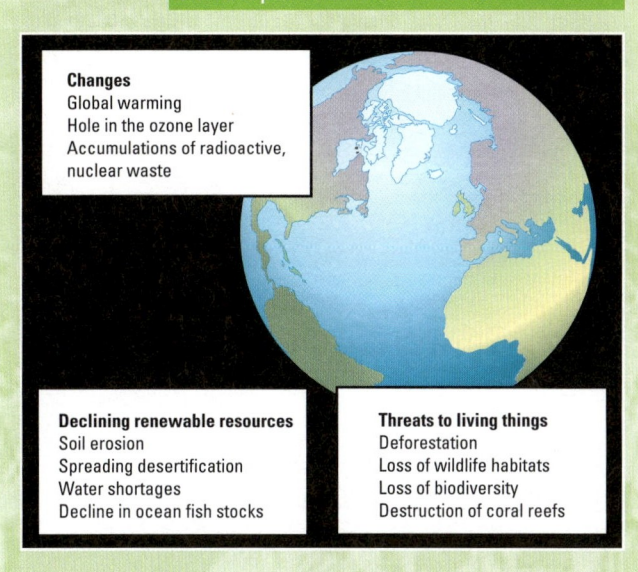

As a result of so much damage to natural environments, there are also many signs of non-sustainable development among human populations. Many of the people affected live in LEDCs. Some of the social signs of non-sustainability are given in Source 2.

Source 2 | Social (human) signs of non-sustainable development in the world

Continuing deprivation
- 850 million adults are illiterate
- Nearly 3 billion lack sanitation
- Almost 1.5 billion are without clean water
- About 1 billion are malnourished

Social changes and decline
- Over 1 billion are unemployed
- A widening gap between rich and poor
- Continuing poor status of women
- Repeated wars and conflicts

Swelling population
- 6 billion people in the world
- Rapid population increase
- Unplanned growth of cities
- Shortage of family planning

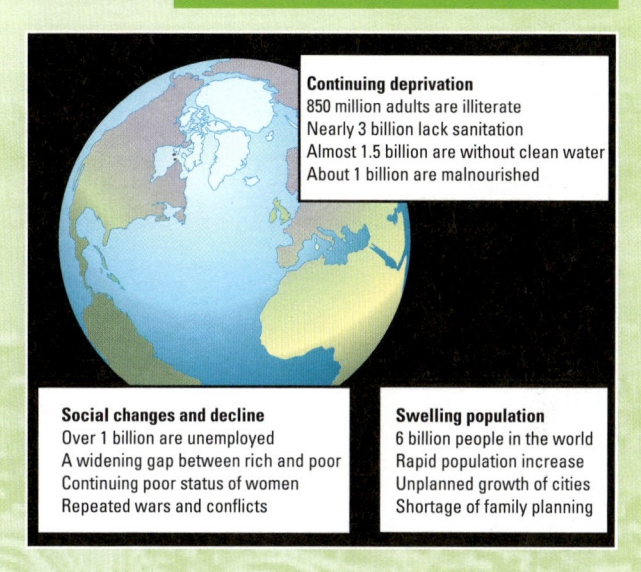

How can people behave responsibly and protect the earth and its resources for future generations? One example of acting sustainability is given in Source 3. In recent years the Namibian government has held national conferences and workshops about the problems of overusing the land that may eventually lead to desertification. With global problems, as with diseases, prevention is better than cure. It is best if desertification can be stopped before it starts.

Source 3 | Looking after the land: planning for the future in Namibia

- Provide cheap alternatives to wood for building and fuel.
- Plan the location of new boreholes carefully.
- Improve the management of land and pasture to prevent overuse.
- Plan for drought, rather than just react to it. Be prepared to decrease cattle numbers quickly during drought, and increase numbers only when rains return.
- Educate schoolchildren and train local people to protect resources.
- Use EIA (Environmental Impact Assessment) methods before introducing new developments.

12.9 A National Park in the UK
the Lake District

The 11 areas designated National Parks in England and Wales are shown in Source 1. All contain areas of beautiful and relatively wild countryside. They were designated National Parks for two purposes:

- to preserve and, wherever possible, increase their natural beauty
- to allow people to enjoy the countryside during their leisure time and holidays.

Source 1 The National Parks of England and Wales

The Lake District is the largest of the National Parks both in terms of area and population. As its name suggests, the large glacial lakes such as Windermere, Coniston and Ullswater are the main visitor attraction. Altogether there are 16 large lakes on the valley floors and many smaller tarn lakes in the mountains. The largest lake, Lake Windermere, offers the greatest opportunities for taking part in a wide variety of water activities. Lakes located towards the west are less accessible to motorways like the M6; Wastwater (Source 2) is visited by fewer people for this reason. For some visitors the mountains are a bigger attraction. England's highest mountains are in the park – Scafell Pike, Helvellyn and Skiddaw. These attract walkers and climbers.

Source 2 Wastwater is famous for its scree slopes

The Lake District receives over 20 million visitors each year. This results in severe damage to the environment from visitor pressure in some of the most popular sites, which are called **honeypots** because of the way great numbers flock to them. One common sign of visitor pressure is footpath erosion. Thousands of people following the same track deepen and widen the path, leading to unsightly scars up valleys and across hillsides.

Managing environments

Conflicts arise between different groups of people (Source 3). Often there are conflicts of interest between visitors on the one hand and those who live and work in the park on the other. Many are farmers. Making a living from keeping sheep in a mountainous area such as the Lake District is difficult at the best of times. However, when visitors allow their dogs to roam freely at lambing time, or when visitors climb over and knock down dry-stone walls, or spread litter everywhere, the farmer's job becomes much more difficult, verging on the impossible. Visitors complain about quarries as great scars on the landscape, but they are an important source of employment for people living in the park.

Source 3 Conflicts between different groups within the Lake District National Park

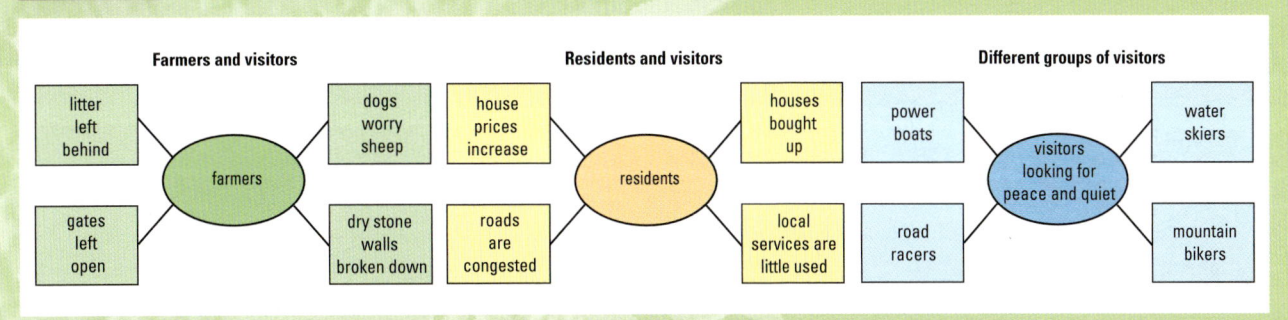

Farmers and visitors
- litter left behind
- gates left open
- farmers
- dogs worry sheep
- dry stone walls broken down

Residents and visitors
- house prices increase
- roads are congested
- residents
- houses bought up
- local services are little used

Different groups of visitors
- power boats
- road racers
- visitors looking for peace and quiet
- water skiers
- mountain bikers

In order to protect the natural environment and to make human developments sustainable, management is essential. Some methods of management are positive:

- undertaking conservation work
- providing facilities for visitors such as information centres, car parks and picnic sites
- making new paths and repairing those that are worn out.

In contrast, some management methods are negative:

- stopping the building of new houses and extensions
- diverting footpaths and limiting access to certain areas
- restricting activities, such as water-skiing, on the lakes.

Some of the management restrictions are very unpopular with local residents. For example, it is difficult to obtain planning permission to build new houses. This is to keep as much countryside as possible for visitors to enjoy. The shortage of new houses means that prices of existing houses in the Lake District have risen sharply. Also more and more houses are being bought up by rich city dwellers as second homes (holiday homes); the local people cannot match the prices city dwellers can afford for any property up for sale. Villages with many second homes in them are dead during the week and outside the holiday season. Second-homers don't use local services and are not popular with many of the local people (Source 4). However, how do you solve this kind of conflict?

Source 4 Conflicts between the old and new village residents

"It'll be perfect for the odd weekend"

"I wish our son could afford to buy a house"

12.10 A National Park in a LEDC
Etosha National Park, Namibia

Etosha National Park in Namibia is one of the oldest and largest game parks in Africa. It measures 300 km from east to west and 100 km north to south (Source 1). Part of it was once a huge lake which gradually dried out to leave a deep, white salty depression or pan. This can be seen today and covers almost a quarter of the total area.

Summers are very hot (40°C) and winters are cool (16°C). Almost no rain falls in winter (May to September). The main vegetation is **savanna** grassland and shrub, with some woodland.

How Etosha developed
The park, created in 1907, is now only a third of its original size, no longer stretching to the Atlantic coast. The constant threat of drought led to many new boreholes being drilled in the 1950s (Source 2). This successfully increased the number of animals in the park, especially elephants and lions. A **game fence** was built, keeping animals in and hunters and diseases out.

However, there have been problems. The new fences interfered with traditional migration routes of wildebeest and zebra, whose numbers fell by 90 per cent and 60 per cent respectively. The park suffered its worst drought in 100 years in 1983. Many animals died; others escaped in search of food and were shot.

Source 1 Etosha National Park, Namibia

The management of the National Park
The park is managed and run by the Ministry of Environment and Tourism (MET). Their job is to:

- balance the needs of wildlife, local people and visiting tourists
- preserve the park's natural vegetation
- provide sufficient water for all users
- deal with conflicts between park users.

The number of visitors is strictly controlled. Permits and accommodation have to be booked in advance.

Source 2 Zebra and springbok graze near the salt-pan

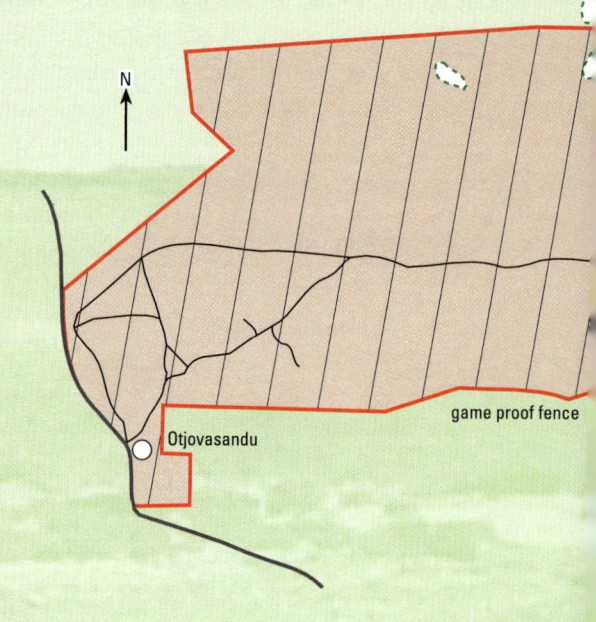

Source 3 Accommodation at the Okaukuejo camp

Managing environments

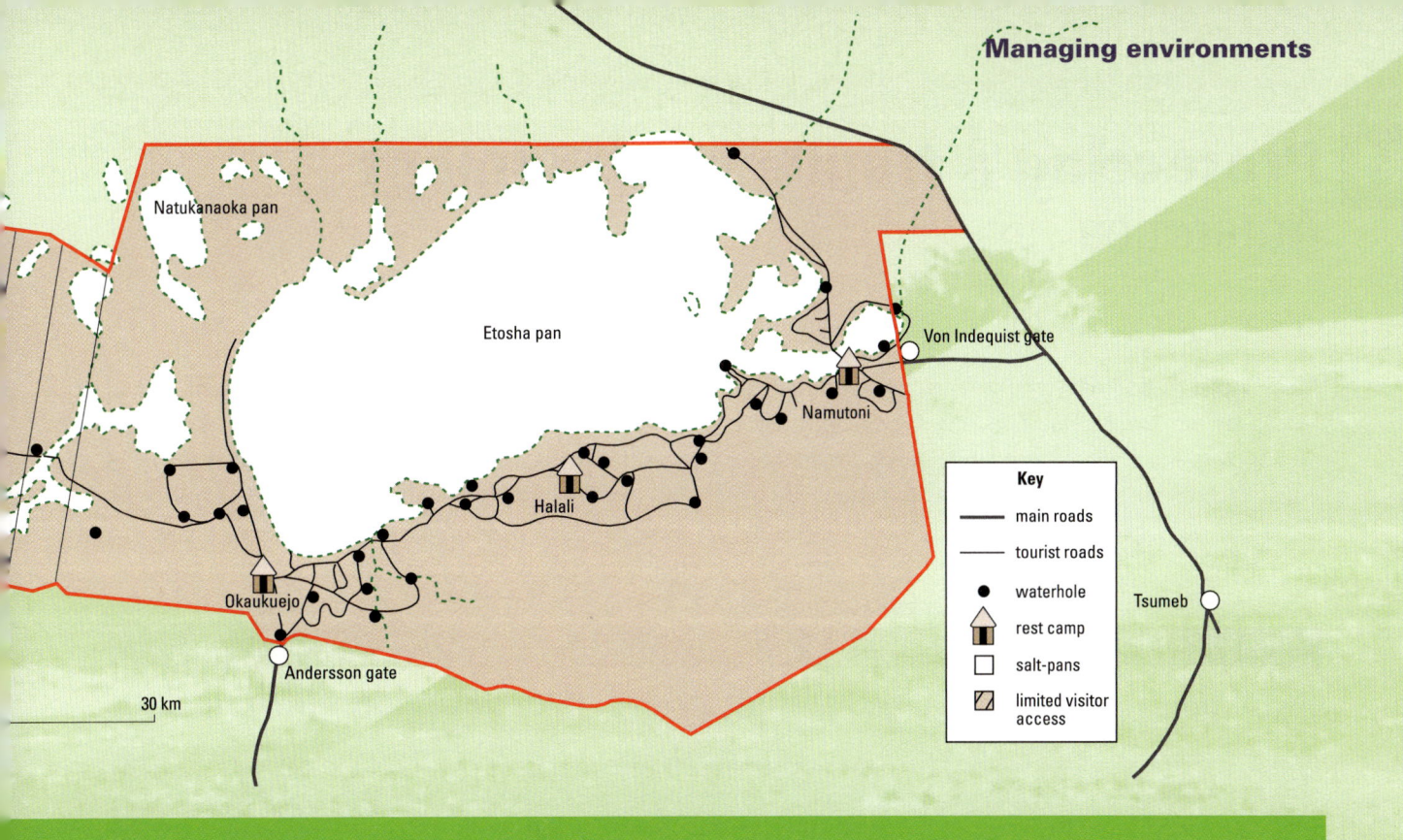

Key
- main roads
- tourist roads
- ● waterhole
- rest camp
- salt-pans
- limited visitor access

The park has three rest camps (Source 3) where visitors can stay overnight. They include areas for tents and caravans, luxury air-conditioned bungalows, restaurants, shops, swimming pools and floodlit waterholes where visitors can watch wild animals night and day.

The main attraction is, of course, the wildlife. Outside the camps visitors can drive around the 700 km of gravel road in search of four of Africa's 'big four' game animals, which are found in Etosha (elephant, lion, leopard and rhino). Visitors must stay inside their vehicles, which have to keep to the roads.

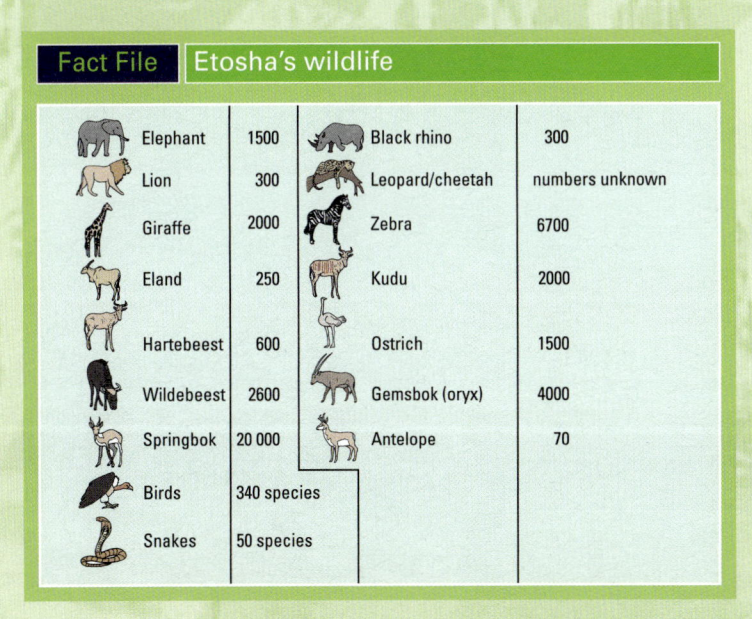

Fact File — Etosha's wildlife

Animal	Number	Animal	Number
Elephant	1500	Black rhino	300
Lion	300	Leopard/cheetah	numbers unknown
Giraffe	2000	Zebra	6700
Eland	250	Kudu	2000
Hartebeest	600	Ostrich	1500
Wildebeest	2600	Gemsbok (oryx)	4000
Springbok	20 000	Antelope	70
Birds	340 species		
Snakes	50 species		

Problems

Despite the MET's efforts, Etosha still has problems.

1. Very little rain has fallen since the drought of 1983, leading to poor vegetation growth.
2. Water is in very short supply throughout Namibia. While local communities may go without, tourists and wildlife are supplied with water piped from the River Kunene in the north.

The future

The potential for tourist growth in Namibia is great and Etosha is a leading attraction. At present only the south-eastern section is open. More tourists may mean new areas being opened up. A controversial fourth rest camp is already planned. The provision of water is an ongoing, expensive problem as is the upkeep of the many gravel roads in the park. The MET has to conserve the wide range of animals and vegetation under very difficult environmental conditions. The conflicting needs of local people, visitors and wildlife make this a hard task.

12.11 Protecting a fragile environment
Antarctica

Many world maps hardly show Antarctica, yet at 13.5 million square km it is the fifth largest continent with 10 per cent of the world's land area. It is permanently covered by snow and ice 2000 to 3000m deep, which is 60 per cent of the world's fresh water! Average temperatures range from −40°C near the centre to −15°C around the edge. There is no permanent human population, just scientists and researchers working on scientific bases. Many of these bases are maintained by countries who have made claims to the land (Source 1). It is a true wilderness because it is still dominated by the forces of nature.

Source 1 Territorial claims on Antarctica

Source 2 Antarctica – a wilderness

Antarctica is a vast outdoor laboratory relatively untouched by humans (Source 2). Scientists from across the world study here. Rises in pollution can be measured, and research continues into Antarctica's natural resources. Beneath the ice and rock is a wide range of minerals including oil, coal, gas, copper, silver and uranium. The surrounding oceans are rich in fish and birdlife.

Managing environments

The threat to Antarctica

In 1961 the first Antarctic Treaty (Source 3) was signed by 32 countries. As the treaty neared the end of its 30 years, Antarctica was increasingly under threat. Why?

- Damage to the **ozone layer** causes an increase in the amount of UV light. This can cause **plankton** at the bottom of the food chain (Source 4) to die.
- As global warming raises temperatures, ice will start to melt. Huge icebergs may break away from Antarctica, eventually melting into the oceans and helping the sea level to rise.

Source 4 | Antarctic food chain

seals — large fish — penguins — small fish — krill — plankton — whales — seabirds

Antarctica's future

During 1990 and 1991 discussions took place over Antarctica's future. Organisations like Greenpeace wanted it to become a world park, with mining banned. Some people also felt that the United Nations should take responsibility for the continent. A new treaty (Source 3) was signed by 26 countries in 1991.

The mining ban cannot be lifted unless all voting members agree. It is also designed to protect plants and animals and restrict tourism and pollution. Although the idea for a world park has not been agreed, a number of countries are in favour of it. The future of this fragile continent remains in doubt.

Source 3 | The Antarctic Treaties 1961 – 2041

Main provisions of the 1961 – 1991 treaty
- to be used only for peaceful purposes
- freedom for scientific study, with information shared
- no recognition of existing territorial claims
- nuclear explosions/nuclear waste disposal banned
- treaty to be reviewed after 30 years

Main provisions of the 1991 – 2041 treaty
- no mining for at least 50 years
- a committee for environmental protection to be set up
- waste to be returned to its country of origin
- restrictions and monitoring of tourism
- wildlife protection in force

Tourism in Antarctica

Despite its remoteness, over 10 000 tourists go to Antarctica each summer, mainly on cruise ships. They go to see the magnificent scenery, the millions of nesting penguins and the icebergs. To reduce the chances of damage to the fragile land environment, cruise operators work to the guidelines drawn up by IAATO (the International Association of Antarctic Tour Operators). Whenever tourists go ashore, they are supervised to ensure that they leave no litter, don't walk on the lichens, don't disturb the wildlife in any way and stay more than 5 metres away from nesting penguins.

This is an example of **ecotourism**, or sustainable tourism, because the emphasis is placed upon protecting the environment. Everything possible is done not to disturb or damage plants and wild animals. Tourists are educated to leave the area in the same state of wilderness that they found when they arrived. The greater the number of people who have knowledge of an area like Antarctica, the greater the chance that it will be preserved as it is for future generations. This is the real meaning of sustainable development.

12.12 Activities

1 a i On a large outline world map, locate and label the environmental problems referred to in the newspaper headlines around the sides of Source 1 on pages 230–1.
  ii Add the names of other areas which are experiencing environmental problems today.
 b Explain why environmental problems are worldwide – in the seas, on the land and even in uninhabited places such as Antarctica.

2 a Write about the causes and consequences of:
  i the greenhouse effect
  ii acid rain
  iii the hole in the ozone layer.
 b In what ways is the greenhouse effect different from damage to the ozone layer?

3 a In the UK 80 per cent of freight goes by road.
  i Why is this such a convenient method of transport?
  ii Suggest how alternative methods of transport could be encouraged and developed.
 b Make a table summarising the advantages and disadvantages of building the Newbury bypass.

4 a Why do some people see nothing wrong in dumping waste in seas and oceans?
 b Explain why it is a bad sign if:
  i great masses of algae are seen in the water
  ii there is a line of plastic bottles on the beach.
 c Write notes about the *Sea Empress* disaster as a case study of an oil spill.
  Use the following headings:
  • When and where did it happen?
  • Damage caused by the spill to:
   – marine life
   – neighbouring land areas
   – income of the local people.

5 a i What is the difference between a desert and desertification?
  ii Describe the main causes of desertification on Namibian farms.
  iii Explain two ways in which it may be possible to prevent desertification from occurring.
 b i What is meant by sustainable development?
  ii It has been said that 'Sustainable development is like living on earth for all time, not just for the weekend'. Can you explain what this statement means?
 c Choose one item showing non-sustainability from each of the six boxes in Sources 1 and 2 on page 239. For each item, give further information about it, such as:
  • where it occurs
  • why it happens
  • what effects it has
  • why it is regarded as non-sustainable.
 d Design a poster to show some of the results of humans not practising sustainable development.

6 a i What is meant by a National Park?
  ii Why does the Lake District attract over 20 million visitors a year?
 b For one of the conflicts shown in Source 3 on page 241:
   i state who the conflict is between
   ii explain why it arises
   iii suggest what can be done to reduce or stop it.
 c Explain as fully as you can the reasons for the conflict shown in Source 4 on page 241.
 d i Describe the distribution of National Parks shown in Source 1 on page 240.
   ii Name one area without any National Parks and suggest why none are found there.
 e i Name the National Park which is closest to where you live.
   ii Describe its attractions for visitors.

7 a Make a poster to show the attractions of the Etosha National Park in Namibia for visitors. The poster can be of the type that the Tourist Office would produce.
 b i Describe some of the ways in which the park is being managed.
   ii What makes management of the park difficult?
 c i Draw up a Development Plan for Etosha. You should consider the needs of the local people, tourists, wildlife and the environment.
   ii Should a new fourth rest camp be built? Explain your views on this.

8 a i What is meant when an area is described as a wilderness?
   ii Using the photographs on page 229 and in Source 2 on page 244, explain as fully as you can why Antarctica can be described as a wilderness.
   iii What threats are there to Antarctica as a wilderness?
 b i What is meant by ecotourism?
   ii Give reasons why increasing numbers of tourists are visiting Antarctica each year.
   iii Do you think that Antarctica is being damaged by tourists visiting it? Explain your views.

9 Look at Source 1 below.

| Source 1 | Pollution spoils the natural environment in Antarctica |

 a Describe what Source 1 shows.
 b Why do people dump instead of recycle?

12.13 Sample examination questions

1 a Look at Source 1 which shows an area in the tropics changed by recent human action.

Source 1 A landscape damaged by human action

   i In a frame, draw a labelled sketch to describe what can be seen in Source 1. (*4 marks*)
   ii Explain how the area has been damaged by recent human action. (*2 marks*)
 b Outline the possible long-term global effects of human action shown in Source 1. (*4 marks*)
 (Total: *10 marks*)

2 Read the newspaper report in Source 2.

Source 2 December 2000

ROAD RAGE

Environmentalists are getting ready for a battle in Hastings over plans to build a bypass through an area of outstanding natural beauty. It is the first of about 30 new road schemes to be considered during the next few months and environmentalists are very worried. They claim that the Hastings bypass will lead to the loss of untouched countryside, containing abundant wildlife. By crossing a flood plain, the bypass will increase run off and the risk of flooding; there have already been several major floods in the area this year. Traffic levels will rise leading to an increase in greenhouse gas emissions. It will also increase the pressure to build a new business park on a greenfield site north west of Hastings.

In a survey, over 80% of the local people were in favour of the bypass. Hastings is among the bottom 30 poorest towns in Britain, despite being located within the generally prosperous South East of England. The bypass will bring new jobs. At least 1000 people will be employed in the business park. The bypass is needed to stop traffic clogging up the narrow streets in the town centre. It will improve the environment in the city centre and along the sea front by creating more space for cyclists and pedestrians.

 a State three arguments against building the Hastings bypass. (*3 marks*)
 b State three arguments in favour of building the Hastings bypass. (*3 marks*)
 c Should the bypass around Hastings be built? Give your view, supporting it with information from the newspaper article. (*4 marks*)
 (Total: *10 marks*)

3 a What is the difference between sustainable and non-sustainable development? (*2 marks*)
 b Name and describe one way in which energy needs can be met sustainably. (*4 marks*)
 c For one area visited by many tourists, describe the methods used to try to make sure that tourism remains a sustainable activity in the area. (*4 marks*)
 (Total: *10 marks*)

Glossary

Unit 1

constructive plate margin where two plates move away from each other

destructive plate margin where two plates collide with each other

epicentre point on the earth's surface directly above an earthquake's focus

extrusive volcanic activity lava pours out on to the surface of the earth

fault fracture in the earth's crust

focus underground source of an earthquake

intrusive volcanic activity magma solidifies beneath the surface of the earth

lava molten rock on the earth's surface

magma molten rock beneath the earth's surface

tectonic plates large segments of the earth's crust which move across the globe

Unit 2

abrasion process of river erosion in which pebbles are used to break off pieces of rock from the bed and banks of the river

attrition process of river erosion in which particles are reduced in size as they are being transported

condensation water vapour in the air is converted into water droplets by cooling

corrosion process of river erosion in which rocks are worn away by chemical action

evaporation when water droplets are heated up to be converted into water vapour

evapo-transpiration when water droplets from trees and vegetation are converted by heat into water vapour in the air

hydraulic action process of river erosion in which the force of the water breaks off rock

infiltration water seeping vertically downwards through the soil

precipitation water from the atmosphere in any form; rain and snow are examples

runoff water that flows overland across the surface into and in rivers

Unit 3

arch wave-cut passage through headland

backwash return of water to sea after wave breaks on beach

constructive waves waves that build beach store

corrasion wearing away of cliffs by particles carried by waves

destructive waves waves that remove beach store

longshore drift wave-carried movement of sand and pebbles along a beach

rock platform solid rock at base of cliff

spit a narrow low-lying strip of sand or pebbles projecting into the sea formed by longshore drift

stack rock left standing out at sea after wave erosion has separated it from the mainland

swash forward movement of wave on a beach

Unit 4

arête sharp, knife-edged ridge formed where two corries meet back to back

boulder clay an unsorted mixture of sand, clay and stones, deposited by a glacier

corrie armchair-shaped hollow high on a hillside, eroded by ice

drumlin mound of boulder clay which has been moulded by the ice

erratic large boulder deposited by the ice in an area which has a different rock type

glacial trough U-shaped valley, flat floored and steep-sided, formed by a glacier

glacier river of moving ice confined in a valley

ice sheet large mass of ice covering a landscape and moving slowly away from its central point

misfit stream small stream in a large glaciated valley

moraine deposits of boulder clay laid down by the ice

Unit 5

convectional rainfall rain produced by rising pockets of hot air which cool

depression a low pressure system; it brings cloud and rain to the UK

desertification process by which the deserts increase in size

front marks the zone where two air masses meet

hurricane a severe tropical storm with winds over 120 km/hour and very heavy rain

latitude distance from the Equator

leaching the washing out of minerals from a soil profile

overgrazing/overcultivation overuse of land by too many animals or crops

rain shadow area in the lee of a mountain range which receives less rainfall

relief rainfall rain produced by air being forced to rise over a mountain barrier

Unit 6

birth rate the number of live births per 1000 people per year

death rate the number of deaths per 1000 people per year

demographic transition model diagram which shows the relationship between birth rates and death rates

density number of people per square kilometre

dependency ratio the ratio between those of working age and those of non-working age

distribution (of a population) where people are found and where they are not found

migration movement of people

natural increase the difference in number between those who are born and those who die in a year

refugees people forced to move from where they live to another area

structure (of a population) the relative percentages of people of different age groups, usually shown on a population pyramid

Unit 7

CBD Central Business District or city centre

gentrification improving the quality and appearance of property so that it attracts people who are wealthier than those who had previously been living in the area

green belt areas of countryside around a city in which most new types of building are forbidden

morphology layout and features which can be seen

rural-urban fringe area around the edge of a town or city where the built-up area ends and the countryside begins

settlement a place where people live

site the actual place where the settlement is located

situation the location of a settlement in relation to the land and features around it

sphere of influence area served by a particular settlement, shop or service

urbanisation growth of towns and cities leading to an increasing proportion of a country's population living there

Unit 8

assisted regions areas of industrial decline and high unemployment, making them eligible for government aid

footloose industries industries that are not tied to a particular location

greenfield location area of land that has not been developed for industry

import substitution when a country tries to produce all its own goods and services in order to limit its imports

quaternary industries these include industries that provide specialist information and expertise

science parks large areas of land, often away from urban areas, where hi-tech industries are located

subcontract where a large company arranges for its goods to be produced by another company

trade deficit where a country imports more goods than it exports

transnational corporations large companies which have branch plants throughout the world; their headquarters are often found in more economically developed countries

Unit 9

agribusiness large-scale intensive commercial farms

famine a shortage of food causing malnutrition and hunger

genetically modified crops crops whose make-up has been altered genetically to increase their yield and resistance to diseases and pests

irrigation the artificial watering of the land

monsoon the rainy season in south-east Asia

padi field a flooded field where rice is grown

plantation a large estate where one main cash crop is grown, often run by a transnational corporation

reclaimed land an area of drained land which was once under the sea

set-aside a European Union farming policy whereby farmers are paid to leave some of their land fallow

subsidies financial support to assist an industry or business to remain competitive

Unit 10

aid loans and goods given to the LEDCs by the MEDCs

balance of trade the value of exports minus the value of imports, there may be a trade surplus or a trade deficit

bilateral aid aid given by one government directly to another

emergency aid aid given after a natural disaster such as a flood or earthquake

exports goods sold abroad

Gross National Product (GNP) the total value of goods and services produced by a country

imports goods bought from abroad

multilateral aid money given by several governments to international institutions who pass it on to the LEDCs

tariffs customs duties charged on imported goods

trading blocs groups of countries who join together for trading purposes

Unit 11

acid rain a cocktail of chemcals (e.g. sulphur and nitrogen oxide)

bio-degradable applies to a material that can be decomposed by the action of living organisms

biogas a methane type gas produced by fermenting animal dung, which can be used as a source of energy

biomass the total amount of organic matter in an ecosystem

deforestation the removal of forest by burning or cutting

fossil fuels coal, oil and natural gas

soil erosion the wearing away or loss of soil mainly due to the action of wind, rain or running water

Unit 12

algae a group of simple plants, mainly found in water (e.g. seaweed)

bush encroachment grazing land is lost and replaced by bushes

CFCs chlorofluorocarbons, a greenhouse gas

ecotourism an environmentally friendly form of tourism

global warming an increase in the average temperature of the world's atmosphere

non-biodegradable material that cannot be decomposed

ozone layer layer of the atmosphere which protects the earth from ultra violet radiation which can cause skin cancer and destroy organisms

plankton microscopic organisms living in the sea, which are food for many fish

savanna natural, open tropical grassland with scattered trees and bushes

SSSI Site of Special Scientific Interest

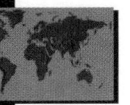

Index

acid rain 230, 233
Adriatic Sea 60–1
agriculture see farming
aid 153, 206–7, 197
air masses 85
alternative energy 216–7, 220
Antarctica 244–5
anticyclones 85, 89
appropriate technology 186
arable farming 174

Bangladesh 38–9, 151, 206–7
beach 52–3
biomes 95
birth rates 108
Brazil 99, 100, 200, 203

California 187
central business district (CBD) 128, 130
Chicago 125
China 119, 222–3
circle of hunger 178
cities 130–5, 140–5
    changes 130–3
    growth 134–7
    land use zones 128–9
    problems 144–5
cliffs 48–51
climate 84–91
    factors 84–5
    graphs 86–7, 96, 180, 186
    United Kingdom 88–9, 173
    world zones 86–7
coasts 47–63
    changes 48–57
    landforms 48–53, 56–7
    pollution 59–61, 230, 236–7
    processes 48–53
coffee growing 182–3
cold continental climate 87
Common Agricultural Policy (CAP) 177
coniferous forest ecosystem 95
conservation, environment 59, 76–7, 240–5

death rates 108
deforestation 100–1, 230, 238
delta 38–9
deposition
    coasts 49, 56–7
    glaciers 70–1
    rivers 26–31
depressions 85, 89
desertification 97, 238
development 191–207
    contrasts 191, 200–3
    measurement 192–3
Devon 52–3
Dominica 205
Dorset 50–1
drainage basin 27

earthquakes 5–6, 10–13
earth's crust 6–7
East Anglia 174
ecosystems 94–9
employment structure 150–1
energy 211–25
    consumption 213, 225
    non–renewable 214–15
    renewable 216–17
    United Kingdom 218–19

environments 229–45
    conservation 240–5
    problems 230–4, 236–44
equatorial climate 86
erosion
    coasts 48–51, 56–7
    glaciers 68–9, 72
    rivers 28–31
    soil 172
Europe 236

fair trade 179
famine 178–9
farming 169–87
    changes 176–7
    commercial 170, 174–5, 182–3, 185, 187
    subsistence 170, 180–1
faults 10
fiords 54–5
floodplains 38–9
floods 32–3
forests 95, 99, 100–1
fossil fuels 212–13
France 118
fuelwood 215, 221

glaciation
    landforms 69–73
    processes 68–70
glaciers 68–72
global warming 230–2
grassland ecosystem 98
greenhouse gases 232
Gross National Product (GNP) 192

hill farming 175
hydro–electric power 216, 222–3
hydrological cycle 26–7

ice landscapes 68–71
Iceland 18
India 11, 162–3, 180–1
industry 149–165
irrigation 186–7
Italy 19, 60–1, 201–2

Japan 12–3, 204, 225

Kielder Water 43
Killari earthquake 11
Kobe earthquake 12–13

lahars 15
Lake District 75–7, 175, 220, 240–1
lakes, glacial 72–5
less economically developed countries (LEDCs) 11, 134, 140–1
    industry 160, 162–3
    population 111–13
Lima 145
London 91, 136–7

Malaysia 100–1
Manchester 142–3
market gardening 174, 185
meanders 31
MetroCentre 139
Mexico 120–1
migration 110–1, 116–7
Milford Haven 58–9, 237
moraines 70–1, 74
more economically developed countries (MEDCs) 111–3, 151, 178–9
Mount Pinatubo 14–15
Mount Vesuvius 19

Namibia 242–3
Netherlands 185

New York 107
newly industrialising countries (NICs) 161
non–renewable energy 214–15
nuclear energy 215, 224–5

oil pollution 59, 230–1, 237
Orford Ness 56
out–of–town shopping 138–9
ozone layer 230–1, 233, 245

Peru 110, 145, 186
Philippines 14–15
plate tectonics 6–7
pollution
    coasts 59–61, 230, 236–7
    oil 59, 230, 237
    rivers 60–1
population 105–21
    change 108–9, 113, 118
    distribution 106, 114–15
    structure 112–13, 118–19
Prairies 98
primary product dependency 205

renewable energy 216–17
rias 54–5
rice farming 180–1
River Ganges 38–40
River Ouse 42
River Po 60–1
River Rhône 34
River Tay 36–7
rivers 25–35

Sahel 96–7, 221
San Andreas fault 10
Scotland 55
settlement 125–45
    classification 126
    land use 128–9
shanty town 145
Sierra Leone 198
soils 92–3
Somalia 179
subsidies, farming 174–5
Suffolk 56–7

Tanzania 62–3, 182–3
tectonic hazards 12–15
tectonic plates 6–7
Thames Barrier 34
trade 194–5
transport development 234–5
tropical cyclones 90
tropical desert climate 87
tropical rainforest 99

United Kingdom 88–9, 206–7, 218–19, 234–5
    farming 173–5
    industry 151–5
    population 112, 114–16
urban see cities
USA 120–1, 187

valleys
    lowlands 30–1, 36
    uplands 28–9, 36
volcanic activity 7–9, 14–17

Wales 58–9, 158–9, 237
waterfall 25, 29
waves 48–9
weather 88–9
    measurement 82–3
wind power 217, 220

Zanzibar 63